American Institute
of Parliamentarians

Standard Code *of* Parliamentary Procedure

Published by:
American Institute of Parliamentarians
AIPparl.org

Copyright © 2023 by American Institute of Parliamentarians

ISBN: 978-1-958850-02-2

All rights reserved. No part of this publication may be reproduced, scanned, uploaded, stored in a retrieval system, or transmitted, in any form or by any means, electronic, mechanical, photocopying, recording, or otherwise, without the prior written permission of the publisher.

Typesetting and cover by Gary A. Rosenberg
www.thebookcouple.com

Printed in the United States of America

Contents

Introduction 1
    Authorship Team and Contributors 3
    Enabling Language 7
    Citing this Parliamentary Authority 7

INTRODUCTION TO PARLIAMENTARY LAW

Chapter 1. Parliamentary Law 10
    What Is Parliamentary Law? 10
    Why Is Parliamentary Law Necessary? 11
    Organizations That Use Parliamentary Law 11
    Where Parliamentary Rules Are Found 12
    Abuse of and Misconceptions Regarding Parliamentary Law 12
    The Parliamentary Authority 13

Chapter 2. Fundamental Principles of Parliamentary Law 14
    The Purpose of Parliamentary Law 14
    Right of Association and Assembly 16
    Equality of Rights 16
    Majority Decision 17
    Minority Rights 17
    The Right of Discussion 18
    The Right to Information 18
    Fairness and Good Faith 18

Chapter 3. Rights and Responsibilities of Members and Organizations 20
    Relationship Between Member and Organization 20
    Rights of Members 20
    Member in Good Standing 22

Rights of Organizations...23
Relationship of Individual and Organizational Rights................23
Resignations...25

Chapter 4. Governing Documents: Charter, Bylaws, and Rules......26

Rules Governing Organizations..26
Types of Charters..26
Constitution and Bylaws..28
Function of Bylaws...29
Interpreting Bylaws and Rules..36
Temporary and Standing Rules of Order................................37
Adopting a Parliamentary Authority...................................38
Adopted Principles...39
Administrative Procedures..40
Supplementing Procedural Rules by Motions............................41
Custom and Precedent...41
Emergency Rules..42

VOTING

Chapter 5. Votes Required for Valid Actions..........................46

Significance of a Majority Vote......................................46
Abstentions..51
Plurality Vote...52
Unanimous Vote...53
Tie Vote...54
Vote of the Presiding Officer..54
Computation of a Two-Thirds Vote.....................................55
Computing a Majority for Separate Questions..........................55
Computing a Majority When Electing a Group...........................56
Voting Separately for Equal Positions................................57
Double Threshold...58
When Members Should Not Vote...58

Chapter 6. Methods of Voting 60
   Voting Is a Fundamental Right 60
   Voting in Meetings 60
   Acting by General Consent 61
   Methods of Voting.. 62
   Changing a Vote.. 75
   Announcing the Result of a Vote 76
   All Votes Are Binding During a Meeting 76

MOTIONS

Chapter 7. Classification of Motions 78
   Classes of Motions 78
   Classification of Unlisted Motions 80
   Changes in Classification of Motions 81

Chapter 8. Ranking of Motions 83
   Order of Precedence.. 83
   Basic Rules of Ranking..................................... 83
   Motions Without Rank....................................... 84
   Example of Ranking... 84

Chapter 9. Rules Governing Motions 87
   The Basic Rules of Motions 87
   Can the Motion Interrupt a Speaker? 87
   Does the Motion Require a Second?.......................... 88
   Is the Motion Debatable? 89
   Can the Motion Be Amended?................................. 90
   What Vote Does the Motion Require?......................... 91
   What Is the Rank (Precedence) of the Motion? 91
   To What Other Motions Can the Motion Apply?................ 92
   What Other Motions Can Be Applied to the Motion?........... 93
   Can a Motion Be Renewed?................................... 94

Repeal by Implication 95
Changing Main Motions Already Voted On 96

Chapter 10. Processing Motions 97
Processing a Motion 97
Steps in Presenting a Motion 97
Consideration of the Motion 101
Steps in Voting and Announcing Results of the Vote 101
Skipping Steps in Processing Motions 104

Chapter 11. Debate 106
The Right of Debate 106
Extent of Debate on Motions 106
Rules of Decorum and Conduct in Debate 107
Obtaining the Floor for Debate 108
Priority of Recognition of Members During Debate 108
Relevance in Debate 109
Addressing Members During Debate 110
Dilatory Tactics 110
Speaking More Than Once 110
What Is Not Debate? 111
Presiding Officer's Duties During Debate 112
Time Limits on Debate 113
Closing Debate 113
Bringing a Question to Vote 113

Chapter 12. Main Motions 115
The Main Motion 115

Chapter 13. Specific-Purpose Main Motions 121
Purpose 121
Motion to Adopt in Lieu Of 121
Motion to Amend a Previous Action 123
Motion to Ratify 125

Motion to Recall from a Committee 127
Motion to Reconsider 129
Motion to Rescind 132

Chapter 14. Subsidiary Motions 135
Motion to Amend 135
Motion to Refer to a Committee 149
Motion to Postpone to a Certain Time 153
Motion to Limit or Extend Debate 157
Motion to Close Debate and Vote Immediately 160
Motion to Table 164

Chapter 15. Privileged Motions 167
Question of Privilege 167
Motion to Recess 171
Motion to Adjourn 173

Chapter 16. Incidental Motions 179
Motion to Suspend the Rules 179
Point of Order 183
Motion to Appeal 186
Inquiries 189
Request to Withdraw a Motion 193
Division of the Question 196
Consider by Paragraph 198
Verification of a Vote 200
Division of the Assembly 200
Motion for a Counted Vote 201

MEETINGS OF ORGANIZATIONS

Chapter 17. Types of Organizations 204
Temporary and Permanent Organizations 204
Form of Organization 204

  Unincorporated Associations..206
  Meeting to Form an Unincorporated Association......................206
  Corporations...208
  Statutory Requirements..209
  Differences Among Nonprofit, Tax-Exempt, and
    Charitable Organizations..210

Chapter 18. Types of Meetings..212
  Meetings and Conventions..212
  Regular Meetings...212
  Special Meetings...213
  Canceling or Changing a Scheduled Meeting...........................214
  Continued Meetings..215
  Closed Meeting...216
  Electronic Meetings..217
  Actions Without a Meeting..217
  Failure to Call Meetings...218

Chapter 19. Electronic Meetings...219
  Characteristics of an Electronic Meeting................................220
  Notice..221
  Quorum..222
  Fairness in Seeking and Obtaining Recognition.......................222
  Making Motions..223
  Points of Order and Appeals...224
  Debate...224
  Voting..225
  Legal Requirements...226
  Other Considerations...227

Chapter 20. Notice of Meetings and Proposals...........................230
  Importance of Notice..230
  Notice Protects Members..230
  Notice of Meetings..230

Notice of Proposed Actions and Scope of Notice.....................233
Waiver of Notice...234

Chapter 21. Order of Business and Agenda 235
Usual Order of Business 235
Agenda...236
Flexibility in the Agenda..237
Consent Agenda...238
Priority Agenda 239
Items on the Usual Order of Business...............................240

Chapter 22. Quorum 245
Requirement for a Quorum...245
Quorum Requirements 245
Computing a Quorum 247
Raising a Question on Quorum 247
Presumption of a Quorum..248

Chapter 23. Minutes 249
Importance of Minutes..249
Responsibility for Accurate Minutes................................249
Minutes Format 250
Minutes Preparation..250
Access to Minutes 250
Content of Minutes...251
Items That Should Not Be Included in Minutes 252
Closed Meeting Minutes...253
Disposition of Minutes...253
Approval of Minutes by a Minutes Approval Committee 255
Published Meeting Reports..256
Retention of Minutes...256
"Dispensing with the Reading of the Minutes" 256
Committee Minutes..257

Chapter 24. Conventions and Their Committees 258
    Delegates and Alternates 258
    Delegate Nominees 260
    Convention Committees 260
    Credentials Committee 261
    Convention Rules Committee 264
    Program Committee 265
    Tellers Committee 266
    Bylaws or Governance Committee 266

Chapter 25. Reference Committees 268
    Composition and Appointment 269
    Introduction of Resolutions and Referral 270
    Hearings 271
    Development of Recommendations 274
    Reference Committee Reports 275
    Consent Agenda in Conventions 277
    Priority Agenda 279
    Action on Reports 279
    Motion to Adopt in Lieu of 281
    Reference Committee Influence 284

ORGANIZATION LEADERSHIP

Chapter 26. Nominations and Elections 286
    Choosing Organization Leaders 286
    Bylaw Provisions on Nominations and Elections 286
    Nominations from the Floor 287
    Closing Nominations 287
    Debating Nominations 288
    Voting for Candidates Not Nominated 288
    Selecting a Nominating Committee 288
    Duties of a Nominating Committee 289

Qualifications of Nominees..290

Nomination to More Than One Office 290

Nominating Committee Members as Candidates....................291

Single and Multiple Nominees for a Position.......................291

Election Committee 292

Counting Ballots..293

Security and Privacy of Balloting...................................293

Determining Validity of Ballots 294

Report of Election Committee or Tellers 294

Vote Necessary to Elect 296

Alternatives to a Ballot Vote Election 297

Motion to Make a Vote Unanimous 298

When Elections Become Effective 298

Challenging the Right to Vote 298

Challenging an Election...299

Incomplete Elections 301

Chapter 27. Officers 302

The President 302

The President-Elect...305

The Vice President..306

The Secretary 307

The Treasurer 309

Appointed Officers..309

Honorary Officers..310

Immediate Past President..311

Powers of Officers..311

Delegation of Authority by Officers, Boards,
    and Committees...311

Term of Office 312

Vacancies..313

The Executive Director 314

Chapter 28. The Skill and Art of Presiding 316
   Skill and Art 316
   Foundations 316

Chapter 29. The Professional Parliamentarian 323
   Meeting or Convention Parliamentarian 323
   Professional Presiding Officer..................................325
   Drafting/Amending/Revising Bylaws....................326
   Written Opinions and Expert Testimony................327
   Teaching 328
   Parliamentarians as Consultants 329
   Floor Parliamentarian...329
   Contractual Issues..330

Chapter 30. Boards..331
   Definition...331
   Members of the Board...331
   Duties, Powers, and Responsibilities 332
   Procedure in Boards..332
   Confidentiality and Minutes 333
   Committees of the Board..333
   Conflicts of Interest 334
   Fiduciary Duty of Board Members..........................335
   Statutory Provisions Related to Public Boards
      and Other Organizations 336

Chapter 31. Committees and Committee Reports.....................337
   Importance of Committees 337
   Standing Committees 338
   Special Committees 338
   Selection, Removal, and Replacement of Committee Members 340
   Ex Officio Members of Committees 341
   Composition, Powers, Rights, and Duties of Committees 341
   Working Materials for Committees 342

Attendance at Committee Meetings...................................343
Procedure in Committee Meetings......................................343
Committee Hearings...345
Form of Committee Reports and Recommendations 346
Agreement on Committee Reports.......................................348
Presentation of Committee Reports....................................349
Consideration of Committee Reports...................................350
Record of Committee Reports..351
Minority Reports...352
Presentation of Committee Recommendations........................352

Chapter 32. Finances..354
Setting Up Financial Records...354
Report of the Treasurer..354
Report of a Financial Review or Audit................................355
Financial Safeguards...356

Chapter 33. Discipline of Members and Officers......................359
Discipline and Expulsion of Members..................................359
Removal of an Officer for Cause......................................361
Removal of an Officer Without Cause..................................363
Other Disciplinary Sanctions...363
Remedies for Improper Removal..364

Chapter 34. Glossary of Parliamentary Terms........................365

APPENDICES

Appendix A. Bylaws Checklist...384
Name and Purpose...384
Membership Provisions..384
Membership Meeting Provisions..385
Governance Provisions 385
Administrative Provisions..387

Appendix B. Sample Emergency Bylaws 390
    Model Set of Emergency Bylaws 390

Appendix C. Sample Proxy Form. 392

Appendix D. Sample Convention Rules for a Hybrid Meeting. 394

Appendix E. Model Minutes—Example 396

Appendix F. Minutes Template—Subject Format 399

Appendix G. Useful Tools for Preparing Minutes 402
    Minutes Template 402
    Action Log 403

Appendix H. Tellers' Report—Elections 404

Appendix I. Adopt in Lieu of Flowchart. 405

Appendix J. Notes and Citations 407

Index 417

Introduction

0.1   Meeting procedures are sometimes viewed as esoteric, complicated, baffling, and irritating. Some consider them a waste of time. Yet, they are a valuable tool to be used in meetings to ensure fairness, justice, and consistency in making decisions in an environment where people have different opinions and are not shy in expressing those opinions. This book is written to untie what is complicated, to enlighten and simplify the procedure, and to make the procedure accessible, not just to a few, but to all members of an organization. It is also designed to dispel some of the common myths and misnomers about parliamentary procedure. It is easily readable, strips away unneeded and overly complex procedures, and does not burden the meeting attendee with archaic and obtuse language. The book has evolved with the ever-changing state of the common parliamentary law. Overall, it provides for a simplified, yet complete, set of procedural rules that can be used by organizations of all sizes.

0.2   Alice Sturgis, in 1950, produced a book on procedure titled *Sturgis' Standard Code of Parliamentary Procedure* that dramatically simplified meeting procedures with the intent of making the rules understandable by all. The procedure was simple, used plain language, dropped archaic procedure and terminology, yet was complete and usable by most organizations, and was based in the law. The American Institute of Parliamentarians (AIP) continues the philosophy of Alice Sturgis through the book entitled *American Institute of Parliamentarians Standard Code of Parliamentary Procedure*, now in its second edition.

0.3   The legal citations throughout this book support the underlying philosophy of specific concepts and rules. Two major changes in this book are based on evolutions in the state of parliamentary procedure, as well as the world. The pandemic in 2020 clearly demonstrated that the default position regarding electronic meetings should be changed from "not allowed unless stated in your governing documents" to "allowed unless prohibited in your governing documents." Many organizations were simply unable to meet due to this prohibition in most parliamentary authorities.

0.4   A second major change is the addition of default rules when the organization's governing documents are silent on a matter. The experience of the authorship team led to the conclusion that despite being stated that certain information "should be included" in the governing documents, it almost never was. These default rules will not suit every organization, and each organization is free to deviate by developing standing rules of order.

0.5   This authorship team resolved to revise the book to represent common, not theoretical, practice for both peaceful and contentious meetings. The team committed to honoring traditional parliamentary writings as much as possible while not being so resistant to change that it could not embrace innovation and change such as occurred with the introduction of the Gordian Knot and Adopt in Lieu of Motions in the last edition. One practice, that of allowing the consideration of a motion or topic informally, was deemed to no longer be sound practice and was removed.

0.6   Alterations of procedure to prevent their abuse or misuse were implemented as well as clarification on what makes up unfinished business. Additional information, innovations, and changes from prior parliamentary books are introduced in the hope of providing a useful reference that is consistent with modern meeting needs and practices. These include:

Changes related to governance and fundamentals:
1. changing the default provision to amend bylaws changed from previous notice and majority vote to previous notice and a two-thirds vote
2. removing member discipline information from "Rights and Responsibilities of Members and of Organizations" to form a new chapter
3. establishing a process for handling individual bylaw amendments to existing bylaws should a revision fail
4. providing sample emergency bylaws

Changes related to motions:
5. replacing the concept of restricted debate with a requirement that debate be germane to the motion at hand;
6. making Close Debate and Vote Immediately amendable as to the motions to which it applies;
7. removing the debatability of motions that limit debate;
8. removing the concept of a substitute amendment because a substitute was already treated as an amendment to strike out and insert; and
9. establishing that after debate has been closed, Factual Inquiries are not permitted, although a Parliamentary Inquiry may be.

Changes related to meetings:

10. clarifying the methodology and motions used to create a continued meeting;
11. clarifying rules related to the formation of a convention or house of delegates, particularly those related to credentials;
12. providing sample rules for a hybrid meeting;
13. establishing electronic notice as a default permission, unless prohibited by statute or the bylaws;
14. establishing that electronic meetings are allowed, unless prohibited by statute or the bylaws; and
15. providing that a change from in-person to virtual, or vice-versa, does not invalidate a notice, provided all members are notified.

0.7   Finally, great effort was made to adjust nomenclature to the common meaning of the words and eliminate the overuse of the word *special*.

1. Specific Main Motions were changed to Specific-Purpose Main Motions.
2. Special Orders were renamed Scheduled Orders.
3. Standing and Special Rules of Order were changed to Standing Rules of Order and Temporary Rules to describe their purposes more accurately.

AUTHORSHIP TEAM AND CONTRIBUTORS

0.8   The AIP Board of Directors commissioned the revision of the book in 2019 and selected a committee to make recommendations for an authorship team. The board selected the authorship team as outlined below. The charge of the authorship team was to update the book, remove any conflicts, and abide by the fundamental guidelines of simplicity and clarity in congruence with both the law and the original work of Alice Sturgis.

0.9   All authorship team members hold at least a Certified Parliamentarian (CP) credential; many are Certified Professional Parliamentarians (CPP). These credentials, offered by AIP, may also have an additional -T, indicating a teacher designation. Most members also hold the Professional Registered Parliamentarian (PRP) credential, offered by the National Association of Parliamentarians (NAP). All are practicing professionals in the field and have a wide range of experience through their clients and AIP. The team includes two returning members from the last edition: Barry Glazer and Michael Malamut, as well as Lucy Hicks Anderson, CJ Cavin, Al Gage,

Glen Hall, Atul Kapur, Shannon Sun, and the Project Manager, Kay Allison Crews. Here is a short description of each:

0.10 **Barry Glazer:** Barry M. Glazer is a CPP-T and served AIP as 2004–2006 President. As a member of the AIP Revision Committee for the fourth edition of *The Standard Code of Parliamentary Procedure*, he also served on the authorship team for that book's successor, *The American Institute of Parliamentarians Standard Code of Parliamentary Procedure*. Barry has been an active member of NAP since 1992 and frequently teaches at both AIP and NAP events. Glazer is a retired anesthesiologist, and he works as a full-time parliamentarian, primarily doing convention work and teaching presiding workshops.

0.11 **Michael Malamut:** Michael E. Malamut, JD, CPP-T, PRP, CGT, is trained as a lawyer and professional parliamentarian. Malamut has been active in nonprofit issues in the American Bar Association, serving as Chair of the Business Law Section's Nonprofit Organizations Committee (2011–2014). He is currently an advisor to the Boston Bar Association Working Group on Revision of the Massachusetts Nonprofit Corporation Act.

0.12 Malamut has also obtained the highest credentials as a professional parliamentarian and a governance trainer. He is currently serving as Chair of the Opinions Committee of AIP (member since 2000, Chair since 2008) and is the past Parliamentary Research Editor/Questions & Answers Committee Chair for NAP (2017–2019). He was President of the American College of Parliamentary Lawyers from 2009–2012.

0.13 Malamut was a member of the authorship team for several publications, including the first edition of the *American Institute of Parliamentarians Standard Code of Parliamentary Procedure* (2012) and Ray E. Keesey's *Modern Parliamentary Procedure* (American Psychological Association, 2d ed. 2018). He is credentialed as a Certified Governance Consultant by BoardSource, and as a PRP and a CPP-T.

0.14 AIP granted Malamut the President's Award for Parliamentary Writing twice (2000 and 2020) and named him Robert W. English Lecturer (2018). In addition, he is an adjunct professor at the University of Massachusetts School of Law. He received his undergraduate degree in Public and International Affairs from Princeton University and his JD cum laude from Harvard Law School. He is currently serving as an Associate Justice of the Massachusetts Trial Court.

0.15 **Lucy Hicks Anderson:** Lucy Hicks Anderson, JD, CP-T, PRP, has served as a member of the Board of Directors and as Chairman of the Bylaws and Standing Orders Committee for AIP. For NAP, she served as a member of the Board of Directors and President of the Texas State Association of Parliamentarians from 2010–2011. She has conducted numerous workshops and presentations and has mentored students in the study of parliamentary procedure for completion of parliamentary certification exams.

0.16 **CJ Cavin:** CJ is a CPP-T and a PRP, and a licensed Oklahoma attorney.

0.17 CJ serves as the Chief Parliamentarian for the Oklahoma House of Representatives and has worked with local, state, national, and international organizations. CJ often teaches about virtual meetings, electronic voting, and the use of technology to improve meeting procedures.

0.18 CJ has also served as the chair for the Commission on Credentialing with NAP, as parliamentarian for AIP, and as vice president for the American College of Parliamentary Lawyers.

0.19 **Al Gage:** Al is a CPP-T, a PRP, and a Professional Accredited Parliamentarian from the Society of Agricultural Education Parliamentarians. Al is a professional practicing parliamentarian with a wide variety of national, state, and local clients that include many nonprofits, corporations, boards, and political parties at all levels, including serving as one of the parliamentarians for the Republican National Committee since 2014, and agriculture organizations. He is also a high school parliamentary procedure coach who has coached national championship Career and Technical Student Organization teams in both the Future Farmers of America and Health Occupation Students of America contests. Al has served as the president of AIP and the Society of Agricultural Education Parliamentarians.

0.20 **Glen Hall:** Glen is a general dentist practicing in Abilene, Texas, who is a CP-T. He has served on the Board of Directors of the Texas Dental Association. He was elected and served as Speaker of the House of Delegates for the Texas Dental Association for twelve years, after which he was elected as Speaker of the House of Delegates for the American Dental Association, serving in that office for seven years. Additionally, he served as the Parliamentarian on the Board of Trustees of the American Dental Association for seven years. He served as Parliamentarian for AIP for six years and is now serving as Parliamentarian for the Texas Dental Association in addition to parliamentary consulting for other organizations.

0.21 **Atul Kapur:** Atul Kapur, MD, is a CPP-T. He serves on the Executive Committee of AIP and on the Opinions Committee, which provides interpretations and explanations on detailed, complicated, or advanced questions. Atul is also a PRP and member of the Bylaws Committee of NAP. Providing a broad range of parliamentarian services for organizations across North America, Atul is frequently invited to teach other parliamentarians. Outside his parliamentarian roles, Atul is an emergency physician in Ottawa, Ontario, Canada.

0.22 **Shannon Sun:** Shannon Sun is a CPP-T and PRP. She has served as meeting parliamentarian and consultant for various organizations, including unions and professional associations. Shannon has taught numerous workshops and classes related to parliamentary procedure. She is a member of the AIP Accrediting Department. She is also currently admitted to practice law in the state of New Jersey.

0.23 **Kay Allison Crews:** Project Manager Kay Allison Crews was President of AIP from 2015–2019. She is both a CPP-T and a PRP. In 2020, Kay was chosen as the Chair of the Joint Committee on the Review of the Code of Ethics, a committee populated by professional parliamentarians representing both NAP and AIP. That committee drafted and adopted the Joint Code of Professional Responsibility, which is used by all members of professional parliamentary associations. Her client base includes labor unions, state and local governments, political parties, and others. In addition to serving as a member of the revision team for Ray E. Keesey's *Modern Parliamentary Procedure* (American Psychological Association, 2d ed. 2018), she has served as project manager of this revision since its inception. She is also the Accrediting Director for AIP.

0.24 The members of this team are eminently qualified as individuals and as a group to have written this book. The team has also called on others for support. The advisors listed below have provided specific, detailed guidance on some of the chapters and support for the efforts of the team.

0.25 **Roger Hanshaw:** The Honorable Roger Hanshaw, JD, CPP, PRP, is the Speaker of the West Virginia House of Delegates. He was recognized by West Virginia Super Lawyers as a Rising Star, and by Chambers USA as one of America's Leading Business Lawyers (Environment).

0.26 **W. Craig Henry:** W. Craig Henry, CPP-T, PRP, has served as a facilitator, expert witness, professional presiding officer, teacher, and organizational strategist. He has worked with commercial businesses, governmental organizations, and nonprofit associations to provide management training and services, primarily focusing on governance, leadership development and strategic planning.

0.27 **Evan Lemoine:** Evan Lemoine is a PRP, a Rhode Island–based CPA, and an adjunct lecturer in accounting. He has extensive experience with not-for-profit organizations as an auditor and tax professional. He frequently presents on topics of financial governance and internal control matters, and he has served as AIP Treasurer.

0.28 **Shawn Paine:** Shawn Paine is a PRP through NAP and a licensed Oklahoma attorney. Shawn serves as the Deputy Parliamentarian for the Oklahoma House of Representatives and has done work for local, state, and national organizations.

0.29 **Clyde Waggoner:** Clyde is a retired Oral and Maxillofacial Surgeon (DMD), a CP, and a PRP. He has served on the Board of Directors of AIP and is commencing his ninth year serving as the Speaker of the House of Delegates for the American Dental Society of Anesthesiology.

ENABLING LANGUAGE

0.30 This book is designed to be an easy-to-use set of default rules to prevent an organization from having overly detailed and cumbersome governing documents. Many organizations will want to adopt this book as their parliamentary authority. One method to accomplish this is to place a statement in their bylaws, such as the following:

> In all matters not covered by applicable law, its constitution, bylaws, standing rules of order, or temporary rules, this organization shall be governed by the current edition of the *American Institute of Parliamentarians Standard Code of Parliamentary Procedure.*

0.31 It is the intention of the authorship team that, although the book is published in 2023, that the effective date for this to be deemed the "current" edition shall be January 1, 2024.

CITING THIS PARLIAMENTARY AUTHORITY

0.32 In order to accommodate electronic publication, this reference book has gone to a chapter-paragraph numbering system. Additionally, both footnotes (indicated with superscript symbols) and endnotes (indicated with superscript numbers) are used. Footnotes are used for material of broad interest to most readers, and endnotes are used for legal citations and information of interest to parliamentary scholars and historians.

0.33 References to this parliamentary authority should be cited using the paragraph number system as follows:

1. AIPSC (2nd ed.) 3.12 [This references Chapter 3, Paragraph 12]
2. AIPSC (2nd ed.) 13.41.2 [This references Chapter 13, Paragraph 41, item #2 in the list]
3. AIPSC (2nd ed.) 8.8–12 [This references Chapter 8, Paragraphs 8 through 12]
4. AIPSC (2nd ed.) 4.1fn* [This references Chapter 4, Paragraph 1, the fn noted "*"]
5. AIPSC (2nd ed.) 2.19en3 [This references Chapter 2, Paragraph 19, endnote #3]

0.34 The first instance of a term defined in Chapter 34, Glossary of Parliamentary Terms, is italicized.

INTRODUCTION TO PARLIAMENTARY LAW

CHAPTER 1. Parliamentary Law

Procedure is more than formality. Procedure is, indeed,
the great mainstay of substantive rights....
Without procedural safeguards ...liberty would rest on
precarious ground and substantive rights would be imperiled.
—William O. Douglas[1]

The history of liberty has largely been the history
of observance of procedural safeguards.
—Felix Frankfurter[2]

WHAT IS PARLIAMENTARY LAW?

1.1   *Parliamentary law* is the code of rules and ethics for working together in groups. It has evolved through the centuries out of the experience of individuals working together for a common purpose. It provides the means of translating beliefs and ideas into effective group action. Parliamentary law includes:

1. law, as found in adopted statutes and regulations;
2. common law, the body of principles, rules, and usages that has developed from court decisions; and
3. generally accepted *procedural rule*s that can be found in bylaws, *standing rules of order* and *temporary rules*, parliamentary authorities, and *custom*.

1.2   Parliamentary law is expressed more specifically in the form of meeting procedures. The purpose of meeting procedures is to allow members at *meetings* to reach informed decisions in an effective, efficient, orderly, courteous, and fair manner. Meeting procedures allow the members making the decisions to work as a cohesive group, while being respectful of the other members, and to reach decisions through *debate* and *majority* vote. Meeting procedures facilitate group decisions and help attain the organization's objectives.

WHY IS PARLIAMENTARY LAW NECESSARY?

1.3   As stated above by two justices of the Supreme Court of the United States, both our freedoms and our rights can exist only if safeguarded by sound procedures, exactly, conscientiously, and impartially enforced.

1.4   Parliamentary law is the procedural safeguard that protects the individual and the group in their exercise of the rights of free speech, free assembly, and the freedom to unite in organizations for the achievement of common aims.

1.5   While originating in—and still used by—Parliaments, Congress, and other legislatures of democratic nations, the principles of parliamentary law also apply to associations, boards, commissions, labor unions, and lower-level government bodies, such as school boards, municipal councils, and government commissions. The rights of members in these bodies, such as the rights to attend, debate, and vote, are protected through well-defined processes that also include mechanisms for their enforcement, for example, the ability to raise a point of order and to appeal a *ruling* of the chair.

ORGANIZATIONS THAT USE PARLIAMENTARY LAW

1.6   Government bodies at the highest levels of democratic nations, such as the US Congress or Canadian Parliament, and their state or provincial counterparts, use parliamentary procedure suited specifically to their needs. These have evolved over the centuries into complex sets of procedures that are suitable for their unique roles but would be inappropriate for most non-legislative organizations.

1.7   Lower-level government bodies, such as school boards, municipal councils, and government commissions, and other associations, such as homeowners, property owners, or condominium boards, commissions, labor unions, voluntary organizations, as well as political parties, religious groups, and nonprofit corporations, all use parliamentary law either because it is deliberately chosen or because it is required by statute, common law, or a superior body.

1.8   These organizations define which deliberative bodies within their own structure make decisions for the organization. The two main deliberative bodies within an organization are the meeting of members, sometimes known as the *assembly*, and the *board of directors* or *governing board* if there is one. While a meeting of members is generally the highest governing body in an organization, the members, in their wisdom, often delegate to the governing board substantive *powers* to carry on the work of the organization between meetings of members. In many cases there are *standing committees* and *special committees* that are mostly advisory to the two main bodies.

WHERE PARLIAMENTARY RULES ARE FOUND

1.9   The four basic sources of the parliamentary rules governing a particular organization, in the order of their rank, are:

1. Law. The law, consisting of the common law and the statutory and regulatory law enacted by federal, state/provincial, or local governments, is the highest source of parliamentary rules for any organization.
2. Charter. The *charter* or *articles of incorporation* granted by a government to an incorporated organization ranks second as a source. The charter granted by a parent organization to a *constituent or component unit* of the organization ranks next to its charter from government.
3. *Bylaws* and Adopted Rules. Any provisions of the bylaws of a parent organization that regulate the constituent or component units of the organization rank ahead of the bylaws adopted by the units. The bylaws and other adopted rules of an organization rank next, with the bylaws being superior.
4. Adopted *Parliamentary Authority*. The book, such as this one, adopted by an organization as its authority on all procedural questions not covered by the law or its charters, bylaws, or adopted rules completes the sources of the parliamentary rules governing an organization.

1.10   If there is a conflict between sources, the higher-ranking source prevails. By way of adopting standing rules of order or temporary rules, an organization can supplement or override the rules in the parliamentary authority; in this way, the organization can tailor its procedures to meet its specific needs.

ABUSE OF AND MISCONCEPTIONS REGARDING PARLIAMENTARY LAW

1.11   A member or group of members may use specific procedural rules to thwart the will of the assembly, even though the use of the rules may, on the face of it, appear to be used properly. Continual use of procedures, for example, for no other reason than to delay the proceedings of the meeting, is an abuse of the rules. It is important that such tactics not be tolerated by the *presiding officer* and the other attendees at the meeting.

1.12 These abuses are the source of misconceptions that may result in resistance to the use of parliamentary procedure. Misuse of parliamentary procedure may give the impression that it is a method for some to improperly impose their will on the organization or deprive others of their rights.

1.13 Similarly, too strict a focus on the details of the procedure may actually detract from its purpose by imposing an unnecessary formality that hinders decision-making without benefit. The procedures must be used and enforced impartially and in accordance with their purpose.

THE PARLIAMENTARY AUTHORITY

1.14 A parliamentary authority is usually a book with a written set of principles and specific procedural rules that can be adopted by motion or stated in bylaws that would determine the rules to be followed in all meetings of the organization. The parliamentary authority can be superseded by other rules adopted by the organization. These are called standing rules of order or temporary rules. These rules are often small in number compared to the multitude of rules contained in the parliamentary authority.

1.15 This book, *American Institute of Parliamentarians Standard Code of Parliamentary Procedure* 2nd Edition, is a comprehensive parliamentary authority that can be adopted by any organization. Standing rules of order or temporary rules, which differ from or augment the rules contained in the book, can then be adopted separately to cover the specific needs of the organization.

CHAPTER 2. Fundamental Principles of Parliamentary Law

2.1   Knowledge of the *fundamental principles* of parliamentary law provides a basis for understanding most parliamentary procedure questions. When the basic principles are understood, it clarifies the subject of parliamentary procedure and makes it easier to apply the rules because they follow logically from the principles. This understanding can also help reason out an appropriate solution when there is no explicit rule.

2.2   The principles are simple and so familiar that we sometimes fail to recognize their importance. They are the same principles on which democracies are based.

2.3   Some fundamental principles are based on law and others on centuries of democratic practice. While an organization may choose to adopt a rule that is contrary to the fundamental principles, consideration should be given to whether such a rule is permissible under applicable law. If permissible, such a rule should be adopted only with serious consideration of the fundamental principles and the basis for their broad historical acceptance. The most appropriate placement for a rule that deviates from the fundamental principles is in the bylaws or in a document referenced in the bylaws.

2.4   Occasionally, the fundamental principles, which have no order of *precedence*, may seem to conflict with one another. Often, when this is the case, the parliamentary authority will provide a specific rule to resolve the apparent conflict: for example, when the majority, which has a right to decide matters, wishes to end debate while the minority wishes to exercise the right to full and free discussion, this book resolves the conflict of these principles by requiring a *two-thirds vote* to close debate.

2.5   Some of the important principles of parliamentary law are listed below. These basic principles serve as a foundation for the framework of democratic group procedures.

THE PURPOSE OF PARLIAMENTARY LAW

2.6   The purpose of parliamentary procedure is to facilitate the orderly transaction of business and to promote cooperation and harmony. The philosophy of parliamentary law is constructive. Parliamentary law makes it easier for people to work together effectively and is designed to help organizations and members accomplish their purposes.

2.7 Parliamentary procedure should not be used to awe, entangle, or confuse the uninitiated.[3] The rules should be used only to the extent necessary to observe the law, to expedite business, to avoid confusion, and to protect the rights of members.

2.8 Some basic procedural rules have been developed to ensure that simple and direct procedures for accomplishing a purpose are observed. For example, some classes of motions have a definite order of precedence, each motion having a fixed rank for its introduction and its consideration.

2.9 This precedence or priority is based on the relative urgency or necessity of each motion in relation to the efficient transaction of business.

2.10 It is this principle of orderly and definite precedence that prevents motions from piling up in confused entanglement. With each motion holding a fixed *rank* for its introduction and consideration, business can move ahead smoothly and swiftly. To illustrate, if a *Main Motion* is being considered, a Motion to *Amend* is in order and takes precedence over the main motion. This is the proper sequence because it is necessary to correct or perfect the motion before it is voted on.

2.11 Another example of this basic principle is the rule that only one *question* is considered at a time.

2.12 In the interests of orderly procedure this principle is fundamental. When one motion is under consideration, it can be superseded by a motion having a higher precedence, which then becomes the motion under consideration. This latter motion can in turn be superseded, but each motion is considered separately and in turn so that only one question is before the assembly at a time. By following the fundamental rule of considering one question at a time, the assembly will find its way clearly through complex situations.

2.13 At times, in pursuit of efficiency, a group of motions may be processed by a single motion. The motions to Adopt in Lieu of and adopting a group of motions on a *consent agenda* are examples of this seeming inconsistency; however, in both cases, a single main motion is pending that addresses the group of motions.

RIGHT OF ASSOCIATION AND ASSEMBLY

2.14 Individuals have the right to associate with others in organized groups to promote and pursue their common interests and aspirations.[4] In forming or joining such organized groups, the members choose the terms of their relationship with one another by agreeing, through democratic processes, to a set of bylaws and other governing documents for the association. The governing documents form an agreement in the nature of a contract between all members and the association. This agreement may be amended from time to time as the needs of the association and the members change. Members of the association have equal rights and are expected to be loyal to the association, to promote and defend their common interests and aspirations, and to pay any membership fees as required. Members also have a right not to associate and may resign at any time subject to the association's rules at that time.

2.15 Individuals or groups have a right to assemble to promote their common interest. The right of assembly is inherent in the right to associate. Associations may protect this right to assemble by securing their assembly location and environment from interference from others, including their own members, to ensure privacy, quiet enjoyment, and security of property and person. In addition, the assembly controls those who may and may not attend, whether the person is a regular member, a *delegate*, or a nonmember, such as a guest or observer. This protection can be enforced through rules of the association and, as a last resort, through outside agencies such as law enforcement.

EQUALITY OF RIGHTS

2.16 **All members have equal rights, privileges, and obligations.** Every member has an equal right to propose motions, speak, ask questions, nominate, be a candidate for office, vote, or exercise any other privilege of a member. Every member has equal obligations, including the obligation to insist on the protection of the rights of all members. The rights of members present as well as the rights of members who are absent must be safeguarded.

2.17 The presiding officer defends this equality by conducting meetings impartially and by acting promptly to equally protect all members in the exercise of their rights and privileges. The general rule that the presiding officer does not take part in debate while *presiding*, except in small boards and in *committees*, is based on the principle of the presiding officer's impartial conduct.

2.18 The presiding officer can best serve the interests of an organization by being strictly impartial toward members or groups in the organization and should assist the organization in reaching its decisions.

MAJORITY DECISION

2.19 **The majority vote decides.** The ultimate authority of an organization is, as a general matter, vested in a majority of its members.[5] This is a fundamental concept of democracy.

2.20 A primary purpose of parliamentary procedure is to determine the will of the majority. By the act of joining a group, a member agrees to be governed by the vote of its majority. Until the vote on a question is announced, every member has an equal right to voice opposition or approval and to seek to persuade others. After the vote is announced, the decision of the majority becomes the decision of the organization, and it is the duty of every member to accept and to abide by that decision.

2.21 Whenever more than a *majority vote* is required to take an action, the minority is given the power to defeat the will of the majority. Thus, if a two-thirds vote is required, the will of the group can be defeated by any number exceeding one-third of its members.

2.22 When the members of an organization elect or appoint *officers*, boards, or committees and delegate authority to them, this selection and delegation should be by the democratic process of majority vote. Democracies operate not by direct participation of every member in every process of democracy but by the delegation of power to a few who are chosen by a vote of the majority. Power is delegated to committees, to boards, to officers, and to representatives, but this delegation must be made directly or indirectly by the democratic process of a majority vote.

MINORITY RIGHTS

2.23 **The rights of the minority must be protected.** Democratic organizations always protect certain basic rights belonging to all members. The rights to present *proposals*, to be heard, and to oppose proposals are valued rights of all members. However, the ultimate authority of decision rests with a majority, except when a higher vote is required to balance the rights of the majority with those of the minority. The members who are in the minority on a question are entitled to the same consideration and respect as members who are in the majority.

2.24 The minority of today is frequently the majority of tomorrow. A member of the majority on one question may be in the minority on the next. The protection of the rights of all members, minority and majority alike, is the responsibility of every member.

THE RIGHT OF DISCUSSION

2.25 **Full and free discussion of every proposition presented for decision is an established right of members.** Each member of an assembly has the right to express an opinion freely without interruption or interference, provided that the rules of debate and decorum, applicable to all members, are observed. This right to speak freely is as important as the right to vote. The democratic concept of freedom of speech is so important that a two-thirds vote is required to restrict that right by adopting motions to limit or close debate, thus providing a balance between the rights of the minority and the principle of *majority rule*. Even when a two-thirds vote is attainable, it may be prudent not to suppress debate prematurely; the exchange of information and opinions is the basis for better decision-making. Additionally, the minority may be more accepting of an action, even if they do not prevail, if there was an opportunity to present opposing facts and opinions.

THE RIGHT TO INFORMATION

2.26 **Members are entitled to information that will facilitate good decisions.** Every member has the right to know the meaning of the question before the assembly and what its effect will be. The presiding officer should always keep the *pending motion* clearly before the assembly and, when necessary, should explain it or may call on another to do so. Any motion and its effect should be explained if there are members who do not understand it. Members have the right to *request* information from or through the presiding officer on any motion they do not understand so that they may cast an informed vote. This principle underlies a member's right to rise to a Factual or Parliamentary Inquiry.

FAIRNESS AND GOOD FAITH

2.27 **All meetings must be characterized by fairness and good faith.** Trickery, bullying or coercion, taking advantage of the lack of parliamentary knowledge of others, overemphasis on minor technicalities, *dilatory tactics*, indulgence in personalities, and applying pressure by rushing—also known as *"railroading"* or *"gaveling through"* a measure—threaten the spirit and practice of fairness and *good faith*. If a meeting is characterized by fairness and good faith, a minor procedural error is not likely to invalidate an action that has been taken by an organization. But fraud, unfairness, or absence of good faith may cause a court to hold any action invalid. The primary responsibility to ensure fairness and good faith belongs to the presiding officer, but it is also the duty of every member.

2.28 Parliamentary strategy is the art of using parliamentary principles, rules, and motions to support or defeat a proposal. It includes, for example, such important factors as timing, wording of proposals, choice of supporters, selection of arguments, and manipulation of proposals by other motions. Strategy, ethically used, is constructive; however, if it involves deceit, fraud, misrepresentation, intimidation, railroading, or denial of the rights of members, it is destructive and possibly unlawful.

2.29 In 1776, John Hatsell, the Chief Clerk of the House of Commons of the British Parliament, wrote, "the motives for it were thought to outweigh the objections of form."[6] The interpretations of the courts make it clear that the intent and overall good faith of the group are of more importance than the specific procedure used in a given instance.[7] The effectiveness and, in fact, often the existence of an organization can be destroyed if its officers or members condone unfairness or lack of good faith.

2.30 An important corollary to this principle of fairness and good faith is that the simplest and most direct procedure for accomplishing a purpose should be followed. In other words, members have a right to an efficient meeting. Not only does this save time and effort on the part of all the members and officers, but it can also avoid confusion. A presiding officer should generally rule motions *out of order* if they present needless complications or when, as Thomas Jefferson said, "[T]he same result may be had more simply…"[8] However, fairness outweighs efficiency.

2.31 If a member undertakes a circuitous approach to a problem, the presiding officer should suggest the most direct and simplest procedure for accomplishing the purpose.

CHAPTER 3. Rights and Responsibilities of Members and Organizations

RELATIONSHIP BETWEEN MEMBER AND ORGANIZATION

3.1   When a member joins an organization, an implicit relationship is formed between the two parties. Parliamentary law requires no procedure to establish this relationship so long as a mutual understanding as to membership is reached. Most often the membership requirements are outlined in the bylaws of the organization. An organization may have prerequisites that a potential member has to meet before receiving full benefits. Membership orientation or initiation ceremonies may be a required part of acceptance as a new member. A person who joins an organization accepts the organization as it exists at that time. The current charter, bylaws, and other rules of the organization are a part of the implicit agreement binding the members and the organization.

3.2   A member's rights do not necessarily remain unchanged forever. Privileges of membership may be taken away by the decision of the voting body, or other privileges may be added. Fees and dues can be changed and assessments levied if provided for in the bylaws, but vested rights, those that have been acquired because of the fundamental agreement between the member and the organization, cannot be taken away.

3.3   All changes to the rights and privileges of members and all amendments to the rules of the organization must be made according to the provisions for making such changes contained in the bylaws or parliamentary authority.

RIGHTS OF MEMBERS

3.4   In addition to the rights a member has as a person, there are also associational rights, property rights, and parliamentary rights, all of which may be protected by law. A member's associational rights stem from membership in the organization. For example, a member has the right to fair and equitable treatment from the other members of the organization. Reciprocally, members have the responsibility to treat other members in a fair and equitable way.

3.5 Property rights also may be involved with membership in the organization, such as an interest in a clubhouse, boat dock, cemetery plot, or other assets owned by the group; however, membership in an organization in and of itself may not automatically convey property rights.

3.6 All members also have the following fundamental rights under *common parliamentary law*, subject only to any specific limitations contained in the bylaws:[9]

1. to be notified of meetings;
2. to attend meetings;
3. to make motions;
4. to debate motions;
5. to vote;
6. to run for office, and to nominate and elect officers and directors of the organization;
7. to propose and vote on amendments to the governing documents;
8. to insist on the enforcement of the rules of the organization and of parliamentary law;
9. to resign from an office or from the organization itself;
10. to remain in the organization, even when on the losing side of a particular proposition;
11. to be presented with *charges* and have a fair *hearing* before expulsion from membership;
12. to receive or have the right to inspect copies of the bylaws, charter, rules, *minutes*, or other official records of the organization; and
13. to exercise any other rights or privileges given to the members by the law, the bylaws, or the rules of the organization.

3.7 The rights of membership may vary depending on the bylaws. An organization may have different classifications of membership; if they are to have different rights, that must be delineated in the bylaws.

3.8 If any of the associational, property, or parliamentary rights of a member are violated, legal action may be taken against the organization or its representatives.[10] Generally, however, courts will not adjudicate such actions until the member has exhausted the means provided for enforcing such rights under the rules of parliamentary procedure and the bylaws of the organization.[11]

3.9 All members have the responsibility to respect and support these rights of other members, and to support the properly determined goals and decisions of the organization.

MEMBER IN GOOD STANDING

3.10 Organizations often use the term *member in good standing* and variations of it in their documents of authority. A member in *good standing* can usually exercise all the rights of membership while loss of good standing may result in loss of one or more rights of membership. Loss of good standing usually differs from suspension or expulsion in that it often may occur or terminate automatically or through administrative steps rather than through consideration of charges against the member as described in Chapter 33, "Discipline of Members and Officers."

3.11 The term has some basis in law, but each organization should provide its own definition, which should clearly describe:

1. the events that lead to loss of good standing and the conditions, if any, that must be met to maintain good standing;
2. the consequences of loss of good standing; and
3. the conditions that must be met to restore good standing.

3.12 A common condition for maintaining good standing is the payment of financial obligations to the organization, such as dues and assessments. Loss of good standing might occur automatically at a given interval after such obligations are due, or such arrears may cause some other process to occur, which, if carried out to completion, will then lead to loss of good standing. A less common condition leading to loss of good standing might be failure to comply with a meeting attendance requirement.

3.13 Consequences of loss of good standing might include the loss of some of or all the rights of membership; for this reason, these details should be placed in the bylaws or in another document or set of rules authorized by the bylaws.

3.14 Restoration of good standing might occur automatically upon removal of the conditions leading to the loss, such as payment of financial obligations, or additional steps might be required to restore good standing. Usually, action by the full assembly is not required for loss of good standing to occur or for it to be restored.

RIGHTS OF ORGANIZATIONS

3.15 The implicit agreement between the organization and the member is not a one-way street. An organization also has rights. These rights are exercised by the decision of the organization as provided in its governing documents. Some of the fundamental rights of an organization are:

1. to carry out its mission and to exercise any of the rights or authority granted it by law;
2. to change its purpose if permitted by law and its charter;
3. to merge with another organization or to dissolve;
4. to establish eligibility requirements and procedures governing the admission of members and to grant or refuse membership according to its adopted rules and within the law;
5. to establish and to amend, through changes in its bylaws, the rights, privileges, and obligations of its members either by extension or by limitation;
6. to delegate authority, within legal limits, to officers, boards, committees, and employees;
7. to select its officers, directors, and committee members;
8. to discipline, suspend, or expel members, directors, and officers in accordance with its bylaws, the parliamentary authority, and within the law; and
9. to purchase and hold property and to defend against or commence litigation in its own name if permitted by applicable law.

RELATIONSHIP OF INDIVIDUAL AND ORGANIZATIONAL RIGHTS

3.16 The rights of each member should be definite and, to the extent they are definite, are protected by law;[12] they must, however, be regarded in relation to the rights of other members and the organization. To successfully assert the rights of membership, the member must choose the appropriate time and forum.[13] The members must also follow the proper procedures. For example, a member has the right to have correct procedure followed; however, the *demand* for this enforcement must be timely and appropriate. Also, a member has the right to present any proposal within the organization's purposes to the assembly, but this is not an unlimited right and cannot be exercised at a *special meeting* by proposing a motion that is not stated in the call for the special meeting.

3.17 Similarly, a member has the fundamental right to speak on any debatable question before the assembly. However, the member's right to discuss gives way to the organization's right to set and enforce its own rules. For example, a member does not have the right to debate in the following circumstances:

1. when the motion has not yet been stated by the presiding officer;
2. for a second time when others desire to speak;
3. when some other member has the *floor*;
4. after debate has been terminated by adoption of a motion to Close Debate and Vote Immediately; or
5. before being recognized by the presiding officer.

3.18 If the rights of an individual member or a minority of members conflict with the rights of the majority of the assembly, the rights of the majority ultimately must prevail unless the governing documents protect the minority provision. For example, a minority has the right to be heard, but if the minority attempts to be heard when a majority has adopted a Motion to *Adjourn*, the minority's right must give way to that of the majority. Yet, some member rights are so fundamental that they cannot be overridden by the majority. Rules denying some of these rights require a higher vote and must apply to every member, such as the rules for limiting or closing debate. Other rights cannot be overridden by any vote—for example, notice or *quorum* requirements.

3.19 The right of members to oppose ideas and candidates does not extend to the right to undermine the organization itself. If, after the majority has made a decision, some members continue to act in opposition to or act in conflict with that decision, to the point where the organization has difficulty functioning or is in danger of being harmed or destroyed, the organization should protect itself by taking proper disciplinary action. This does not mean, however, that a member does not have the right to attempt to influence fellow members to change policy, thereby creating a new majority.

3.20 In some cases members may attempt to use meetings to gain an improper personal advantage. For example, a member may use information gained in meetings, perhaps even in a *closed meeting* where the information is to be protected, for a private interest so that the member may gain a personal advantage through this information. While a member may have a right to information, that information cannot be used for private gain, and using it for that purpose is an abuse of the privileges of membership. This type of behavior is not allowed and the sanctions against such behavior must be swift and direct.

RESIGNATIONS

3.21 A member has the absolute right to resign from an organization at any time. A provision in the bylaws that a member's dues must be paid up before the member resigns cannot prevent a resignation. There is no practical way in which an ordinary society can compel a delinquent member to continue as a member, nor can it persist in assessing and collecting dues. There are exceptions in law to this rule, such as property ownership where there is a need to own property to maintain membership.

3.22 A resignation from membership becomes effective immediately unless some future time is specified by the resigning member, and no acceptance of it is necessary to make it effective unless the bylaws say otherwise.

3.23 The bylaws, when addressing discipline, should also address the situation where a member resigns from membership but does so with disciplinary charges pending and before the applicable disciplinary process has been completed. If the bylaws are silent, the board decides, by motion, whether the disciplinary process should continue.

3.24 An officer or director may resign from office at any time. A written resignation is not required. An implied resignation, such as when a member moves out of the jurisdiction of the organization and is no longer eligible for membership, must be confirmed at least verbally by the affected individual before it is effective. A bylaws provision that an officer shall hold office "until a successor is elected" does not prevent the officer from resigning, nor can it be used to force a person to remain in office.

3.25 A resignation effective at some future date may be withdrawn until the effective date of the resignation; if, however, the resignation is intended to become effective immediately, it cannot be withdrawn.

3.26 After the resignation becomes effective, an officer or director who has resigned either orally or in writing cannot simply resume office because of a change of mind. A person who has resigned from office can be restored to that office only pursuant to the applicable *vacancy* filling provision. After resigning, an officer or director continues to be liable for actions taken before resignation.

CHAPTER 4. Governing Documents: Charter, Bylaws, and Rules

RULES GOVERNING ORGANIZATIONS

4.1   An organization may be governed by statutes, a charter, a *constitution*, bylaws, and/or standing rules of order. If the organization is incorporated, the primary rules under which it operates are the corporate laws of the jurisdiction in which it is incorporated. Organizations that are not incorporated may operate under other general laws applicable to that type of organization, such as unincorporated association law or a community association statute.* In addition, the following governance documents, when applicable, are ranked in the following order: the rules included in its *corporate charter*, the charter from a parent organization, the constitution, the bylaws, and any standing rules of order. Governing documents with these functions may have different names in different jurisdictions and different organizations, but their essential characteristics remain the same regardless of their name. The parliamentary authority adopted by the organization, typically specified in one of the governing documents, controls in all matters not covered by these governing documents. The graphic following paragraph 4.5 shows the relative rank of each of these documents.

TYPES OF CHARTERS

4.2   An organization looks to the law as its highest source of guidance on procedure and to its charters and bylaws as the next-ranking sources. Charters are of two types—charters of incorporation from the government and charters from a parent organization. Some organizations hold charters of both types. In that case, the charter from the government ranks above the charter from a parent organization.

4.3   The charter of an incorporated organization is a government grant, usually by a state, province, or territorial government, and occasionally by a national government, to a group of persons who have the right to *incorporate* and operate for specific purposes under the laws governing

---

* See Chapter 17 for further explanation of the types of organizations and their requirements.

corporations. In many jurisdictions, this charter is referred to by different terms, such as *articles of incorporation* or *certificate of incorporation*. The corporate charter of a nonprofit corporation usually contains its name and business address, a statement of the purposes of the organization, whether the organization is to be run as a membership organization or a board-only organization, and provisions relating to the organization's tax-exempt status. After a corporation is formed, the laws of the jurisdiction of incorporation continue to govern the corporation, regardless of where the corporation is doing business. This is called the internal affairs doctrine.[14]

4.4 The corporate laws of most jurisdictions provide the method for amending the corporate charter. No amendment to the charter is effective until it has been approved in the manner prescribed by law, usually provided by the corporation statute. Organizations in such jurisdictions should include a charter provision requiring amendments to their charters to be adopted by rules and procedures at least as strict as those required by the organization for amendments to its bylaws.

4.5 The charter from a parent organization, sometimes called a superior or central organization, is a certificate issued to a group of persons giving them the right to operate as a subordinate unit of the parent organization, which may be a constituent unit operating as an independent legal *entity* subject to the general supervision of the parent or a component unit organized as an internal division of the parent. Only the parent organization may amend the charter from the parent, although the bylaws may provide that amendment of certain provisions require the assent of the subordinate unit. A subordinate unit cannot amend a charter from a parent organization, although it can petition the parent organization to change the charter. Typically, the subordinate charter contains provisions regarding the relationship of the unit to the parent organization, often including provisions for parent organization approval of amendments to the subordinate charter. If permitted by the applicable corporate law, the corporate charter should contain a provision reserving the parent organization's right to approve amendments to the corporate charter. Unless otherwise provided in its governing documents, the subordinate unit is subject to the provisions in the charter or bylaws of the parent organization that relate to similar subordinate units. Changes required by the parent organization supersede contrary provisions of a subordinate organization's bylaws just as with any other higher ranking governing document.

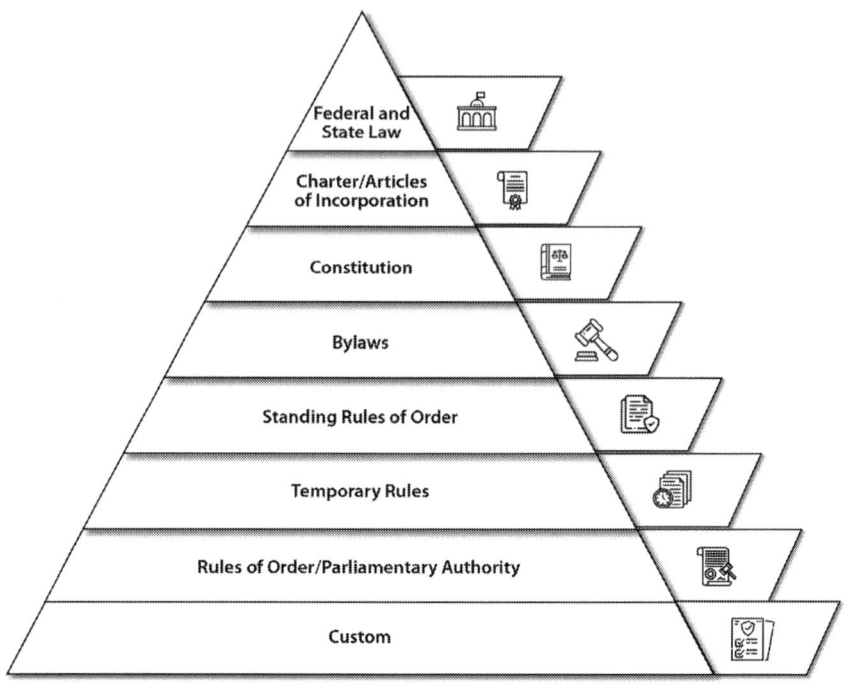

CONSTITUTION AND BYLAWS

4.6   Some organizations have adopted both a constitution and bylaws as two separate documents. If so, the constitution establishes the fundamental framework of the organization, and its amendment should be more difficult than amendment of the bylaws. Most corporate statutes recognize only bylaws, in which case the constitution is considered a higher-ranked form of bylaws within the organization's internal documents. Most newer organizations prefer to consolidate the provisions usually contained in the two documents into a single document, usually called bylaws or constitution and bylaws. A single document is preferable as it reduces the potential for duplication and conflict between the two documents. In an unincorporated association with both constitution and bylaws, the constitution should address those issues otherwise addressed in a corporate charter, such as name, purpose, and requirements for tax-exempt status in addition to the organization's fundamental framework. The bylaws supplement these fundamental provisions with additional detail and should be easier to amend. An organization planning on consolidating its separate constitution and bylaws should ensure that the amendment requirements of both prior governing documents are complied with and include a provision clarifying that the new unified document supersedes all prior governing documents.

FUNCTION OF BYLAWS

4.7   Bylaws are adopted and maintained by an organization to define the privileges secured and the *duties* assumed by the members, and to set up the governance framework of the organization. An organization has the right to adopt such bylaws as the members may agree on, so long as they are not contrary to the law or a higher-level governing document.[15]

Drafting Bylaws

4.8   Drafting original bylaws should be done by a committee large enough to include those concerned with the creation of a new organization. The services of a *parliamentarian* are useful in developing proper language and form. More information on the services of a parliamentarian can be found in Chapter 29. If the group plans on incorporating, an attorney should be consulted. Accuracy is essential in writing bylaws with each section carefully thought out and stated clearly and concisely, using correct grammar and punctuation. When the final draft is developed, it should be agreed on by a majority of the committee. Adopted bylaws should be written so there is only one possible interpretation because they will become a legal document.

4.9   The bylaws contain all the details necessary to make the organization function and are considered a contract between the organization and its members, among the members in a corporation,[16] and among the members in an unincorporated association.[17] Members, once they have joined an organization, are legally bound by its bylaws. Meeting procedures specific to the organization are enumerated in the standing rules of order and administrative details in adopted procedures rather than the bylaws. Bylaws are written to meet the needs of that organization. A provision that works well for one organization may be entirely unsuitable for another. Bylaws should be concise and are best arranged in outline form. All bylaws dealing with the same general subject should be grouped together under one article, which in turn is divided into sections.*

---

* *See* Appendix A, Bylaws Checklist.

4.10 If not otherwise provided by applicable corporate statutes, a provision for dissolution of the organization should be included in the bylaws to protect the assets of the organization. Nonprofit, tax-exempt organizations cannot distribute profits to their members in the form of dividends and cannot distribute the assets to their members during the life of the organization. If the organization is incorporated, it dissolves under the laws of incorporation; if not incorporated, it dissolves by adoption of a *resolution* to do so, which should include how any assets may be disposed of. A motion to dissolve is, in essence, a motion to rescind the bylaws and, if not otherwise provided for by law or in the bylaws, should follow the same procedure as required for amendment of the bylaws.

4.11 An organization may need the assistance of an attorney on legal matters. An attorney should be involved in the creation of a new organization if organized as a corporation or trust; the filing of legal documents; and the review of proposed documents with legal implications. The initial bylaws should be drafted in consultation with an experienced parliamentarian.

Adoption of the Original Bylaws

4.12 When the presiding officer of an *organizing meeting*, sometimes called a *mass meeting*, calls for the report of the committee appointed to draft the bylaws, the committee chair first moves the adoption of the proposed bylaws to bring the document before the assembly for consideration and discussion.* The presiding officer states the motion, "It has been moved that the bylaws be adopted. The committee chair will read the first section."**

4.13 The process used is to *consider by paragraph*.*** The committee chair reads the first section of the first article, and the presiding officer calls for discussion, questions, or amendments to it. If an amendment to the section is proposed, the presiding officer states it to the assembly, and, after discussion, it is voted on. Only the proposed amendments, not articles or sections, are voted on. The presiding officer then calls for the reading of the next section and follows the same procedure. When the reading and amendment of each individual bylaw section is completed, the presiding officer opens all sections for further amendment or discussion.

---

* For more information on the organizing meeting, *see* Chapter 17.

** No second is required for motions from a committee.

*** *See* Chapter 16.

4.14 When there are no further amendments or debate, the presiding officer takes the vote on the motion to adopt the bylaws. A majority vote is required for adoption of the original bylaws.

When Bylaws Go into Effect

4.15 The bylaws, and any proposals to amend the bylaws, go into effect immediately with the announcement of the vote adopting the document. Alternatively, some organizations may have a bylaw provision or a standing rule of order providing a standardized default effective date for all bylaw amendments, such as at the end of the meeting at which it is adopted, thirty days after adoption, or by a particular date each year.

4.16 From time to time, however, the body may wish for a specific bylaw to have a different effective date than those described in the previous paragraph. For example, "I move that the bylaws be adopted as amended, provided that Article VII, Section 8, adding a standing committee on strategic planning, not go into effect until September 1." The name for a provision that changes the effective date of a bylaw amendment is called a *proviso*.

4.17 In no circumstance can a bylaw amendment have a retroactive effect.

4.18 Even if the effective date is later, an amendment or revision of the bylaws, together with any implementing proviso, becomes a part of the bylaws immediately upon the announcement of the vote adopting it. Therefore, once approved, neither a bylaw amendment, bylaw revision, nor an applicable proviso can be reconsidered.

Provisions for Amending Bylaws

4.19 It is considered a best practice for an organization to include in its bylaws specific requirements covering the following:

1. how and by whom amendments to bylaws may be initiated and proposed;
2. the form in which proposed amendments should be stated;
3. the date before which proposed amendments must be received, and to whom they are to be addressed;
4. the required notice to members of proposed amendments; and
5. the vote required to adopt the amendment.

Proposing Amendments to the Bylaws

4.20 An organization must be able to adapt to changing conditions by being able to amend its bylaws. However, to provide for stability and security in the purpose and function of the organization, it is recommended that the organization make amending the bylaws more difficult than amending standing rules of order or policies.

4.21 In many local groups, any member may rise while new business is being considered and offer a proposal to amend the bylaws simply by stating the proposal and giving a copy of it to the secretary. In most groups, the proposal is then referred to the bylaws committee or *reference committee*, which studies it and reports the recommendation of the committee to the voting body at a later meeting. The bylaws of most organizations require *previous notice* for proposals and may require review by a bylaws or reference committee.* Most organizations require at least a two-thirds vote for adoption. Some groups also restrict consideration of bylaw proposals to the *annual meeting*.

4.22 State, national, and international organizations ordinarily require that amendments to the parent governing documents be proposed by an elected delegate of the organization, a constituent or component unit, a committee, or a board of the parent organization. These organizations typically require that such proposals be submitted by a certain date preceding a *convention*.

4.23 When a motion for which notice is required is pending, the maker of the motion may request of the assembly that the motion be withdrawn, just as any other motion may be requested to be withdrawn. However, any other member may then choose to make the same motion in that member's own name, and no additional notice is required.**

Form for Proposed Amendments to Bylaws

4.24 Unless the bylaws provide differently, a proposed amendment must be stated in such language that, if adopted, it may be incorporated directly into the bylaws and is sent in this form as a notice to all members.

---

* Reference committees are explained more fully in Chapter 25.

** For issues involving withdrawal of bylaw amendments before or during the meeting, see the chapter on Notice, Chapter 20.

4.25 The following is a simple method of stating a proposed amendment:

> **Proposed Amendment to Article VI, Section 1, of the Bylaws**
>
> To Amend Article VI, Board of Trustees, Section 1, Membership, by striking out "three members elected by the House of Delegates" and inserting in their place "five members elected by the General Assembly."
>
> If amended, the section will read: Section 1, Membership. The board of trustees shall consist of the president, vice president, secretary, treasurer, and five members elected by the General Assembly.

4.26 The three-column format is commonly used to present proposed bylaw amendments as shown below.

Existing Language	Amendment	If Amended
Section 1, Membership. The board of trustees shall consist of the president, vice president, secretary, treasurer, and three members elected by the House of Delegates	Section 1, Membership. The board of trustees shall consist of the president, vice president, secretary, treasurer, and five members elected by the General Assembly	Section 1, Membership. The board of trustees shall consist of the president, vice president, secretary, treasurer, and five members elected by the General Assembly

Considering Amendments to Bylaws

4.27 Proposals to amend the bylaws are an example of the Specific-Purpose Main Motion to Amend a Previous Action. Because of their unique proposition to change the bylaws, unlike the usual Motion to Amend a Previous Action, they require previous notice and a two-thirds vote for their adoption unless a different requirement is stated in the bylaws.

4.28 If proper notice of a proposal to amend the bylaws has been given, and the decision is delayed to another meeting, then the notice should be provided again, if possible, of the proposal and the meeting at which it will receive further consideration. If referred to a committee and the committee recommends amendments outside the original *scope of notice*, notice of the proposal must be given as though it were a new bylaw amendment.[*]

---

[*] Incorporated organizations should check their jurisdiction's corporation statute for the default voting requirement.

4.29 The member offering the proposal reads the first proposal as it is stated in the notice and moves its adoption. It may be amended, and secondary amendments are also *in order*. The vote required to adopt amendments to the proposal is a majority and requires no notice, even though the adoption of the proposal requires previous notice, and a two-thirds vote.

4.30 When notice has been given, the subject covered by the proposal has been opened to change and gives the assembly discretion in offering amendments to the proposal. Parliamentary law, however, provides that:

1. The amendment must be germane to the proposed bylaw amendment.
2. Amendments can only be considered if they can reasonably be implied by the notice given on the proposal. This is often referred to as an amendment within the scope of the notice. Further restrictions on the extent or type of amendments to proposals must be included in the bylaws.*

4.31 Once notice of the proposal to amend the bylaws has been given, members are aware that a particular subject will be open to subsidiary amendment at the meeting without further notice. For example, if a proposal adds associate membership to the bylaws, members know that the proposal may be amended by providing or changing the qualifications, rights, and privileges of those associate members. However, amendments pertaining to other classes of membership would not be in order since the scope of the notice does not state or imply changes to any class of membership except associate membership.

4.32 A Motion to Amend another part of the bylaws not specified in the notice is admissible if it is reasonably implied by the notice. Using the same example, the original proposal provides for an associate membership class. Fixing the dues for associate members would be implied, although the subject of dues is covered in another part of the bylaws and might have been omitted unintentionally in the proposal. A Motion to Amend the bylaws to establish dues for associate members would be within the scope of notice.

4.33 If a proposal conflicts with an existing provision elsewhere in the bylaws, an amendment to the conflicting provision in the bylaws should be included in the original notice; however, if that is not done, the conflicting provision can be amended to conform to the newly adopted proposal

---

* See Chapter 20 for further information on scope of notice.

without additional notice. Similarly, if a proposal is adopted, clerical changes for consistent numbering of the bylaws and other non-substantive conforming changes are implicit in the amendment. The implementation of such conforming changes is delegated to the secretary unless a motion or rule grants authority to others.

4.34 Other amendments to a proposed bylaw amendment are not in order if they go beyond the range between the current bylaw provision, the status quo, and the proposed bylaw amendment. As an example: The existing bylaws specify dues of forty-five dollars. The proposal is to raise the dues to fifty dollars. It is not in order to amend the proposal to an amount less than forty-five dollars or more than fifty dollars.

Revision of Bylaws

4.35 After bylaws have been in place for a considerable period, it may be necessary to amend many portions of them. A *revision* can be a substantive rewriting of the bylaws, a restatement of the current bylaws for clarity or reorganization, or a single document including a series of amendments that proposes a substantial number of changes that may considerably affect the structure of the organization. The simplest method of revision, when extensive changes are required, is to establish a special committee for this purpose or instruct the bylaws committee to study the bylaws and submit a revision. The recommendation of a special revision committee or a bylaws committee constitutes a revision when the notice presents a substantive rewriting of the entire bylaws or a complete restatement of the current bylaws.

4.36 A copy of the proposed revision with notice of the date when it will be considered and voted on should be sent to each member in advance of the meeting or convention. Rationales or necessary explanations may be provided as a separate document. A revision committee may be appointed or elected and should have the same qualifications stated for those creating new bylaws. The committee may hold hearings so that members may submit and justify suggested changes.

4.37 A revision proposes, in effect, a new set of bylaws, and the revision is presented and considered in the same manner as adoption of original bylaws, which are considered by paragraph. Scope of notice does not limit amendments to a revision if the revision was authorized in advance by the body that will vote on the adoption of the revision, or the board or *executive committee* of the organization. A revision, however, requires the same vote and advance notice that is required to amend the bylaws. The original bylaws, which are still in effect, are not amendable by the assembly while the revision is being considered.

4.38 The revision is considered first, and should the *bylaws revision* fail, separately noticed amendments to the existing bylaws may be considered. If the revision is adopted, the existing bylaws have been replaced. Any separately noticed amendments may be considered if they can be easily adapted to the revised bylaws.

INTERPRETING BYLAWS AND RULES

4.39 Organizations frequently have difficulty agreeing on the interpretation of ambiguous provisions of their own bylaws and rules. It is wise to assign the initial duty of interpreting the bylaws and rules to the committee on bylaws or to the board of directors. The interpreting group may seek the advice of an attorney, a professional parliamentarian, or both. The final decision on an interpretation of the bylaws and rules, when they are ambiguous, rests with the membership unless the bylaws assign this authority to another body.* Once an ambiguity has been identified and resolved by an interpretation, the bylaws should be amended to remove the ambiguity. Bylaws that are not ambiguous must be followed until they are amended.

4.40 Some general rules to be considered when interpreting ambiguous provisions of bylaws or rules, often called *canons of construction*, include:[18]

1. The purpose of interpretation is to ascertain the intent of the drafters of the ambiguous provision.
2. The bylaws (or rules) are to be read together as a whole and words used in one place in the bylaws should have a similar interpretation elsewhere in the bylaws (or rules).
3. Every clause or provision of the bylaws (or rules) should be given effect.
4. Weight should be given to the customary practice of the organization in carrying out the provision.

---

* If the membership does not meet regularly, then the bylaws ambiguity may be resolved on a temporary basis by the body that encounters the ambiguity in a meeting.

5. Words (other than legal or technical terms) are to be given their standard meanings, not a forced or artificial construction.
6. When legal or technical terms are used in the bylaws in a technical sense, they are to be given their legal or technical meaning.
7. The bylaws or rules should not be construed to lead to an absurd or infeasible result.
8. If a word is included in a list, it is to be interpreted to be used similarly to the other words in the list.
9. When a list contains several specific items, other similar items are intended to be excluded.
10. When general words follow specific words in a list, the general words are considered to cover items like those of the specific words.
11. A provision requiring something to be done implies authority and reasonable means necessary to carry the action out.
12. A specific provision prevails over a general provision.
13. A mandatory provision prevails over a permissive provision.
14. An authorization for a greater action includes within it the power to take lesser included actions. Likewise, a prohibition of a lesser action prohibits any similar greater action.
15. *Penalty* clauses, such as fines and disciplinary provisions, are to be interpreted narrowly.

TEMPORARY AND STANDING RULES OF ORDER

4.41 Organizations sometimes adopt rules governing procedure and conduct in meetings that add to or deviate from the rules of parliamentary law as stated in their adopted parliamentary authority. The rules that are temporary and intended to meet a current or special situation are termed *temporary rules*.[*] The rules that are intended to stand until revoked are termed *standing rules of order.* Temporary and standing rules of order cover meeting procedures and are of higher rank than those in the parliamentary authority. Convention rules deal with organizing and conducting business at a *convention* and are discussed in Chapter 24, "Conventions and Their Committees."

---

[*] In prior editions, *temporary rules* were referred to as *special rules*, which many found confusing.

4.42 Organizations have the right to adopt standing rules of order or temporary rules by majority vote without notice and to abolish or amend them by a two-thirds vote without notice. When a standing rule of order or temporary rule is abolished, the rule defaults to the rule contained in the *American Institute of Parliamentarians Standard Code of Parliamentary Procedure*.

ADOPTING A PARLIAMENTARY AUTHORITY

4.43 Every deliberative organization is presumed by law to be governed by the rules of parliamentary law. The charter, constitution, bylaws, and standing rules of order of the organization are its highest authority; in all matters not covered by these rules, the organization is governed by parliamentary law.

4.44 An organization can adopt any code or book of rules on parliamentary procedure to govern it, typically called a parliamentary authority, but sometimes called a meeting guide or meeting manual. The name of the authority should be included in the bylaws or standing rules of order. This bylaw is usually stated in a form similar to the following:

> In all matters not covered by applicable law, its constitution, bylaws, standing rules of order, or temporary rules, this organization shall be governed by the current edition of the *American Institute of Parliamentarians Standard Code of Parliamentary Procedure.*

4.45 Great care should be given to the selection of the parliamentary authority because the courts do not excuse any organization from its legal requirements because of errors, omissions, or ambiguities in the authority that may have been adopted. Ignorance of the correct rules of procedure is not a valid defense against legal entanglements or action.[19]

4.46 The parliamentary authority does not have the force and effect of bylaws. If state or federal law requires that something be allowed or prohibited in the bylaws, and it is allowed or prohibited in the parliamentary authority, this does not satisfy the legal requirement.

4.47 Unique circumstances occasionally arise that are not directly addressed in an organization's adopted parliamentary authority. In such cases, many times the answer to the question lies in an analogy to another similar situation covered by the text or may be found by relying on the fundamental principles detailed in Chapter 2. When no answer is otherwise clear, provisions found in other parliamentary authorities may prove persuasive on how to address a situation not directly covered by the adopted authority. Under the *AIP Standard Code of Parliamentary Procedure,* other parliamentary authorities may be referred to if the relevant provisions are consistent with the simplified and modernized approach of this book.*

ADOPTED PRINCIPLES

4.48 *Principles*, as used in this parliamentary authority, define the beliefs and philosophy of the organization, and bylaws define the structure.** Organizations frequently adopt principles that are as important in determining the action of the group as are its bylaws or other rules. Principles are usually formulated to meet recurring problems that come up for decision. Most successful businesses have written principles that have developed from experience and that guide their operations. Many organizations develop principles that have an equally powerful influence on their effectiveness.

4.49 Once a principle has been developed and adopted, it sets a standard for judging and deciding all new proposals dealing with the subject or situation covered by the principles. If a proposal is contrary to an adopted principle of the organization, it should not be considered unless the principle is first amended to permit such a proposal.

4.50 Organizations that use guiding principles should provide in their bylaws for their adoption, the vote required, and the method for amending and reviewing those principles. Unless otherwise specifically stated in the bylaws, however, principles require only a majority vote to adopt or to change.*** Some organizations review their principles each year, or every several years, to see whether changes or new principles are required. Many organizations provide for a standing committee on principles that maintains a list of currently effective principles, considers and makes recommendations on proposed principles, reviews all principles periodically, and interprets them when requested. Other organizations may require

---

* If none of these approaches yields a clear answer, inquirers may submit questions through www.AIPparl.org.

** Organizations often call these *principles, position statements, belief statements, purposes, objects, mission, vision*, or other similar terms.

*** Unless rules categorized as principles are more difficult to amend than ordinary main motions with continuing effect, they can be overridden under the principle of Repeal by Implication. See Chapter 9.

committees to review periodically all principles that relate to their scope of work and determine whether any should be amended or rescinded.

4.51 Principles should not be included in the bylaws but should be compiled separately and stated appropriately. The following are examples of principles:

1. This association believes that, because its fundamental purpose is to educate senior citizens on proper use of medications, its programs should not include speakers on political topics.
2. This organization shall adhere to the principle of raising our professional standards by strict screening of applicants for membership. The professional character of our organization can best be advanced by gradually increasing, but never lowering, the eligibility requirements of applicants for membership.
3. This organization believes that current services to members are its most important function. Our principle is that profit from convention registration fees should not be saved, accumulated, or invested for future use, but that all revenue from convention profits should be used to provide a constantly improving and expanding current program of services to our members.
4. To avoid any perception of a *conflict of interest*, this organization adheres strictly to the principle that no member may give gifts or gratuities to any employee of the organization, and that no employee or board member may receive gifts from a supplier of services to the organization.

ADMINISTRATIVE PROCEDURES

4.52 There are many details of administrative procedures outside of a meeting that are necessary to carry out the provisions of the charter, bylaws, and adopted rules. These detailed procedures should not be included in the bylaws as they will add length and confusion.* They can be changed more frequently than the bylaws or more important rules and require only a majority vote to adopt or change. They should be classified under suitable headings—for example, "Convention Credentials Committee Procedures" or "Reimbursement of Expenses."

4.53 Policies and procedures may not be used to restrict the rights of members unless the bylaws specifically authorize such restrictions, such as a

---

* Organizations often call these *policies, procedures, guidelines, protocols*, or other similar terms.

bylaw provision that "Qualifications for elected office shall include those stated in the Election Policy."

SUPPLEMENTING PROCEDURAL RULES BY MOTIONS

4.54   An organization has the inherent power to take any action that is not in conflict with the law or its charter, bylaws, or adopted rules. This includes the power to adopt motions regulating the conduct of its current business. Since many situations arise that are not covered by rules, it is essential that the details of transacting business be determined by motions. During proceedings, motions are frequently necessary to facilitate the method, manner, or order of transacting business. For example, if a committee has submitted five recommendations relating to the same subject, and the committee chair has moved that the first recommendation be adopted and it is being considered, some member might move that the fifth recommendation be considered and decided first because it contains a general statement on which the other four recommendations depend.

4.55   The power of an organization to adopt any motions for the conduct of current business is particularly important during *elections*. For example, when there are several candidates for an office and no candidate receives the required majority vote, it is often impractical to require that successive votes be taken until one candidate receives the necessary majority vote. An organization has the power to adopt motions to enable it to complete the election within a reasonable time. Organizations sometimes vote, for example, to drop the candidate having the lowest number of votes from the list of candidates after each successive vote. Or an organization may decide to reopen nominations for the office, to secure a candidate on whom a majority can agree. Organizations have wide leeway in adopting motions to determine the conduct of pending business.

CUSTOM AND PRECEDENT

4.56   *Custom* and *precedent* are related concepts. Custom is a rule that is based on usage and is not written down. Precedent is a rule based on interpretation of the rules through a presiding officer's ruling on a point of order or the assembly's vote on an appeal or other motion to interpret its rules. Precedents should be included in the organization's minutes but are often difficult to locate because minutes are typically not indexed.

4.57 A procedure established by custom or precedent will prevail until a contrary written rule is brought to the attention of the assembly. A custom, when questioned, becomes a precedent when the presiding officer rules on a point of order or the assembly votes on an appeal. An assembly may also adopt a main motion that incorporates the organization's customary practice into a rule. Precedent may be overridden by a majority vote to establish a new rule.

EMERGENCY RULES

4.58 Every organization should have a set of procedures in place to allow the organization to continue functioning, to the extent feasible, in case of emergency. Because there are so many different types of emergencies, no one set of rules is likely to meet the needs of every situation. Flexibility is important because a snowstorm or a hurricane on the date of an annual meeting may call for a different response than social distancing requirements during a months-long pandemic.

4.59 An emergency may require temporary governance measures as well as special meeting procedures. Therefore, an organization needs to check at all levels of governing documents as to what measures are permitted. Many nonprofit corporation laws include special emergency provisions, which may include both defaults and mandates. In addition, statutes addressing recurring emergency situations may grant the executive branch of the government power to issue emergency edicts, often called executive orders or decrees. Sometimes, legislatures adopt special legislation intended to deal with a specific emergency expected to last for several years or more, for example a pandemic or cleanup after a major flood, fire, storm, or earthquake.

4.60 Before any organization takes actions outside the standard course during an emergency, it should check any applicable emergency statutes and executive orders to verify that the intended actions are authorized. Regarding internal governance, the jurisdiction where the group was organized should be consulted, but the jurisdiction of the location of a scheduled meeting controls health and safety precautions about how an emergency affects the ability to meet.

4.61 Certain necessary actions during emergency situations may require authorization in the bylaws. Emergency bylaws should be included in the body of the standard bylaws, although some groups place them in an appendix. If included in an appendix, emergency bylaws are still bylaws and must comply with applicable law. They require the same vote to adopt as standard bylaws, and the same vote to amend as any other part of the bylaws unless they include a separate, typically lower, threshold for amendment. Before drafting emergency bylaws, an organization should check to determine which emergency bylaws are permitted in the jurisdiction where the group was organized. Any emergency rules that qualify as standing rules of order or adopted procedures should be adopted at the most flexible level.

4.62   Issues to address in emergency bylaws include:

1. who is to determine whether an emergency exists and is applicable to the organization and the criteria to use to make that decision, e.g., government emergency declaration or determination by the board or an officer; often board or officer determination is limited to occurrence of certain circumstances, such as a quorum of the board being unable to meet;

2. when and by whom a meeting can be postponed or canceled, and rescheduled;

3. how and by whom *notice of meetings*, postponements, or cancellations are to be given;

4. whether quorum requirements should be relaxed;

5. whether the board should be delegated certain powers by the members, including amending the bylaws;

6. whether to deviate from or add additional officers to the standard order of succession of officers due to vacancy or incapacity; to extend officers' and directors' terms; and, if vacancies occur, including temporary emergency-related vacancies, to fill those vacancies in a more expeditious manner than otherwise provided in the bylaws;

7. whether (i) proxies or (ii) telephonic or electronic meetings should be permitted if otherwise prohibited by the bylaws;

8. whether to relocate the corporate office;

9. how the board and members are to be notified of action taken outside the standard course during the emergency; and

10. whether and how soon after the emergency ends the standard procedures will resume effect.

4.63 In general, it is a best practice:

1. to postpone any major decisions that are not necessary until after the emergency is over and take only those actions necessary to continue the essential operations of the organization during the emergency;
2. to conform any emergency rules as closely as reasonably possible in the circumstances to the standard rules;
3. to ratify any actions that were taken using emergency procedures; and
4. to allow the relevant body to undo any changes to governing documents made during the emergency and revert to pre-emergency procedures on a majority vote.

4.64 It is important to note that the purpose of the rules is to serve the will of the organization and not to restrain it.[20] It would be absurd for an organization to be unable to fulfill its purposes or carry out its essential operations because it failed to provide in its rules for every unforeseen event.[21] Therefore, when an organization's adopted governing rule is impossible to carry out in the circumstances and this prevents the organization from functioning, the only thing that can be done is to change that provision to a reasonable one, complying, in making the change, with the spirit of the existing rules as nearly as possible.[22]

4.65 For a sample set of emergency bylaws, see Appendix B.

VOTING

CHAPTER 5. Votes Required for Valid Actions

SIGNIFICANCE OF A MAJORITY VOTE

5.1   One of the fundamental concepts in a democracy is that the ultimate authority lies in the citizens of the democracy. Likewise, in an organization, the ultimate authority lies in a majority of the members when they meet to act through the majority vote. This fundamental principle of voting allows the members to operate their organization democratically and legitimately through the will of the members of the organization. A majority vote is required to take action.[23] A *majority vote* in this book, unless otherwise qualified, is defined as more than half the legal votes cast by members present and voting. Abstentions are not considered votes cast. Thomas Jefferson said, "The voice of the majority decides…. [T]he former law is not to be changed but by a majority."[24] To permit less than a majority to decide for any group would subject the many to the rule of the few, and this would be contrary to the most basic democratic principle. Democratic peoples universally accept decision by majority vote.

5.2   If a majority agrees, that is an agreement by the body since all members by the act of joining the organization have agreed that the majority should govern.[25] For more discussion on the relationship between members and the organization, see Chapter 3.

5.3   As a general principle of good governance, an organization should not authorize less than a majority to decide anything. Likewise, more than a majority, sometimes called a *supermajority*, also should not be required for most decisions. Some organizations, however, do adopt a rule that permits a mere plurality—one vote more than any other candidate receives—to elect an officer or director. Others go to the opposite extreme of requiring a high vote, sometimes as high as an 80 percent vote, on certain proposals. An 80 percent vote to *adopt* a measure allows one-fifth of the members to control the organization's decision. Sometimes such policies may be justified, but they should be used with great caution as under either of these rules the minority, not the majority, controls.

5.4   Any requirements permitting decisions by less than a majority vote (for example, by plurality in an election) or requiring more than a majority vote (for example, a two-thirds vote on a substantive proposal) are not valid unless they are required by statute, the charter, or bylaws. An exception is made for procedural rules in the parliamentary authority or standing rules of order or temporary rules, where, for example, closing debate may require more than a majority vote. These procedural exceptions are in place to protect the rights of the minority to participate in the deliberative process.

Requiring More Than a Majority Vote

5.5   Sometimes members mistakenly assume that the higher the vote required to take an action, the more democratic the process; however, the opposite is true. Whenever a vote of more than a majority is required to take action, control is taken from the majority and given to a minority. For example, when a two-thirds vote is required, the minority needs only to cast more than one-third of the votes to defeat the proposal. Thus, a minority is permitted to overrule the will, not only of the majority, but of up to two-thirds of the members. If a two-thirds vote is required to pass a proposal and 65 members vote for the proposal and 33 members vote against it, the 33 members have won; the 65 have been defeated. This is minority rule, not majority rule. For a substantive decision, this allows a minority to preserve the status quo, which may be desirable in certain circumstances. For example, many organizations require notice and a two-thirds vote to amend the bylaws in order to safeguard the underlying principles and basic structure of an organization from hasty change due to the passions of a temporary majority.

5.6   The higher the vote required, the smaller the minority to which control passes. The requirement of a *unanimous vote* means that one member can overrule the will of all other members.

5.7   Thomas Jefferson clearly recognized that a decision by a majority vote is an integral and vital element of democracy in a letter to Baron von Humboldt in 1817:[26]

> The first principle of republicanism is that the *lex majoris partis** is the fundamental law of every society of individuals of equal rights; to consider the will of the society enounced by the majority of a single vote, as sacred as if unanimous, is the first of all lessons in importance, yet

---

* Law of the majority.

the last which is thoroughly learnt. This law once disregarded, no other remains but that of force, which ends necessarily in military despotism.

5.8   One exception to the principle of requiring only a majority vote is when a vote has an adverse impact on the rights of the members. For example, members have the right to full and free discussion. This right can be limited but only by a two-thirds vote, such as required by the Motions to Limit or Extend Debate or to Close Debate and Vote Immediately. Another exception is when there is an immediate need to suspend the rules of order to do something that could not be done under the current rules. While the urgency may be real, common parliamentary practice requires a two-thirds vote to suspend the rules to avoid abuse of such a powerful rule by a slim majority. Another exception is when the rights of absentees are involved. For example, most organizations stipulate in their bylaws that the bylaws can be amended only by a two-thirds vote with advance notice to protect absentees. Bylaws of some nonprofit corporations (and some corporation codes) require a two-thirds vote to buy or sell real estate or to mortgage property owned by the organization.

5.9   Generally, it is unwise to require more than a majority vote to commit the organization to a course of action because of the power it gives to a minority to override the majority's wishes.

Requiring Less Than a Majority Vote

5.10   The effect of deciding proposals or electing candidates by less than a majority vote is similar to requiring a higher vote than a majority. It takes away the power of decision from the majority and gives it to a minority.

5.11   Electing a candidate or deciding a proposal by *plurality vote* (more votes than any other candidate or alternative proposal) means that officers may be chosen by a minority and that they therefore may not have the support that is behind a candidate chosen by a majority. If there are a large number of candidates for an office, the candidate elected might be chosen by only a small fraction of the members of the organization. A candidate can only be elected to office and a proposal can only be decided by a majority vote unless the bylaws provide otherwise.

Importance of Defining the Vote Required

5.12   The term *majority vote* sometimes causes controversy when the basis for computing the majority is not stated clearly. Hundreds of cases have wound up in the courts because of the resulting confusion. The common parliamentary law is that decisions are made by a *majority of the legal votes cast* unless clearly stated otherwise. For this reason, whenever such terms as *majority, two-thirds, three-fourths*, and *unanimous vote* are used without specifying a basis, for users of this parliamentary authority, the basis is assumed to be the legal votes cast by members present and voting, excluding abstentions.

5.13   Every organization should state in its bylaws the vote required for elections and also the vote required for those decisions it wishes to have decided by other than a majority vote. Whenever not defined in statute, charter, or bylaws, the basis on which a vote must be computed is a majority of the legal votes cast by members present and voting, excluding abstentions.

5.14   An organization that wishes to calculate a vote on a basis other than the default must be careful to use precise language that clearly and unambiguously reflects the intent. An organization that means to use the default basis, by contrast, should simply use the term *majority vote* because any further specification is likely to create confusion regarding the intent.

Different Calculations for a Majority Vote

5.15   A majority vote, or any other vote, may be qualified or defined in many ways. Clear and unambiguous language is required to ensure that the votes are defined as the organization desires. For example, assume an organization consisting of 100 membership positions (limited to 100 members) that currently has 80 members in total, 75 of whom are in good standing, with a quorum requirement of one-eighth of all the membership positions, which is 13. If there are 70 members present at a meeting and only 10 members vote, a majority vote could be variously computed as follows:

A majority of all the membership positions (100) is	51
A majority of the membership or the members (80) is	41
A majority of the members in good standing (75) is	38
A majority of the members present (70) is	36
A majority of a quorum (13) is	7
A majority of the legal votes cast (10) is	6

5.16 A *majority vote of all the membership positions* is often required to act in organizations having a fixed number of memberships. When this rule is applied to a board of education that has eight membership positions, a majority is five. If there are two vacancies, reducing the actual number of members to six, the required vote is still five because a majority of the eight membership positions of the board is necessary to adopt a proposal.

5.17 A *majority vote of all the members in good standing* means a vote of more than half of all the members in good standing both present and absent. Such a vote is often required in organizations in which the members serve in a representative capacity, such as a house of delegates or an *executive board*.*

5.18 A *majority vote of the members present* is sometimes required to act, often on corporate boards where directors have a *fiduciary duty* of care to the organization and are expected to be familiar with meeting materials. Under this rule, the failure of some members to vote does not reduce the number of *affirmative votes* required. If there are 75 members present, an affirmative vote of 38 is necessary to act, regardless of the number voting. In large assemblies a vote based on a majority of the members present can cause problems if votes are generally close and an ongoing tally of those arriving or leaving the assembly is not maintained.

5.19 A *majority vote of the quorum*, or a majority of the minimum number of members who are authorized to act for the organization, is an alternative minimum affirmative vote that some organizations require to make a decision. It means a *majority of those present and voting*, assuming a quorum is present, with the further stipulation that the affirmative vote must be at least a majority of the number required for a quorum. For example, suppose a board consisting of nine members with a quorum of five (a majority of the quorum being three) is governed by this requirement. There are five members present at the meeting and two vote for a proposal, one votes against it, and two *abstain* from voting. Because the passage of a motion requires at least three affirmative votes, the motion would fail—even though it has a two-thirds vote of those "present and voting" at a legally constituted meeting. In essence, in this example, those abstaining have the same impact on the outcome as if they had voted in the negative, whereas in normal voting their abstentions would have no impact on the outcome.

---

* For a definition of *good standing*, see the Member in Good Standing section in Chapter 3.

5.20 A majority of the legal votes cast, also referred to as a majority of those present and voting, is the requirement that most commonly approves a motion or elects a candidate. When the term *majority* is not defined and no other type of majority is specified, the law holds that a majority of the legal votes cast is required. This legal decision has been agreed on to resolve some of the confusion that resulted when the basis for counting a majority was not defined. Unless it is qualified in some way, a majority vote means a majority of the legal votes cast by members present and voting, excluding abstentions. Unless stated otherwise, this is the meaning of a majority vote when used in this parliamentary authority. For a discussion of what constitutes a *legal ballot*, see the section Determining the Validity of Ballots in Chapter 26.

5.21 The legal theory under which the decisions of an organization may be made by a majority of those present and voting is that all members have the right to attend meetings and to vote. They may choose to exercise those rights if they wish. The members who fail to attend or vote are presumed to have waived the exercise of their rights and to have consented to allow the will of the organization to be expressed by those present and voting. The result of a vote is based on the number of members present and voting.

5.22 It is possible for a majority to consist of only one vote. A member may propose a motion that is of little interest to other members, and when the presiding officer calls for a vote, the proposer votes "Aye" and no one votes "No." The question is adopted because it received a majority of the legal votes cast. A single affirmative vote, when there are no other votes cast, has been held by the courts to approve a motion because that vote is the majority of the legal votes cast.

ABSTENTIONS

5.23 A member has the right to abstain from voting on any motion. A member abstains whenever the member is present when a vote is taken and does not vote in the affirmative or the negative or, in an election, for a candidate. A member abstains when the member is present during a roll call and responds "Abstain," "Present," or "Not voting," or simply fails to respond. An abstention is not considered a vote and therefore is not counted in determining the result. A member who abstains has, in fact, relinquished his or her vote.

5.24 This can cause confusion because it is common to say that an abstention has the effect of a no vote when the voting threshold is a majority or two-thirds of the members present. In that situation, abstentions, while not votes, have the negative effect because only affirmative votes count in reaching that threshold.

PLURALITY VOTE

5.25 A *plurality vote* means more votes than the number received by any other candidate or alternative proposition. There is no requirement in plurality voting that a candidate or any proposition receive a majority vote. Thus, it may be less than a majority, and often is when there are more than two choices. A plurality vote does not elect a candidate or adopt a motion except when the bylaws provide for decision by plurality vote. For example, the result of a vote might be:

Candidate A	100
Candidate B	90
Candidate C	80

5.26 The total number of votes is 270. The first candidate has a plurality, but no candidate has received a majority vote (136). If the election to office is by plurality vote, Candidate A is elected. But if the election requires a majority vote to elect, no candidate is elected, and another ballot must be taken.

5.27 While election by plurality is simpler and quicker, it is usually not advisable. In the above example, for instance, Candidate A might represent an extreme viewpoint, whereas Candidates B and C both represent a moderate viewpoint, and perhaps a majority of the members would consider either candidate preferable to Candidate A. Nevertheless, with plurality voting, the wishes of the majority in such a case would be thwarted, and Candidate A would be elected with 37% of the vote. In subsequent votes, as would be necessary with a majority required to elect, one of the moderate candidates might pick up enough votes from the other to win, or as often happens, the weakest candidate, recognizing a hopeless situation, might withdraw. In either case, the will of the majority decides.

5.28 For the foregoing reason, when a majority is required to elect, repeated voting is required unless the bylaws or rules of the organization or an adopted motion has designated some method other than repeated voting. One such method is to omit the candidate receiving the lowest number of votes on the second ballot, and if that fails to produce a majority, the process of eliminating the candidate with the lowest number of votes is repeated. Another method is the "runoff" system, with the second ballot being limited to the two candidates who receive the most votes. Before an election takes place, the organization should establish a clear rule stating what shall be done if no candidate obtains a majority. This prevents the assembly from determining rules at the last minute in the middle of an election or important vote.

UNANIMOUS VOTE

5.29 A unanimous vote on a proposal is a vote in which all the legal votes cast are on the same side, whether affirmative or negative.

5.30 A unanimous vote for a candidate for a particular office is a vote in which one candidate receives all the legal votes cast for that office.

5.31 A proposal is adopted unanimously if one vote is cast for it and no vote is cast against it or is defeated unanimously if no vote is cast for it and one vote is cast against it.

5.32 If the term *unanimous vote* is qualified in some way, the qualification determines the meaning of that particular unanimous vote. For example, the unanimous vote of "all the members of the board" means that all the members of the board must be present and that each member must vote on the same side of a proposal. A unanimous vote of all the "members present" means that all the members who are present must vote and that all members present must vote on the same side of a proposal.

5.33 A requirement of a unanimous vote to adopt an action is an example of decision by a minority—in this case a minority of one—and is a violation of the democratic principle of decision by a majority. It gives the minority "an absolute, permanent, all-inclusive power of veto."[27] Three centuries ago, in 1693, the court of the King's Bench ruled that "the major number must bind the lesser, or else differences could never be determined."[28] The requirement of a unanimous vote is seldom necessary or wise.

TIE VOTE

5.34 A *tie vote* on a motion means that the same number of members have voted in the affirmative as in the negative. A majority vote, or more than half the legal votes cast, is required to adopt a motion; an equal or tie vote means that the motion is defeated. A tie vote on a motion is not a *deadlock* vote that must be resolved; it is simply not a majority vote, and the motion is defeated.

5.35 In an election, a tie vote may constitute a deadlock that must be resolved. If there are only two candidates, balloting must continue until the deadlock is resolved when a single candidate receives a majority of the legal votes cast.

5.36 This also occurs when two or more positions are being voted on at the same time and more candidates than there are positions receive the same number of votes in sufficient quantity to be elected. Then no candidate is elected. Such a tie vote results in a deadlock, and the vote must be retaken until the tie vote is resolved by additional voting or is resolved by some other method that the assembly may choose. If no candidate has received a majority, regardless of whether there is a tie or not, voting must continue until a candidate has received a majority of the legal votes cast, or other actions are taken as defined in Chapter 26.

VOTE OF THE PRESIDING OFFICER

5.37 No officer relinquishes the rights of membership by accepting office, except that the presiding officer of an assembly should not propose motions or generally participate in debate. The presiding officer, if a member of the assembly, does have the right to cast a vote, but in an assembly the presiding officer customarily exercises that right only when the vote is by ballot or when his or her vote will make a difference in the result. This preserves the presiding officer's duty of impartiality and objectivity. The presiding officer cannot be required to cast a vote.

5.38 In case of a tie vote on a motion requiring a majority for adoption, the presiding officer, if a member of the assembly, may vote with either side, provided that the presiding officer has not already voted. If the presiding officer chooses not to vote, the motion is defeated.

5.39 If a motion is about to be adopted by a single vote, the presiding officer may choose to vote against it, thereby *creating a tie*, in which case, lacking a majority, the motion is defeated.

5.40 Although a tie vote is not an issue in matters requiring a two-thirds or other supermajority vote for decision, nevertheless, there are again situations in which the presiding officer, not having voted, may wish to do so to change the outcome of the vote.

5.41 Ballot voting. When voting is by ballot, the presiding officer (if a member of the organization) votes as everyone else, casting a ballot at the same time as other members. But in such cases, if a tie results, the presiding officer cannot break the tie by voting a second time unless the bylaws provide that this may be done. Such a provision in bylaws is often based on a misunderstanding that a tie vote cannot decide a proposal, and that the tie must therefore be resolved. This assumption may apply to elections but does not apply to most motions. If this is the only basis for such a provision, it may be unwise to give the presiding officer a vote in excess of that of any other member.

COMPUTATION OF A TWO-THIRDS VOTE

5.42 To determine quickly whether a two-thirds vote has been attained or not attained, the presiding officer should double the number of negative votes. If the affirmative vote is equal to or higher than the number of negative votes doubled, the proposal has obtained the necessary two-thirds vote and is adopted.

5.43 For example, if the vote is 87 in favor and 44 opposed, the motion fails, because two times 44 is 88, and the affirmative vote is one short of that number. Using a calculator to multiply the total vote by .67 or by .66 can lead to rounding errors and should be avoided.

COMPUTING A MAJORITY FOR SEPARATE QUESTIONS

5.44 When more than one question is voted on at the same time, or on the same ballot, the number of votes cast is counted separately for each question. A majority of the legal votes cast on each question is required to approve that question.

5.45 In an election, when candidates for more than one office are voted on at the same time, a majority of the legal votes cast for each office is required to elect a candidate to that office.

5.46 In both instances, abstentions are not counted; abstentions are not votes.

COMPUTING A MAJORITY WHEN ELECTING A GROUP

5.47 Frequently candidates for several positions or offices of equal rank, such as members of a board, committee, or group of delegates, are voted on at the same time. With offices of equal rank and no differentiation between the offices, the majority vote required to elect is computed differently.

5.48 When several equal positions are voted on simultaneously, the majority vote is based on the total number of legal ballots cast for those positions, which contain at least one legal vote, for the group of equal offices, not the number of votes cast for each position. Even if some ballots contain a vote for only one nominee, these ballots are counted in determining a majority of the total ballots cast. A ballot with votes for more than the number of positions available is an *illegal ballot* and is not counted in determining a majority. Ballots without a vote for any candidate are abstentions and are not counted in computing the results of the vote.

5.49 When several offices of equal rank are being voted on simultaneously and require a majority vote, there are two requirements for election. The nominee must:

1. receive a majority vote based on the total number of legal ballots cast for all the equal offices; and
2. rank among those candidates receiving the highest number of votes above the number required to elect, which is the total number of offices to be filled.

5.50 A candidate who receives a majority vote but fails to rank high enough to place within the number of offices to be filled is not elected. Similarly, a candidate who ranks among the highest candidates but does not receive a majority vote is not elected.

5.51 For example, if five board members are to be elected at the same time and there are seven nominees for these five positions, with 95 members voting, the vote might result as follows:

Nominee	Vote
A	80
B	79
C	75
D	75
E	69
F	52
G	43

5.52 Six members received the necessary majority vote (48), but only the top-ranking five are elected. The two nominees who tied for third and fourth place were both elected. Therefore, there is no necessity to break this tie vote. However, had there been a tie between the fifth and sixth places, it would have been necessary to vote again to determine which of those two is elected.

5.53 If only three of the nominees had received a majority vote, only those three would be elected; it would then be necessary to take another vote to fill the two remaining vacancies. Unless the assembly adopts a motion to the contrary, all nominees except the three already elected remain candidates on the second ballot, whether it is needed to resolve a tie or complete an election in which an insufficient number of candidates were elected.

5.54 If the governing documents or standing rules of order are silent regarding electing multiple candidates to equal positions, this method is used instead of others.

VOTING SEPARATELY FOR EQUAL POSITIONS

5.55 Some organizations favor differentiating between equal positions by numbering each position and nominating candidates separately for each position, instead of voting on the candidates as a group as discussed above. For example, with two available at-large board positions for equal terms, candidates A, B, and C might be nominated as candidates for Board Vacancy No. 1 and candidates D and E for Board Vacancy No. 2. In this case, a majority of the legal votes cast for each position would elect a candidate. This practice risks a highly regarded candidate being defeated and a different candidate being elected. In the example given, candidates A, B, and C might be much more highly regarded than the other candidates, but two are sure to be defeated while with candidate D or E, one will surely be elected, even if not as highly regarded.

5.56 Sometimes the reason for differentiating is that one of the terms is, for example, for two years and the other one is for one year. A common way of handling this situation is for the two candidates receiving the highest vote to be declared elected, with the allocation of terms to be determined by lot, or with the successful candidate or candidates receiving the highest vote obtaining the longest term or terms and the successful candidate or candidates with the next highest vote receiving the next longest term or terms. If the method is not specified in the bylaws or in the standing rules of order, a motion clarifying the procedure should be made prior to the election.

DOUBLE THRESHOLD

5.57 Some organizations consist of individual members organized in caucuses or delegations, often by geographic region. On large expenditures or important decisions that significantly affect the organization, a *double threshold vote* may be required to adopt a proposal. A double threshold means that a majority of the individual members and a certain alternative threshold, such as one-third or a majority of the regional caucuses, must vote in favor of the proposal for it to be adopted. This type of voting may be seen as fair when the caucuses represent important concerns not equally distributed throughout the membership. For example, a national organization may have a constituent unit with ten divisions, and one of those divisions has 60% of the total members. A double threshold vote requirement, such as a majority vote and at least four divisions voting in favor, may balance the influence between the constituent units and, in addition, may ensure that group decisions are acceptable to a broader base of support.

WHEN MEMBERS SHOULD NOT VOTE

5.58 Membership in an organization carries with it the fundamental right to vote on proposals. However, as a general principle, a governing board member or member of a legislative or other delegate body having a direct personal or financial interest in a matter should not vote on it, because board members owe fiduciary obligations to the organization and members of legislative and delegate bodies act in a representative capacity for others. For example, if a motion is made to award a contract to a director, the director should not vote on it. See the section, Conflicts of Interest, in Chapter 30.

5.59 Many nonprofit corporation codes have detailed conflict-of-interest provisions for directors and officers. Corporations should adopt procedures and forms that make compliance with the applicable provisions straightforward. Most nonprofit corporation codes have recognized an exception to this rule when the board is authorized to fix the compensation of its members; otherwise, it would be impossible to vote to fix the compensation.

5.60 In an assembly of the members, in contrast, a member with a financial or personal interest should abstain from voting but can only be required to do so pursuant to the bylaws, charter, or statutory requirements.

5.61 A member who would otherwise be disqualified from voting under the rules may still vote on a question involving the whole organization when others are equally affected by the vote, even though the member has a direct personal or financial interest. For example, every member has the right to vote on a motion that determines convention expenses to be paid to delegates by the organization. Another example is elections, which are considered to affect the whole organization because all members share an interest in serving the organization and electing the best officers, directors, and committee members to do so.

5.62 When charges have been preferred against a member, that member cannot vote on the charges. However, if other members are also named in the charges, all members can vote on the charges. This rule prevents a small proportion of members from gaining control of an organization by filing charges against the majority of the members.

CHAPTER 6. **Methods of Voting**

VOTING IS A FUNDAMENTAL RIGHT

6.1   A member of any democratic body has the right to participate in electing officers and in deciding propositions. The right to vote in determining the will of an assembly is a fundamental right of a member.[29] A vote is a formal expression of the will of the assembly. While it is the right of each member to vote on every question, in ordinary assemblies the members cannot be compelled to vote. The proposer of a motion has the same right as any other member to speak for or against the motion, or to vote for or against it because the proposer's opinion may have changed during debate, or the motion itself may have been changed by amendment.

VOTING IN MEETINGS

6.2   When not prescribed in the bylaws, the method of voting on a motion or candidate is usually determined by the presiding officer. At any time before the vote is taken, the assembly may also determine the method of voting by majority vote without debate as an *incidental motion*. The usual methods of voting are:

1. *general consent*;
2. *voice vote*;
3. *standing vote* or show of hands;
4. counted standing vote or show of hands;
5. roll call; and
6. ballot.

6.3   If more than one method is proposed, the alternatives proposed are voted on in the order in which they are proposed by the method used for *filling blanks*.*

6.4   As a practical matter, it is best that visitors and nonvoting members be seated in different parts of the meeting room from the voting members to ensure that only voting members speak and vote. Some organizations provide for such seating arrangements through a standing rule of order

---

* See Chapter 14.

or a temporary rule. The alternative methods of voting discussed in this chapter relate to voting at an in-person meeting. Some are well suited to modification for the electronic context (including telephone meetings) and others less so. Voting in electronic meetings is discussed in greater detail in Chapter 19, "Electronic Meetings."

6.5 When visitors or others who are not entitled to vote are seated with voting members, voting methods should be used to ensure that only voting members participate in voting. Such methods include requiring the use of a voting card, electronic keypad, or taking a *roll call vote*.

6.6 In taking a vote by any method, the presiding officer must always call for the affirmative vote first and, when giving the results of the vote, announce the affirmative side first.

6.7 The negative vote must always be called for, even if the affirmative vote appears to be overwhelming or unanimous. The only exception is a courtesy vote. For example, the presiding officer should call for only the affirmative vote on a motion thanking a speaker for participating.

ACTING BY GENERAL CONSENT

6.8 Routine or noncontroversial questions are often decided by general consent, without taking a formal vote. When members are in general agreement, this method (sometimes called *unanimous consent*) saves time and expedites business. Whenever an action requires a vote (even if higher than a majority), and a *ballot vote* is not required, general consent is a valid method to adopt the motion. Motions adopted by general consent are included in the minutes, just as any other adopted motion would be.

6.9 For example, if a member moves "that the minutes be approved by a minutes approval committee," the presiding officer may respond, "Is there objection to the minutes being approved by a minutes approval committee?" If any member says, "I object," no reason need be given, and a vote must be taken on the motion. Otherwise, the presiding officer states, "There is no objection, and the minutes will be approved by a minutes approval committee."

6.10 The presiding officer may propose action by general consent without either a formal motion or second or may proceed by assuming general consent and moving on with business at the meeting. For example, if a member asks to make an announcement at an unusual time, the presiding officer may say, "If there is no objection, the member will be allowed to make an announcement now." Even when the presiding officer has announced that an action has been taken by general consent, if any member immediately objects, the question must be stated and voted on. If no one objects promptly, the motion is adopted by general consent and the presiding officer moves on to other business. The *objection* to general consent is simply the way to require a vote of affirmative and negative on that issue; therefore, the member need not state any other reason for the objection.

6.11 If the motion has not been opened for debate prior to the objection, the motion can be debated at this point; however, if debate has occurred and the motion is being put to a vote, the objection does not grant additional rights to debate.

METHODS OF VOTING

Voice Vote

6.12 Voting by voice is the most commonly used method of voting and is the method used by default except in electronic meetings. The presiding officer determines the result of the vote by the volume of voices.* When in doubt as to how the majority voted, the presiding officer should call for the vote again, asking for a standing vote (a *Division of the Assembly*) or a show of hands.

6.13 Any member who believes that a voice vote is inconclusive or that the presiding officer has not announced the outcome of a voice vote correctly may interrupt and demand a division of the assembly to have the vote taken by another method. This right continues even after the vote has been announced and another speaker has claimed the floor, but the right must be exercised before the speaker has begun to speak.

Standing Vote and Counted Standing Vote

6.14 A standing vote (also called a rising vote) may be used by the presiding officer to verify an inconclusive voice vote or in response to a call from a member for a division of the assembly. The vote on a motion requiring a definite number or proportion of votes, such as two-thirds, is taken initially by a standing vote to make the determination easier, as determination of fractional votes by voice would be inherently difficult.

---

* See Chapter 10 for sample language.

6.15 When the standing vote is close, the members' votes should be counted; they must be counted if there is any doubt in the mind of the presiding officer as to the result of the vote. A counted standing vote can also be ordered by a majority vote of the assembly. It is always the duty of the presiding officer to ensure that the stated result of the vote expresses the will of the body.

6.16 The presiding officer usually assigns other members to assist with a counted vote. In a convention or a large meeting, the presiding officer usually appoints several *tellers*, including a head teller, to assist. Each teller or pair of tellers counts a particular section of voters and reports the numbers to the head teller, who aggregates the results and reports the total vote to the presiding officer. The presiding officer then announces the totals and the result: "There are 99 in the affirmative, 101 in the negative. The negative has it and the motion is defeated."

6.17 In many assemblies, one way of ensuring accuracy in counting a standing vote is a *serpentine count*. Members in favor stand; then, beginning with the first row, each person counts off and sits down, with the count running back and forth along the rows in serpentine fashion. When all who voted in the affirmative are seated, the same is done with the negative vote. This minimizes the risk of any error in the count, increases confidence in the result of the vote, and is conducted quickly when the assembly is accustomed to this method.

Show of Hands

6.18 In boards, committees, and small assemblies, the presiding officer will usually ask for a show of hands rather than a standing vote. And even in large assemblies, a show of hands may be used at the discretion of the chair because it is usually quicker and simpler. In a large assembly, however, when a vote needs to be counted, a standing vote usually ensures greater accuracy.

6.19 Many organizations issue voting cards to voting members of the assembly. The voting cards are often colored and are of sufficient size to be visible to the chair. The members use the voting cards by raising them to accentuate their vote. This makes it easier for the presiding officer to determine the result of the vote and to assure that only those allowed to vote have done so.

Roll Call Vote

6.20 A *recorded vote* is often advantageous when members vote as representatives of others—for example, delegates, proxies, or members of governmental boards or commissions. A vote by roll call may be required by the bylaws or standing rules of order or may be ordered by the assembly. As with all motions to determine the voting method, a majority vote without debate is required to order a roll call.

6.21 When a roll call is taken, the presiding officer states the question on a roll call as follows: "The motion is… As your name is called, those in favor of the motion will say 'Aye'; those opposed will say 'No.' The secretary will call the roll."

6.22 The names are called in alphabetical order, in the numerical order of districts, or in some other appropriate order. The name of the presiding officer is usually called last. A member who does not wish to vote may remain silent or answer "Present" or "Abstaining." When the voting threshold is based on the number of votes cast, a member who remains silent or responds with "Present" or "Abstaining" will not affect the outcome of the vote and will not affect the number of votes required to adopt. These responses will document the presence of the member, which may be important to show the presence of a quorum. The secretary should always have lists of names ready for use in calling the roll and should repeat each member's vote, including those who respond "Present" or "Abstaining," to ensure that it is recorded correctly. The roll call record is included in the minutes.

6.23 Another form of roll call vote is a signed ballot. In this method of voting a member is provided with a ballot, often with the stated question or proposal typed on it. The member then votes by printing his or her name (or constituency or assigned identification number if required) on the ballot if the ballot does not come with the name or number preprinted, signing the ballot, and voting for the preferred choice. The ballots are then collected. When this method is used, an unsigned ballot is counted as an illegal vote. For each ballot, the teller records the name of the voter and how that member voted on the proposal. The count is tallied, and the presiding officer announces the result. How each member voted is entered in, or attached to, the minutes as well as the result as announced by the presiding officer. The recording of the vote in the minutes is identical to a roll call vote. The advantage of this form of roll call is that no member knows how another member has voted during the balloting; additionally, the assembly can usually move on to other business while the votes are being counted, as opposed to a roll call vote.

Ballot Vote

6.24 Voting by ballot is the only method that enables members to express their decisions without revealing their opinions or preferences. The use of a voting machine or electronic keypads, or any other method in which the person expressing a choice cannot be identified with the choice expressed, is considered a form of voting by ballot.* Secrecy is implicit in a ballot vote, and an election requiring a ballot vote may be invalidated by the courts if it is shown that it would be possible for the organization casting the votes to determine how an individual voted—such as numbering ballots in a way that would identify the voter.[30]

6.25 A ballot vote is usually required in contested elections and frequently in voting on important proposals. If a ballot vote on a particular proposal is not required by the bylaws, it may be ordered by adoption of a motion by majority vote, without debate. If a vote by ballot is required by the bylaws, a motion to dispense with the ballot vote, or to suspend the provision requiring such a vote, is not in order, even if there is only one nominee, unless this suspension is provided for in the bylaws.[31]

6.26 The presiding officer should give careful instructions as to how the members should prepare their ballots and should ask before the voting begins whether anyone is without a ballot.

6.27 When voting by ballot (or voting by electronic means, including internet voting), the organization needs to ensure that the following occurs: only those entitled to vote actually vote; members only vote once; if secrecy is a requirement for the vote, the secrecy of the vote is maintained; members should ensure that their ballot accurately reflects their desires prior to the votes being cast; and members are given clear written instructions, and if necessary, some training on how to vote for their preferences, especially when the vote is by electronic means, by internet, or by some form of *preferential voting*.

---

* Voting in electronic meetings is discussed in greater detail in Chapter 19, "Electronic Meetings," which includes a discussion on forms of voting that are equivalent to ballot voting.

6.28 An alternative method of balloting, called the *Texas ballot*, allows voters to indicate the candidate that they do *not* wish to be elected in an election for several positions of equal rank, as for several at-large director positions. It can be efficiently used when there are many positions open for a specific office and there are slightly more candidates than the number of positions open. Depending on the rules, each member may have one **no** vote or up to a number equal to the excess of candidates above the available positions. Those candidates with the most **no** votes are eliminated until the number of remaining candidates matches the number of available positions.

6.29 The opposite, more positive, method of ballot voting is called *approval voting*. This method allows members to vote in favor of all candidates that are acceptable to them with no limit on the number of affirmative votes in an election for several positions of equal rank, as for several at-large director positions. Those candidates with the most affirmative votes, provided that they are a majority, up to the number of available positions, are elected.

6.30 Either of these methods, if used for the election of officers or directors, must be authorized in the governing documents.

Voting by Mail

6.31 In organizations whose members are scattered over a wide area or who work during different hours, provision is sometimes made for members to vote on important questions by mail. Voting by mail cannot be used unless it is authorized in the bylaws.

6.32 Voting by mail has certain disadvantages. When voting by mail, the members do not have the opportunity to discuss or listen to debate on proposals or to amend them. In elections, there is no opportunity to nominate candidates from the floor. Typically, with mail balloting, *write-in votes* are prohibited by a standing rule of order. That prohibition applies in organizations adopting this parliamentary authority.

6.33 Voting by mail by some members who cannot attend a meeting cannot be combined successfully with voting at a meeting or convention by those who attend and is therefore prohibited. Since proposals and amendments to bylaws can be discussed and amended at a meeting or convention, those voting by mail and those voting at a convention might each be voting on quite different proposals or amendments. Similarly, when candidates are being elected, members voting by mail would have no chance to nominate additional candidates from the floor, to consider candidates nominated from the floor, to discuss the qualifications of the candidate, or to vote for another candidate if their candidate withdraws or is eliminated from the ballot.

6.34 An organization's bylaws must clearly authorize voting on proposals or amendments to the bylaws by mail, thereby foregoing the right to discuss, amend, and vote on them at a meeting or convention. Similarly, the bylaws must clearly authorize voting for candidates by mail, thereby foregoing the right to nominate additional candidates from the floor. For those who have adopted this parliamentary authority, if voting is permitted by mail in the governing documents, those topics voted on by mail may not be discussed, amended, or voted on at a meeting or convention; similarly, should voting for candidates be conducted by mail, there shall be no right to nominate additional candidates from the floor.

6.35 Any method of voting by mail may be followed so long as it ensures that voters fully understand the issues to be decided and the instructions for returning their votes. Unless the bylaws provide for a particular plan, a ballot containing proposed measures, or amendments to bylaws, or a list of candidates is mailed to each member together with voting directions from the election committee. When mailing the ballot, some organizations enclose information concerning the qualifications of candidates, which may include whether a candidate has been nominated by the nominating committee or by *petition*, and arguments for and against each proposal to be voted on. The organization should adopt procedures to resolve challenges related to the information accompanying the ballots and make clear who can resolve such challenges. When mail balloting is required by the bylaws, those responsible for distributing mail ballots cannot thwart a properly submitted proposal by refusing to send out mail ballots. The board can act in that case to ensure that the ballots go out by an alternative means.

6.36 The ballot must be marked and returned within a specified time. The usual way to preserve secrecy in a mail vote is to provide each member with a blank envelope that has no mark of identification on it. The marked ballot is placed inside the unmarked envelope, which is then sealed. The unmarked sealed envelope, in turn, is enclosed in another envelope that the member signs and seals, so that the member's name may be checked against the list of members eligible to vote. The blank inner envelope is removed and delivered, still sealed, to the tellers or election committee, maintaining the chain of custody of the ballots. Ballots returned without the unmarked envelope, but that are otherwise valid ballots, are still counted; the member has waived any right of secrecy but has not waived the right to vote.

6.37 In the case of an election by mail, if the law, charter, or bylaws do not specify the requirement to elect a candidate to office, the requirement is a majority of the legal votes cast, no matter the number of votes received.

6.38 In recent years, casting ballots electronically, typically on the internet, has become more common. Most considerations involved with voting by mail also apply to voting online. See Chapter 19, "Electronic Meetings," for more information.

Acting by Proxy

6.39 A *proxy* is a written authorization empowering another person to act, in a meeting, for the member who signs the proxy. This means that a particular person, who may or may not be a member, is authorized to act on behalf of an absent member in a meeting or convention, which includes voting for the absent member. The term *proxy* may mean either the statement authorizing another to act in place of the member signing it or the person who attends the meeting in the place of the absent member. To avoid confusion, the member giving the proxy statement is often called the *proxy giver* while the person who will act for the proxy giver is called the *proxy holder*. Unless restricted by the bylaws or standing rules of order, the proxy holder need not be a member. The proxy holder may cast votes to the same extent that the absent member(s) represented could if such member were in attendance. In addition to voting, unless otherwise restricted by the proxy, the proxy holder may act in all ways for the absent member, including speaking in debate and making motions.

6.40 In business corporations, in which ownership interests are typically widely dispersed and obtaining a wide representation of the shareholders at meetings is important because of their investment interest, voting by proxy is commonly used.

6.41 In nonprofit corporations, voting by proxy is authorized by statute in most jurisdictions unless prohibited in the charter or bylaws. In other jurisdictions, the charter or bylaws of the organization must specifically authorize the use of proxies. Those drafting bylaws for incorporated organizations should check with legal counsel to determine the laws applicable to their organization regarding proxies. In a voluntary (unincorporated) association, proxies are not allowed unless specifically authorized in the bylaws. While statutes and bylaws may permit members (proxy givers) to give their authorization to another to act on the member's behalf in a meeting, the organization, if not disallowed by statute, can restrict the number of proxies that a proxy holder may carry and vote, and may restrict who may be a proxy holder. The most common restriction is that the proxy holder must be a member. Any such restriction must be clearly stipulated in the bylaws.

6.42 Proxies are not generally used in nonprofit organizations with active and engaged membership unless members have a financial interest in the organization, as with community property associations. Use of proxies authorized by a statutory default provision, when the bylaws are silent and proxies have not been used in the past, can upset the settled expectations of members.[32] Organizations that do not expect to use proxies should therefore include a bylaw provision prohibiting them. Organizations that expect to use proxies should authorize that use in the bylaws and indicate whether the board or the members should adopt standing rules of order and procedures governing their use. To the extent that applicable statutes permit an organization to prohibit proxies by a rule outside the bylaws, they are prohibited in organizations adopting this parliamentary authority.

6.43 Directors or board members in most jurisdictions cannot attend or vote by proxy in their *board meetings*. Directors are bound by their fiduciary duties (the duties of care, loyalty, and obedience) and their requirement to act in good faith when carrying out their duties as a director. Transferring these duties to another through a proxy would be contrary to their responsibilities toward the organization.

6.44 A proxy may be given in almost any form if its meaning is clear.[*] It may be limited to one meeting; one motion, issue, person, or time; or it may be unlimited (often called a general proxy). Many nonprofit corporation statutes set a maximum effective period for proxies. A proxy holder may be given full discretion to vote on all matters during the meeting or can be instructed to vote in the affirmative or the negative; to abstain on a specific proposal; or to vote for specific candidates running for office.

---

* See Appendix C for a sample Proxy Form.

Proxies with specific voting instructions are often called *directed proxies*.* Directed proxy holders are required to honor the intention of the proxy giver in exercising the proxy. It is strongly recommended that directed proxies not be used in conjunction with a deliberative membership meeting, with the possible exception of elections. Mail and electronic balloting are recommended instead to obtain widespread organizational input when membership meeting attendance is possibly unrepresentative. A mix of physical attendance with directed proxies can result in a loss of the deliberative nature of the assembly. For example, a significant number of votes directed in advance could render any additional voting by those attending in person unnecessary. Conversely, those sending directed proxies will not have the opportunity to hear debate, which might change that member's opinion, nor will such member be able to change a directed vote as a result of amendments to the motions.

6.45 Generally, proxies in nonprofit organizations are revocable by the proxy giver, although it is helpful to provide explicitly on the proxy statement that it is revocable when that is the case. A proxy procedure requiring advance registration of proxies should include provisions addressing how to revoke a proxy after it has been registered.

6.46 Even though a proxy may give specific instructions on how a proxy holder may vote on a resolution that will come before the meeting, the resolution may have amendments applied to it. If the organization uses this parliamentary authority, the proxy holder has discretion to vote on such amendments or other such *subsidiary motions* within the directions given by the proxy giver unless the proxy statement, the bylaws, or the standing rules of order say otherwise. This discretion flows from the authority of the proxy holder to vote on the resolution or main motion.

6.47 Some nonprofit corporation statutes allow proxies to be used to establish a quorum and therefore a legal meeting. If an organization allows proxies, the bylaws should specify whether they count toward establishing a quorum. If the organization does not have a rule, then proxies count toward the quorum.[33] Some organizations choose to have two quorum requirements, both of which must be satisfied to conduct business: (1) a minimum number of members that need to be present in person, and (2) a

---

* Although it is not advised, some organizations allow absentee voting by ballots submitted in advance of a meeting regarding previously noticed Main Motions and elections. This can be considered equivalent to making the secretary the member's proxy holder and directing the secretary to vote as instructed.

somewhat higher number that includes members present in person and by proxy to establish a quorum.

6.48 The organization must carefully set up procedures to receive proxies, ensuring that they are valid proxies from members. The process whereby the authenticity of each proxy is validated is crucial to the integrity of the overall proxy process. Only after a proxy has been verified can the proxy holder receive a voting card and ballots—if votes are to be taken by ballot. The proxy holder will receive as many voting cards and ballots as are warranted by the proxies held.

6.49 Proxies that are simply made out to an unnamed holder of the proxy have historically caused numerous problems in verifying their authenticity. This abuse of the proxy process can be mitigated if the organization adopts a proxy procedure requiring all proxies to be registered with the organization a specified number of days before the meeting.

6.50 If used, all proxies must conform strictly to the provisions of the statutes, charters, bylaws, and rules of the organization, including any restrictions on the number of proxies a proxy holder can carry.

Preferential (Ranked Choice or Instant Runoff) Voting

6.51 Sometimes an organization does not wish to conduct repeated ballots if an election is not won by majority vote on the first ballot. Rather than permit the winner to be determined by plurality on the first ballot, the election can be conducted by a preferential ballot, which will result in an election by majority vote under that system.

6.52 There are many preferential voting systems.[34] Preferential voting can be used, not only to select among many candidates in an election, but also to select among many choices in deciding any other matter. When conducting preferential voting, the method of dealing with any ties that may occur should be determined in advance of the voting; in fact, to avoid disgruntled candidates and their supporters, the question of how to resolve ties is best determined in advance before voting occurs by any method unless the assembly wants to re-ballot until the election is complete.

6.53 The preferential voting system described below, often called *Instant Runoff Voting*, is the default for those organizations that use this parliamentary authority and that require preferential voting for single position elections. In such an election, members mark their ballots to indicate their first, second, third, and subsequent choices among the candidates. Tellers count the ballots and report the result based on first choice votes only. If no candidate receives a majority of the ballots on this basis, the candidate with the fewest first choice votes is eliminated from further consideration. Ballots listing the eliminated candidate as the first choice are allocated to the candidate with the voters' second choice ranking, adding these ballots to the original totals for those candidates who received "second choice" ranking.* If no candidate has a majority after this (or any subsequent) count, the process is repeated, dropping the lowest candidate and distributing that candidate's votes among the remaining candidates until one has received a majority. A preferential ballot need not rank every candidate, but the order must be sequential from the first choice. If rankings are skipped (i.e., rank 1, 2, 3, 5, 6, 7), the rankings after the gap (ranks 5, 6, 7 in this example) are illegal votes . As in any vote, illegal votes may lower the number required for a majority. Unranked candidates count as abstentions.

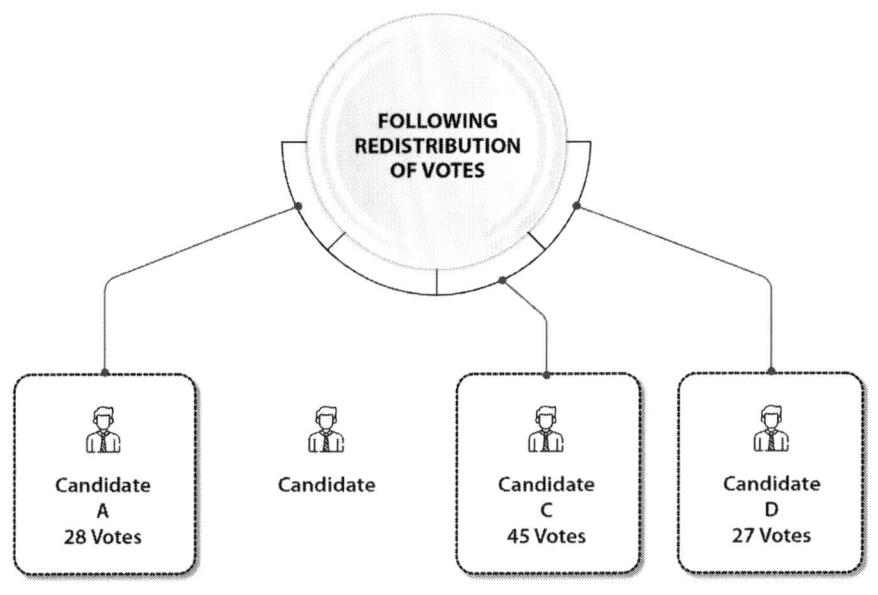

---

* If there are two or more candidates tied for the lowest number of votes, all those candidates are dropped, and the ballots are distributed accordingly. Organizations adopting this method of voting should be aware that this could result in an unintended outcome, such as when a ballot results in a vote count of 300-250-250, and the candidate with 300 votes would automatically be declared the winner. In situations where this method would be infeasible, the assembly can make a decision by a procedural vote.

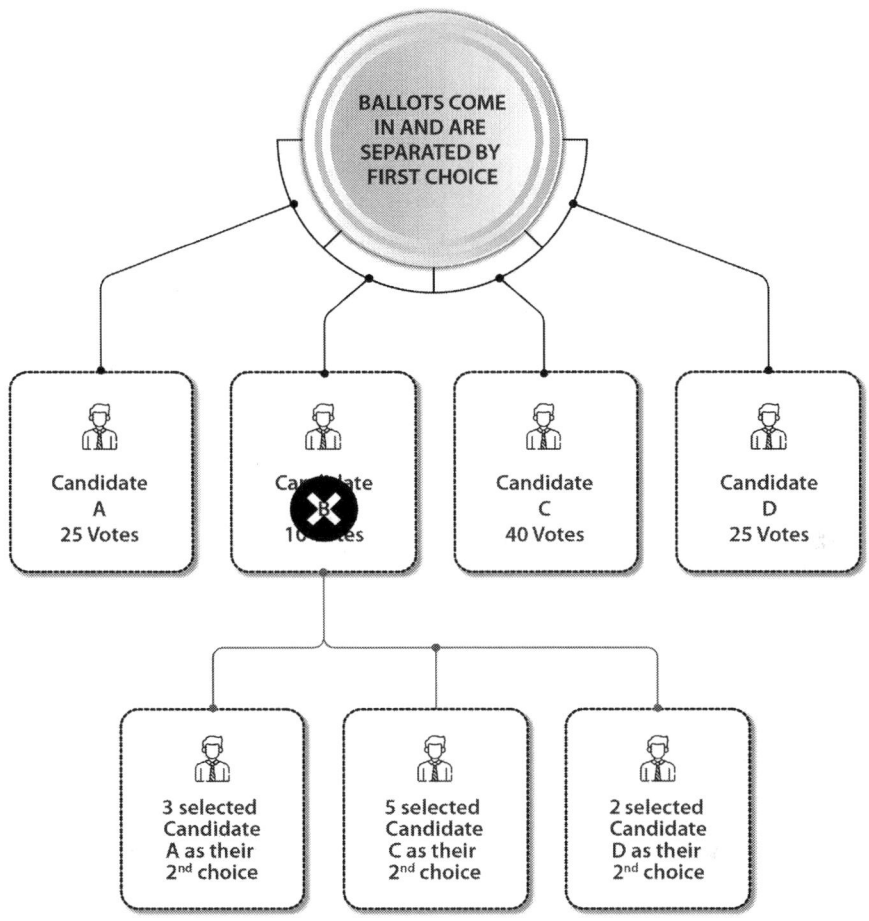

In the above example, Candidate B is eliminated, and those votes are redistributed as follows:

1. Three selected Candidate A as their second choice
2. Five selected Candidate C as their second choice
3. Two selected Candidate D as their second choice

6.54   This is essentially equivalent to in-person voting when no candidate receives a majority vote on the first ballot, and subsequent ballots are then taken, dropping the candidate with the lowest number of votes each time until one candidate does receive a majority vote. It is useful when a mail ballot is necessary, or when a meeting will end before counting is completed, and the members cannot be reconvened for additional balloting.

6.55 This method of voting sometimes produces unusual results under certain circumstances and should be used only when necessary. Instant Runoff Voting is not appropriate for electing a number of positions of equal rank, as for several at-large director positions. There are a number of variations of preferential voting that handle this type of election, some of which suffer from random redistribution effects or electing candidates without true majority support. More sophisticated variations using computer technology can be fairer and quicker to count. Because the issue is complex and the available methods are subject to change as technology develops, unless otherwise provided for in the bylaws or standing rules of order, organizations choosing preferential voting for multiple position elections should empower their board to select an appropriate method and provide the members with training in its use before implementation.

6.56 When using preferential voting, the presiding officer and the tellers committee should be instructed in explaining to members how to cast their votes, how the tellers are to count votes, how votes are to be allocated to the candidates, and what is to happen when the last place candidate is dropped and how those votes are redistributed. When the number of voters is large, it would be wise to use computer technology to ensure an accurate result.

Borda Count Voting

6.57 *Borda Count voting* was championed by J. C. Borda, a French scientist of the eighteenth century, who devised the method to overcome anomalies in elections and, in particular, elections held by plurality. In modern times, it has been shown by mathematical analysis that the Borda Count best achieves the fairness goal in elections when more than two candidates are running.

6.58 The Borda Count method of voting is not a majority voting system; it is based on a points system. For example, if there are four candidates running for office, the member ranks each candidate on the ballot in accordance with his or her preference, one, two, three, or four. The member's first choice candidate will receive four points, the second choice candidate three points, third choice candidate two points, and the fourth choice candidate one point. The tellers committee will tally all the points for each candidate. The candidate with the most points is elected. If the bylaws require preferential voting, Borda Count is not a permissible alternative.

6.59 There are several variations on the Borda Count method. Organizations should pick the most appropriate method for the organization's needs. There should be a provision in the bylaws or standing rules of order, or the bylaws should provide that the board can make the choice among the methods.

Bullet Voting

6.60 *Bullet voting* is a voting strategy by which certain members choose to abstain from voting for candidates other than their first choice to focus a member's voting power on a single candidate in an election for several positions of equal rank, as for several at-large director positions. A member casts a single vote for a single candidate and abstains from using any additional votes for anyone else. Because a member has a right to abstain, bullet voting is permitted unless prohibited by the governing documents.

Cumulative Voting

6.61 *Cumulative voting* is another method used to elect a number of positions of equal rank, as for several at-large director positions. It allows a member to place multiple votes for a single candidate instead of casting single votes for several different candidates. Typically, each member is assigned a number of votes equal to the number of open positions. Instead of being limited to one vote for each candidate, the member can assign any number of available votes to any candidate. Those candidates with the most votes, up to the number of available positions, are elected. This allows members with strong preferences to enhance the likelihood of their preferred candidate's election. It is often used to ensure that a minority faction can have a representative on the board. Many jurisdictions prohibit cumulative voting in nonprofit corporations. Organizations should check with legal counsel before using this method. This form of voting must be authorized in the governing documents.

CHANGING A VOTE

6.62 When a vote is taken by voice, a show of hands, or by standing, members may not change their votes. When a vote is taken by roll call or by counted vote, members may change their votes up until the time that the result of the vote is finally announced. When voting is by ballot, including by electronic balloting, a member may not change the ballot after it has been placed in the ballot box or cast electronically.

ANNOUNCING THE RESULT OF A VOTE

6.63 It is the duty of the presiding officer to announce the result of the vote according to the facts.[35] However, an incorrect or untrue announcement of the vote cannot change the outcome as determined by the votes if timely challenged.[36] An incorrect announcement must be challenged promptly by raising a point of order when the vote is announced or else the challenge will be considered waived. In case of a disputed vote, the courts will examine the facts to determine whether the vote as announced is correct.

ALL VOTES ARE BINDING DURING A MEETING

6.64 A few organizations follow the improper practice of taking an informal test, or *straw vote*, in meetings, which they interpret to be a vote that is not binding. Such a vote is sometimes used to influence members to reach a consensus. A unity of opinion, if it is reached without coercion, is desirable, but informal votes cannot properly be taken during a meeting.

6.65 No organization, board, or committee can, during its meeting, properly take a vote that is not binding. If an assembly wishes to vote to recess to determine the probable vote of the members, it may do so because, under the law, all votes taken during a meeting are binding.

MOTIONS

CHAPTER 7. Classification of Motions

CLASSES OF MOTIONS

7.1   *Motions* are classified into five groups according to their purposes and characteristics:

1. Main Motions;
2. *Specific-Purpose Main Motions*;
3. Subsidiary Motions;
4. *Privileged Motions*; and
5. Incidental Motions.

Main Motions

7.2   Main Motions are the most important and most frequently used motion. The Main Motion is the foundation of the conduct of business. Its purpose is to bring substantive proposals before the assembly for consideration and action. After it is stated by the presiding officer, the main motion becomes the subject for deliberation and decision. An example would be, "I move that the installation dinner attire be business casual."

Specific-Purpose Main Motions

7.3   There are six main motions that have specific names and are governed by somewhat different rules. They are referred to as Specific-Purpose Main Motions because they perform unique and specific functions. They do not present a new proposal but concern proposals or actions known to be coming before the assembly or actions that were previously taken by the assembly. The Specific-Purpose Main Motions are:

1. *Adopt in Lieu of*;
2. Amend a Previous Action;
3. Ratify;
4. Recall from a Committee;
5. *Reconsider*; and
6. Rescind.

Subsidiary Motions

7.4 Subsidiary motions alter the main motion or delay or hasten its consideration. Subsidiary motions are usually applied to the main motion, but some may also be applied to certain other motions, in which case they are subsidiary to the motion to which they are applied.

7.5 The six subsidiary motions are listed in order of precedence (from highest to lowest in rank):

1. *Table*;
2. Close Debate and Vote Immediately;
3. Limit or Extend Debate;
4. Postpone to a Certain Time;
5. Refer to a Committee; and
6. Amend.

Privileged Motions

7.6 Privileged motions have no direct connection with the main motion before the assembly. They are motions of such urgency that they are entitled to immediate consideration subject to precedence. They relate to the members, to the organization, and to the meeting as a whole rather than to *items of business*. Privileged motions would be main motions but for their urgency. Because of their urgency, they are given the privilege of being considered ahead of other motions that are before the assembly.

7.7 The three privileged motions are listed in their order of rank (from highest to lowest):

1. Adjourn;
2. Recess; and
3. Question of Privilege.

Incidental Motions

7.8 Incidental motions only arise tangentially out of business before the assembly. They do not relate directly to the Main Motion or Specific-Purpose Main Motions but usually relate to matters that arise from the conduct of the meeting. Because of their nature, they may interrupt business and may sometimes interrupt the speaker. Incidental motions may be offered at any time when they are applicable, have no rank of precedence among themselves, and are disposed of prior to the business out of which they arise.

7.9   Some of the frequently used incidental motions include:

1. Inquiries: Factual or Parliamentary;
2. Point of Order;
3. Motion to Appeal;
4. Motion to Suspend the Rules;
5. Motion to Withdraw;
6. Division of the Question; and
7. Division of the Assembly.

CLASSIFICATION OF UNLISTED MOTIONS

7.10   The motions within each class—Main, Specific-Purpose Main Motion, Subsidiary, Privileged, and Incidental—differ somewhat but have similar purposes and characteristics. Only the more commonly used motions in each class are typically listed in charts and classifications. There are many other motions that may be proposed, and the presiding officer must know how to classify motions to determine whether they are in order and what rules govern them. Therefore, it is essential to understand the purposes and characteristics of each type of motion to classify those that are not specifically named in the lists.

7.11   For example, while a Main Motion is being considered, a member might move "that the vote on the motion be taken by roll call." This might appear to be a main motion. It is, however, an incidental motion because it arises tangentially out of business before the assembly. It would therefore be in order and would be decided immediately. As a second example, a member might move "that the article in today's newspaper, explaining the reason for a city sales tax increase, be procured and read to the assembly before we vote on the question under consideration." This would be considered immediately as a Question of Privilege because of its urgency. Without an understanding of the classification of motions, the presiding officer might mistakenly think that the examples just cited are main motions and rule them out of order because another main motion is pending.

7.12 The name given a motion by its proposer is not the determining factor in classifying the motion because the proposer may name the motion incorrectly. For example, someone might move "to table the motion until ten o'clock." This is a Motion to Postpone to a Certain Time, not a Motion to Table, since a time is specified, and the proposer does not intend to kill the main motion.

CHANGES IN CLASSIFICATION OF MOTIONS

7.13 A motion that usually is listed in one classification may belong in another if it is proposed in a different situation. The classification of a motion is usually based on the relationship of that motion to the main motion. The main motion is the foundation motion that determines the classification of other motions.

7.14 Usually, a main motion is already pending when a subsidiary, privileged, or incidental motion is proposed. However, certain subsidiary, privileged, or incidental motions may be proposed when no main motion is pending. In this situation the subsidiary, privileged, and incidental motions are classified and processed as main motions, subject to debate and amendment, except they retain the same voting requirement as their counterparts.

7.15 The following sections provide examples of subsidiary, privileged, and incidental motions that may be proposed when no business is pending, with an example of a possible form in which each might be proposed.

Subsidiary Motions Moved When No Business Is Pending

7.16 **Refer to a Committee.** I move that the president appoint a committee of three to review the condition of all office equipment and report its recommendations for any upgrades that may be needed at the May meeting. (This motion would require a majority vote.)

7.17 **Postpone to a Certain Time.** I move to postpone reports of officers until after the mayor's speech. (This motion would normally require a majority vote. If the motion includes making the item a *scheduled order*, it would require a two-thirds vote.)

7.18 **Limit or Extend Debate.** I move that debate on the bylaws amendments be limited to 45 minutes. (This motion would require a two-thirds vote.)

7.19 **Table.** I move to table the motion submitted in advance to authorize the Treasurer to spend $5,000 on new computer equipment. (This motion would require a two-thirds vote.)

Privileged Motions Moved When No Business Is Pending

7.20 **Question of Privilege** (presented as a motion). I move that we enter into a closed meeting with our attorney to consider motions related to marketing our services and possibly employing consultants.

7.21 **Recess.** I move that we recess for twenty minutes. Or I move that after the report of the nominating committee, we recess the meeting until tomorrow morning at 8 a.m.

7.22 **Adjourn.** I move that we adjourn. Or I move that we adjourn this evening at 6 p.m.

Incidental Motions Moved When No Business Is Pending

7.23 **Appeal.**

Presiding Officer:	Your demand to discuss the reserve funds is not in order because no motion is pending.
Member:	I appeal from the decision of the chair.

7.24 **Suspend the Rules.** I move that we suspend the rules to allow invited guest experts to speak when the strategic plan and the budget are considered.

CHAPTER 8. Ranking of Motions

ORDER OF PRECEDENCE

8.1 The rank, also known as precedence, of motions is important. The rank of a motion determines the priority with which it may be proposed, and the sequence in which it must be considered and disposed of. The purpose of the rank of a motion is to ensure that each motion is dealt with consistently and without confusion. The precedence of motions is logical and is based on the relative urgency of each motion.

8.2 From the highest ranking to the lowest ranking, the order of rank of the motions is:

8.3 **Privileged Motions**:

1. Adjourn;
2. Recess; and
3. Question of Privilege.

8.4 **Subsidiary Motions**:

4. Table;
5. Close Debate and Vote Immediately;
6. Limit or Extend Debate;
7. Postpone to a Certain Time;
8. Refer to a Committee; and
9. Amend.

8.5 **Main Motions**:

10. The Main Motion and Specific-Purpose Main Motions.

BASIC RULES OF RANKING

8.6 There are two basic rules:

1. **When a motion is being considered, any motion of higher rank may be proposed, but no motion of lower rank may be proposed.** For example,

when a Main Motion (10) is pending, a member may move to refer the motion to a committee (8). Another member may move to recess (2). There will then be three motions pending at the same time. Since the proper order of rank was followed in proposing motions, there will be no confusion in considering and disposing of them. A Motion to Postpone to a Certain Time (7), would not be in order since it is of a lower rank than the Motion to Recess (2).

2. **Motions are considered and voted on in reverse order to their proposal.** The motion last proposed, which is the highest ranked motion pending, is considered and disposed of first. For example, if motions (10), (8), and (2) are proposed in that order and are pending, they are considered and decided in the reverse order, which is (2), (8), and (10).

MOTIONS WITHOUT RANK

8.7 **Incidental Motions** have no order of precedence. They can arise tangentially out of the immediately pending business at any time. Incidental motions must be decided as soon as they arise. For more information on incidental motions, see Chapter 16.

EXAMPLE OF RANKING

8.8 Complicated problems regarding the ranking of motions should rarely occur. Quite frequently, however, two or more motions are awaiting a decision by the assembly. All motions that have been proposed and stated to the assembly but are not yet decided are called pending questions or pending motions.

8.9 The motion being considered by the assembly that is next to be voted on in the order of precedence is called the *immediately pending question* or the immediately pending motion.

8.10 Suppose that a member proposes a Main Motion (10): "that the club sponsor ten students attending the summer music camp." While this motion is pending, another member moves to amend (9) it by striking out the word *ten* and inserting the word *fifteen*. While the amendment is being discussed, another member moves to "limit debate (6) on the amendment to one speech per member for no more than two minutes per speech."

8.11 Another member now moves to postpone (7) the main motion until the next meeting. Immediately, a member rises to a point of order (an incidental motion, which can be made whenever necessary), and states that the Motion to Postpone to a Certain Time (7) is not in order because it is of lower rank than the immediately pending Motion to Limit Debate (6). The presiding officer rules the member's point "well taken" and declares the Motion to Postpone to a Certain Time (7) not in order, stating that the immediately pending motion is "to limit debate" (6) A member then moves "that we take a recess (2) for twenty minutes."

8.12 All these motions, except the one ruled out of order, have followed the correct ranking and are (therefore) in order. The following four motions are pending:

Motions Pending	Rank
Recess	2
Limit or Extend Debate	6
Amend	9
Main Motion	10

8.13 The presiding officer first takes a vote on the Motion to Recess (2). If the Motion to Recess is defeated, the presiding officer calls for a vote on the Motion to Limit or Extend Debate (6). If the Motion to Recess (2) is adopted, the Motion to Limit or Extend Debate (6) will be pending when the members return from recess. After the Motion to Limit or Extend Debate (6) has been adopted or defeated, the Motion to Amend (9) becomes the immediately pending question. After it has been discussed and voted on, the presiding officer calls for discussion on the Main Motion (10).

8.14 While the assembly is considering any of the four motions in their order of rank, a member may present another motion, provided that it has a higher rank than the one that is currently being considered. For example, while the Motion to Limit or Extend Debate (6) is pending, a Motion to Close Debate and Vote Immediately (5) would be in order, but a Motion to Refer to a Committee (8) would not.

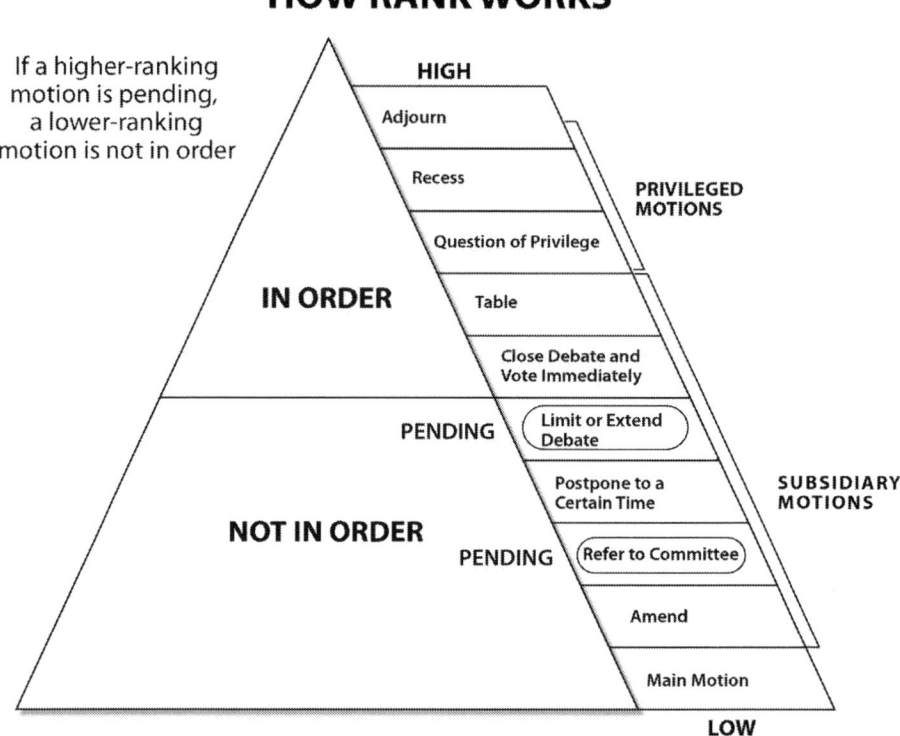

8.15 It is the duty of the presiding officer, with assistance from the secretary or parliamentarian, to keep the assembly clearly informed as to what motion is immediately pending. This is most readily accomplished by repeated statements of which motion is immediately pending as the presiding officer calls for debate and again immediately prior to taking the vote.

CHAPTER 9. Rules Governing Motions

THE BASIC RULES OF MOTIONS

9.1   Orderly procedure requires that basic rules of motions be strictly and uniformly applied. Understanding the basic rules of motions begins with understanding the purpose and logic of the rules. Nothing is more essential to procedure in which full justice is accorded each member than applying all rules with uniformity and certainty.[37]

9.2   The basic questions that must be answered to understand each motion are the following:

1. Can the motion *interrupt* a speaker or the proceedings?
2. Does the motion require a *second*?
3. Is the motion debatable?
4. Can the motion be amended?
5. What vote does the motion require?
6. What is the ranking of the motion?
7. To what other motions can the motion apply?
8. What other motions can be applied to the motion?
9. Can the motion be renewed?

CAN THE MOTION INTERRUPT A SPEAKER?

9.3   Motions normally cannot interrupt a speaker; however, there are two types of motions that, because of their urgency, can interrupt a speaker or proceedings: those that are subject to a time limit to move the motion and those that present a question requiring immediate attention.

9.4   The first are those motions that must be proposed and decided within a specific time limit: Reconsider, Appeal, Division of the Assembly, and request to *Withdraw a motion*. The Motion to Reconsider must be made during the same meeting or convention at which the vote to be reconsidered was taken and may be moved by any member.[38] This motion can be made at any time within its time limits but cannot interrupt a speaker who is speaking in debate. An Appeal and a demand for Division of the Assembly must be made before another item of business is taken up by the assembly. A proposer who wishes to Withdraw the motion may interrupt the presiding officer who is stating, or is about to state, the motion. After the motion has been stated by the presiding officer, the proposer may interrupt another speaker to request the withdrawal of the motion. The withdrawal must be requested before the motion is voted on.

9.5   The second are those motions that relate to the immediate rights and privileges of a member or of the assembly: Question of Privilege, Point of Order, Factual Inquiry, and Parliamentary Inquiry.

9.6   A question of privilege involving the immediate convenience, comfort, or rights of the organization or its members may be so urgent that it justifies interrupting a speaker. An example is noise that prevents the member from hearing the speaker. A Point of Order involving a mistake, error, or failure to comply with the rules can interrupt a speaker if the point relates to the speaker or to some error that cannot await the completion of the speech for its determination.

9.7   To justify interrupting a speaker, a factual inquiry or parliamentary inquiry must relate to the speaker, to the speech, or to some other matter that cannot be delayed until the completion of the speech. A factual inquiry that interrupts a speaker is only appropriate in extreme situations. If an immediate answer would prevent erroneous interpretation of the information and prevent the development of a substantive problem with the question being debated, an interrupting inquiry would be appropriate. The chair should not allow a factual inquiry or parliamentary inquiry that is being used in a dilatory fashion, as an opportunity to disrupt a speaker, or for any minor corrections of fact. After debate is closed, a factual inquiry is not in order.

9.8   A parliamentary inquiry is similar to a point of order in that it raises a question about procedure that may be immediately addressed.

DOES THE MOTION REQUIRE A SECOND?

9.9   Motions normally require a second. To justify the consideration of the assembly, a proposal must have the support of at least two members: one who makes the motion and another, the seconder, who indicates a willingness for the motion to be considered. The second indicates only that the member believes the motion should be considered and does not mean that the seconder agrees with the proposal. The name of the person seconding the motion does not appear in the minutes unless the assembly has a standing rule of order to that effect, or the assembly orders it done.

9.10 There are exceptions to this rule: in small meetings of committees, boards or assemblies, or some governmental bodies, seconds are not required.[39] Organizations that do not believe that a requirement for seconds is necessary may remove the requirement by adopting a standing rule of order.

9.11 A few actions do not require seconds because, although technically classified as motions, they are requests or demands that are decided or disposed of by the presiding officer. These are Point of Order, Factual and Parliamentary Inquiries, Withdraw a Motion (when offered prior to the motion being stated), Division of the Question (as a request), Division of the Assembly, and Question of Privilege. Questions of Privilege, Division of the Question, and Withdrawal of a motion are sometimes presented as motions instead of requests, in which case they require seconds. Once debate has begun and more than one member has participated, the lack of a second is irrelevant because multiples members have shown that they wish to consider the matter.

IS THE MOTION DEBATABLE?

9.12 Some motions are open to *full debate*, others are open to *limited debate*, and some are not debatable. All debate is subject to the principle of germaneness as discussed in Chapter 11. The only motions that are fully debatable are Main Motions, amendments to fully debatable Main Motions, and motions to Ratify, Adopt in Lieu of, Amend a Previous Action, Rescind, and Appeal.

9.13 Main Motions are debatable because they present substantive propositions requiring the consideration and decision of the organization. Amendments to debatable motions involve a part of the motion itself and are therefore debatable. The Motion to Ratify is fully debatable because the members must fully understand what is being ratified. Adopt in Lieu of is fully debatable as the members need to understand the main motion that is being presented in lieu of other main motions. The Motions to Amend a Previous Action and to Rescind a Main Motion that was previously adopted are debatable because they change or repeal an action taken earlier, and members need to understand the action that is being proposed. An Appeal from a decision of the chair is debatable because the presiding officer should give reasons for the presiding officer's ruling and the member appealing has a right to present reasons for appealing that decision.

9.14 Five motions are open to limited debate: Refer to a Committee, Postpone to a Certain Time, Recall from a Committee, Reconsider, and Amend. Limited debate means discussion is confined to specific points relative to the purpose of the motion itself. Thus, debate on the Motion to Refer to a Committee is limited to the advisability of referral and to the selection, membership, and duties of the committee, or instructions to it. Debate on the Motion to Postpone to a Certain Time is limited to discussion of the advisability of postponing and of the time to which the matter would be postponed. Debate on the Motion to Recall from a Committee is confined to the reasons for the removal from a committee's or board's consideration. Debate on the Motion to Reconsider is confined to the reasons for reconsidering. Debate on amendments to any of these motions is subject to the same limitations on debate.

9.15 Debate is not permitted on the subsidiary motions to Limit or Extend Debate or to Close Debate and Vote Immediately when the primary purpose of those motions is to change the rules for debate or end debate entirely. Likewise, debate is not permitted on the Motion to Table as the sole purpose of the motion is to remove the main motion from consideration without further debate.

CAN THE MOTION BE AMENDED?

9.16 A simple test determines whether a motion can be amended. If the motion contains wording that can be varied, then it is amendable. For example, the motion "I move that we recess for ten minutes" could have been stated, "I move that we recess for thirty minutes." The motion "I move that we limit debate on this question to one more speech on each side" could have been stated, "I move that we limit debate to two more speeches on each side." Such motions therefore are amendable.

9.17 However, if the motion contains wording that cannot be varied, it cannot be amended. Examples include the Motions to Table and to Reconsider.

9.18 The only motions that can be amended freely are Main Motions and Amendments to Main Motions, subject to germaneness; some motions can be amended with limitations, and some other motions cannot be amended.

9.19 Six motions can be amended only within limitations: Refer to a Committee, Postpone to a Certain Time, Limit or Extend Debate, Close Debate and Vote Immediately, Recess, and Adjourn. Refer to a Committee can be amended only as to the standing committee to which the matter is referred or, if a special committee is desired, the method of selection, size, membership, duties, and instructions to the committee. Postpone to a Certain Time, Limit or Extend Debate, and Recess can be amended only as to time or manner of restriction. Close Debate and Vote Immediately can be amended only as to which motions it applies. Adjourn can be amended to establish a *continued meeting* or change the time or place of a proposed continued meeting.

WHAT VOTE DOES THE MOTION REQUIRE?

9.20 The foundation of parliamentary procedure rests upon decisions made by the majority. For this reason, most motions require a majority vote. Motions that affect the rights of members require a two-thirds vote. These motions change the rights of members to propose, discuss, and decide proposals and include Motions to Limit or Extend Debate, Close Debate and Vote Immediately, Table, and Suspend the Rules. An organization's bylaws may provide that certain other motions require a two-thirds vote. For example, most bylaws require a two-thirds vote for their amendment, and in some states the law may require a two-thirds vote for a nonprofit membership corporation to buy, sell, or lease real estate or to mortgage substantially all its property.[40]

WHAT IS THE RANK (PRECEDENCE) OF THE MOTION?

9.21 To avoid confusion, each motion is assigned a definite rank or priority. This rank is based on the urgency of the motion. Motions are listed in the order of their rank in Chapter 8, "Ranking of Motions." When a motion is before the assembly, any motion is in order if it has a higher rank than the immediately pending motion, but no motion having a lower rank is in order. Motions are considered and decided in reverse order to that of their proposal.

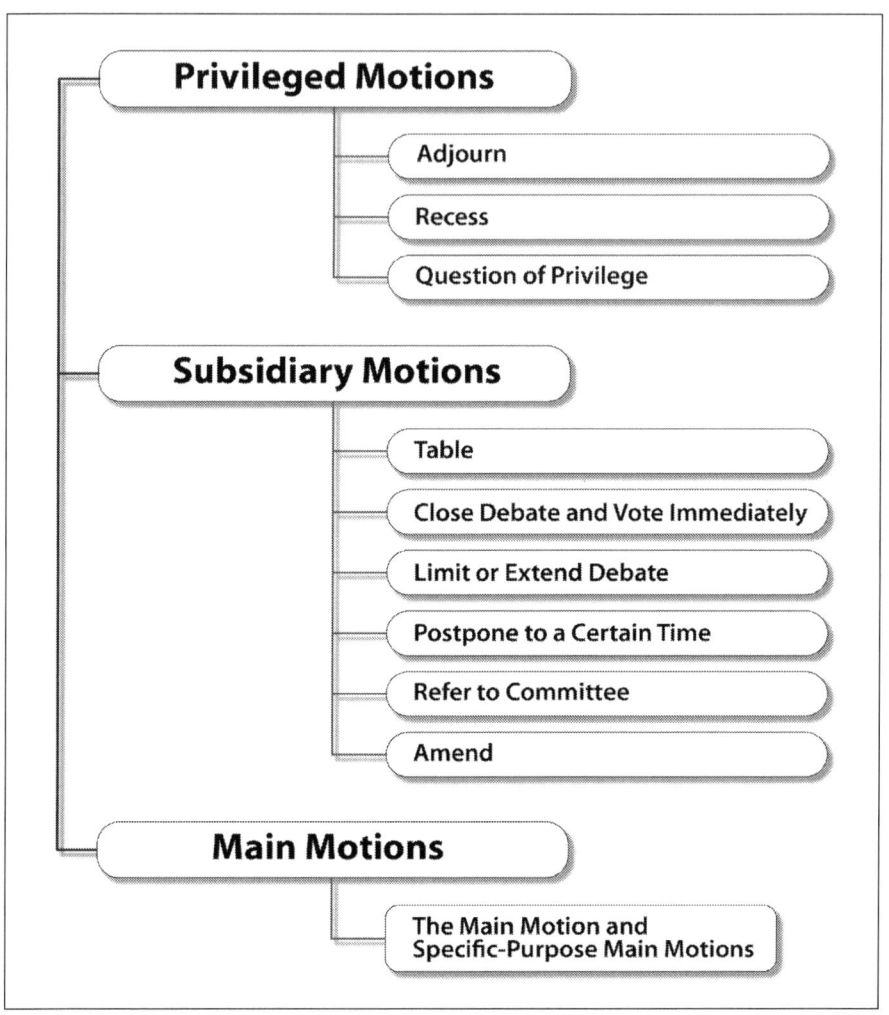

9.22 The general order of rank gives privileged motions the highest rank, subsidiary motions second, and the Main and Specific-Purpose Main Motions the lowest. Incidental motions have no order of rank among themselves. Incidental motions may be proposed at any time they are needed and are decided immediately.

TO WHAT OTHER MOTIONS CAN THE MOTION APPLY?

9.23 A motion is said to *apply* to another motion when it is used to alter, dispose of, or affect the underlying motion in some way. For example, if a main motion is being considered, and a member moves "to postpone the consideration of the motion until Friday at three o'clock," the Motion to Postpone to a Certain Time applies to the main motion. Subsidiary motions apply to main motions and other applicable motions. The subsidiary Motion to Limit or Extend Debate applies to debatable motions and the Motion to Close Debate and Vote Immediately applies to debatable or amendable motions. The subsidiary Motion to Amend applies to:

1. a Main Motion;
2. the Specific-Purpose Main Motions to Amend a Previous Action, Rescind, and Adopt in Lieu of;
3. the subsidiary motions to Amend, Refer to a Committee, Postpone to a Certain Time, Limit or Extend Debate, and Close Debate and Vote Immediately; and
4. the privileged motions to Recess and Adjourn.

9.24 Privileged motions relate to the organization and the welfare and rights of its members rather than to items of business and therefore do not apply to any other motion.

9.25 Incidental motions do not apply to other motions, except that the Motion to Withdraw applies to any motion. Division of the Question applies to the Main Motion and Specific-Purpose Main Motions if they are divisible. Division of the Assembly applies to voice votes on motions.

9.26 Apart from Adopt in Lieu of, which applies only to two or more main motions that are to be presented as a group,* Specific-Purpose Main Motions deal with previously adopted motions and are not applied to pending motions.

WHAT OTHER MOTIONS CAN BE APPLIED TO THE MOTION?

9.27 When a motion is being considered, it is important to know what other motions can be applied to it. The following rules determine what motions may be applied to each individual motion:

1. All motions can have the Motion to Withdraw applied to them.
2. All debatable motions can have the Motions to Close Debate and Vote Immediately and to Limit or Extend Debate applied to them. All

---

* See Chapters 13 and 25 for further information and examples.

amendable motions can have the Motion to Close Debate and Vote Immediately applied to them.

3. All motions that may be worded in more than one way, thereby producing different results, can have the Motion to Amend applied to them.

4. All subsidiary motions can be applied to the Main Motion.

5. Applying subsidiary motions to Specific-Purpose Main Motions varies according to the nature of the Specific-Purpose Main Motion. All subsidiary motions can be applied to four of the Specific-Purpose Main Motions—to Amend a Previous Action, to Rescind, and to Adopt in Lieu of. The Motions to Ratify, to Recall from a Committee and to Reconsider cannot be amended, but the Motions to Limit or Extend Debate and to Close Debate and Vote Immediately can be applied to them. The Motions to Refer to a Committee and to Postpone to a Certain Time can be applied to the Motion to Rescind.

6. The application of other motions to privileged motions is limited to the following: the Motions to Amend and to Close Debate and Vote Immediately can be applied to the Motions to Recess and to Adjourn.

7. Incidental motions can only have the Motion to Withdraw applied to them, except the Motions to Close Debate and Vote Immediately and to Limit or Extend Debate can be applied to the Motion to Appeal.

CAN A MOTION BE RENEWED?

9.28 Generally, when a main motion has been disposed of, the same—or substantially the same—motion cannot be proposed again at the same meeting or convention. Parliamentary law recognizes, however, that an assembly may change its mind, just as an individual may, and that some method must be provided for changing a decision which has been made. In the case of a main motion the matter can be brought before the assembly again at the same meeting or convention by the Motion to Reconsider, which is discussed in Chapter 13, "Specific-Purpose Main Motions." Approval of the Motion to Reconsider cancels the earlier vote and enables the assembly to debate and amend the motion, if desired, and to take another vote.

9.29 If the motion in question was adopted at an earlier meeting or convention, it cannot be reconsidered. It may be repealed, however, by the Motion to Rescind, which nullifies the earlier decision, or it may be amended by the Motion to Amend a Previous Action. Unlike the Motion to Reconsider, the

Motions to Rescind and Amend a Previous Action have no time limit and can be proposed at any subsequent meeting.

9.30 If a main motion was defeated at an earlier meeting or convention, it may be renewed by being introduced as a new main motion at a subsequent meeting or convention.

9.31 All motions that are procedural rather than substantive may be *renewed* at the discretion of the presiding officer, subject to appeal. The presiding officer should judge the likelihood of a different outcome if the *procedural motion* is renewed. This is often based on a *change in the parliamentary situation*, which may occur after progress in debate or by amendment of the main motion, so that the motion now applies to essentially a different question. For example, a defeated Motion to Refer to a Committee may now be more likely to be adopted if the underlying motion has changed, or if repeated attempts to amend or further debate has made it apparent that the motion may be more complex than previously realized, and that referral may have merit now, despite the assembly's earlier decision not to refer.

REPEAL BY IMPLICATION

9.32 In addition to the nine questions about each motion that have been summarized in this chapter, there is one additional procedural question that should be understood: How does a main motion that is currently pending affect previously adopted main motions that are on the same subject and are still in effect? This is explained through the concept of *repeal by implication*.

9.33 A main motion that has been adopted can be affected by a new main motion that has been introduced later. Repeal by implication automatically results from the adoption of a motion that conflicts in whole or in part with another motion or motions previously adopted.[41] The first motion is repealed only to the extent that its provisions cannot be reconciled with those of the new motion; portions of the previous action that are not in conflict with the newly adopted action remain in effect.

9.34 Members may be unaware of related motions previously adopted, or those motions may have been overlooked. Before a member proposes a new main motion, it is considered a best practice to search the records for adopted main motions that may still be in effect but with which the new motion might conflict. Such motions that are still in effect should be rescinded or amended before a new motion is adopted. Repeal by implication is intended to correct inadvertent conflicts, not to be a blanket method for disposing of previously adopted main motions without voting directly on their repeal.

9.35 Repeal by implication applies to any previously adopted motion or rule that conflicts with a newly adopted motion or rule. If the new motion conflicts with a provision in a source of higher authority, for example, a charter, bylaws, or rule, it is out of order, and, if it is adopted, its adoption is null and void unless the new motion is one to amend a source of higher authority.

CHANGING MAIN MOTIONS ALREADY VOTED ON

9.36 The table below describes how a previously considered Main Motion can be affected:

Action	May Be Used:	Applies to:
Motion to Reconsider	Only at same meeting or convention	Any main motion adopted, defeated, or tabled
Motion to Rescind	At any meeting or convention	Any main motion adopted at an earlier meeting or convention
Amend a Previous Action	At any meeting or convention	Any main motion previously adopted
Renew by new main motion	At any subsequent meeting or convention	Any main motion defeated or tabled
Repeal or amend by implication	At any meeting or convention	Any main motion previously adopted that conflicts with a current main motion

CHAPTER 10. Processing Motions

PROCESSING A MOTION

10.1 A motion is a formal statement of a proposal to an assembly to act or express certain sentiments. Once stated, a motion may be referred to as a question, proposal, motion, or proposition, depending on context. Longer or more complex motions may be presented in the form of a written resolution.

STEPS IN PRESENTING A MOTION

10.2 Motions may take on many forms, but the initial presentation follows a generally accepted procedure. Presenting a motion to the assembly usually requires the following steps:

1. A member rises and addresses the presiding officer.
2. The member is recognized by the presiding officer.
3. The member proposes or "moves" the motion.
4. Another member seconds the motion.
5. The presiding officer states the motion to the assembly.

Addressing the Presiding Officer

10.3 Any member has the right to present a motion. Addressing the presiding officer indicates that the member wishes to obtain the floor, that is, to have the right to present a motion or to speak. To do this, the member rises and addresses the presiding officer by his or her official title. If the member does not know the official title of the presiding officer, the terms *Mr. Chair* and *Madam Chair* are always correct unless the organization has adopted a different style of address. After addressing the presiding officer, the member waits for *recognition*.

10.4 In assemblies where a microphone system is used, members form a line at the appropriate microphone, and the presiding officer recognizes the members based on the microphone number or location.

10.5 Seeking recognition in an electronic meeting will vary according to the features of the electronic meeting platform and according to the meeting rules that are established by the assembly. A method to seek recognition to speak should be clearly defined. See Chapter 19 for additional information.

Recognition by the Presiding Officer

10.6 The presiding officer should recognize all members in the same manner to avoid the perception of favoritism. For instance, if the presiding officer does not know every member by name, then another form of recognition must be used. This may include "speaker at microphone A," "the member in row four," or "the member in the red jacket."

10.7 Members, when recognized, should identify themselves by name and, if applicable, their state, district, or other unit represented, and the purpose for which recognition is sought. For example, "Bill Brown, delegate from Wyoming. I speak in favor of the motion."

10.8 Having received formal recognition from the presiding officer, a member is said to "have the floor" and is entitled to present a motion or speak. Other members who were also seeking recognition should be seated as soon as one member is recognized. If a microphone system is being used, members in line may keep their places in line but should step back to avoid crowding the member who has the floor.

Proposal of a Motion by a Member

10.9 The correct form for *stating a motion* is "I move that…" or "I move to…" followed by a statement of the proposal that the member wishes to bring before the assembly: For example, "I move that this organization have a fundraiser for the community park." The enacting clause "I move…" gives notice to the presiding officer and to the assembly that the speaker is submitting a proposal for decision. Avoid forms such as "I so move," "so moved," or "I make a motion that." Statements beginning "I think we should" or "I suggest" should be treated as debate and not as motions. However, the presiding officer may ask if the member wishes to put the statement in the form of a motion.

10.10 If the meaning of the motion is not clear to the members, the presiding officer should ask the member to restate the motion more clearly. The presiding officer may assist members in clarifying the wording of motions.

A member who clearly wishes to make a proposal for action should never be prevented from doing so based on a lack of knowledge of the proper form.

10.11 Aside from an occasional brief explanatory remark, no discussion is permissible until the presiding officer states the motion to the assembly.

10.12 It is critically important that the presiding officer and the assembly understand the exact wording of every motion. If the motion is not initially clear, the presiding officer has the responsibility to assist the maker in clarifying the motion. In doing so, the presiding officer must take care not to propose any substantive changes to the motion or otherwise suggest that the presiding officer might have an opinion on the matter being proposed.

10.13 The presiding officer may require that any motions be submitted in writing, via email or other designated format. A lengthy, complicated, or important motion, such as a resolution, should always be prepared in writing. If submitted in writing, a motion should be distributed to the presiding officer, the secretary, the parliamentarian, and, if applicable, the staff member who will arrange for its projection on a screen for all to see.

Seconding a Motion

10.14 After the maker has proposed the motion, another member may, without waiting for recognition, say, "I second the motion" or "Second." Seconding a motion is not necessarily an expression of support for the motion but indicates that the member wishes the motion to be considered by the assembly.

10.15 If the motion is not seconded, the presiding officer asks, "Is there a second to this motion?" If there is no response, the presiding officer states, "There is no second, the motion is not before the assembly" or "There is no second, the motion will not be considered," and proceeds to other business.

10.16 The presiding officer may proceed without a second on routine items of business if that is the custom of the organization. If any member objects to the lack of a second, the presiding officer must call for one unless debate by more than one member has already occurred, in which case the purpose of the second, indication that more than one member wishes the motion to be considered, has been fulfilled.

10.17 A second is not required for motions when submitted by a committee to the assembly. When moved in a small committee or board, motions do not require a second.

Statement of a Motion by the Presiding Officer

10.18 When a motion has been moved and seconded, the presiding officer states the motion to the assembly as correctly and clearly as possible. If the presiding officer decides that the motion is not in order, the presiding officer makes that ruling without stating the motion. If the presiding officer makes an error in stating a motion, the proposer should immediately raise a point of order to correct the error. If there is a difference of opinion as to the exact wording of a motion during consideration of the motion, the motion as stated by the presiding officer is the official motion.

10.19 The presiding officer states the motion as follows: "It has been moved and seconded that [state the motion]" or "It has been moved and seconded that the following resolution be adopted: Resolved, [state the resolution]."

10.20 It is useful to have motions submitted to an assistant or staff member who will project the motion for all members to see on a large screen. In such situations, the presiding officer may dispense with restating the entire motion and direct the assembly to the screen. If this is done, the presiding officer should first confirm that the wording of the projected motion is correct. The motion as displayed becomes the official wording of the motion.

10.21 If there is a difference between the motion as projected and the motion as stated by the chair, the version that members can see is the final wording of the motion, and is what is recorded in the minutes as the motion considered by the assembly. If the motion displayed cannot be altered to accurately reflect the motion, perhaps due to the presentation software, the display should be discontinued, and the assembly considers the motion as stated by the chair.

10.22 After a motion has been stated to the assembly by the presiding officer, it is open for discussion if it is debatable. From the time a motion is stated by the presiding officer until it is disposed of, it is called a pending question or pending motion.

Example of the Presentation of a Motion

10.23 An example is shown in the table below, with each step identified:

Step	Language
1. A member rises and addresses the presiding officer.	**Member A:** Mr. President.
2. The member is recognized by the presiding officer.	**Presiding Officer:** Member A.
3. The member proposes the motion.	**Member A:** I move that this organization begin a campaign to raise funds for equipment for the community park.
4. Another member seconds the motion.	**Member B:** (remaining seated and not waiting for recognition) I second the motion.
5. The presiding officer states the motion to the assembly.	**Presiding Officer:** It has been moved and seconded "that this organization begin a campaign to raise funds for equipment for the community park." Is there any discussion?

CONSIDERATION OF THE MOTION

10.24 After the motion has been stated by the presiding officer, it is open to consideration, which may include debate (see Chapter 11), amendment (see Chapter 14), or other procedural motions.

STEPS IN VOTING AND ANNOUNCING RESULTS OF THE VOTE

10.25 The final step in processing a motion is to take the vote. Voting on a motion usually requires the following steps:

1. The presiding officer restates or "puts" the pending question (puts the question to a vote).
2. The presiding officer takes the affirmative vote.
3. The presiding officer takes the negative vote.
4. The presiding officer announces which side prevailed.

5. The presiding officer announces whether the motion was adopted or defeated.
6. The presiding officer announces what will be done as a result of the vote.
7. The presiding officer introduces the next item of business or calls for further business.

Step	Language
1. The presiding officer restates or "puts" the pending question (puts the question to a vote).	**Presiding Officer:** The pending motion is "that this organization undertake a campaign to raise funds for equipment for the community park." Is there any (further) discussion?
2. The presiding officer takes the affirmative vote.	**Presiding Officer:** Those in favor of adopting the motion, say "Aye."
3. The presiding officer takes the negative vote.	**Presiding Officer:** Those opposed to adopting the motion, say "No."
4. The presiding officer announces which side prevailed.	**Presiding Officer:** The Ayes/Noes have it.
5. The presiding officer announces whether the motion was adopted or defeated.	**Presiding Officer:** The motion is adopted/defeated.
6. The presiding officer announces what will be done as a result of the vote.	**Presiding Officer:** The organization will/will not raise funds for equipment for the community park.
7. The presiding officer introduces the next item of business or calls for further business.	**Presiding Officer:** The next business in order is…

Putting the Question

10.26 Stating the motion to the assembly for the purpose of taking a vote on the motion is referred to as *"putting the question."* The presiding officer must be sure that the members understand the effect of adoption or defeat prior to taking the vote. Prior to taking the vote, the presiding officer should restate, or put, the motion exactly as it is pending at the time. The motion as put by the presiding officer prior to voting is the official language of the motion for inclusion in the minutes. Great care should be taken by both the presiding officer and the assembly to ensure the accuracy of the motion. If the presiding officer makes an error in putting the question, a member of the assembly should rise to a point of order to ensure accuracy.

Taking the Affirmative Vote

10.27 The presiding officer takes the affirmative vote in the following manner: For a voice vote, the presiding officer says, "Those in favor, say 'Aye.'" It is not acceptable to take a vote by saying "Those in favor" without completing the instruction by indicating the action to be taken.

10.28 For a vote by division or for a two-thirds vote, the presiding officer says, "Those in favor, rise. (pause) Be seated." In small groups, the presiding officer may ask members to raise their hands instead of rise from their seats.

10.29 For a vote by other methods, the presiding officer clearly instructs the members how to indicate their preference, especially in electronic meetings. For more information on methods of voting, see Chapter 6.

Taking the Negative Vote

10.30 Following the completion of the affirmative vote, the presiding officer must always take the negative vote, even if it appears that the affirmative vote is unanimous. The method used should parallel the procedures used in the affirmative vote. Calling for "the same sign" is never acceptable. For example, for a voice vote, the presiding officer says, "Those opposed, say 'No.'" The presiding officer, in taking the negative vote, must ensure that there is no perception that the presiding officer has a preference as to how members should vote. The language should never discourage members who wish to vote against a proposal from doing so; for example, "Anybody opposed?" or "Are there any opposed?" is unacceptable.

Announcing Which Side Prevailed

10.31 The presiding officer determines which side prevailed and announces it; for example, "The Ayes have it" or "The Noes have it." If the presiding officer is uncertain which side prevailed, the vote must be repeated using a more definitive method, for example, a division or a counted vote. It is essential that this determination be certain, and that the members have confidence in the announcement of which side prevailed. There is nothing more damaging to an organization and its meetings than a feeling by some members that the outcome of one or more votes was announced incorrectly.

Announcing Whether the Motion Was Adopted or Defeated

10.32 The presiding officer announces the effect on the motion; for example, "The motion is adopted" or "The motion is defeated."

Announcing What Will Happen–the Effect of the Vote

10.33 The presiding officer explains what will happen as a result; for example, "This organization will (or will not) undertake a campaign to raise funds for the scholarship for the local swim team."

Introducing the Next Business

10.34 It is the responsibility of the presiding officer to keep the assembly informed on the item of business that is pending and what will be considered next. If a subsidiary or other motion has been voted on, the presiding officer presents the next pending motion, in order of precedence, for consideration by the assembly; for example, "The Motion to Refer to a Committee is defeated; is there further discussion on the main motion, which is [states the main motion]?" Of course, if the referral is adopted, the next business would be another main motion or the introduction of the next *agenda* item.

10.35 If a main motion has been voted on, and an adopted agenda designates the next item of business, the presiding officer places that item of business before the assembly; for example, "The next item of business is [announces the next business in order]."

SKIPPING STEPS IN PROCESSING MOTIONS

10.36 While all the steps in processing a motion should ordinarily be followed, there are often situations where either the rules or the circumstances allow steps to be skipped.

10.37 For example, if the rules applicable to a motion allow the maker to interrupt the proceedings in some way, the steps in which a member seeks and is granted recognition might be skipped. For a motion that does not require a second, that step would be skipped.

10.38   In routine matters, almost all the steps in processing a motion might be skipped. As an example, if the minutes have been previously distributed, the presiding officer might say, "Are there corrections to the minutes as distributed? (pause) There being no corrections, the minutes are approved as distributed." In this example, the presiding officer *assumes the motion* to approve the minutes. That is, no one seeks recognition, no one is recognized, no one makes the motion, and the motion is not seconded; even the statement of the motion by the presiding officer is implied rather than explicit. In taking the vote, general consent is presumed, and all the steps are compressed into the indicated statements by the presiding officer. The presiding officer may assume a motion at any time that the parliamentary situation makes it obvious to the presiding officer that a motion is required.

10.39   It is a common practice to make an exception to taking a formal vote on motions honoring or thanking members, in which case it is not unusual for the assembly to demonstrate its approval by applause and in such cases, the presiding officer may simply declare such motions adopted.

10.40   Even without skipping steps, each step does not need to be identified discretely and they can be combined into one statement. For example, after taking the vote on an amendment to the main motion, the presiding officer might say, "The Ayes have it, and the amendment is adopted; the main motion now reads [states the main motion as amended]. Is there discussion?" Thus, the presiding officer will have combined the last four steps of voting into a concise but clear and complete statement.

10.41   If any member finds the omission of steps confusing, that member should raise a point of order, and the presiding officer can either correct the omissions or explain how steps have been combined. While it can be tedious to follow every step in processing every motion, at no time should steps be omitted to rush business through the assembly, nor should steps be omitted if it will create an impression that such rushing is occurring.

10.42   It is important to remember that although steps are skipped, for example, if a motion is adopted by general consent, the assembly is still taking an action, or permitting an action to be taken by the body. That action must be included in the minutes, just as if each of the steps in the motion-making process were followed individually.

CHAPTER 11. **Debate**

THE RIGHT OF DEBATE

11.1 The purpose of deliberative bodies is to secure the collective judgment of the group on proposals submitted to it for decision. This purpose is best served by free exchange of information and opinions through discussion before making a final decision on the pending question.

11.2 The right of every member to participate in the discussion of any matter of business that comes before the assembly is one of the fundamental principles of parliamentary law. Every member has the right to speak for or against any debatable motion; this includes the right of the maker of a particular motion to speak in debate against that same motion.

11.3 Debate is regulated by parliamentary rules to assure every member a reasonable and equal opportunity to speak. Knowledge of the rules governing debate is essential to every member wishing to exercise that right.

EXTENT OF DEBATE ON MOTIONS

11.4 Motions that are debatable are those that may require discussion for decision. All debate must be *germane* to the immediately pending motion. If it is a main motion, the debate must be germane to the merits of the motion—the merits of adopting or not adopting the motion. If it is a subsidiary motion, debate must be germane to the merits of that motion. For example:

1. debate on a Motion to Amend must be germane to the amendment only;
2. debate on the Motion to Refer to a Committee must be germane to the merits of referring only; and
3. debate on the Motion to Postpone to a Certain Time must be germane to the merits of postponing.

11.5 Except for the Motion to Appeal, all other incidental motions are not debatable and must be put to a vote immediately.* This is due to their urgency, as with incidental or privileged motions, or because debate would

---

* See the section on Point of Order in Chapter 16 for the limited times this motion may be debatable.

defeat the purpose of the motion. For example, to permit debate on the Motion to Close Debate and Vote Immediately would defeat the purpose of the motion.

RULES OF DECORUM AND CONDUCT IN DEBATE

11.6   The following are the rules of decorum in debate:

1. Members must be recognized to debate.
2. Debate must be germane to the immediately pending question.
3. Debate is directed to or through the presiding officer.
4. Dilatory tactics are not in order.
5. Debate must be impersonal.
6. Debate should be concise and non-repetitive.
7. Remarks presented in debate should be courteous.
8. Members should listen to debate attentively and courteously.

11.7   Debate must be impersonal. All discussion is addressed to or through the presiding officer and must never be directed to any individual. The motion, not the advocate, is the subject of debate. A motion—its nature or consequences—may be attacked vigorously. It is the duty of the presiding officer to quickly stop any member who engages in personal attacks, discusses the motives of another member, or speaks or acts in a discourteous manner. Debate must address the merits of a motion, not people.

11.8   Out of respect for the time of other members, arguments and opinions should be stated as concisely as possible. A speech is made, not for the pleasure of the speaker or for the entertainment of others, but to assist the assembly in arriving at a decision on the question under discussion.

11.9   A member is more likely to be effective in debate when demonstrating courtesy toward the presiding officer and other members. Anyone who uses improper language or acts in a disorderly manner must be corrected promptly by the presiding officer. When a point of order is raised concerning a speaker's conduct, the speaker must be seated until the point of order is decided by the presiding officer.

11.10   A member who fails or refuses to speak in an orderly and courteous manner may be denied recognition by the presiding officer. If necessary, the assembly may eject such a member from the meeting for a period up to the end of the meeting or convention by a majority vote, without debate. The motion to eject the member may be moved by any member or assumed by the presiding officer.

11.11   Members who do not have the floor must listen attentively and respectfully to the remarks of the speaker. Good decision-making is more likely if members judge the speaker's remarks on their merits and not on the perceived merits of the person presenting those remarks.

OBTAINING THE FLOOR FOR DEBATE

11.12   As soon as a debatable motion has been stated to the assembly by the presiding officer, any member has the right to discuss it after obtaining the floor. A member waits until no one has the floor, then rises, addresses the presiding officer, and waits for recognition. The floor is obtained in this manner whether the purpose is to present a motion or to participate in debate. In a large meeting or convention, convention rules may be adopted describing the method used to obtain the floor, for example, keeping a speakers list or assignment by order of lining up at microphones.

11.13   A member who has been recognized is entitled to be heard, provided that the rules of debate are observed.

PRIORITY OF RECOGNITION OF MEMBERS DURING DEBATE

11.14   Usually, the first person who rises and asks for recognition, when no member has the floor, is entitled to recognition. When more than one member seeks recognition at the same time, the following rules help the presiding officer decide which member is recognized first:

1. The person who has proposed a motion or the committee member who has presented a report is allowed the first opportunity to explain the motion or report, and usually is given the opportunity to speak again after it appears all others who wish to do so have spoken.

2. A member who has not spoken on the immediately pending motion has priority over one who has already spoken on the motion. Similarly, a member who seldom speaks is given preference over one who claims the attention of the assembly frequently.

3. The presiding officer recognizes members for debate, alternating between proponents and opponents of a motion whenever possible. When there are opposing opinions, the presiding officer may inquire of

a member seeking recognition which viewpoint the member will present or may ask if there are members wishing to speak to the position opposite that of the member who has just spoken. Thus, the presiding officer can divide the opportunities to speak more equitably.

11.15 A member who seeks recognition for a purpose that can properly interrupt needs to indicate this so that the presiding officer can recognize the member first. For example, a member wishing to raise a point of order may interrupt business, and even a speaker, by calling out (without prior recognition) "Mr. President, Point of Order!" and then awaiting recognition before proceeding.

RELEVANCE IN DEBATE

11.16 All discussion must be relevant or germane to the motion before the assembly. A member who is given the floor may only use that privilege for the purpose of discussing the pending question or making a permissible motion or both. Discussion that departs from the subject is out of order. Short illustrations or stories may be used in discussing a point so long as they are relevant to the motion under discussion.

11.17 Discussion is always limited so far as possible to the immediately pending motion. When a motion is under discussion and a motion of higher rank is made, discussion is confined to the motion of higher rank until it is decided, or until a higher-ranking motion is proposed. Occasionally, brief mention of lower-ranking motions may be appropriate while debating the immediately pending motion; for example, with an amendment immediately pending, its impact on the general intent of the main motion may be considered germane. With a Motion to Refer immediately pending, a brief statement of a preference for adoption of a pending amendment to the main motion may be germane. Another example is the occasion when the urgency of adoption of the main motion might sometimes be germane to the need for referral.

11.18 If a speaker departs from the subject, the presiding officer's role is to interrupt and request that the speaker's remarks be limited to the pending motion and to remind the speaker and the assembly of exactly which motion is immediately pending. If the presiding officer fails to do this, any member may rise to a point of order and call the attention of the presiding officer to the speaker's digression. The presiding officer then directs the speaker to limit discussion to the motion before the assembly.

ADDRESSING MEMBERS DURING DEBATE

11.19   In meetings conducted using formal parliamentary procedure, members should address one another by last name, or in the third person, even though ordinarily on a first-name basis. In a large group, this adds a note of formality, which keeps the discussion at a higher level. In recent years, however, with the trend toward greater informality, this practice is often ignored, especially in small groups and in social organizations in which all members are on a first-name basis. Under no circumstances, however, should the presiding officer call some members by their first names and others by their last, as this may create a perception of favoritism for a group composed of close friends of the presiding officer and another group of comparative strangers.

11.20   In very large assemblies, it is often the custom to avoid the use of names altogether by referring to members by such terms as *the previous speaker*, or *the maker of the motion*, or *the delegate from Arizona*. This helps to keep the discussion impersonal. Another purpose of this formality is to create an atmosphere that is conducive to more respectful behavior of the members toward one another, which is mandatory no matter the size or relationship among the members.

DILATORY TACTICS

11.21   Dilatory tactics—that is, delaying the proposal or the vote on a subject by, for example, making unnecessary motions, asking pointless questions, reading extensively from papers without the approval of the assembly, or talking around and not on the question—are always out of order. As soon as it is evident that a member or group of members is using dilatory tactics, the presiding officer rules that such conduct is not in order. If members persist in dilatory tactics, the presiding officer must either refuse to recognize them or rule the dilatory motions out of order.

SPEAKING MORE THAN ONCE

11.22   It is important that the debate be balanced. No member, or small group of members, is to be permitted to monopolize the discussion on a question. It is the duty of the presiding officer to prevent a group of members from dominating debate to the extent that only one side of the issue is presented, and even more so if that group then attempts to close debate before opposing opinions are heard. In the interest of balanced participation, good decision-making, and the protection of the rights of the minority, the presiding officer must ensure that such strategies are not allowed.

11.23 Other members wishing to speak have a right to be recognized in preference to the member who has already spoken on a question. However, if no other members seek recognition, a member who has already spoken may be recognized again.

11.24 Sometimes a few members who are interested in and informed on the subject being discussed will speak several times on that question. This is permissible if it is not repetitive and members who have not already spoken are not seeking recognition.

WHAT IS NOT DEBATE?

11.25 Debate or discussion refers to any comments made about the motion and is usually put forth to persuade others to support the speaker's position.

11.26 A brief comment or remark by the proposer of a motion before stating it is generally permissible and is not considered debate. Similarly, a very brief explanatory remark or a question is sometimes permitted on an undebatable motion. For example, a member could say, "Having heard several speakers on each side of the pending motion, I move to close debate and vote immediately." An inquiry, or a brief suggestion or explanation, is not debate. The presiding officer must be careful that this is not abused or allowed to become debate.

11.27 When there is a limitation on debate, by adopted motion or rule, and a member who does not already have the floor responds to a question asked through the presiding officer, both the question and the reply are not debate. When the member who has the floor is interrupted by an inquiry and is recognized and responds to the inquiry, the question and the reply are not considered debate and the time is not subtracted from the time allotted to the speaker. However, in both situations the presiding officer must ensure both the question and answer are as brief as possible and that neither expands into debate.

11.28 During debate, every member is entitled to know precisely what the question is, to know what its effects will be, to ask for a reasonable explanation, or to raise a Factual or Parliamentary Inquiry. Such inquiries are not considered debate. A member has the right to have a motion restated before voting or at any time when there is uncertainty about its meaning or wording, and such a request is not debate. The presiding officer has a duty to ensure that these rights of members are not abused and the will of the assembly in proceeding to a vote is followed. For this reason, Factual Inquiries are not in order after a Motion to Close Debate and Vote Immediately has been adopted.

PRESIDING OFFICER'S DUTIES DURING DEBATE

11.29   The presiding officer has the responsibility of controlling and expediting debate. A member who has been assigned the floor has a right to the undivided attention of the assembly. It is the duty of the presiding officer to protect the speaker in this right by suppressing disorder; by intervening when others are distracting the assembly or the member speaking by, for example, whispering or walking about; and by preventing annoyance, heckling, or unnecessary interruption. The presiding officer should remind members to be attentive to the business before the assembly. The assembly owes respectful attention to the presiding officer and to each speaker.

11.30   It is also the presiding officer's duty to keep the subject clearly before the members, to rule out any irrelevant discussion, and to restate the motion whenever necessary. The presiding officer must make sure the assembly is aware of the immediately pending motion at all times.

11.31   If there are important aspects of the motion that are being overlooked, the presiding officer may offer or solicit factual information that would otherwise be unknown to members of the assembly, thus leading to a better-informed decision by the assembly. The presiding officer must remain impartial when providing information or questions.

11.32   The presiding officer must refrain from participating personally in debate, other than debate on an appeal from the chair's ruling. If the presiding officer wishes to participate in debate, which should occur rarely, the presiding officer must vacate the chair and call on someone else, in accordance with any provisions in the bylaws, to preside. In such a case, the presiding officer does not resume the chair until the pending main motion is disposed of.[42] The able presiding officer takes considerable care to assure that bias is not exhibited from the chair on any pending business, especially while presiding.

TIME LIMITS ON DEBATE

11.33   Parliamentary law fixes no limit on the length or number of speeches during debate. Each organization has the right to establish limits on debate if the members wish to do so. Debate can ordinarily be kept within reasonable time limits by the presiding officer's insistence that all discussion be confined strictly to the subject. However, especially in meetings with large memberships and extensive agendas, assemblies may find it necessary to adopt limits on the duration or number of speeches that members may make on any pending motion. Such limitations often increase the opportunities for more members to participate in debate and the likelihood of timely completion of the assembly's business.

11.34   If debate has been limited, time allocated to one member cannot be transferred to another member. In legislative bodies, members may yield portions of debate time to other members, but this is not permitted in ordinary societies.

CLOSING DEBATE

11.35   While members have a right to debate, the assembly has the right to determine how much debate is necessary. It is generally unwise to make a practice of cutting off or preventing debate on most debatable questions; members who are frequently denied the right to participate in its deliberations cannot be expected to maintain interest in the organization. Further, assemblies cannot be expected to make good decisions if voting occurs before there is an adequate opportunity to learn the facts that bear on the pending motion and to hear the opinions of others. The presiding officer should be prepared to manage such occurrences when they are used to prevent opposing views from being presented.

BRINGING A QUESTION TO VOTE

11.36   When it appears that all the members who wish to speak have done so, the presiding officer inquires, "Is there any further discussion?" After confirming that there is no further discussion, the presiding officer takes the vote on the pending question.* The presiding officer never ends discussion unilaterally. It is ended only by the assembly, whether by general

---

* For information on the Motion to Close Debate and Vote Immediately, see Chapter 14.

consent, by adoption of a Motion to Close Debate and Vote Immediately, or by a previously adopted limitation on debate.

11.37   The presiding officer does, however, have a responsibility to assist the assembly in disposing of its business efficiently. If all debate has been limited to one side of an issue, and the presiding officer has called for debate on the other side with no response, it may be appropriate to ask the assembly, "Are you ready to vote?" Likewise, when debate has become repetitive, the presiding officer should ask, "Is there any **new** discussion (or debate)?" If no one responds, the presiding officer proceeds to the vote. Members still seeking the floor, seeing no opposition to their position or having no new points to raise, may be willing to proceed directly to a vote, or a member may move to close debate and vote immediately.

11.38   After the presiding officer has begun to take the vote, no further debate or inquiries are permitted. However, if the presiding officer starts to put the question to a vote prematurely, this does not cut off the right of a member to speak. A member, if reasonably prompt in seeking recognition, may be granted the right to speak at any time before the vote is taken.

CHAPTER 12. Main Motions

THE MAIN MOTION

12.1 A Main Motion is a substantive proposal presented to the assembly for consideration, discussion, decision, and action. It is usually originated by an individual member or a committee. It is the basic motion for the transaction of business. Because it is a fundamental principle of parliamentary law that only one subject can be considered at one time, a main motion can be proposed only when no other motion is before the assembly.[43] While the main motion is the most important kind of motion, it is also the lowest ranking motion in the precedence of motions.

Purpose and Effect

12.2 The purpose of a main motion is to propose an action to the assembly for a decision. The effect of adopting a main motion is to commit the organization to the proposed action stated by the motion or to express the sentiment in the motion.

Examples of a Main Motion

Member:	I move that we organize a campaign to elect our past president to the national board.
Presiding Officer: (after the motion is seconded)	It has been moved and seconded that we organize a campaign to elect our past president to the national board. Is there any discussion?

12.3 Alternatively,

Member:	I move that we organize a campaign to elect our past president to the national board, and that we ask our members to contribute to a fund to finance the campaign at the national convention.

Presiding Officer: (after the motion is seconded)	It has been moved and seconded that we organize a campaign to elect our past president to the national board, and that we ask our members to contribute to a fund to finance the campaign at the national convention. Is there any discussion?

12.4 Or to propose adoption of a resolution (see below for further details on resolutions):

Member:	I move the adoption of the following resolution: **Resolved,** that we organize a campaign to elect our past president to the national board.
Presiding Officer: (after the motion is seconded)	It has been moved and seconded that we adopt a resolution to organize a campaign to elect our past president to the national board. Is there any discussion?

Phrasing the Main Motion

12.5 The main motion is a proposal of action that a member presents for consideration by the assembly. Because of the many kinds of actions that may be taken, the wording of main motions varies greatly, and wide latitude is permitted. However, all motions must be introduced by the words "I move that" or "I move to." A motion should be concise and clear. If a member presents a confusing motion or one that is longer or more complicated than necessary, the presiding officer may ask the proposer to rephrase the motion. The presiding officer has a duty to assist a member in the proper phrasing of a motion if this process does not unduly consume the time of the assembly. If this process becomes complicated or prolonged, the presiding officer should rule that the motion is not in order as proposed. The presiding officer cannot change the intent of the motion and can rephrase it only in wording that is approved by the member who proposed the motion.

12.6 If a motion is long, complicated, or controversial, it is wise to submit it in writing. The presiding officer has a right to require that any motion be submitted in writing.

12.7 The proposer of a main motion may rephrase or withdraw the motion at any time before it is stated by the presiding officer to the assembly. If the presiding officer has stated it incorrectly, the member may correct the wording of the presiding officer until the wording is correct according to the member. After the motion is stated by the presiding officer, it is owned by the assembly. From that time, it may be changed or withdrawn only with the permission of the assembly.

12.8 The main motion should generally be stated in the affirmative since the negative form often confuses members in voting. If a motion is presented in the negative, the presiding officer may request that the proposer rephrase the motion, or the presiding officer may rephrase it with the consent of the proposer. For example, the motion "that we do not permit any member to stay on the hospitality committee after not attending three consecutive meetings" is more clearly stated affirmatively as "that any member of the hospitality committee who misses three consecutive meetings be discharged from the committee."

The Main Motion in Resolution Form

12.9 Main motions that express sentiments or are a formal statement of the opinions of the assembly are usually stated in the form of resolutions. Resolutions may have two portions: optional "Whereas" clauses that state the rationale for the actions to be taken, and "Resolved" clauses that state the action to be taken. Resolution form is also used when the proposal is highly important or is long and involved. A resolution should be in writing and is usually introduced in such a form as:

12.10 I move the adoption of the following resolution:

Whereas, The executive director has led the association through tumultuous times; and

Whereas, The executive director has established and led processes that resulted in repaying the association's mortgage loan five years early; be it

Resolved, That this organization expresses its appreciation for the outstanding service rendered by our executive director during the past ten years; and be it further

Resolved, That we give the executive director a $5,000 bonus at a reception held in her honor during our annual convention.

Preamble

12.11 While not required, often a resolution is prefaced by statements, each introduced by the word *whereas*, that state the background to or the reasons for the resolution: The statements set forth why the action in the resolution is being proposed. This part of a resolution is called the *preamble*. If the preamble contains any statements that would be out of order in debate, the presiding officer must rule the entire resolution out of order. Such a resolution may be resubmitted if the offending language is removed.

12.12 The statements contained in the whereas clauses sometimes are the cause of disagreement. Members frequently desire to debate and amend these prefacing statements, often to the neglect of the substantive "resolved" clauses; therefore, whereas clauses should be limited to only what is necessary to present the rationale and should be factual as much as possible rather than expressing opinion.

12.13 Debate and amendment occur first on the resolved clauses and then on the whereas clauses if necessary. Whereas clauses are useful mainly when the organization plans to publicize the resolution and wishes the background and reasons for its adoption to be read with it. Whereas clauses are included in the minutes of the meeting unless the assembly decides otherwise, either on an individual basis or by the adoption of a standing rule of order or a temporary rule.

Debate on the Main Motion

12.14 As soon as the main motion has been formally stated to the assembly by the presiding officer, it is open for debate. It cannot be debated before this formal statement by the presiding officer. Discussion on the main motion must conform to the rules governing debate. For additional information on the rules of debate, see Chapter 11.

Disposition of the Main Motion

12.15 Whenever the main motion has been stated to an assembly by the presiding officer, some action must be taken on it and recorded in the minutes. The main motion may be decided by adopting, defeating, or tabling it; it may be withdrawn; or it may be disposed of temporarily by some other motion such as Motion to Refer to a Committee or Postpone to a Certain Time. A main motion cannot be ignored; definite action must be taken on it.

12.16 When a main motion has been acted on and defeated or tabled, it cannot be renewed in the same or substantially the same words at the same meeting or convention, but it may be reconsidered at the same meeting or convention or presented as a new motion at a later meeting or convention. Likewise, an adopted motion may not be revisited at the same meeting except by a Motion to Reconsider. At a subsequent meeting an adopted motion may only be revisited by the Motions to Amend a Previous Action or to Rescind. See the table below for a comparison of the ways in which motions can be disposed of.

Method of Disposal	Outcome	Revisiting the Decision–Same Meeting	Revisiting the Decision–Later Meeting
Permanent Disposal–Adoption	The motion is adopted and remains in effect in the absence of subsequent action	Only by use of the Motion to Reconsider	The motion may be rescinded or changed by the Motion to Amend a Previous Action
Permanent Disposal–Defeat	The motion is defeated and is not in effect	Only by use of the Motion to Reconsider–otherwise may not re-introduce the same or substantially the same motion	The motion may be renewed (re-introduced) at any subsequent meeting
Permanent Disposal–Table	The motion is disposed of as though defeated.	Only by use of the Motion to Reconsider applied to the tabled main motion	The motion may be renewed (re-introduced) at any subsequent meeting
Temporary Disposal–Refer to a Committee	The motion is referred to a committee and may not be re-introduced at the same meeting or subsequent meetings until permanently disposed of	Only by use of the Motion to Recall from a Committee	Automatic consideration of the motion occurs when the committee reports, or by use of the Motion to Recall from a Committee
Temporary Disposal–Postpone to a Certain Time	Consideration of the motion is stopped until the designated time or event arrives, and it may not be re-introduced at the same meeting until consideration under the postponement has occurred	Automatic at the time (or event) to which the motion is postponed, or by a motion to take the postponed item up immediately or at an earlier time (unless it has been postponed and made a scheduled order)	Automatic under unfinished business if postponed to the subsequent meeting, or at the designated time if postponed as a scheduled order. Otherwise, by renewal (re-introduction)

Basic Rules Governing the Main Motion

12.17 The rules governing the Main Motion are that it:

1. cannot interrupt a speaker;
2. requires a second;
3. is debatable;
4. is amendable;
5. requires a majority vote;
6. takes precedence over no other motions;
7. applies to no other motion;
8. can have applied to it all subsidiary motions and the incidental motions to Withdraw, Division of the Question, and to Consider by Paragraph; and
9. cannot be renewed as to the same question at the same meeting or convention but can be reconsidered.

CHAPTER 13. Specific-Purpose Main Motions

PURPOSE

13.1 There are certain defined main motions that permit an assembly to revisit actions previously taken by the assembly, or that otherwise deal with unique situations related to the previous or pending actions. These six Specific-Purpose Main Motions are listed in the table below, with the motions or actions to which they can be applied:

Specific-Purpose Main Motion:	Can Be Applied to:
Adopt in Lieu of	Motions with closely related content
Amend a Previous Action	A main motion that was adopted at a previous meeting or convention
Ratify	An action that was taken or a motion that was adopted without proper authority or without a quorum present
Recall from a Committee	A main motion (with any pending amendments) or a topic that was referred to a committee or board
Reconsider	A main motion that was adopted, defeated, or tabled at the same meeting or convention
Rescind	A main motion that was adopted at a previous meeting or convention

13.2 These six Specific-Purpose Main Motions have defined names, perform a unique function in the meeting, have somewhat different rules, but have the rank of main motions. They are explained below.

MOTION TO ADOPT IN LIEU OF

Purpose and Effect

13.3 In special circumstances, when the body is presented with several main motions that are related, one main motion is introduced with the intent that its adoption will also defeat any other related main motions that are known to be coming before the assembly as happens when main motions are required to be submitted in advance of a meeting.

13.4 The Motion to Adopt in Lieu of allows an assembly to adopt one motion while simultaneously disposing of other motions dealing with the same subject. Conversely, a defeated Motion to Adopt in Lieu of defeats the main motion, but leaves available for consideration the other related main motions.

Example

13.5 The Motion to Adopt in Lieu of is moved in the following manner: "I move the adoption of Resolution X in lieu of Resolutions A, B, and C." A full script of this motion is provided in Chapter 25.

13.6 The Motion to Adopt in Lieu of has the following two features:

1. If adopted, a main motion introduced in this manner not only enacts the motion itself but also defeats the other motions specified. It should be noted that debate on the other motions is not in order at this time except that comparative remarks may be made in speaking to advocate for the adoption or defeat of the immediately pending resolution or motion.
2. If the Motion to Adopt in Lieu of is defeated, the motion thus proposed is defeated and any of the other related motions specified may be introduced by a member for consideration by the proposal of a subsequent Adopt in Lieu of Motion and vote by the assembly.

13.7 Other than the above two unique features, the Motion to Adopt in Lieu of is a Specific-Purpose Main Motion that has almost the same basic rules as a Main Motion.

Basic Rules Governing the Motion to Adopt in Lieu Of

13.8 The rules governing the Motion to Adopt in Lieu of are that it:

1. cannot interrupt a speaker;
2. requires a second;
3. is debatable;
4. is amendable;
5. requires a majority vote;

6. takes precedence over no other motions;
7. applies to designated motions with closely related content;
8. can have applied to it all subsidiary motions and the incidental motions to Withdraw, Division of the Question, and Consider by Paragraph; and
9. cannot be renewed as to the same question at the same meeting or convention but can be reconsidered.

MOTION TO AMEND A PREVIOUS ACTION

Purpose and Effect

13.9 The Motion to Amend a Previous Action modifies a main motion that was adopted at any prior meeting. The effect of adopting this motion is to change the portion of an adopted motion that has not been executed.

Example

| Member: | I move to amend the motion, which was adopted at the previous meeting, to create a scholarship fund for youth, by striking out "youth" and inserting "students enrolled at least half-time in an accredited college or university." (Another member seconds the motion.) |

What Previous Actions Can Be Amended?

13.10 A main motion adopted at a previous meeting or convention can be amended without notice by majority vote unless the adopted motion required notice or a higher vote for its original adoption, in which case the same notice and vote are required to amend the motion. Since a Motion to Amend a Previous Action is a Specific-Purpose Main Motion, it is subject to primary and secondary amendments, as is any other main motion.

13.11 The Motion to Amend a Previous Action, if adopted, affects the present and future only, and is not retroactive. As an example, if a motion has been adopted to assess members a fine for missing meetings, the Motion to Amend a Previous Action could be used to change the amount of the fine or the number of meetings missed before a fine is due, but any fines already due or paid would remain properly due or collected. A separate motion, or a motion combined with the Motion to Amend the

Previous Action, could be considered to forgive or refund some or all the previously due or paid fines.

13.12 Should a Motion to Amend a Previous Action be made that would have the effect of rescinding the previous action, the motion is ruled not in order by the presiding officer, and the maker may be encouraged to make the Motion to Rescind. Likewise, any amendment offered to the Motion to Amend a Previous Action that has the effect of rescinding the previous action should be treated in this same manner.

Basic Rules Governing the Motion to Amend a Previous Action

13.13 The rules governing the Motion to Amend a Previous Action are that it:

1. cannot interrupt a speaker;
2. requires a second;
3. is debatable;
4. is amendable;
5. requires the same vote as was required for adoption of the original motion; if notice was required for adoption of the original motion, the same notice is required for a Motion to Amend a Previous Action;
6. takes precedence over no other motions;
7. applies to main motions adopted or actions taken at a previous meeting or convention;*
8. can have applied to it all subsidiary motions and the incidental motions to Withdraw, Division of the Question, and Consider by Paragraph; and
9. cannot be renewed as to the same question at the same meeting or convention but can be reconsidered.**

---

*To alter a decision made at the current meeting or at a convention, which may consist of more than one meeting, the proper motion is the Motion to Reconsider; to completely cancel a main motion approved or action taken at a previous meeting or convention, the proper motion is the Motion to Rescind.

**Although a different amendment could be proposed to the same previous action.

MOTION TO RATIFY

Purpose and Effect

13.14 The Motion to Ratify is used to confirm and thereby validate an action. The assembly has the authority to Ratify any action or motion that it would have otherwise had the authority to adopt in a properly called meeting or convention with a quorum present. Actions that can be ratified may include action taken when a quorum was not present; action taken in an improperly called meeting; action taken in excess of the authority of an officer, board, employee, or third party; action taken without a meeting; action taken in excess of the notice of a special meeting; or the action or decision of an affiliate body.

Example

13.15 Member: I move to ratify the action taken by the homeowner and the president on June 11 to spend $500 to upgrade the internet in our club house. Or

13.16 Member: I move to ratify the decision made at the April meeting, when a quorum was not present, to establish August 1 as our roll-out date for our long-planned upgrade to our website. Or

13.17 Member: I move to ratify the new advertising and communication strategy as adopted by the International Association. Or

13.18 Member: I move to ratify the budget adopted at the annual meeting of the national organization when no quorum was present.

Need for Ratification

13.19 The officers and members of an organization sometimes make decisions when it is not possible to obtain the permission of the body that has authority to act. A committee sometimes may have to take action that exceeds its authority. In a meeting that lacks a quorum, it is sometimes necessary to take action that cannot be delayed until a special meeting can be called or until the next *regular meeting*. In some cases, it is not possible to hold a meeting at all, even though action is required. These actions may be challenged if they are not formally approved and should be ratified as soon as possible, at a meeting with a quorum present, by the body with authority to approve the otherwise improper action.

13.20 In such situations, the body may only adopt or defeat the Motion to Ratify; however, the question to be ratified may be divided through the Motion for a Division of the Question. Once divided, it is possible to ratify one portion of the action while not ratifying the other. Therefore, an organization may choose to ratify the purchase of a new computer, but defeat the ratification of the purchase of a new monitor.

13.21 Another form of ratification occurs when organizations require that specific actions taken by one body be approved by another level or affiliate body of the organization. This may be ratification by a parent body or by a subsidiary body before the action becomes official. Should ratification of certain actions by a parent body or by a subsidiary body be desired, provisions defining those actions that must be ratified and time frames for that ratification must be included in the bylaws of the parent body and may be included in the bylaws of the subsidiary body.

13.22 If an action is taken on behalf of the organization that would require prior authorization, and the ratification is not achieved, there could be unforeseen consequences.[44]

Basic Rules Governing the Motion to Ratify

13.23 The rules governing the Motion to Ratify are that it:

1. cannot interrupt a speaker;
2. requires a second;
3. is debatable;
4. cannot be amended;
5. requires a majority vote unless the action requiring ratification would regularly require a higher vote (if notice was required for the original action, the same notice requirement applies to the Motion to Ratify);
6. takes precedence over no other motions;
7. applies to actions taken without proper authority or in the absence of a quorum, or to any other actions that require ratification before taking effect (Ratify may apply to actions taken by an affiliate body that require ratification to be effective);
8. can have applied to it all subsidiary motions except the motion to amend and the incidental motions to Withdraw and Division of the Question; and

9. cannot be renewed as to the same question at the same meeting or convention but can be reconsidered.

MOTION TO RECALL FROM A COMMITTEE

Purpose and Effect

13.24 The Motion to Recall from a Committee enables an assembly to remove a previously referred motion or subject from a committee or board and place it before the assembly for consideration. The effect of the adoption of this motion is to place the original main motion and any proposed amendments before the assembly again or to place the subject matter before the assembly for consideration.

Example

Member:	I move to recall the motion to create new standards for accreditation from the education committee. (Another member seconds the motion.)
Presiding Officer:	It has been moved and seconded to recall the motion to create new standards for accreditation from the education committee. Is there any discussion on the Motion to Recall the referred motion? (No one seeks recognition.)
Presiding Officer: (continues)	Those in favor of recalling the referred motion, say "Aye." Those opposed, say "No." The Ayes have it and the Motion to Recall the referred motion is adopted. The motion to create new standards for accreditation is again open for discussion.

13.25 Or, to recall a subject from a committee, assume that the following motion was adopted at a prior meeting: "To refer the subject of Bill 2022-43 concerning money laundering to our legislative affairs committee for study and recommendation regarding our response, if any:"

Member:	I move to recall the subject involving Bill 2022-43 concerning money laundering that had been referred to our legislative affairs committee for study and recommendation. (Another member seconds the motion.)

Presiding Officer:	It has been moved and seconded to recall the subject involving Bill 2022-43 concerning money laundering, which had been referred to our legislative affairs committee for study and recommendation. If this motion is adopted, the subject concerning money laundering will immediately come before the assembly for consideration. Is there any discussion? (No one seeks recognition.)
Presiding Officer: (continues)	Those in favor of recalling the referred subject, say "Aye." Those opposed, say "No." The Ayes have it; the Motion to Recall the referred subject is adopted. The subject has been recalled from the legislative affairs committee. (The presiding officer calls for the next business in order.)

Need for the Motion to Recall from a Committee

13.26   An assembly that has referred a pending main motion or subject to a committee or board may have reasons to remove the motion or subject from the committee or board. The assembly, if it desires, can then act, which may include final disposal of the matter or referral to a different committee.

Basic Rules Governing the Motion to Recall from a Committee

13.27   The rules governing the Motion to Recall from a Committee are that it:

1. cannot interrupt a speaker;
2. requires a second;
3. is debatable and debate is limited to the reasons for recalling the motion or subject;
4. cannot be amended;
5. requires a majority vote;
6. takes precedence over no other motions;
7. applies to any main motion or subject that has been referred;
8. can have applied to it the Motions to Postpone, Limit or Extend Debate, Close Debate and Vote Immediately, and Withdraw; and
9. can be renewed at the same meeting or convention if there is a change in the parliamentary situation.

MOTION TO RECONSIDER

Purpose and Effect

13.28 The Motion to Reconsider enables an assembly to set aside the final disposition on a main motion that has been adopted, defeated, or tabled at the current meeting or convention or the disposition on the Motions to Adopt in Lieu of, Amend a Previous Action, Ratify, or Rescind at the same meeting or convention and to consider the motion again as though no vote had been taken on it. The effect of adopting the Motion to Reconsider is to cancel the disposition of a Main Motion or Specific-Purpose Main Motion, and to bring that motion before the assembly again.

Example

Member:	I move to reconsider the motion, which was adopted earlier in the meeting, to donate $500 from our reserve funds to the Community Relief Fund. (Another member seconds the motion.)
Presiding Officer:	It has been moved and seconded to reconsider the motion, which was adopted earlier in the meeting, to donate $500 from our reserve funds to the Community Relief Fund. Is there any discussion on the motion to reconsider? (No one seeks recognition.)
Presiding Officer: (continues)	Those in favor of reconsidering the motion, say "Aye." Those opposed, say "No." The Ayes have it and the motion will be reconsidered. The motion to donate $500 from our reserve funds to the Community Relief Fund is again open for discussion.

What Dispositions Can Be Reconsidered?

13.29 Main motions are occasionally adopted, defeated, or tabled by the assembly because of a misunderstanding or lack of adequate information, and sometimes later events at the meeting or convention cause the assembly to change its mind.

13.30 The disposition of a main motion can be reconsidered at the same meeting or convention, except when something has been done because of the vote that cannot be undone. For example, when an affirmative vote has resulted in a contract, when money has been paid, or when a time limit has passed, the vote cannot be reconsidered.

13.31   The Motion to Reconsider can be applied only to the final disposition of the Main Motion; the Specific-Purpose Main Motions Adopt in Lieu of, Amend a Previous Action, Ratify, and Rescind; and Main Motions that have been tabled. Reconsider cannot be applied to itself or to the Motion to Recall.

13.32   A Motion to Amend cannot be reconsidered because an amendment can be offered changing the language back to its original form or further amending it if, in the judgment of the presiding officer, subject to an appeal, the assembly seems to want additional changes. An example of this is an amendment that lowered the designated fee for an event that is later discovered to be insufficient and in need of an increase.

13.33   The same result is accomplished for all other motions by more simple and direct means. Procedural motions can be proposed again or renewed if, in the judgment of the presiding officer and subject to an appeal, the vote might result differently. For more information on renewal of motions, see Chapter 9.

Proposal of the Motion to Reconsider

13.34   The Motion to Reconsider is a Specific-Purpose Main Motion that can be offered at any time during a meeting. It is unusual in that, unlike a main motion, it may be proposed when other business is under consideration. Proposal of the Motion to Reconsider, when seconded, suspends any action provided for in the motion to be reconsidered until the Motion to Reconsider is decided. When a Motion to Reconsider is proposed and seconded while other business is pending, the presiding officer directs the secretary to record its proposal, but the Motion to Reconsider is not considered until the pending business has been handled. The Motion to Reconsider is then considered and decided immediately. If the meeting adjourns before the Motion to Reconsider is reached or adopted, then the Motion to Reconsider is no longer pending and its suspending effect ends. If the Motion to Reconsider is offered when no other business is pending, it is considered immediately.

Who Can Move to Reconsider?

13.35   Some parliamentary authorities allow the Motion to Reconsider to be proposed only by a member who voted on the prevailing side when the main motion was originally adopted or defeated. The limitation has, on occasion, led to deceitful maneuverings and, as far back as 1856, Luther Cushing, the eminent lawyer and parliamentarian, wrote, "a motion to Reconsider may be made at any time or by any member, precisely like any other motion."[45]

13.36 This parliamentary authority upholds Cushing's position, and in the absence of a provision to the contrary in the organization's bylaws or in its parliamentary authority, the Motion to Reconsider may be offered by any member.

13.37 The proponents of restricting the proposal of the Motion to Reconsider to those who voted on the prevailing side argue that this prevents the dilatory use of the motion. The purpose of this limitation, however, is defeated because under such a rule:

1. Any member can vote on the prevailing side for the sole purpose of being eligible to move to reconsider.
2. Even if a member fails to vote with the prevailing side, a vote can be changed just prior to the final announcement of the vote, making the member eligible to move reconsideration.
3. Except in the case of a roll call, it is impossible to determine accurately how anyone has voted.
4. In a ballot vote, no one can be asked how he or she voted because the inquiry would violate the fundamental principle of the secret vote.

13.38 This parliamentary authority permits any member to propose the Motion to Reconsider. The Motion to Reconsider is useful when new information becomes known, a decision should be changed, or when errors have been made by hasty decisions. The presiding officer can rule a Motion to Reconsider out of order if the presiding officer finds it to be dilatory. If members disagree with the presiding officer's ruling, the decision can be appealed and the final decision rests with the assembly.

Debate on the Motion to Reconsider

13.39 The Motion to Reconsider is debatable, but debate is limited to reasons for reconsidering the motion proposed to be reconsidered. Debate on that main motion must wait until the assembly has voted affirmatively to reconsider it.

13.40   Since the proposal and second of the Motion to Reconsider suspends action on a motion that has already been voted on, the Motion to Reconsider should be decided immediately, or as soon as any pending main motion is disposed of and cannot be postponed to a later meeting or to a later time within the same meeting.

Basic Rules Governing the Motion to Reconsider

13.41   The rules governing the Motion to Reconsider are that it:

1. can interrupt proceedings but cannot interrupt a speaker;
2. requires a second;
3. is debatable and debate is limited to the reasons for reconsideration;
4. cannot be amended;
5. requires a majority vote;
6. takes precedence over no other motions;
7. applies to Main Motions that have been finally disposed of and the Specific-Purpose Main Motions Adopt in Lieu of, Amend a Previous Action, Ratify, and Rescind;*
8. can have applied to it the Motions to Close Debate and Vote Immediately, to Limit or Extend Debate, and to Withdraw; cannot be applied to itself; and
9. cannot be renewed at the same meeting or convention.

MOTION TO RESCIND

Purpose and Effect

13.42   The Motion to Rescind is used to repeal a main motion adopted at a previous meeting. The cancellation of the motion begins when the Motion to Rescind is adopted and does not apply to portions of the motion that have already been carried out.

---

*To change or alter a decision adopted at a previous meeting, the correct motion is to either the Motion to Rescind or the Motion to Amend a Previous Action.

Example

Member:	I move to rescind the motion that the club host a golf tournament for youth each September, which was adopted at last month's meeting. (Another member seconds the motion.)
Presiding Officer:	It has been moved and seconded to rescind the motion that the club host a golf tournament for youth each September, which was adopted at last month's meeting. Is there any discussion? (No one seeks recognition.)
Presiding Officer: (continues)	Those in favor of rescinding the motion, say "Aye." Those opposed, say "No." The Ayes have it and the Motion to Rescind is adopted. The motion that the club host a golf tournament for youth each September is rescinded.

What Motions Can Be Rescinded?

13.43 Any main motion that was adopted, no matter how long before, may be rescinded, but the rescission does not affect action taken after adoption of that main motion but before adoption of the Motion to Rescind.

13.44 The Motion to Rescind, if adopted, affects the present and future only; it is not retroactive.[46] For example, if a motion to assess special fees from members were rescinded, those fees would no longer be imposed; however, the fees already collected would be retained and fees that were assessed before the motion was rescinded would still be collectible.

13.45 If a member believes that the existing policy should be continued with some revisions instead of rescinding it, the member should explain that if the Motion to Rescind is defeated, a Motion to Amend a Previous Action will be presented.

13.46 A Motion to Rescind requires the same notice and vote as the motion being rescinded. Usually, this is a majority vote without notice.

Basic Rules Governing the Motion to Rescind

13.47 The rules governing the Motion to Rescind are that it:

1. cannot interrupt a speaker;
2. requires a second;

3. is debatable and opens to debate the motion it proposes to Rescind;
4. cannot be amended;
5. requires the same vote as was required for adoption of the original motion; if notice was required for adoption of the original motion, the same notice is required for a Motion to Rescind;
6. takes precedence over no other motions;
7. applies to main motions adopted at a previous meeting or convention;[*]
8. can have applied to it all subsidiary motions, except the Motion to Amend; it can also have the incidental motion to Withdraw applied to it; and
9. cannot be renewed at the same meeting or convention but can be reconsidered.

---

[*] To reach a motion adopted or defeated at the current meeting, the correct motion is the Motion to Reconsider.

CHAPTER 14. Subsidiary Motions

14.1 Subsidiary motions apply to the main motion and help change the main motion, dispose of the motion, and control the debate on the motion. Some subsidiary motions also apply to other motions as described in the sections below. The six subsidiary motions are Amend, Refer to a Committee, Postpone to a Certain Time, Limit or Extend Debate, Close Debate and Vote Immediately, and Table.

MOTION TO AMEND

Purpose and Effect

14.2 The subsidiary motion to Amend modifies the wording of a motion that is being considered by the assembly so that it expresses more satisfactorily the will of the members. The adoption of a Motion to Amend changes the wording of the original motion as the amendment provides.

Types of Amendments and Examples

14.3 There are three types of amendments:

1. amendment by *inserting*;
2. amendment by *striking out*; and
3. amendment by *striking out and inserting*, sometimes referred to as amendment by substitution.

14.4 An example of each type is applied to the following motion:

14.5 Pending Main Motion: That the organization use its reserve funds to purchase a headquarters building and hire an executive director.

Example: Amendment by Inserting:

Member:	I move to amend the main motion by inserting the word *half* before the word *its*. (Another member seconds the motion.)
Presiding Officer:	It has been moved and seconded to amend the main motion by inserting the word *half* before the word *its*. The main motion, if amended, would read: "that the organization use half its reserve funds to purchase a headquarters building and hire an executive director." Is there any discussion on the amendment to insert the word *half* before the word *its*? (Proceeds to discussion and determines when it has concluded.) Is there any further discussion on the amendment? (No one seeks recognition.)
Presiding Officer: (continues)	The amendment is to insert the word *half* before the word *its*. The main motion, if amended, would read: "that the organization use half its reserve funds to purchase a headquarters building and hire an executive director." Those in favor of the amendment to insert the word *half* before the word *its*, say "Aye." (pause) Those opposed to the amendment say "No." (pause) The Ayes have it. The amendment is adopted, and the main motion as amended now reads: that the organization use half its reserve funds to purchase a headquarters building and hire an executive director.
Presiding Officer: (continues)	Is there any discussion on the main motion as amended?

Example: Amendment by Striking Out:

Member:	I move to amend the main motion by striking out the words *and hire an executive director*. (Another member seconds the motion.)
Presiding Officer:	It has been moved and seconded to amend the main motion by striking out the words *and hire an executive director*. The main motion, if amended, would read: "that the organization use its reserve funds to purchase a headquarters building." Is there any discussion on the amendment to strike the words *and hire an executive director*? (Proceeds to discussion and determines when it is concluded.) Is there any further discussion on the amendment? (No one seeks recognition.)

Presiding Officer: (continues)	The amendment is to strike out the words *and hire an executive director*. The main motion, if amended, would read: "that the organization use its reserve funds to purchase a headquarters building." Those in favor of the amendment to strike out the words *and hire an executive director*, say "Aye." (pause) Those opposed to the amendment say "No." (pause) The Ayes have it. The amendment is adopted, and the main motion as amended now reads: "that the organization use its reserve funds to purchase a headquarters building."
Presiding Officer: (continues)	Is there any discussion on the main motion as amended?

Example: Amendment by Striking Out and Inserting:

Member:	I move to amend the main motion by striking out the word *purchase* and inserting the word *lease*. (Another member seconds the motion.)
Presiding Officer:	It has been moved and seconded to amend the main motion by striking out the word *purchase* and inserting the word *lease*. The main motion, if amended, would read: "that the organization use its reserve funds to lease a headquarters building and hire an executive director." Is there any discussion on the amendment to strike out the word *purchase* and insert the word *lease*? (Proceeds to discussion and determines when it has concluded.) Is there any further discussion on the amendment? (No one seeks recognition.)
Presiding Officer: (continues)	The amendment is to strike the word *purchase* and insert the word *lease*. The main motion, if amended, would read: "that the organization use its reserve funds to lease a headquarters building and hire an executive director." Those in favor of the amendment to strike the word *purchase* and insert the word *lease*, say "Aye." (pause) Those opposed to the amendment say "No." (pause) The Ayes have it. The amendment is adopted, and the main motion as amended now reads: "that the organization use its reserve funds to lease a headquarters building and hire an executive director."
Presiding Officer: (continues)	Is there any discussion on the main motion as amended?

14.6 Amendment by striking out and inserting is sometimes referred to as an amendment to *substitute*; however, it is handled in the same way as shown above.

Amendments Must Be Germane

14.7 Amendments must be *germane* to the pending motion; that is, they must be relevant to and have direct bearing on the subject of the pending motion that the amendment seeks to change.[47] For example, a motion "that the association contract with a national internet service provider to provide leased equipment for a five-year period" could be amended by adding the words *not to exceed $12,000 for the contract period*. These additional words relate closely to purchasing a lease and would therefore be germane to the motion.

14.8 However, an amendment to add the words *and that we contract with an employment agency to provide twenty hours of secretarial work per week* would not be germane to the subject of the motion. The presiding officer must immediately rule this amendment not in order, stating: "The chair rules the amendment not in order as it is not germane to the pending main motion."

14.9 Germaneness is often a matter of both the context established by the underlying issues being addressed by the main motion and judgment. The presiding officer should exercise judgment in deciding and ruling on the germaneness of a proposed amendment; however, the presiding officer may wish to allow broad latitude in making this determination. If the assembly disagrees, the ruling of the presiding officer may be appealed.

14.10 There is an option for the presiding officer to ask the assembly to decide a question of germaneness rather than to make a ruling on the matter. This approach runs the risk that members will vote based on the underlying substance of the decision at hand rather than truly voting based on the question of germaneness.

14.11 If an amendment is determined not to be germane, the intent of the amendment should be sufficiently unrelated to the existing motion so that it would later be in order as a new main motion that would not be considered as dealing with a matter already decided.

Amendments May Be Hostile

14.12 An amendment may be hostile. This means that it may be directly opposed to the actual intent of the original motion. It is a common misconception that an amendment cannot change the intent of the underlying motion, but this is not correct. It may change completely or even counteract the original intent of the motion. For example, the motion "that we write a letter to the city council condemning its decision to deny employees the right to organize as a labor union" might be amended by striking out the word *condemning* and inserting the word *endorsing*. Thus, the intent of the original motion would be reversed by a *hostile amendment*. This amendment would be germane to the subject of the main motion, which is to express the organization's attitude toward the action of the city council, and therefore is in order.

Improper Amendments

14.13 An amendment that would change one type of motion into another type of motion is never in order. For example, if a member moves "that the main motion be postponed until next month's meeting," it would not be in order for a member to move "that the motion be amended by striking out the words *postponed until next month's meeting* and inserting the words *referred to the board of trustees.*" This would change the motion from a Motion to Postpone to a Certain Time to a Motion to Refer to a Committee, which has a different rank in the order of precedence. This type of amendment is therefore not in order.

14.14 An amendment that merely changes an affirmative statement of a motion to a negative statement of the same motion is not in order. For example, a motion "that we form a committee to investigate a new location for headquarters" cannot be amended by inserting the words *do not* before the word *form*. Such a motion is not in order because the same result can be attained by voting against the main motion. It also provides for an ambiguous result if the motion with the words *do not* is defeated. The negative wording of the motion can also confuse members who are casting votes.

14.15 An amendment whose adoption would render the main motion out of order is also improper. For example, at a meeting on January 22, a motion to host a dance on February 14 would be rendered out of order by the adoption of a Motion to Amend the date to January 14.

The A.M.P. Method of Stating Amendments

14.16 One of the fundamental duties of the presiding officer is to ensure that every member understands the pending motion. There is a method of stating amendments and putting amendments to vote that helps members understand a pending amendment. It is called the A.M.P. method. In a continuous three-part process, the chair states the proposed Amendment, then repeats the Motion as it would read if amended, and then states the immediately Pending motion that is the amendment. This method avoids confusion on the part of the assembly as to what they are discussing or voting on. This action is performed as the motion is being stated by the presiding officer and again immediately prior to the vote on the amendment. Here is an example with the A.M.P. capitalized in its entirety for reference.

14.17 Pending Main Motion: That the organization purchase a new computer and telephone system from XYZ Providers:

Member:	I move to amend the main motion by striking out the word *telephone* and inserting the word *communication*. (Another member seconds the motion.)
Presiding Officer:	It has been moved and seconded to AMEND the main motion by striking out the word *telephone* and inserting the word *communication*. The main MOTION, if amended, would read: "that the organization purchase a new computer and communication system from XYZ Providers." Is there any discussion on the PENDING amendment to strike out the word *telephone* and insert the word *communication*? (No one seeks recognition.)
Presiding Officer: (continues)	The AMENDMENT is to strike the word *telephone* and insert the word *communication*. The main MOTION, if amended, would read: "that the organization purchase a new computer and communication system from XYZ Providers." Those in favor of the PENDING amendment to strike the word *telephone* and insert the word *communication*, say "Aye." (pause) Those opposed to the amendment say "No." (pause) The Ayes have it. The amendment is adopted, and the main motion as amended now reads: "that the organization purchase a new computer and communication system from XYZ Providers."
Presiding Officer: (continues)	Is there any discussion on the main motion as amended?

Primary and Secondary Amendments

14.18 Amendments are of two levels. Those applied to the original motion are primary amendments, and must relate directly to the motion to be amended.

14.19 Amendments to a pending primary amendment are secondary amendments and must relate directly to the pending primary amendment. No amendments to secondary amendments are in order.

14.20 Only one amendment of each level can be pending at one time to any given motion. When a primary amendment to a motion is pending, another primary amendment to that same motion is not in order, but a secondary amendment is in order. Whenever a secondary amendment is immediately pending, another secondary amendment to that primary amendment is not in order.

14.21 After an amendment of either level is adopted or defeated, another amendment of the same level is in order. Several primary amendments and secondary amendments may be offered in succession, but only one amendment of each level may be pending at the same time to a particular motion.

14.22 If the motion "that the organization sponsor a drive to raise funds for the City Youth Club" is pending, and someone moves to amend it by adding the words *during the month of September*, this is an amendment to the main motion or a primary amendment. If, during discussion on this amendment, someone proposes that the amendment be amended by inserting the words *first week of the* before the words *month of September*, this is a secondary amendment and is in order. However, while the primary amendment is pending, if a member proposes an amendment to strike out the words *sponsor a drive* and insert the words *hold an auction*, this is not in order currently because it is another primary amendment. When a primary amendment is pending, no other amendment of that same level is in order until the pending amendment is disposed of.

14.23 Nothing in this section on amendments prevents an assembly from revisiting words that have already been amended. The purpose of amending a motion is to achieve the best possible expression of the intent of the assembly. If, in the chair's judgment, the proposal of such an amendment is being used for delay or dilatory tactics, the chair rules the amendment not in order subject to an appeal.

14.24 Although the motions to amend the bylaws or to amend a previous action both use the word *amend* in their title, they are not forms of the subsidiary motion to amend but are examples of the Specific-Purpose Main Motion to Amend a Previous Action. As such, they are subject to amendments of both levels.

Accepting Amendments

14.25 The ability of the proposer of a motion to "accept" an amendment depends on whether or not the presiding officer has stated the motion.

14.26 If the presiding officer has not yet stated the motion, and a member is able to obtain recognition before the statement occurs, that member may propose an amendment that the maker of the motion may wish to accept, and the maker may save time by saying, "Madam President, the mover accepts the amendment." The consent of the seconder is not necessary. The proposed amendment becomes part of the main motion by this acceptance, and the presiding officer should confirm the wording of the amended motion with the maker and then state it to the assembly.

14.27 If the original motion has already been stated by the presiding officer, and an amendment is proposed as described above and accepted by the maker of the motion to be amended, then the consent of the assembly is needed to include the amendment. The presiding officer asks the assembly if there is an objection to the amendment. If no objection is made, the presiding officer states that the motion is amended by general consent. If anyone objects, the motion must be formally stated by the presiding officer, debated, and voted on in the usual manner. Note that a second to such an amendment is not necessary; the purpose of a second is to assure that more than one member wishes to discuss the proposal, and this has been accomplished by the proposer of the amendment and the proposer of the original motion agreeing to the change.

14.28 Amendments proposed in such an informal manner are sometimes called *friendly amendments*. When a member proposes a friendly amendment, the member is usually implying support for the motion to be amended but thinks it can be improved by the suggested amendment. The procedure for considering a friendly amendment is that described previously. If the motion has not yet been stated by the presiding officer, the proposer of the motion may accept the amendment, and the motion as amended is then stated by the presiding officer. If the motion has already been stated by the presiding officer, the acceptance of the friendly amendment requires the approval of the assembly, provided by majority vote or general consent.

14.29 Friendly amendments offered after the chair has stated the motion are handled exactly the same as any other Motion to Amend.

14.30 Even if not "accepted" by the proposer of the original motion, an amendment can sometimes be processed quickly by the chair by asking for general consent to accept the amendment and, if an objection is expressed, obtaining a second and stating the amendment formally for debate and vote.

Debate on Amendments

14.31 The debatability of an amendment is dependent on the debatability of the motion being amended. Amendments to debatable motions are debatable. Amendments to undebatable motions are not debatable.

14.32 When an amendment to a motion is proposed, discussion is limited to that amendment. When an amendment to the primary amendment is proposed, discussion is limited to the resulting secondary amendment.

14.33 Because debate must be germane to the immediately pending motion, reference to the main motion is permissible only for the purpose of explaining the amendment or its effect. When opposing an amendment, it is in order to say that, if the amendment is defeated or withdrawn, the speaker will propose another amendment, which may be stated briefly.

Withdrawing Amendments

14.34 As with any other motion, the proposer of an amendment has the right to modify or withdraw the amendment at any time before the presiding officer has stated it to the assembly for consideration. As soon as it has been stated to the assembly by the presiding officer, it belongs to the body, and the proposer of the amendment can withdraw it only by a majority vote of the assembly or by general consent. Further discussion of the Motion to Withdraw is in Chapter 16, "Incidental Motions."

Voting on Amendments

14.35 Amendments are voted on in the reverse order of their proposal. Note in the following illustration the main motion is made first, followed by a primary amendment and a secondary amendment, made in that order.

14.36 The secondary amendment is voted on first. The vote is then taken on the primary amendment and, finally, on the main motion.

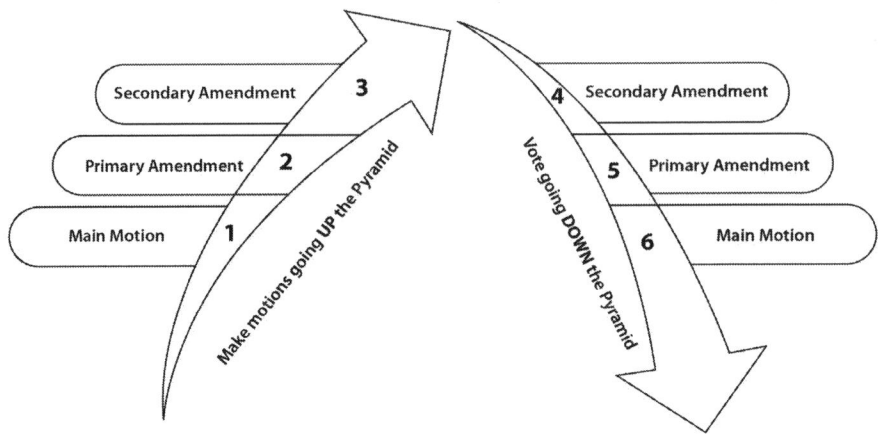

14.37 If a debatable motion, a primary amendment, and a secondary amendment are pending, the procedure for disposing of them is as follows:

1. Discussion is called for on the secondary amendment, and when discussion is complete or debate is closed, a vote is taken on it.

2. Discussion is then called for on the primary amendment, either as amended if the secondary amendment has been adopted, or as originally proposed if the secondary amendment was defeated. Other secondary amendments may be moved at this time. When discussion of the primary amendment is complete or debate is closed, a vote is taken on it. A vote adopting an amendment to a main motion—even an amendment that completely replaces the original motion with an entirely new motion—does not adopt the motion, and a final vote on the adoption of the motion itself is required as shown in step 3.

3. Discussion is called for on the main motion, either as amended if the primary amendment has been adopted or as originally proposed if the primary amendment is defeated. Other amendments may be moved at this time. When discussion on the main motion is complete or debate is closed, a vote is taken on the main motion.

Vote Required on Amendments

14.38 An amendment to any pending motion or amendment requires only a majority vote, even though the motion being amended may require a higher vote for adoption.⁴⁸ An amendment to the bylaws requires whatever vote the bylaws dictate but amendments to proposed bylaw amendments, or to a pending revision of the bylaws, require only a majority vote.

Motions with Pending Amendments

14.39 When a main motion that has amendments pending is referred to a committee or is postponed to a certain time, all pending amendments go with it. When the main motion comes before the assembly from the committee, the amendments are also before the assembly for consideration.

Subsidiary Motions That Can Be Amended

14.40 The Motion to Amend can be applied to subsidiary motions as shown in the table below:

Subsidiary Motion	Possible Amendments
Close Debate and Vote Immediately	To which motions it applies
Postpone to a Certain Time	Time, date, or event to which the motion is postponed
Limit or Extend Debate	Length of speeches, the number of speeches, the number of people who may speak on each side, when the vote will be taken following debate, and to which motions it applies
Refer to a Committee	Committee name, number of members, method of selection of the committee, the instructions to the committee, the time the motion is to be reported back to the assembly

Filling Blanks

14.41 Filling blanks is a procedure that allows for alternative proposals and is therefore like amending but also has similarities to elections. Filling blanks is an alternative way to consider multiple competing options, instead of a series of primary and secondary amendments.

14.42 Motions or resolutions are sometimes submitted with blank spaces for details such as names, dates, numbers, or other variables with the blank spaces to be filled by allowing members to propose suggestions. Sometimes the presiding officer creates a blank by general consent based on the parliamentary situation. A member may also move to strike out a variable part of a motion to create a blank. The motion to create a blank requires a second and is not debatable.

Member:	I move to purchase _____ chairs for the conference room. (Another member seconds the motion.)
Presiding Officer:	It has been moved and seconded to purchase _____ chairs for the conference room. Are there any suggestions to fill the blank?

OR

Member A:	I move to purchase 6 chairs for the conference room. (Another member seconds the motion.)
Presiding Officer:	It has been moved and seconded to purchase 6 chairs for the conference room. Is there any discussion?
Member B:	I move to strike out "6" and insert "8." (Another member seconds the motion.)
Presiding Officer:	It has been moved and seconded to strike out "6" and insert "8" so that if the amendment is adopted the main motion will read that we purchase 8 chairs for the conference room. The pending question is to strike out 6 and insert 8. Is there any discussion?
Member C:	I move to strike out "8" and insert a blank. (Another member seconds the motion.)
Presiding Officer:	Is there any objection to striking out 8 and inserting a blank? (pause) There is no objection, and the blank is inserted in the main motion. The proposals for filling the blank are 6 and 8; are there further suggestions?

OR

Member A:	I move to purchase 6 chairs for the conference room. (Another member seconds the motion.)

Presiding Officer:	It has been moved and seconded to purchase 6 chairs for the conference room; however, the presiding officer is aware that there has been discussion about the number of chairs to be purchased. Therefore, the presiding officer suggests inserting a blank for the number of chairs. Is that acceptable to the maker?
Member A:	Yes, it is.
Presiding Officer:	The motion is to purchase ___ chairs for the conference room. The first suggestion to fill the blank is "6." Are there other suggestions?

14.43 Any proposals that have been struck to create the blank become the first suggestions for filling the blank. Members call out suggestions for filling the blank without seconds, as if calling out suggestions for candidates in an election for some organizations. When no more suggestions are offered, the presiding officer opens discussion on the suggestions as a group, followed by a separate counted vote on each suggestion in the order of their proposal.

14.44 Each member may vote on each suggestion, casting a vote for or against each separate suggestion. For example, if five cities have been proposed as a convention site, a member who preferred three of the cities suggested could vote for each of those three and against the other two.

14.45 If the vote involves members of the assembly, and an individual declines, that suggestion is automatically withdrawn from consideration. Suggestions that do not involve members of the assembly may be withdrawn with the consent of the assembly at any time before voting begins.

14.46 Votes are generally taken on suggestions in the order they were made although the presiding officer may propose a different logical order. After the votes have been completed on all suggestions, the suggestion receiving the highest number of affirmative votes, provided that it is a majority, is inserted in the blank. If multiple suggestions all receive the same highest number of affirmative votes, creating a tie, then the tied suggestion receiving the lowest number of negative votes is inserted in the blank.

14.47 Abstentions in this type of voting may alter the outcome in an unintended way. As an example, if the vote is 13–3 in favor of Kansas City and 13–2 for New Orleans, New Orleans fills the blank on the tiebreaker because it has a lower negative vote due to an abstention on the vote for New Orleans.

14.48   If the negative votes are also tied, then the voting is repeated on only those suggestions involved in the tie.

14.49   If a tie persists on this subsequent vote, then voting on all suggestions is repeated unless the assembly adopts a motion to use another procedure. If the blank is not successfully filled because no suggestion received a majority on the first attempt, a motion can be offered to reopen suggestions or debate to increase the likelihood of a decision. If suggestions are reopened, the original suggestions remain for consideration. After the blank has been filled, further discussion of the motion or resolution with the blank filled is allowed, and then a vote is taken on the motion as a whole.

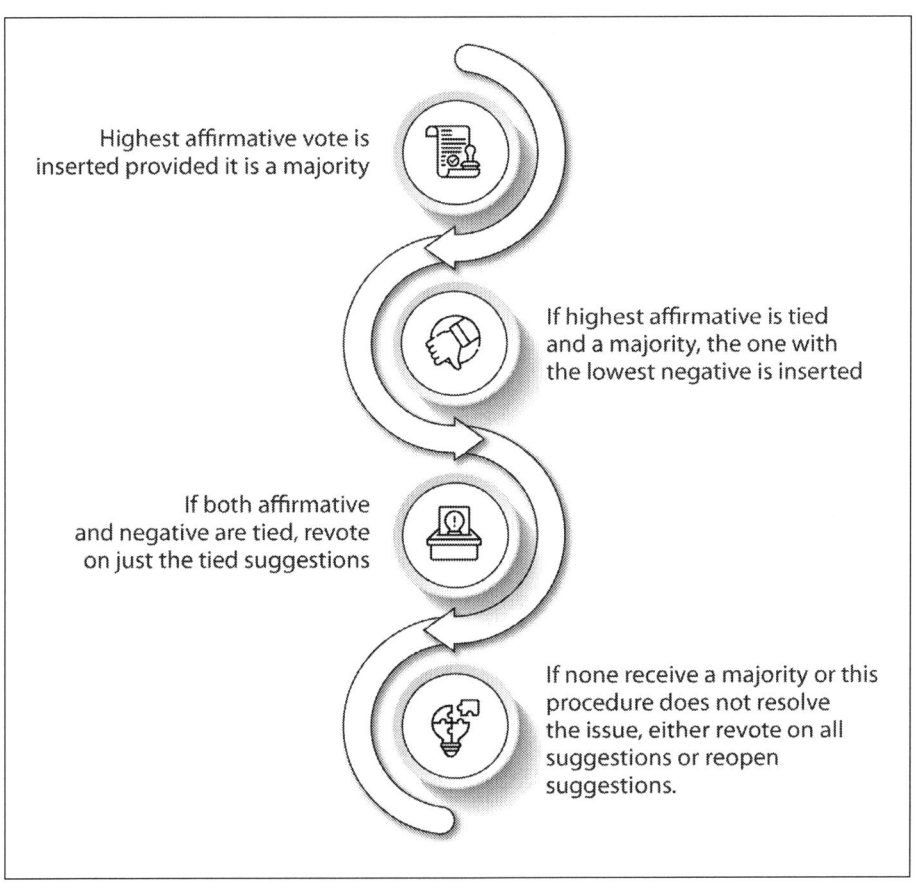

Highest affirmative vote is inserted provided it is a majority

If highest affirmative is tied and a majority, the one with the lowest negative is inserted

If both affirmative and negative are tied, revote on just the tied suggestions

If none receive a majority or this procedure does not resolve the issue, either revote on all suggestions or reopen suggestions.

14.50 Ballot voting can be used for filling blanks, but write-ins are inappropriate in such a case. Each ballot contains a for and against option for each suggestion, and the member may vote for or against each of the suggestions as the member deems acceptable. The rules stated above for tiebreaking also apply when voting by ballot.

Basic Rules Governing the Motion to Amend

14.51 The rules governing the Motion to Amend are that it:

1. cannot interrupt a speaker;
2. requires a second;
3. is debatable unless applied to an undebatable motion;
4. is amendable;
5. requires a majority vote, even if the motion to which it applies requires a higher vote;
6. takes precedence over the main motion; when applied to other motions, it takes precedence over the motion it proposes to amend;
7. applies to motions that may be stated in different ways: Main Motions; Motions to Amend a Previous Action; Motions to Amend, to Refer to a Committee, to Postpone to a Certain Time, to Limit or Extend Debate, to Close Debate and Vote Immediately, and to Recess; and to the privileged Motion to Adjourn to create a continued meeting;
8. can have applied to it the Motions to Close Debate and Vote Immediately, to Limit or Extend Debate, to Amend, and to Withdraw; and
9. can be renewed at the discretion of the presiding officer.

MOTION TO REFER TO A COMMITTEE

Purpose and Effect

14.52 The purpose of a Motion to Refer to a Committee is to transfer a motion that is pending before the assembly to a committee for reasons that may include:

1. to investigate or study the proposal, make recommendations on it, and return it to the assembly;
2. to conserve the time of the assembly by delegating the duty of deciding

the proposal, and sometimes of carrying out the decision, to a smaller group;

3. to ensure privacy in considering a delicate matter; or
4. to provide a hearing on the proposal.

14.53 The adoption of a Motion to Refer transfers the main motion and any pending amendments to the designated committee immediately. See Chapter 31 for consideration of motions in committee and committee reports.

Example

Member:	I move to refer the motion to the standing committee on certification with instructions to report at the annual meeting. (Another member seconds the motion.)
Presiding Officer:	It has been moved and seconded to refer the motion to the standing committee on certification with instructions to report at the annual meeting. Is there any discussion on the motion to refer the motion to the standing committee on certification?

14.54 Or to refer to a special committee with the *power to act*:

Member:	I move to refer the motion to a committee composed of member X, member Y, and member Z with full power to act. (Another member seconds the motion.)
Presiding Officer:	It has been moved and seconded to refer the motion to a committee composed of member X, member Y, and member Z with full power to act. Is there any discussion on the motion to refer the motion to member X, member Y, and member Z?

14.55 Or to refer to a special committee for study and to report back:

Member:	I move to refer the motion to a special committee of five members to be appointed by the president with instructions to consult with legal counsel, to conduct a hearing for members to provide input, and to report back at the annual meeting. (Another member seconds the motion.)

Presiding Officer:	It has been moved and seconded to refer the motion to a special committee of five members to be appointed by the president with instructions to consult with legal counsel, to conduct a hearing for members to provide input, and to report back at the annual meeting. Is there any discussion on the motion to refer the motion to a special committee of five members to be appointed by the president with instructions to consult with legal counsel, to conduct a hearing for members to provide input, and to report back at the annual meeting?

Provisions Included in the Motion to Refer to a Committee

14.56 A member may propose the motion in the simple form, "I move to refer this motion to a committee," or the member may include provisions such as the name of the standing committee or, if a special committee, the number of members, how those members are to be selected, and the committee chair. Regardless of the type of committee, any instructions should be included in the Motion to Refer. If the committee is to have the power to act on behalf of the organization, the wording of the Motion to Refer must provide for this power.* Empowering the committee is important if the committee is expected to act. If these provisions are not specified in the motion, the presiding officer must ask the assembly to determine the detailed provisions either before or after the Motion to Refer to a Committee is voted on. These provisions may be included in the Motion to Refer if the maker of the motion accepts them before the Motion to Refer is stated by the presiding officer. They may also be proposed as amendments to the Motion to Refer to a Committee, or in a main motion proposed at any time after the Motion to Refer has been adopted.

14.57 If the pending motion concerns a subject that is within the scope of a particular standing or reference committee, that committee must be the one to which any referral is made.

14.58 Debate on the Motion to Refer, or on amendments to it, is limited to a discussion on the advisability of referring or to such details as the selection, membership, or duties of the committee or instructions to it. Similarly, an amendment is restricted to these same limitations.

---

* See the section, Delegation of Authority by Officers, Boards, and Committees, in Chapter 27 for a discussion on ministerial powers and discretionary powers, and how (or if) those can be delegated.

14.59 Instructions from the assembly may be given to a committee as a part of the Motion to Refer or by a separate motion. The president or another officer may be empowered by the governing documents to give directions to a committee. Additional instructions may be given to the committee by the assembly or, if so empowered, the president or another officer at any time before its report is submitted. After the report is submitted, the motion or committee assignment may be referred to the committee again with or without additional instructions.

Recalling a Motion from a Committee

14.60 An assembly that has referred a motion or a matter to a committee may, by use of the Motion to Recall, vote at any time to return the motion or matter to the assembly, after which the assembly may dispose of the motion by any proper actions as though the motion had never been referred.*

Refer as a Main Motion

14.61 If no main motion is pending, and a member moves to refer a subject or problem to a committee, moves to create a new committee, or moves to give instructions to an existing committee, this motion is a main motion rather than the subsidiary motion to refer.

Basic Rules Governing the Motion to Refer

14.62 The rules governing the Motion to Refer are that it:

1. cannot interrupt a speaker;
2. requires a second;
3. is debatable and debate is limited to discussion on the advisability of referring and to the committee selected, its membership, duties, or instructions to it;
4. is amendable and amendments are limited to such details as the committee selected, its membership, duties, powers, or instructions to it;
5. requires a majority vote;
6. takes precedence over the main motion and amendments to the main motion;

---

* See Chapter 13 for more information on the Motion to Recall from a Committee.

7. applies to main motions only, along with any pending amendments;
8. can have applied to it the Motions to Close Debate and Vote Immediately, to Limit or Extend Debate, to Amend, and to Withdraw; and
9. can be renewed after a change in the parliamentary situation.

MOTION TO POSTPONE TO A CERTAIN TIME

Purpose and Effect

14.63 The purpose of a Motion to Postpone to a Certain Time is to delay consideration, or further consideration, of a pending main motion and to designate a point for its future consideration.

14.64 The adoption of a Motion to Postpone to a Certain Time postpones consideration of the pending main motion to a designated time, date, meeting, position on the agenda, or after a specified event.

14.65 When a main motion is postponed, any pending subsidiary motions, for example, an amendment or a Motion to Refer are also postponed along with the main motion. When the main motion and any subsidiary motions are again before the assembly, the question is considered in the same form as it existed at the time of postponement.

Example

Member:	I move to postpone the motion until after the presentation by the management consultant who will arrive later at this meeting. (Another member seconds the motion.)
Presiding Officer:	It has been moved and seconded that the motion be postponed until after the presentation by the management consultant who will arrive later in this meeting.

14.66 Other examples of the Motion to Postpone to a Certain Time include:

14.67 Member: I move to postpone the motion until after the recess that has been scheduled for midmorning. (Another member seconds the motion.) Or

14.68 Member: I move to postpone the question until the next regular meeting. (Another member seconds the motion.) Or

14.69   Member: I move to postpone the motion to the next regular meeting and make it a scheduled order for 7:30 p.m. (Another member seconds the motion.)

Limitations on the Motion to Postpone to a Certain Time

14.70   A main motion cannot be postponed in the following situations:

1. to a meeting that is not already scheduled, for example, to a special or continued meeting that has not been established;
2. to any time that would be too late for the proposed motion to be effective if adopted. For example, a motion "that the organization participate in this year's annual talent show to raise funds for the City Youth Club" cannot be postponed to a meeting that will occur after the talent show;
3. from one convention of delegates to the next convention; and
4. from a meeting other than the annual meeting to beyond the next annual meeting; furthermore, a main motion cannot be postponed from one annual meeting to the next annual meeting. For example, a motion could be postponed from a monthly meeting in March to the annual meeting in January but not to the February meeting.

14.71   A pending motion cannot be postponed from one convention to the next convention. The next convention may be composed of different delegates who can begin anew any consideration of the matter, instead of dealing with motions developed by an assembly that no longer exists.

14.72   Additionally, because most organizations change officers in conjunction with the convention, postponement beyond that time is not permitted. A convention may defer action to a convention by referring the matter to a committee, which is ordered to submit a report at the next convention detailing, at minimum, the motion that was referred and any related recommendations. Similar rules would apply to a body holding an annual meeting instead of a convention.

14.73   At a meeting, a pending motion cannot be postponed beyond the next annual meeting. The next annual meeting may be composed of different members who can begin anew any consideration of the matter, instead of dealing with motions developed by an assembly that no longer exists.

Types of Postponement

14.74 Any main motion that is postponed to a certain time becomes the next item of business at that time. When that time arrives, if no other item of business is pending, the presiding officer states the postponed motion to the assembly for consideration. If another item of business is pending when the time arrives, the presiding officer states the postponed motion as pending to the assembly as soon as the current pending item of business has been disposed of.

14.75 When a main motion is postponed within the same meeting or convention dependent on an event occurring, such as the arrival of a member or another agenda item having been disposed of, the main motion comes automatically to the floor when the event occurs without requiring the motion to be made again. If another item of business is on the floor, that business continues until completed. The presiding officer then states the postponed main motion, and consideration of the previously postponed motion resumes.

14.76 To postpone a main motion and designate it for a specific time requires a majority vote. A motion postponed to a certain time may again be postponed to a later time or day by a majority vote.

14.77 Instead of simply postponing a motion to a specific time, the assembly may vote to make it a scheduled order. This means that when the specified time arrives, the matter must be taken up immediately, regardless of whether something else is pending at that time. Any motion or proceeding that is interrupted by the scheduled order is simply put aside until the scheduled order is disposed of, at which point consideration of the interrupted motion is resumed.

14.78 Because a scheduled order interrupts pending business, a two-thirds vote is required to postpone a main motion and make it a scheduled order.

14.79 Because individuals may have arranged activities outside the meeting, the assembly may not take up a scheduled order prior to the time of postponement.

14.80 Before the time established for a scheduled order, if the assembly does not want to take up consideration of a scheduled order at the prescribed time, it may order further postponement but only with a two-thirds vote. However, once the scheduled order is pending before assembly, a member may rise and move postponement with a majority vote.

14.81   A main motion may be postponed:

1. to a later time in the same meeting or convention; or
2. to a later meeting for a specific time, as a scheduled order, or as an item of business to come up under unfinished business at the specified meeting. If a motion is postponed to a particular meeting but not to a specified time, it comes up under unfinished business at the meeting to which it was postponed.

14.82   A main motion may be postponed in the regular form (as shown in the example) or as a scheduled order to a time that is not stated but that is dependent on some other item of business. For example, a main motion might be postponed "until after the report of the special committee appointed to plan the organization's centennial celebration and is to be a scheduled order at that time."

Consideration of Postponed Motions

14.83   If a motion that was postponed to a certain time or until an event occurs, or postponed as a scheduled order, is not taken up at the meeting for which it was set, it can be proposed as new business at a subsequent meeting but is not treated as unfinished business.

14.84   When a motion that has been postponed to a certain time is sent to the assembly for consideration, it may again be postponed to a later time or day.

14.85   If no main motion is pending and a motion is proposed to postpone a motion or subject to a certain time, the Motion to Postpone to a Certain Time is a main motion.

Basic Rules Governing the Motion to Postpone to a Certain Time

14.86   The rules governing the Motion to Postpone to a Certain Time are that it:

1. cannot interrupt a speaker;
2. requires a second;
3. is debatable and debate is limited to brief discussion on reasons for, or time of, postponement;

4. is amendable and amendments are limited to time of postponement, or to making the postponement a scheduled order;

5. requires a majority vote unless proposed as creating a scheduled order, which requires a two-thirds vote;

6. takes precedence over the Motions to Refer to a Committee, to Amend, and the Main Motion;

7. applies to main motions only and includes any pending subsidiary motions;

8. can have applied to it the Motions to Amend, to Close Debate and Vote Immediately, to Limit or Extend Debate, and to Withdraw; and

9. can be renewed after a change in the parliamentary situation.

MOTION TO LIMIT OR EXTEND DEBATE

Purpose and Effect

14.87 The purpose of a Motion to Limit or Extend Debate is to limit or extend the time that will be devoted to discussion of a pending motion or motions. The Motion to Limit or Extend Debate is also used to modify or remove limitations already imposed on the discussion.

14.88 The adoption of a Motion to Limit or Extend Debate limits discussion on a pending question or extends or removes limitations already adopted.

Example

Member:	I move to limit the time of each member speaking on this motion to two minutes. (Another member seconds the motion.)
Presiding Officer:	It has been moved and seconded that the time of each member speaking on this motion be limited to two minutes. The Motion to Limit Debate can be amended only in terms of the nature of the limitations. (No one seeks recognition.)
Presiding Officer: (continues)	Those in favor of the motion, please rise. Be seated. Those opposed, please rise. Be seated. There are two-thirds in the affirmative, and the Motion to Limit Debate is adopted. Speakers on the motion will limit their comments to two minutes. Member X is appointed as timekeeper.

14.89   Other examples of Motions to Limit Debate include:

14.90   Member: I move to limit debate on this bylaw amendment to a total time of fifteen minutes. (Another member seconds the motion.) Or

14.91   Member: I move that the time of the speaker be extended by two minutes. (Another member seconds the motion.)

Types of Limitations on Debate

14.92   The Motion to Limit or Extend Debate on a pending question or to modify limitations already set up usually relates to the number of speakers who may participate, the number of times a member may debate, the length of time allotted to each speaker, the total time allotted for discussion of the motion, or some variation or combination of these limitations. A common example of a motion extending limitations on debate is one that extends the time allowed for a particular speaker.

14.93   An amendment to the Motion to Limit or Extend Debate may alter the motion as to the number of debates per person, the total number of speakers, the total time for debate, the time at which the vote on the motion will be taken, or any combination of these.

How Limiting or Extending Debate Affects Pending Motions

14.94   The Motion to Limit or Extend Debate may be applied to all pending debatable motions, to any number of successive pending motions that must include the immediately pending motion, or to only the immediately pending motion. To illustrate: if a main motion, a primary amendment, and a secondary amendment are pending, and the proposer of the Motion to Limit or Extend Debate does not specify the motion or motions to which the limit is to apply, only the immediately pending question—in this case the secondary amendment—is affected. If the proposer wishes to specify the motions to which the limit applies, the proposer could specify that it applies to all pending motions or only to the secondary amendment and the primary amendment. The proposer could not specify that it be applied to the secondary amendment and the main motion and not the primary amendment.

14.95   If a main motion is pending and a limitation of debate is applied to that motion, the limitation also applies to any motions applied to that motion. For example, if a main motion was pending and a member made a Motion to Limit or Extend Debate to a total time for debate of 45 minutes and it was adopted, any amendments or other subsidiary motions applied to the main motion would be included in the 45-minute time limitation. A limitation of debate also applies to any and all motions made after adoption of the limitation of debate on that particular item of business unless the original limitation of debate specified otherwise.

14.96 If no main motion is pending and a motion is made to Limit or Extend Debate on a motion or motions that are to come up later, this is a main motion and not the subsidiary motion to Limit or Extend Debate.

Termination of the Effect of the Motion to Limit or Extend Debate

14.97 A motion limiting or extending debate is in force only during the meeting or convention at which it was adopted. If the main motion is postponed until another meeting or referred to a committee, the motion limiting or extending debate is no longer in effect when the motion is taken up again, but a new Motion to Limit or Extend Debate would be in order. A Motion to Table also ends the effect of a motion limiting or extending debate.

14.98 If the limitation of debate sets a time for debate to end, then the limitation is a maximum time for debate, and is open to any subsequent additional Motions to Limit or Extend Debate or to Close Debate and Vote Immediately.

Basic Rules Governing the Motion to Limit or Extend Debate

14.99 The rules governing the Motion to Limit or Extend Debate are that it:
1. cannot interrupt a speaker;
2. requires a second;
3. is not debatable;
4. is amendable and amendments are limited to limitations, extensions, or removal of limitations on debate;
5. requires a two-thirds vote because it limits freedom of debate or modifies already adopted limitations on debate;
6. takes precedence over Motions to Postpone to a Certain Time, to Refer to a Committee, to Amend the Main Motion, and the Main Motion;
7. applies to debatable motions only;
8. can have applied to it the Motions to Withdraw, to Amend, and to Close Debate and Vote Immediately if used to end amendments; and

9. can be renewed after a change in the parliamentary situation.

MOTION TO CLOSE DEBATE AND VOTE IMMEDIATELY

Purpose and Effect

14.100   The purpose of the Motion to Close Debate and Vote Immediately is to prevent or to stop discussion on the pending question or questions, to prevent the proposal of other subsidiary motions, to prevent further Factual Inquiries, and to bring the pending question or questions to an immediate vote. The Motion to Table is still in order even after the Motion to Close Debate and Vote Immediately is proposed or adopted. Once the Motion to Close Debate and Vote Immediately is adopted, the presiding officer takes the vote on the immediately pending motion(s) designated by the motion.

Example

Member:	I move to close debate and vote immediately on the motion. (Another member seconds the motion.)
Presiding Officer:	It has been moved and seconded to close debate and vote immediately on the amendment. Those in favor of closing debate and voting immediately, please rise. Be seated. Those opposed, please rise. Be seated. There are two-thirds in the affirmative, the affirmative has it, and the motion to close debate and vote immediately is adopted. We will now vote on the pending motion, which is the amendment. (Presiding officer restates the motion that will be voted on.) (After this voting is completed, the presiding officer asks if there is any further debate on the main motion since the closure only applied to the amendment.)

14.101   Other examples of Motion to Close Debate and Vote Immediately include:

14.102   Member: I move to vote immediately. (Another member seconds the motion.) Or

14.103   Member: I move to close debate. (Another member seconds the motion.)

14.104   If a member wishes to close debate and vote immediately on all pending issues, a form similar to the one below is used:

Member:	I move to close debate and vote immediately on all pending motions. (Another member seconds the motion.)
Presiding Officer:	It has been moved and seconded to close debate and vote immediately on all pending motions. Those in favor of closing debate and voting immediately on all pending motions, please rise. Be seated. Those opposed, please rise. Be seated. There are two-thirds in the affirmative, the affirmative has it, and the motion to close debate and vote immediately on all pending motions is adopted. We will now vote on the pending motion, which is the amendment to the main motion. (Presiding officer restates the motion that will be voted on.) (After this vote, the presiding officer immediately takes the vote on the underlying main motion without further debate.)

Proposing a Motion to Close Debate and Vote Immediately

14.105 The Motion to Close Debate and Vote Immediately is a powerful tool for expediting business. It may be proposed at any time after the motion to which it applies has been stated to the assembly. It is permissible to debate a motion and conclude debate with a Motion to Close Debate and Vote Immediately; however, some organizations may choose to adopt standing rules of order to modify this practice.

14.106 If the Motion to Close Debate and Vote Immediately is proposed as soon as a main motion has been stated to the assembly, its adoption prevents any discussion of the question, and the vote is taken immediately.

How Closing Debate and Voting Immediately Affects Pending Motions

14.107 If the Motion to Close Debate and Vote Immediately is unqualified—"I move that we close debate," for example—it applies to the immediately pending motion only.

14.108 If more than one motion is pending, the Motion to Close Debate and Vote Immediately should specify the pending motions to which it applies. For example, suppose a main motion, a primary amendment, and a secondary amendment are all pending. If the proposer of the Motion to Close Debate and Vote Immediately wishes it to apply to both the primary amendment and the secondary amendment but not to the main motion, this qualification must be stated, "I move to close debate and vote immediately on the primary amendment and the secondary amendment." If the motion is to apply to all pending motions, this must be stated. In the above example, the motion could not be applied to the secondary amendment and the main motion only, excluding the primary amendment, because the Motion to Close Debate and Vote Immediately must be applied only to successive pending motions and must include the immediately pending motion. If the Motion to Close Debate and Vote Immediately on all pending motions is adopted, an immediate vote must be taken on the secondary amendment, then on the primary amendment, and then on the main motion. A pending Motion to Close Debate and Vote Immediately may be amended to take in either more or fewer motions.

Termination of the Effect of the Motion to Close Debate and Vote Immediately

14.109 The effect of the Motion to Close Debate and Vote Immediately terminates with the adjournment of the meeting or convention at which it is adopted or with its referral to a committee. For example, assume a main motion and a postponement are pending; a member then moves to close debate and vote immediately on all pending motions, and the Motion to Close Debate and Vote Immediately is adopted. A Motion to Table also ends the effect of a motion closing debate.

14.110 After the Motion to Close Debate and Vote Immediately has been adopted, if the main motion is postponed to a later time within the same meeting and is taken up within the same meeting, the effect of the Motion to Close Debate and Vote Immediately still applies, no debate is permitted on the main motion, and it is voted on immediately.

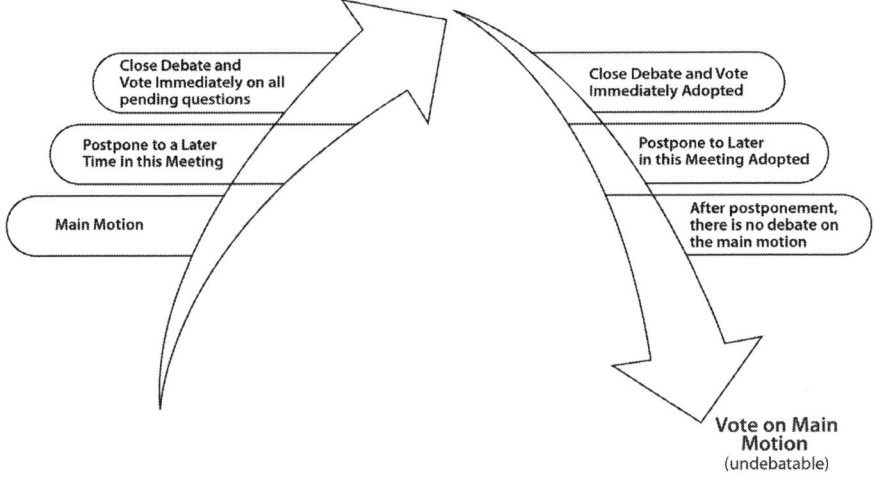

14.111 However, after the Motion to Close Debate and Vote Immediately has been adopted, if the main motion is postponed to a future meeting, the postponed motion is fully debatable at that future meeting.

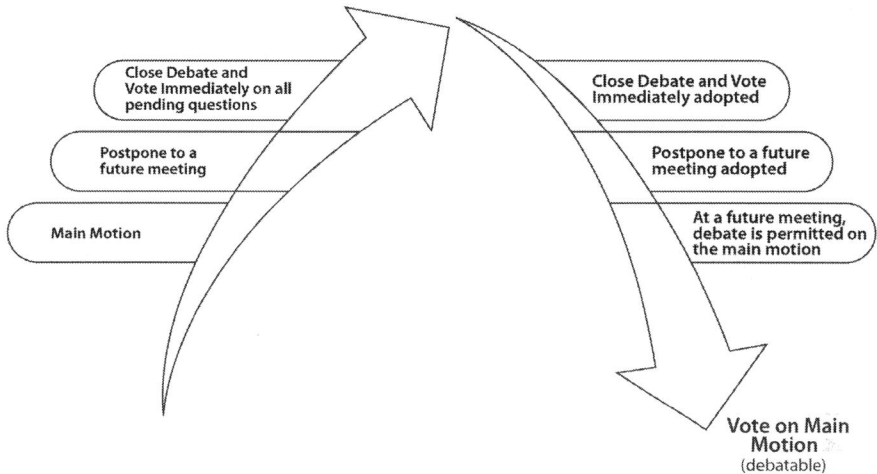

Call the Question!

14.112 The correct way to bring a matter to an immediate vote is to obtain the floor and move to close debate and vote immediately. A common practice, however, is to call out "Call the question!" or even "Question!" without obtaining the floor.

14.113 Calling out "Question" is an informal way to move to close debate and vote immediately, but the practice is not in order unless the member has been properly recognized. If there is no recognition, the presiding officer should ignore the member calling out "Question" or should call the member to order for speaking without recognition, explaining that the Motion to Close Debate and Vote Immediately requires the member to seek recognition and be recognized before the motion can be proposed.

14.114 If a member is properly recognized but does not use the correct language to propose a Motion to Close Debate and Vote Immediately, this does not mean that the motion should be ruled out of order. If the member, for example, says, "I call the question" or "Question!" or "I move the previous question" or "I move that we vote now" or similar phrases because the member wishes to propose the Motion to Close Debate and Vote

Immediately, if seconded, the presiding officer should process the motion after stating it in its correct form.

Basic Rules Governing the Motion to Close Debate and Vote Immediately

14.115 The rules governing the Motion to Close Debate and Vote Immediately are that it:

1. cannot interrupt a speaker;
2. requires a second;
3. is not debatable;
4. is amendable as to the motions to which it applies;
5. requires a two-thirds vote because it ends debate;
6. takes precedence over all subsidiary motions except the Motion to Table;
7. applies to debatable or amendable motions only;
8. can have no motion applied to it except the Motions to Amend and to Withdraw; and
9. can be renewed after a change in the parliamentary situation.

MOTION TO TABLE

Purpose and Effect

14.116 When adopted, the Motion to *Table* disposes of a main motion without a direct vote on the main motion. It suppresses or kills a main motion without further debate, with the intention of avoiding any further action on the main motion in the current meeting.

Example

Member:	I move that the main motion be tabled. (Another member seconds the motion.)
Presiding Officer:	It has been moved and seconded to table the main motion currently before the assembly. Those in favor of tabling, please rise. Be seated. Those opposed, please rise. Be seated. There are two-thirds in the affirmative, the affirmative has it, the main motion is tabled.

14.117 Alternatively, a member could say: I move to table the main motion. (Another member seconds the motion.)

Proposing a Motion to Table

14.118 On occasion, an assembly may wish to dispose of a main motion without any debate, or without further debate, and without a direct vote on the main motion. The main motion could be seen by some members as extremely objectionable, divisive, or clearly unwanted. This may occur even after some debate has taken place and when members come to realize the consequences of further discussion on the matter. It permits the assembly to dispose of an unwelcome issue quickly and decisively.

14.119 It is permissible to debate a motion and conclude your remarks with the Motion to Table. While this parliamentary authority allows this use of the Motion to Table, some organizations may choose to adopt standing rules of order to modify this practice.

Pending Subsidiary Motions Also Tabled and Disposed Of

14.120 When a main motion is tabled, all pending amendments and other subsidiary motions are also tabled and disposed of.

14.121 If the main motion is brought before the assembly again by adoption of a Motion to Reconsider, only the main motion, in the form it was in when it was tabled, becomes pending at that time. The subsidiary motions that were pending when the main motion was tabled are not before the assembly. Any subsidiary motions that were pending at the time the motion was tabled can be renewed. Any amendments that had been adopted remain as part of the main motion. Any limits on or closure of debate that had been adopted would no longer have an effect.

Use of the Term "to Table"

14.122 The practice of killing a motion by tabling it is used frequently by legislative bodies and by most voluntary organizations although it is frowned upon in some other parliamentary manuals. The argument against it is that the Motion to Table, being undebatable, permits a bare majority to kill a proposal without discussion, which violates the principle that debate can be ended only by a two-thirds vote. However, the motion is so convenient a means of ending discussion and setting a motion aside that it continues to be widely used for that purpose, despite efforts to discourage its use. For this reason, in this parliamentary authority, the Motion to Table requires a two-thirds vote to adopt.

14.123   The Motion to Table disposes of the main motion immediately. By the use of the Motion to Reconsider the tabled motion, a majority of the members may, at any time before the end of the meeting or convention, return the main motion to the assembly for further consideration by the members. The main motion can also be renewed at a future meeting or convention.

Basic Rules Governing the Motion to Table

14.124   The rules governing the Motion to Table are that it:

1. cannot interrupt a speaker;
2. requires a second;
3. is not debatable;
4. cannot be amended;
5. requires a two-thirds vote to adopt;
6. takes precedence over all other subsidiary motions;
7. applies to main motions only;
8. can have no motion applied to it except the Motion to Withdraw; and
9. cannot be renewed as to the same question.

CHAPTER 15. Privileged Motions

15.1 Privileged motions deal with basic member rights, actions requiring immediate attention, and actions of the assembly as a whole. These motions affect the comfort or convenience of the assembly or one of its members. Privileged motions do not relate to pending business but when moved take priority over any main motion or pending subsidiary motions.

QUESTION OF PRIVILEGE

Purpose and Effect

15.2 Raising a Question of Privilege allows a single member to request immediate action affecting safety, health, security, comfort, or integrity, including the rights and privileges of a member or members or of the assembly generally, and in some instances to make a motion to take immediate action even when other business is pending.

15.3 The presiding officer acts on a request, or allows the assembly to consider a motion, in order to meet an immediate need or emergency. If stated as a request, the presiding officer rules on the request and, if the ruling is in favor, orders the requested action to be taken. If the request was to present a motion, the member makes the motion, and, if it is seconded, the presiding officer rules whether it is one of privilege. If it is, then the presiding officer states the motion to the assembly for consideration.

15.4 As with other rulings of the presiding officer, the ruling on a question of privilege may be appealed.

Example

Question of Privilege of the Assembly (Request)

Member: (without waiting for recognition)	I rise to a question of privilege of the assembly. (No second is required.)
Presiding Officer:	State your question of privilege.

Member:	May we have the members use a microphone during debate so all may hear?
Presiding Officer:	Yes, the request is granted. The members will use the floor microphone when speaking to the assembly.

Question of Personal Privilege (Request)

Member: (without waiting for recognition)	I rise to a question of personal privilege.
Presiding Officer:	State your question of privilege.
Member:	May I be excused from serving on the election committee since I must leave the meeting early today?
Presiding Officer:	Yes, your request is granted. The chair will appoint another member to serve on the committee.

Question of Privilege to Present a Motion

Member: (without waiting for recognition)	I rise to a question of privilege to present a motion.
Presiding Officer:	State your motion.
Member:	I move that the assembly go into a closed meeting to consider the personnel issues. (Another member seconds the motion.)
Presiding Officer:	The chair rules this to be a motion of privilege, it has been moved and seconded that the meeting go into executive session to consider the personnel issues.

Question of Privilege to Establish a Continued Meeting

15.5 Assuming that a main motion is pending, and further discussion will be warranted:

Member: (without waiting for recognition)	I rise to a question of privilege to present a motion.

Presiding Officer:	State your motion.
Member:	I think we need more time to consider this motion. I move that a continuation of this meeting be scheduled for next Saturday at 2:00 p.m. in this location. (Another member seconds the motion.)
Presiding Officer:	The chair rules this to be a motion of privilege, it has been moved and seconded that a continuation of this meeting be scheduled for next Saturday at 2:00 p.m. in this location.

Question of Privilege (Denial)

Member: (without waiting for recognition)	I rise to a question of privilege.
Presiding Officer:	State your question of privilege.
Member:	I need to respond to what the current speaker is saying. It simply isn't true, and …
Presiding Officer: (interrupting the member)	That is not a proper question of privilege. If you wish to respond to the remarks of another member, you must be recognized for debate. Will the member who was speaking please continue.

Member's Right to Raise a Question of Privilege

15.6 A member has the right to request a decision or action by the presiding officer or by the assembly on urgent questions involving the immediate convenience, comfort, rights, or privileges of the assembly, the requesting member, or another member. A question of privilege may be in the form of a request to be decided by the presiding officer or a motion to be decided by the assembly. The presiding officer may decide that a particular motion is not a proper question of privilege and rule it not in order.

Interruption by a Question of Privilege

15.7 The importance or emergency nature of a question of privilege allows its proposer to interrupt a speaker. When interrupted by a question of privilege, a speaker should relinquish the floor temporarily, sitting down until the matter is settled. The presiding officer must rule immediately on the question of privilege by granting or denying it. The ruling is subject to appeal.

15.8 If the presiding officer decides that the request is a proper question of privilege and of sufficient urgency, the request may be granted, and the request is carried out immediately. However, if the presiding officer decides that it is a proper question of privilege but can wait, the presiding officer explains that the request may be granted when the speaker who was interrupted has finished. If the presiding officer decides that the question of privilege is not a proper request, it is denied.

Privilege of the Assembly vs. Personal Privilege

15.9 Questions relating to a privilege of the assembly have to do with the rights, safety, integrity, comfort, or convenience of the whole assembly. They frequently are concerned with the heating, lighting, or ventilation of the hall, the seating of members, or the control of noise. A question of privilege relating to the assembly takes precedence over a question of privilege relating to a member.

15.10 Questions of personal privilege pertain to an individual member or a small group of members, and usually relate to their rights, reputation, conduct, safety, or convenience as members of the body.

Motions as Questions of Privilege

15.11 Sometimes when one main motion is pending, it is necessary to propose another main motion to take care of an emergency or other urgent matter. This motion can interrupt only as a question of privilege. The presiding officer will usually grant the member the right to propose an urgent motion. If, after hearing the motion and a second, the presiding officer decides that it needs immediate decision, the motion is stated to the assembly and is opened for debate, thus setting aside the pending business temporarily. If the presiding officer decides that the motion is not urgent or that it is not a question of privilege, it is ruled not in order until the pending business is disposed of.

15.12 For example, if during a convention an embarrassing discussion arises that should not be held in public, the presiding officer might allow a member to move, as a question of privilege, "that guests and observers be required to leave the room" or "that the assembly move into a closed meeting."

15.13 When it is decided that the motion presented is to be considered as a question of privilege, it is a main motion now pending for action. It follows all the rules of a main motion except that it has interrupted business. If it is noncontroversial, as it often is, it will usually be handled by general consent. Once the motion considered as a question of privilege has been dealt with, the assembly immediately returns to the business that was interrupted.

Basic Rules Governing a Question of Privilege

15.14 The rules governing a Question of Privilege are that it:

1. can interrupt a speaker if it requires immediate decision and action;
2. requires no second because it is a request;
3. is not debatable because it is decided by the presiding officer;
4. cannot be amended;
5. requires no vote;
6. takes precedence over all motions except to Recess and to Adjourn;
7. applies to no other motion;
8. can have no motion applied to it except the Motion to Withdraw; and
9. can be renewed after a change in the parliamentary situation.

15.15 A main motion introduced as a question of privilege is subject to all the basic rules of a main motion, except that it is allowed to interrupt if sufficiently urgent.

MOTION TO RECESS

Purpose and Effect

15.16 The Motion to Recess orders a break in a meeting immediately and sets a definite time or event for the meeting to resume. Adoption of the motion begins a break, which may be moved for a variety of reasons including comfort, logistics, or strategy.

Example

Member:	I move that we recess for twenty minutes. (Another member seconds the motion.)
Presiding Officer:	It has been moved and seconded that we recess for twenty minutes. Those in favor, say "Aye." Those opposed, say "No." The motion is adopted. The meeting is recessed for twenty minutes.

15.17 Other examples of Motions to Recess include:

15.18 Member: I move to recess until 2:45 p.m.

15.19 Or in a convention or meeting lasting more than a day: Member: I move that we recess until tomorrow morning at 8:30 a.m.

Limitations on the Motion to Recess

15.20 The duration of a recess is usually brief, but there is no definite limitation on its length except that a recess cannot extend beyond the time set for the next regular or special meeting or, in a convention, beyond the time set for the next business meeting or for adjournment of the convention.

15.21 It is usually desirable to set a definite time for reconvening rather than moving to recess "to the call of the chair." This avoids uncertainty about when the meeting will resume and the risk that some members will miss the resumption of the meeting. If a meeting is recessed to the call of the chair, there should be a way to notify members who may have left the immediate area that the meeting is about to resume.

15.22 The Motion to Recess may be amended only as to the time or duration of the recess. The presiding officer should be careful to allow members to offer amendments to the Motion to Recess but should not allow these amendments to become debate.

When Recess Is Not a Privileged Motion

15.23 The Motion to Recess, made when no other business is pending, is a main motion and is subject to all the rules of main motions. Motions to Recess that do not take effect immediately—that is, those that set a time for recess in the future—are not privileged motions but are main motions and subject to the rules regarding a main motion.

Basic Rules Governing the Motion to Recess

15.24 The rules governing the Motion to Recess are that it:

1. cannot interrupt a speaker;
2. requires a second;
3. is not debatable;
4. amendments are limited to the time to reconvene or duration of the recess;
5. requires a majority vote;
6. takes precedence over all motions except to Adjourn;
7. applies to no other motion;
8. can have applied to it the Motions to Amend, to Close Debate and Vote Immediately for the purpose of precluding amendments, and to Withdraw; and
9. can be renewed after a change in the parliamentary situation.

MOTION TO ADJOURN

Purpose and Effect

15.25 The Motion to Adjourn can be offered for one of two reasons:

1. to end a meeting or convention, or
2. to end a meeting or convention and to set a time for a continued meeting (sometimes referred to as an *adjourned meeting*).

15.26 Adoption of the Motion to Adjourn, when privileged:

1. terminates a meeting or convention with the announcement of adjournment by the presiding officer; or
2. adjourns a meeting or convention immediately upon the announcement by the presiding officer and continues the meeting or convention at a later date and time if previously established in the agenda or through setting a time for a continued meeting.

Example

Member:	I move that we adjourn. (Another member seconds the motion.)
Presiding Officer:	It is moved and seconded to adjourn. Those in favor, say "Aye." Those opposed, say "No." The motion is adopted. Are there any announcements? The meeting is adjourned.

15.27 Other examples of Motions to Adjourn include: I move that the Annual Meeting of the American Institute of Parliamentarians adjourn. (Another member seconds the motion.)

15.28 If the member wishes to set a continued meeting and to adjourn immediately:

Member:	I move that we adjourn this meeting to resume as a continued meeting on Friday, February 25, at 7 p.m. in this room. (Another member seconds the motion.)
Presiding Officer:	It has been moved and seconded that we adjourn this meeting to resume as a continued meeting on Friday, February 25, at 7 p.m. in this room. Those in favor, say "Aye." Those opposed, say "No." The motion is adopted. Are there any announcements? The meeting is adjourned to resume as a continued meeting on Friday, February 25, at 7 p.m. in this room.

The Privileged Motion to Adjourn

15.29 When a main motion is pending, the Motion to Adjourn is a privileged motion that takes precedence over all other ranked motions. The Motion to Adjourn is only privileged if it takes effect immediately. The Motion to Adjourn, when privileged, is not debatable, but it may be amended to establish a time and place for the current meeting to continue if adjournment is adopted. Proposal or adoption of an amendment to set a continued meeting does not cause the motion to lose its privileged status.

When Adjourn Is Not Privileged

15.30 If there is no main motion pending, the Motion to Adjourn is not a privileged motion but is a main motion and is subject to all the rules of main motions. Likewise, if the Motion to Adjourn is proposed so that the adjournment will take place other than immediately, it is not in order, and cannot be considered, as a privileged motion but is a main motion and subject to the rules of a main motion. The Motion to Adjourn, when privileged, cannot be amended to take effect at a later time.

Difference Between Recess and Adjourn

15.31 A Motion to Recess interrupts the current meeting until a later time. When an assembly reconvenes following a recess, it resumes the meeting at the point where it was interrupted by the Motion to Recess.

15.32 The Motion to Adjourn, when privileged, terminates the meeting unless the assembly adjourns to a continued meeting. When an assembly meets again following an adjournment, it begins an entirely new meeting, starting with the first step in the regular *order of business*. The only exception to this procedure is when an assembly adjourns to a continued meeting. For more information on this type of meeting, see the section, Continued Meetings, in Chapter 18. This type of adjournment is, in fact, similar to a recess.

15.33 Conventions often transact business for several days, and the series of periods for the transaction of business are actually a series of business meetings. A convention, therefore, may move to recess to the next period for transacting business and then adjourn at the end of the convention.

Completion of Business Before Adjournment

15.34 When a Motion to Adjourn is made, it is the duty of the presiding officer to see that no important business is overlooked before stating the motion. If the presiding officer knows of any important matter that has not been considered and requires action before adjournment, it should be called to the attention of the assembly. If the presiding officer fails to do this, any member may call attention to the oversight. For example, if decisions have not been made for an event that is to be held before the next meeting, it is important that this be done before adjournment.

15.35 When attention is called to some action required before adjournment, the presiding officer usually asks the proposer of the Motion to Adjourn to withdraw the motion until the essential business has been completed. If the member refuses to do so, and if the assembly chooses to disregard the warning of the presiding officer, the assembly has the right to vote to adjourn.

Adjournment to a Continued Meeting

15.36 When an assembly cannot consider all its important business in the time available for a meeting, it may be desirable to continue the meeting at a later time. No exact form is required in stating such a Motion to Adjourn, but it must be clear that the meeting is to continue at a later date, and the time and place of the continued meeting must be specified. The setting of the time to continue the meeting can be done through the Motion to Adjourn or an amendment to the privileged form of this motion, a question of privilege of the assembly to establish a continued meeting, or a main motion dealing only with the establishment of the continued meeting. No additional notice of the continued meeting is required unless provided for in the bylaws. When the date or time or location of the continued meeting is dependent upon information that is not yet known, the current meeting can be adjourned to meet at the call of the chair; in such case, notice of the continued meeting must be given by the same method as a special meeting. Failure to hold a continued meeting before the next regular meeting automatically causes the end of the first meeting to become a regular adjournment.

15.37 The interval between the current meeting and the continued meeting is, in effect, like a recess, and the continued meeting is a part of the original meeting. For additional information, see the section, Continued Meetings, in Chapter 18.

Adjournment and Dissolution

15.38 A final adjournment of an assembly when there is no provision for a further meeting has the effect of dissolving the assembly or closing a convention. This is termed *adjournment sine die*, or adjournment without day, and can only be moved as a main motion. The presiding officer should call the attention of the assembly to the fact that there is no provision for another meeting and that the assembly might, in effect, be dissolved by adoption of the Motion to Adjourn.

15.39 For example, an organization having a meeting of its *House of Delegates* may adjourn sine die. That dissolves the assembly composed of delegates but does not dissolve the organization, which continues to exist, and at a later time, will *convene* another House of Delegates.

15.40 Dissolution of an organization is accomplished as required in the bylaws and applicable statutes. If the bylaws have no provision for dissolution, the requirements for amending the bylaws, such as previous notice and a two-thirds vote, should be applied to the motion "that the organization be dissolved."

Voting on Adjournment

15.41   After the vote on the Motion to Adjourn, the meeting does not end until the presiding officer announces the vote and declares adjournment. Before the presiding officer declares the meeting adjourned, brief announcements may be made. The decision on whether to adjourn, however, is made by the assembly, not the presiding officer. The presiding officer cannot unilaterally declare adjournment.

15.42   A formal vote need not always be taken, however. The presiding officer, sensing that it is time to adjourn, may ask, "Is there any further business to come before the meeting?" If, after a pause, there has been no response, the assembly has, in effect, voted by general consent to adjourn, and the presiding officer may simply say, "Are there any announcements? There being no further business, the meeting is adjourned."

15.43   Frequently there is confusion in phrasing Motions to Adjourn. The presiding officer should find out which type of adjournment the proposer of the motion intends and then rephrase the motion, if necessary, to make it clear. For example, a member may say, "I move that we adjourn until next Thursday at 7:30 p.m." If the next regular meeting is scheduled for that date and hour, the member is merely calling attention to the time of the next regular meeting. The presiding officer should restate the motion as "It has been moved and seconded that we adjourn." In announcing the result, the presiding officer may say, "We are now adjourned. Our next regular meeting will be at 7:30 p.m. next Thursday in Jones Hall." It is good practice for the presiding officer, in declaring any meeting adjourned, to state the time and place of the next meeting.

Adjournment at Previously Set Time

15.44   When a definite hour for adjournment has been set by the adoption of a *program*, by rule, or by a previous motion, it is the duty of the presiding officer, when the hour of adjournment arrives, to interrupt a speaker or the consideration of business and to state that the time set to adjourn has arrived. A member may then propose an incidental motion to set another time for adjournment by majority vote.

Business Interrupted by Adjournment

15.45   Business that is interrupted by adjournment is affected as follows:

1. Business that was interrupted by adjournment of a meeting comes up as the first item under unfinished business at the next meeting.

2. Business that was interrupted by the final adjournment of a convention is dropped.

15.46   Business on the agenda that is never reached and is not introduced is not unfinished business—it is dropped; it may be introduced at a future meeting as new business.

Basic Rules Governing the Privileged Motion to Adjourn

15.47   The rules governing the Motion to Adjourn are that it:

1. cannot interrupt a speaker;
2. requires a second;
3. is not debatable when privileged;
4. can be amended to establish a continued meeting, or to change the time or place of a proposed continued meeting;
5. requires a majority vote;
6. takes precedence over all other motions when privileged;
7. applies to no other motion;
8. can have no motion applied to it except the Motions to Amend, to Close Debate and Vote Immediately for the purpose of precluding amendments, and to Withdraw; and
9. can be renewed after a change in the parliamentary situation.

CHAPTER 16. Incidental Motions

16.1 Incidental motions arise out of the business that is immediately pending before the assembly. They do not relate directly to the Main Motion or to Specific-Purpose Main Motions but instead relate to matters arising from the conduct of the meeting. Because of their nature, they may interrupt business and may, if necessary, interrupt the speaker. Incidental motions may be offered at almost any time, have no order of rank, and are disposed of prior to the business from which they arise.

MOTION TO SUSPEND THE RULES

16.2 When an organization desires to accomplish a specific purpose or to take a specific action and is prevented from doing so by the rules of procedure, it may vote to suspend the rules that interfere with the accomplishment of the particular purpose or action required.

Purpose and Effect

16.3 The Motion to Suspend the Rules permits an assembly to take an action that would otherwise be prevented by a procedural rule. The adoption of the motion immediately suspends the rules to permit the action.

Example

Member:	I move to suspend the rules and allow our invited guests to participate in the debate on the pending motions. (Another member seconds the motion.)
Presiding Officer:	It has been moved and seconded to suspend the rules and allow our invited guests to participate in the debate on the pending motions. Those in favor of suspending the rules, please rise. Be seated. Those opposed to suspending the rules, please rise. Be seated. There are two-thirds in the affirmative, the motion is adopted, and the rules are suspended; our invited guests may participate in the debate on the pending motions. Is there any further debate?

16.4 It is not necessary to state the rule to be suspended. The motion is to suspend the rules to permit an action, or to suspend the rules and take an action, when the procedural rules would not otherwise allow this to be done. Often general consent is used to take an action that would otherwise require an explicit motion and vote to suspend the rules. For example, the presiding officer may state, "If there is no objection, we will allow our invited guests to debate on the pending motions."

16.5 As with any motion, if suspension of the rules is likely to confuse some members of the assembly, the presiding officer must take extra precautions to explain the motion and its effect if adopted or defeated, so that members understand the impact of the motion.

Which Rules Can Be Suspended?

16.6 Only rules of procedure can be suspended.

16.7 Sometimes it is sufficient to suspend the rules to permit consideration of another motion that might not be in order. In this case it would also be permissible to combine the Motion to Suspend the Rules with, not just the consideration, but the adoption of that other motion. For example, "I move to suspend the rules and adopt all the recommendations included in the program committee's written report." Adoption of such a motion by a two-thirds vote would adopt the recommendations without debate.

Which Rules Cannot Be Suspended?

16.8 There is a common misconception that anything can be done by use of the Motion to Suspend the Rules. This is not correct. Suspension of the rules cannot deny a member or members any fundamental right as defined in Chapter 2 whether inherent in parliamentary law or defined by the rules of the organization. As well, an assembly cannot suspend:

1. a rule stated in a statute or regulation, charter, or the organization's constitution or bylaws unless a specific provision in these documents of authority provides for suspension of the rule;

2. rules that protect absentees or a minority of more than one-third, such as those rules governing:

    a. *notice of meeting*,

    b. *notice of motion*, including taking up a scheduled order prior to the time established for its consideration, or

    c. quorum requirements;

3. rules that prohibit taking up business not "noticed" on that agenda or call of a special meeting;
4. vote requirements, such as a majority or a two-thirds vote; and
5. voting methods, such as the requirement for a ballot vote.

Restrictions and Duration of a Suspension of the Rules

16.9 The Motion to Suspend the Rules may be made when no motion is pending, or it may be made when a motion is pending if the suspension is for a purpose related in some way to that motion.

16.10 Rules may be suspended only for a specific purpose and only for the limited time necessary to accomplish the proposed action. Any suspension for a longer period would require an amendment of the rules, not a suspension. For this reason, the object of the suspension must be specified in the Motion to Suspend the Rules, and only the action that is specifically mentioned in the Motion to Suspend the Rules can be taken under the suspension.

16.11 As soon as the purpose for the suspension is complete, the suspended rule again becomes effective.

16.12 A Motion to Suspend the Rules can be moved when no business is pending and retains all the basic rules governing an incidental motion. When moved with no business pending, the motion must clearly specify when the effect of the suspension expires, but it can be no later than the conclusion of the meeting.

Cutting the "Gordian Knot"

16.13 The Motion to "Cut the *Gordian Knot*" is a form of the Motion to Suspend the Rules.* The motion permits the assembly, by a two-thirds vote, to return to a point in the meeting that was less confusing, which may be as extreme as returning to the main motion as initially stated by the

---

* The legend of the Gordian Knot relates to a solution to a problem by Alexander the Great. The yoke of a wagon in the Phrygian capital of Gordium had a rope with a complex knot that had been in place for centuries, unable to be untied, and there was a prophecy that whoever could unfasten the knot would rule all of Asia. Either by removing a linchpin or by cutting the knot with his sword, Alexander was able to solve the problem rapidly and unconventionally. In this parliamentary authority, use of the phrase "Cutting the Gordian Knot" refers to the creative use of the Motion to Suspend the Rules to convert a complex procedural situation into a simple one.

presiding officer or even discarding the main motion and inviting a new main motion. This is a useful motion when the parliamentary situation in a meeting has become so confused that the presiding officer or the members have difficulty in knowing how best to proceed. In such cases, debate can become bitter and counterproductive, focusing on procedure rather than on substance.

16.14 The wording a member may use is "Mr. President, the parliamentary situation has become very confusing. I think it would be best to cancel the pending motions and start over with a new motion. I move to suspend the rules to allow this action." Alternatively, the presiding officer, recognizing that this situation exists, may assume the motion although some words of explanation will likely be helpful.

16.15 Such a motion can usually be adopted by general consent because members on both sides of the question are likely to be equally frustrated and welcome a way out. If, however, a member objects to making the decision to suspend the rules by general consent, a formal Motion to Suspend the Rules can be used.

16.16 This type of motion should rarely be needed, but even groups who are sophisticated in the use of parliamentary procedure can become confused and need a way out of such meeting situations. Cutting the Gordian Knot serves this purpose.

16.17 Another alternative to starting over is for the mover of the main motion to request that the main motion be withdrawn, or another member may ask the mover of the main motion to withdraw the motion. If the main motion is withdrawn, any member may introduce a new motion that might better meet the needs of the assembly.

Basic Rules Governing the Motion to Suspend Rules

16.18 The rules governing the Motion to Suspend the Rules are that it:

1. cannot interrupt a speaker;
2. requires a second;
3. is not debatable;
4. cannot be amended;
5. requires a two-thirds vote;

6. takes precedence as an incidental motion and must be decided immediately;
7. applies only to procedural rules but not to another motion;
8. can have no motion applied to it except the Motion to Withdraw; and
9. can be renewed after a change in the parliamentary situation.

POINT OF ORDER

Purpose and Effect

16.19 A Point of Order calls the attention of the presiding officer and the assembly to an alleged violation of the rules, an omission, a mistake, or an error in procedure and secures a ruling on the question raised.

16.20 A point of order interrupts business until the point of order is disposed of.

Example

Member: (recognition not required)	I rise to a point of order (or point of order!).
Presiding Officer:	State the point of order (or state the point.)
Member:	An amendment to the main motion is not in order because a motion to postpone this until after lunch, which is higher ranking, is pending.
Presiding Officer:	The point of order is well taken. The proposed amendment to the main motion is not in order. Or The point of order is not well taken. The motion to postpone was withdrawn. The member who was speaking on the proposed amendment may continue.

Duty of the Presiding Officer to Enforce Rules

16.21 When a member violates a rule, whether intentionally or not, the presiding officer has a duty to call attention to the violation and either require the member to conform to the rule or declare the member's action not in order. The presiding officer is responsible for enforcing the procedural rules during the meeting.[49]

16.22 If the presiding officer makes an error; fails to enforce a rule of the assembly or of parliamentary procedure; does not notice an error made by a member; or something has been done or attempted to be done in violation of the bylaws or other rules of the organization, it is the right of any member to call attention to the violation by raising a point of order.

16.23 Raising a point of order is a demand by a single member that the presiding officer make a ruling or decision on the point raised by the member. The presiding officer has a duty to rule on the point raised or to refer it to the assembly to decide.

When a Point of Order May Be Raised

16.24 A point of order must be raised immediately after the mistake, error, or omission occurs. It cannot be brought up later in the meeting, or in another meeting, unless the error involves a violation of law or of the bylaws.

16.25 Since it is important that a mistake be corrected immediately, a point of order may interrupt, even though a speaker has the floor and has begun speaking. The member making a point of order may interrupt a speaker by saying, "I rise to a point of order" or, more succinctly, "Point of order." These words let the presiding officer know that the member is entitled to immediate recognition, even though someone else may have the floor or may be seeking the floor.

16.26 It is not proper for members to raise points of order when the violation of the rules is minor or of little or no consequence. For example, if a member's speech has exceeded the limit on debate, but the member is clearly concluding the speech, or if a motion is being debated by someone other than the proposer, thus affirming that more than one member wishes to consider the matter, and there was not a second to the motion, neither of these situations justifies raising a point of order.

Ruling on Points of Order

16.27 When a member has stated a point of order, the presiding officer may clarify the point being raised, or consult with the parliamentarian or knowledgeable staff, before ruling on the matter. When ruling on the point, the presiding officer states the point is "well taken," agreeing with the point raised, or "not well taken," disagreeing with the point raised. The presiding officer may state the reasons for the ruling.

16.28   The ruling of the presiding officer on a point of order may be appealed. See the section, Motion to Appeal, in this chapter.

16.29   While the presiding officer would normally rule on a point of order, if the presiding officer is unsure how to rule because the matter on which the point is raised is obscure, or is related to the bylaws, or may set an important precedent, the ruling may be referred to the assembly to decide by vote. For example, "The member has raised the point of order that the motion just proposed is not in order because it conflicts with the purposes stated in our bylaws. The presiding officer is in doubt and will refer it to the assembly for a decision. The question is, "Is the proposed motion (stating the motion) in order? Is there any discussion? Those who believe that the motion is in order, say 'Aye.' Those who believe that it is not in order, say 'No.' The decision is in the affirmative; the proposed motion is in order."

16.30   A point of order referred to the assembly is open to discussion by the members. A decision of the assembly on a point of order cannot be appealed.

Basic Rules Governing Point of Order

16.31   The rules governing a Point of Order are that it:

1. can interrupt a speaker because a violation of the rules should be corrected immediately;
2. requires no second;
3. is not debatable unless the presiding officer refers it to the assembly for discussion and decision;
4. cannot be amended;
5. requires no vote as it is decided by the presiding officer; if the presiding officer refers it to the assembly, it is debatable and is decided by majority vote;
6. takes precedence as an incidental motion and must be decided immediately;
7. applies to any procedural mistake, violation, or omission;
8. can have no motion applied to it except the Motion to Withdraw; and

9. cannot be renewed as to the same question.

MOTION TO APPEAL

Purpose and Effect

16.32   The purpose of the Motion to Appeal is to enable two members who disagree with the presiding officer's ruling to challenge that ruling and have the assembly decide, by vote, whether the presiding officer's ruling is to be sustained, that is, to be upheld or to be reversed.

16.33   An appeal is a motion that suspends the ruling of the chair as the decision of the assembly until voted on. If the ruling of the presiding officer is sustained, the presiding officer's ruling becomes the decision of the assembly. If the ruling of the presiding officer is not sustained, the decision is reversed and overturns the ruling, which becomes the final decision of the assembly.

Example

Member: (immediately after the presiding officer has announced the ruling, and without waiting for recognition):	I appeal the ruling of the chair. Or I appeal the decision of the presiding officer. (Another member seconds the motion.)
Presiding Officer:	The ruling of the chair (or presiding officer) has been appealed. (Presiding officer states the reasons for the ruling and calls on the member appealing the decision.)
Member:	(States the reasons for the appeal.)
Presiding Officer: (following any other debate)	Those in favor of sustaining the ruling of the presiding officer, say "Aye." Those opposed to sustaining the ruling of the presiding officer, say "No." The (Ayes or Noes) have it and the ruling of the presiding officer (is or is not) sustained.

16.34   Other examples of language the presiding officer might use include: The question is on the ruling of the chair. Shall the ruling of the chair be sustained?

An Appeal Must Be Timely

16.35 Any decision of the presiding officer involving judgment is subject to appeal. In contrast, the presiding officer's statement of a fact, such as announcing the result of a vote, or simply answering a question or providing information, such as a parliamentary inquiry or factual inquiry, cannot be appealed. In addition, rulings of the presiding officer related to an unambiguous provision of the bylaws, rules, or parliamentary authority are not subject to appeal. A ruling made while an appeal is pending may not be appealed.

16.36 An appeal is permissible immediately after the presiding officer's ruling has been rendered; it is too late to appeal if any other business has intervened, such as the introduction of or vote on a motion or resumption of debate on the pending motion. However, if another member has obtained the floor, that member may be interrupted before beginning to speak by a member wishing to move an appeal. The presiding officer should be careful not to rush so fast that a member is unduly prevented from making an appeal.

16.37 A ruling by the presiding officer when no main motion is pending can be appealed. If moved in these circumstances, the Motion to Appeal retains the same governing rules as the incidental motion to Appeal.

Debating an Appeal

16.38 After an appeal has been stated by the presiding officer, the presiding officer states the reasons for the ruling. In doing so the presiding officer is not required to leave the chair. The person who made the appeal may then state their reasons for making the appeal and any member may debate for or against the ruling.

16.39 The presiding officer may speak during or at the end of debate. Though not limited in the number of times to speak, the presiding officer should be careful not to attempt to respond to each speaker individually. The member making an appeal may request to withdraw the appeal after hearing the presiding officer's explanation or after further debate. The presiding officer may change the ruling if the member's rationale for the appeal or the debate on the appeal is convincing. In this case, the appeal is dropped. If the presiding officer does not change the ruling because of the debate, or the appeal is not withdrawn, the members vote after debate.

Vote on an Appeal

16.40 The chair, when putting the question on the appeal, states it in a neutral manner, "Those in favor of sustaining the ruling of the presiding officer…" and not in a biased manner. The appeal must focus on the decision or ruling.

16.41 Correct: "Those in favor of sustaining the ruling of the presiding officer…"

16.42 Incorrect: "Those in favor of sustaining the rules…" or "Those supporting the presiding officer…"

16.43 The presiding officer's initial ruling stands as the decision of the assembly unless the ruling is appealed, in which case the vote of the assembly on the appeal decides the assembly's final ruling.

16.44 The vote is always on sustaining the decision of the presiding officer.

16.45 The chair takes the vote and announces the result. If the result is a majority in the affirmative or tied, the vote affirms the ruling of the chair, and the ruling is sustained. If the vote is a majority in the negative, the ruling of the chair is overturned.

Basic Rules Governing the Motion to Appeal

16.46 The rules governing the Motion to Appeal are that it:

1. cannot interrupt a member who has begun speaking but may interrupt after the floor has been granted but before the member begins speaking;
2. requires a second;
3. is debatable;
4. cannot be amended;
5. is stated as a question on sustaining the ruling of the presiding officer and requires a majority vote or a tie vote to sustain the ruling;
6. takes precedence as an incidental motion and must be decided immediately;
7. applies to rulings of the presiding officer;
8. can have applied to it the Motions to Close Debate and Vote Immediately, to Limit or Extend Debate, and to Withdraw; and
9. cannot be renewed as to the same question.

INQUIRIES

Purpose and Effect

16.47   An Inquiry allows a member (1) to ask the presiding officer a question relating to procedure in connection with the pending motion or with a motion the member may wish to bring before the assembly immediately (Parliamentary Inquiry); or (2) to request substantive information or facts about the pending motion or for information on the meaning or effect of the pending question from the presiding officer or a speaker (Factual Inquiry).

Example: Parliamentary Inquiry

Member: (recognition and second not required)	I rise to a parliamentary inquiry. Or Parliamentary inquiry!
Presiding Officer:	State the parliamentary inquiry.
Member:	Is it in order to move to refer the main motion to a committee now?
Presiding Officer:	Yes, the motion could be offered by someone who has been recognized in debate.

Example: Factual Inquiry to the Presiding Officer

Member: (recognition and second not required)	I rise to a factual inquiry. Or I rise to a request for information.
Presiding Officer:	State the inquiry. Or What information is needed?
Member:	Was the proposed dues increase reviewed by the finance committee and what is the committee's conclusion?
Presiding Officer:	Yes, the finance committee reviewed the proposed increase and agrees that an increase is needed.

Example: Factual Inquiry Through the Presiding Officer to Another Person

Member: (recognition and second not required)	I rise to a factual inquiry. Or I rise to a request for information.
Presiding Officer:	State the inquiry. Or What information is needed?
Member:	May I ask the speaker a question?
Presiding Officer:	Is the speaker willing to answer a question?
Speaker:	Yes.
Presiding Officer:	State the question.
Member: (to the presiding officer)	Will the [asks question]?

16.48   If the speaker does not wish to answer questions, a statement such as "I will answer questions after completing my remarks," or "I do not wish to be interrupted by questions," would mean that the member may not interrupt the speaker, and the speaker would continue with debate.

Processing Inquiries

16.49   A request for an inquiry requires the presiding officer to assist the inquiring member in obtaining the information requested, whether provided by the presiding officer, staff, or another person. When appropriate, the presiding officer may rule that the inquiry is not in order or that it may not interrupt a speaker. No additional business is conducted until a response is provided to the inquiry, even if the response does not provide a direct answer to the inquiry, such as a response of "that information is not available."

16.50   If an inquiry is directed through the presiding officer to a member speaking, the speaker may agree to be interrupted for questions or may refuse to permit such interruptions. If speeches are being timed because of a limitation on debate, neither the time taken to ask the question nor the time taken to answer the question is charged to any member's debate limit.

However, the presiding officer must take care to ensure that both questions and answers are as brief as possible, and that neither the question nor the answer evolves into presentation of information that should be properly offered as debate.

16.51 Inquiries are addressed to the speaker in the third person through the presiding officer: "Does the speaker know the proposed motion's financial impact on the club?" rather than "How much do you think this proposal would cost the club?" The presiding officer should correct a member who does not have the floor and who continues the interruption or begins debating.

16.52 Interrupting a speaker for a question is not a right; it is a privilege that may be granted by the speaker. It is exercised only to obtain information, not to engage in debate, and certainly not to obtain the floor preferentially to provide information.

16.53 Some members misunderstand the term *point of information*, as was previously used in other parliamentary authorities, to mean that information or answers can be provided to questions other members may have asked. These members then attempt to respond by offering a "point of information." Unless called upon by the presiding officer to present such information or answers, the member's offer is not in order; it is considered debate. The presiding officer should not allow such interruptions, even if offered as an innocent error, but especially not purposefully to circumvent rules of recognition to offer debate.

Right of Members to Inquire

16.54 Any member has the right to inquire at any time during the processing of a motion provided a vote has not begun on the motion.* The inquiry must be directly related to a pending motion and can be related to procedural matters or substantive matters regarding the merits of the motion, such as the meaning or effect of the pending motion. Inquiries are requests or questions that form the basis of the democratic process of making decisions and are a right of members in a meeting.

---

* Factual inquiries are not permitted after a Motion to Close Debate and Vote Immediately is adopted although parliamentary inquiries may be permitted.

When an Inquiry Interrupts

16.55 An inquiry may interrupt a speaker only if it requires an immediate answer. A member must not interrupt a speaker with an inquiry if it can reasonably wait until the speaker has finished speaking. In order that the presiding officer may know that a member is rising to an inquiry and may have the right to the floor, the member, without recognition, should clearly state that he or she is rising to a parliamentary inquiry or a factual inquiry.

16.56 If a speaker is interrupted by a parliamentary inquiry and the presiding officer decides that the question does not require an immediate answer, the presiding officer explains that the inquiry will be answered as soon as the speaker has finished, and the speaker should be directed to continue.

16.57 The presiding officer should never allow a Parliamentary Inquiry or a factual inquiry to be used as a method of annoying a speaker who has the floor and should deny recognition to any member who is using inquiries to harass or delay.

Inquiry Addressed to the Presiding Officer

16.58 A Parliamentary Inquiry is always addressed to the presiding officer and is answered by the presiding officer. The presiding officer may consult with the parliamentarian, if there is one, but normally does not ask the parliamentarian to respond directly to the questioner.

16.59 If the request for factual information is related to the meaning or effect of the motion, the presiding officer may answer the question, taking care to exhibit no bias on the matter under consideration, or may recognize an officer or staff member, the proposer of the motion, or another member, as appropriate, to provide the requested information. A request for non-procedural information cannot always be granted as the desired information may not be known by anyone at the meeting and may not be readily obtained.

16.60 The presiding officer should answer inquiries on parliamentary procedure that are pertinent to the pending business. However, the presiding officer should not answer general questions on parliamentary procedure that are not directly related to the business before the assembly.

Basic Rules Governing Inquiries

16.61   The rules governing an inquiry are that it:

1. can interrupt a speaker only if it requires an immediate answer;
2. requires no second because it is a request;
3. is not debatable;
4. cannot be amended;
5. requires no vote because it is a request and is decided by the presiding officer;
6. takes precedence as an incidental motion and the presiding officer must rule if the question is in order and if so, at what point it will be answered;
7. applies to any motion;
8. can have no motion applied to it except the Motion to Withdraw; and
9. cannot be renewed on the same matter.

REQUEST TO WITHDRAW A MOTION

Purpose and Effect

16.62   A request to withdraw a motion enables a member who has proposed a motion to remove it or request it be removed from consideration by the assembly. If the request is granted, the motion is withdrawn from further consideration.

Example: Before the Motion Has Been Stated to the Assembly by the Presiding Officer

Member: (recognition not required)	I withdraw my motion.
Presiding Officer:	The motion has been withdrawn.

Example: After the Motion Has Been Stated to the Assembly by the Presiding Officer

Member: (recognition not required)	I withdraw my motion.

Presiding Officer:	The member asks permission to withdraw the motion. Is there any objection to permitting the withdrawal of the motion? (No one seeks recognition.) There being no objection, the motion is withdrawn.

16.63   If a member objects, the script might read:

Member A: (recognition not required)	I withdraw my motion.
Presiding Officer:	The member asks permission to withdraw the motion. Is there any objection to permitting the withdrawal of the motion?
Another Member: (recognition not required)	I object!
Presiding Officer:	Those in favor of allowing Member A to withdraw the motion, say "Aye." Those opposed, say "No." The Ayes have it, the motion is adopted, and Member A's motion is withdrawn.

Right of the Proposer to Withdraw or Modify a Motion

16.64   Any motion can be withdrawn. Before a motion has been stated by the presiding officer, its proposer may modify it or withdraw it without the assembly's permission, and any member or the presiding officer may request that the maker withdraw it. Usually such a request is made because some more urgent business needs prior consideration, or because the motion was based on erroneous or incomplete information or is not worded clearly. At this point the maker has the right to choose among the options to withdraw the motion, modify the motion, or decline to make any change.

Permission to Withdraw or Modify a Motion

16.65   After a motion has been stated to the assembly by the presiding officer, it becomes the property of that body, and the proposer may withdraw or modify it only with the permission of the assembly, which may be granted through a majority vote or by general consent. If a member objects to the general consent, the presiding officer immediately proceeds to take a vote on whether the motion can be withdrawn or modified. This motion is not debatable and requires a majority vote.

16.66   Once stated, only the mover of a motion has the right to request that it be withdrawn; the consent of the seconder is not necessary. A motion can be withdrawn or modified if there is no objection, or with permission from the assembly, up to the moment the final vote on it is taken, even though other higher-ranked motions affecting the motion may be pending or debate has been limited or closed. When a motion is withdrawn, all motions dependent upon the withdrawn motion are also withdrawn.

Recording Withdrawn Motions

16.67   A main motion that is withdrawn after it has been stated by the presiding officer is recorded in the minutes with a statement that it was withdrawn. No mention is made in the minutes of a motion that is withdrawn before it has been stated to the assembly by the presiding officer.

Basic Rules Governing a Request to Withdraw a Motion

16.68   The rules governing the Motion to Withdraw are that it:

1. can interrupt a speaker;
2. requires no second because it is a request;
3. is not debatable;
4. cannot be amended;
5. requires no vote before the motion is stated by the presiding officer, in which case the request is granted; after the motion is stated by the presiding officer, it requires the approval of the assembly by general consent or a majority vote;
6. takes precedence as an incidental motion and must be decided immediately;
7. applies to all motions;
8. can have no motion applied to it; and
9. can be renewed after a change in the parliamentary situation.

DIVISION OF THE QUESTION

Purpose and Effect

16.69 The Motion for Division of the Question allows a motion composed of two or more parts, each of which can stand independently, to be divided into individual motions that will be considered and voted on separately.

16.70 If the motion is divided, then the first portion is stated by the presiding officer, considered, and disposed of unless the assembly orders another sequence. This is repeated for each of the divided motions in turn until all the divisions of the original motion have been disposed of. The mover and seconder of the original motion are assumed to be the same for each divided motion.

Example

16.71 Assume that the following motion has been introduced: "I move that the club donate $5,000 to the Children's Shelter, and that funds donated to any charity this year be drawn from the reserve account."

Member: (following recognition)	I request that the motion be divided into two motions: (1) that the club donates $5,000 to the Children's Shelter, and (2) that funds donated to any charity this year be drawn from the reserve account.
Presiding Officer: (no second required; motion is divided on demand if it contains more than one distinct and independent proposal)	A member has requested that the motion be divided into two separate motions. The motion will be divided. The motion now before the assembly is "that the club donates $5,000 to the Children's Shelter." Is there any discussion?

Motions Divided by the Presiding Officer

16.72 When a motion contains two or more distinct and independent proposals, any member has the right to demand that it be divided into separate motions. If the presiding officer agrees that the motion contains more than one distinct and independent proposal, the presiding officer rules that it will be divided into two or more separate motions. To be considered as being distinct and independent, each proposal must be capable of standing alone as a reasonable motion that might have been offered independently, and each proposal must be suitable for adoption even if the other motion, or motions, should be defeated. The presiding officer's decision to permit or deny the division of the question is subject to appeal.

16.73 For example, on the one hand, a motion "that the organization promote the use of social media in our public relations efforts and that the association hire an assistant to the executive director" is clearly divisible because the two proposals are distinct and independent.

16.74 On the other hand, a motion "that the association purchase fifteen laptop computers and that the association give one of the computers to each member of the board of directors" cannot be divided because the proposals are not independent: If the motion to "purchase fifteen laptop computers" is defeated, it would be meaningless to consider the motion to "give one of the computers to each member of the board of directors." The presiding officer must deny a request to divide such a motion, explaining the reason for the denial.

16.75 A motion may contain several proposals that are worded such that they cannot be divided easily or without extensive rewriting. In this case, the Motion for Division of the Question should clearly indicate the wording of each of the individual proposals. In important cases, where clarity is required by the assembly, the assembly can refer the original motion to a committee to divide the motion and carefully rewrite its parts so that each can stand alone and be discussed and voted on in a logical manner.

When Division of the Question May Be Proposed

16.76 A request to divide a question is most effective if it is proposed immediately after the introduction of the motion that it seeks to divide. However, since it is an incidental motion, it may be proposed at any time before the vote has begun.

Alternative Proposals for Dividing the Question

16.77 A motion for Division of the Question should state clearly how the question is to be divided. Any member may propose a different division. Such proposed divisions are alternative proposals, not amendments, and should be voted on in the same way as filling blanks: They are voted on in the order in which they are proposed. See Chapter 14 for details on Filling Blanks.

Basic Rules Governing a Request for Division of the Question

16.78   The rules governing the Motion for Division of the Question are that it:

1. cannot interrupt a speaker;
2. requires no second;
3. is not debatable;
4. cannot be amended;
5. requires no vote;
6. takes precedence as an incidental motion and must be decided immediately;
7. applies to divisible motions;
8. can have no motion applied to it except the Motion to Withdraw; and
9. can be renewed after a change in the parliamentary situation.

CONSIDER BY PARAGRAPH

Purpose and Effect

16.79   For some proposals, particularly those that are longer or more complicated, consideration paragraph by paragraph or section by section may be clearer and more efficient. In this process, each paragraph or section is considered and may be amended individually in sequence. After all paragraphs or sections have been considered individually, the entire motion is open to debate and further amendment and is then finally voted on as a whole. If the entire motion is defeated on this final vote, any amendments that may have been adopted during the consideration of individual paragraphs or sections are also defeated and are not in effect.

16.80   The Motion to Consider by Paragraph permits the assembly to focus on one paragraph or section of a proposal at a time and perfect it through amendments before moving on to the next paragraph or section. This usually allows members to follow and understand the effects of amendments more easily than if those amendments are introduced haphazardly, jumping between various parts of the proposal.

16.81   For example, a committee may report a motion with a number of changes, and consideration of each paragraph or section separately can aid in focusing the debate on specific points. After every paragraph has been debated, and amended as necessary, the full motion is opened to further debate and amendment. This step allows any conflicts that have been introduced during the process to be corrected before the motion is finally voted on as a whole. A proposed revision of the bylaws is often considered in this manner.

Example

Presiding Officer:	It has been moved and seconded that we adopt the revised bylaws as presented. Is there any discussion? The chair recognizes Member A.
Member A:	I move that we consider the revision by paragraph. (Another member seconds the motion.)
Presiding Officer:	It has been moved and seconded that we consider the revision by paragraph. Those in favor of considering the revision by paragraph, say "Aye." Those opposed, say "No." The motion is adopted, and we will consider the revision by paragraph.

Considering a Motion by Paragraph

16.82 Any member may move to consider the main motion by paragraph. The motion requires a majority vote or may be approved by general consent. As it is an incidental motion, it requires a second and is not debatable. Alternatively, consideration by paragraph can be implemented by the presiding officer.

16.83 Only the Motions to Amend or to Limit or Extend Debate can be applied to the separate paragraphs. Other subsidiary motions cannot be applied to separate paragraphs as could be done if the question were divided; any other subsidiary motions offered, such as the Motion to Refer or to Postpone to a Certain Time, would apply to the entire main motion.

16.84 During consideration of the motion by paragraph, a member may move that the motion "be considered as a whole." This requires a second, is not debatable, and requires a majority vote. If adopted, the process of considering each paragraph separately is halted and the motion is fully open to debate, amendments, and other subsidiary motions. Amendments already adopted remain as part of the main motion, even if the main motion moves from consideration by paragraph to consideration as a whole, or vice versa.

Basic Rules Governing Consider by Paragraph

16.85 The rules governing the Motion to Consider by Paragraph are that it:

1. cannot interrupt a speaker;
2. requires a second;
3. is not debatable;
4. cannot be amended;
5. requires a majority vote unless implemented by the presiding officer;
6. takes precedence as an incidental motion and must be decided immediately;
7. applies to main motions only;
8. can have no motion applied to it except the Motion to Withdraw; and
9. can be renewed after a change in the parliamentary situation.

VERIFICATION OF A VOTE

DIVISION OF THE ASSEMBLY

Purpose and Effect

16.86 It is the duty of the presiding officer to accurately determine the outcome of a vote by the most efficient method available. Members have the right to request verification of a vote when the results are uncertain or have been incorrectly announced. This may be done by a demand for a Division of the Assembly or a request or Motion for a Counted Vote.

16.87 The purpose of a Motion for a Division of the Assembly is to verify an unclear voice vote by requiring members to rise. If demanded, the presiding officer takes a standing vote on the motion just voted on or, if the presiding officer remains unclear about the results, conducts a counted vote. For more information, see Chapter 6, "Methods of Voting."

Example

Member: (immediately after a voice vote has been taken or announced; recognition not required):	Division!

| Presiding Officer: | A division of the assembly has been called for. Those in favor of the motion that [stating the pending motion], please rise. Be seated. Those opposed, please rise. Be seated. There is a majority in the affirmative, and the motion is adopted. |

16.88 Other examples of Motions for a Division of the Assembly include: "I ask that the vote be verified" or "I ask for a standing vote."

When Division May Be Demanded

16.89 The responsibility of determining the correct outcome of a vote rests with the presiding officer. If in doubt, the presiding officer takes the initiative and conducts a standing vote or, in a small assembly, a show of hands. If still in doubt, or if it would be more efficient to do so directly, the presiding officer conducts a counted vote.

16.90 However, any member, without waiting for recognition, may call for a division of the assembly as soon as a question has been put to a voice vote and even before the vote is announced. This right continues after the vote has been announced and another speaker has claimed the floor, but the right must be exercised promptly and expires when the speaker has begun to speak.

MOTION FOR A COUNTED VOTE

16.91 If, after a standing vote has been held, a member doubts the presiding officer's declaration of the outcome of the vote, the member may request a counted vote. If the presiding officer agrees that the result is in doubt, the presiding officer conducts a counted vote. Otherwise, the presiding officer requires the member to move to take a counted vote. This undebatable motion requires a second and a majority vote to be adopted.

16.92 Any member who feels an uncounted vote has not been correctly announced or reported has the right to request verification, but a member cannot use this privilege to obstruct business by calling for a division or a counted vote on an obviously decisive vote. This request may be made after the vote has been announced and another speaker has claimed the floor, but the right to make the request must be exercised promptly and expires when the speaker has begun to speak.

Basic Rules Governing the Motion for a Division of the Assembly

16.93   The rules governing the Motion for a Division of the Assembly are that it:

1. can interrupt proceedings because it requires immediate decision;
2. requires no second;
3. is not debatable;
4. cannot be amended;
5. requires no vote;
6. takes precedence as an incidental motion and must be decided immediately;
7. applies to a voice vote when, in the opinion of a member, the outcome was not clear or was incorrectly announced;
8. can have no motion applied to it; and
9. cannot be renewed on the same vote.

Basic Rules Governing the Motion for a Counted Vote

16.94   The rules governing the request or Motion for a Counted Vote are that it:

1. can interrupt proceedings because it requires immediate attention;
2. requires a second unless the presiding officer agrees to the request for a counted vote;
3. is not debatable;
4. cannot be amended;
5. requires no vote if the presiding officer agrees to the request for a counted vote; requires a majority vote if a motion is made;
6. takes precedence as an incidental motion and must be decided immediately;
7. applies to a vote with an unclear outcome;
8. can have no motion applied to it other than the Motion to Withdraw; and
9. cannot be renewed on the same vote.

MEETINGS OF ORGANIZATIONS

CHAPTER 17. Types of Organizations

TEMPORARY AND PERMANENT ORGANIZATIONS

17.1 An organization may be established as either a temporary or a *permanent organization*. A *temporary organization* may exist for a few meetings or even a single meeting. It dissolves automatically as soon as the members accomplish the purpose for which they organized. An example of a temporary organization is a group of people gathering to accomplish a specific civic project, such as donating a statue or creating a park.

17.2 A permanent organization is one formed with the intention of functioning over a considerable period of time until it is dissolved.

17.3 A temporary or permanent organization may choose any legal form of entity discussed below, as permitted by applicable statute, but it is most common for temporary organizations to be created as unincorporated associations.

FORM OF ORGANIZATION

17.4 The founders of a new organization, or the members of an existing organization who wish to reorganize, must decide on the type of entity that best suits their purpose. Most nonprofit membership organizations choose to organize either as unincorporated associations or as corporations. Nonprofit corporations may be organized as membership corporations or as board-only corporations. Business entities include partnerships and business corporations (where shareholders are similar to members in nonprofit corporations). Some nonprofits, typically those without individual members, and many businesses choose to organize as trusts (which may be governed by a board of trustees, but more frequently by one or more trustees who are required to act unanimously) or as limited liability companies (an entity that provides considerable governance flexibility but requires consideration of tax-related concerns).

17.5 In general, courts will apply basic principles of common parliamentary law to meetings of the members (or shareholders) and governing boards of all such entities, to the extent not otherwise provided for by the governing documents or applicable statutes,[50] with greater informality in the case of smaller bodies.

17.6 Business entities typically arrange their governance with considerable power concentrated in the hands of management and less member- or shareholder-based decision-making, which is why it is somewhat less frequent for business entities to adopt a parliamentary authority.

Comparison of Legal Options for Nonprofit and Business Organizations					
	Unincorporated Association	Corporation	Trust	Limited Liability Company	Partnership
Nonprofit	Yes	Membership corporation or board-only corporation	Yes	Yes (occasionally)	No
Business	No (joint ventures instead)	Shareholder corporation	Yes	Yes	Yes

17.7 It is difficult for a large assembly to formulate plans. When creating a new organization, a small group or committee of founders should meet to consider and come to decisions on such questions as the purposes of the proposed organization. The following decisions should be given careful consideration:

1. its legal form (temporary or permanent, profit or nonprofit, charitable or non-charitable, incorporated or unincorporated, and category of tax-exempt status);
2. types of membership;
3. financing;
4. policies;
5. temporary officers; and
6. affiliation with other organizations.

17.8 It may be helpful to seek legal advice regarding entity choice and formation, particularly if the choice is anything other than an unincorporated association.

UNINCORPORATED ASSOCIATIONS

17.9   Those unincorporated nonprofit entities that are rather loosely structured and that operate only under their own governing documents are termed unincorporated associations. Unions, political committees, homeowners associations, service associations, and local units of parent organizations are typical of the types of organizations that may be created as unincorporated associations. Unincorporated associations may be somewhat limited with regard to the powers of leasing or owning property, employment, having bank accounts, and receipt of charitable gifts.[51] Many jurisdictions, however, have adopted unincorporated nonprofit association acts that grant unincorporated associations powers similar to those of corporations while allowing them much more flexibility over internal governance matters than corporations.[52] Review of the statutes and/or codes in the jurisdiction of the organization or consultation with an attorney may be useful to see if such a statute is in effect and to determine its applicability to the proposed organization.

MEETING TO FORM AN UNINCORPORATED ASSOCIATION

17.10   At the organizing meeting for an unincorporated association, sometimes referred to as a mass meeting, one of the group members calls the meeting to order and nominates or calls for *nominations* for a temporary presiding officer.[53] If additional persons are nominated, a vote is taken on each candidate. The individual receiving the highest majority vote is elected as explained in Chapter 26. This nominee is then declared the temporary presiding officer who calls for nominations for a temporary secretary to be elected in the same manner. The presiding officer then requests a member of the organizing group to read the call of the meeting, the notice advertising the meeting, and to explain the purpose of the proposed organization.

17.11   If the new organization is forming as a unit of an existing organization, the parent organization may have issued a charter in anticipation of formation. If such a charter has been issued, it constitutes the governing rules for the meetings creating the new organization. Otherwise, the call of the meeting and the rules of common parliamentary law govern the procedures of an organizing meeting unless the body adopts a parliamentary authority, standing rules of order, or both, which is advised if the formation process is expected to be long or complicated. Someone may then present a motion or resolution for forming the organization.

17.12   A resolution for forming a temporary organization might read:

> **Resolved**, That this assembly form a temporary organization, to be known as the Old Town Preservation Committee, for the purpose of promoting creation of a tax-free zone in the downtown area by the Milo City Council; and be it further
>
> **Resolved**, That a committee consisting of five members elected by the assembly be formed to coordinate the efforts of the organization and to call further meetings if needed; and be it further
>
> **Resolved**, That the members of the coordinating committee attend the next meeting of the Milo City Council to present a signed petition promoting creation of the zone; and be it further
>
> **Resolved**, That a copy of this resolution with the reasons for our promotion and a list of members of the coordinating committee be sent to the news media located in this county.

17.13   A motion to form a permanent organization might read:

17.14   I move that we organize as the Woodford County Improvement Association with the following purpose: to advocate for improved infrastructure and economic development of Woodford County.

17.15   A formal resolution or a simpler motion may be used for the creation of either type of organization.

17.16   If this motion is adopted, a member can move to create a committee to draft bylaws consistent with the stated purpose. If the bylaws have already been prepared, they are presented, in which case the proposed purpose clause of the bylaws is sufficient and does not need to be repeated in the organizing motion. As soon as the bylaws have been adopted, which may need to be done at another meeting, or at a continuation of the original meeting if they were not prepared in advance, permanent officers are elected, and the organization is complete. For more information on the adoption of original bylaws, see Chapter 4.

17.17   If the members decide to seek a charter as a unit of an already existing organization and such a charter has not already been granted, they select or authorize the presiding officer to appoint a committee to carry out this procedure.

CORPORATIONS

17.18 While nonprofit membership organizations, whether local, regional, national, or international in scope, may be unincorporated, many are incorporated. The chief advantages of incorporation are:

1. The organization holds a charter from a government, granted by the appropriate agency in the jurisdiction in which the organization incorporated. It operates under the guidance and protection of the applicable laws governing corporations.

2. The purposes of the organization and the powers necessary to carry out these purposes have legal recognition.

3. The individuals or member groups are able to work with greater effectiveness and scope by joining their resources and efforts because of the greater formality afforded by corporate recognition.

4. While the process for dissolution is generally more difficult than for unincorporated associations and must follow statutory formalities, nevertheless, corporate statutes typically provide a method of dissolution when an organization is unable to function because it cannot obtain a quorum after a number of attempts, whereas dissolution of an unincorporated association in such circumstances may be difficult without a specific bylaw provision covering that situation.

5. The corporation is recognized as a legal entity apart from its individual members and thus can do business and hold property of any kind in its own right. Consequently, most jurisdictions require corporations to file contact and leadership information regularly with a government agency, so that parties doing business with the corporation can locate responsible individuals if necessary.

6. Officers, directors, and members are free from personal liability for debts of the organization.

7. The name and seal of the organization are legally protected.

17.19 If an organization chooses to form as a corporation, it should consult legal counsel. Corporate formation must follow statutory requirements that vary with the jurisdiction. Generally, after formation, corporations may operate in any jurisdiction, possibly subject to local filing requirements.

Nonprofits generally tend to incorporate in the jurisdiction where headquartered. If, however, the nonprofit corporation law of that jurisdiction contains onerous requirements incompatible with the intended governance structure of the organization, it may be useful for the organizers to consider incorporating in another jurisdiction.

17.20 One common way for individuals with common interests to form a corporation is to create a temporary organization in the form of an unincorporated association in order to assist in the creation and registration of the corporation. In such a case, the temporary organization's formation resolution should state the intended name and purposes of the corporation and authorize the organizing or coordinating committee to take such steps as are necessary to incorporate the organization.

STATUTORY REQUIREMENTS

17.21 If a nonprofit organization is incorporated, members should be aware that in addition to having their bylaws and practices comply with their corporate charter (sometimes called articles of incorporation), they also must comply with applicable corporation codes. Many of these codes set specific guidelines for such things as quorum requirements, election procedures, notice required for meetings, and proxy voting. An attorney should be consulted when a corporation is established to ensure that the charter and bylaws conform to applicable statutes as well as any requirements for tax-exempt status.

17.22 Most corporation codes do not provide detailed guidance on the conduct of meetings. These codes permit the organization to adopt its own procedural guide, such as this parliamentary authority, and to establish its own bylaws and rules so long as these do not conflict with the corporate charter or with statutory or common law.[54]

17.23 Private-sector labor unions in the United States should be aware that their bylaws must also conform to provisions of federal law, particularly the Labor-Management Reporting and Disclosure Act of 1959, better known as the Landrum-Griffin Act.[55] Public-sector labor unions in the United States are typically covered by similar statutory requirements of the applicable jurisdiction. On procedural matters not covered by these acts, the union should be guided by the basic principles of common parliamentary law and should adopt a parliamentary authority to resolve questions not dealt with in the act or in the union's bylaws.

17.24 Similarly, other organizations, such as political committees, homeowner associations, and public charities, may be subject to statutory governance and filing requirements based on their substantive work regardless of their form of organization.

DIFFERENCES AMONG NONPROFIT, TAX-EXEMPT, AND CHARITABLE ORGANIZATIONS

17.25 Almost all voluntary membership organizations are nonprofit groups, sometimes also called not-for-profit organizations although any distinction between the terms is largely theoretical. Applicable law will determine if the organization qualifies as a nonprofit.[56] In many jurisdictions, special nonprofit corporation statutes may make formation of a nonprofit corporation easier.[57] Nonprofit organizations, whether or not organized as corporations, may have certain advantages or privileges under applicable law. Typical permissible purposes for a nonprofit corporation may be charitable, political, social, governmental, or educational in character. The main requirement is that any income or profit of the organization must be used solely to carry out its legal purposes and cannot be distributed as profit to its members. The organization cannot pay dividends or other remuneration to its members. It can, however, pay reasonable compensation or salaries for services rendered, and in some cases, such as some mutual benefit organizations, it may be able to distribute certain assets to members upon dissolution, but this would be the exception.[58]

17.26 Some nonprofit organizations are charities. The test to determine whether an organization is charitable depends on applicable law and may vary somewhat from jurisdiction to jurisdiction. Generally, organizations with purposes related to health care, education, service to the poor, advancement of science, sports, and the arts and culture qualify as charitable in most jurisdictions. Charitable nonprofits may have additional filing requirements not applicable to other nonprofits, for example, regarding charitable solicitation.

17.27 A nonprofit organization may receive profit incidental to its operations, but that profit must be used for the purposes for which the organization exists. For example, a regional medical association might receive considerable profit from some of its activities; this money could not be distributed as pecuniary gain to its members, but it could be spent for educational or other purposes that would benefit its members and the public.

17.28 A nonprofit organization, whether incorporated or not, may be treated by both the federal and state, territorial, or provincial government as a tax-exempt entity. Tax-exempt status is accorded on the basis of specific statutory and regulatory provisions. While most nonprofit organizations will qualify as tax-exempt, the particular category of exemption, and the consequent benefits and compliance requirements, may not be obvious. Consultation with a lawyer or tax professional is advisable when asserting tax-exempt status. If an organization asserts tax-exempt status, it is important to comply with applicable filing requirements in order not to jeopardize that status.

CHAPTER 18. Types of Meetings

MEETINGS AND CONVENTIONS

18.1 A meeting is an official assembly of the members of an organization or board during which the members conduct business and do not separate except for a recess. It covers the period from the *call to order* until the time of final adjournment.

18.2 An annual meeting, sometimes referred to as an annual general meeting or an annual business meeting, is the meeting open to all members of an organization that is held yearly, usually at the end of the organizational year. Such a meeting is frequently held for the purposes of electing or installing officers and hearing reports.

18.3 A convention is an official assembly of representative delegates rather than all members of the organization. It may be composed of a series of meetings that follow in relatively close succession but is regarded as a single meeting with intervening recess periods, some of which may be from day to day. Information on flag etiquette and on *protocol* for conventions is available at www.aipstandardcode.com.

18.4 A mass meeting refers to an initial gathering or series of gatherings of an unorganized group—one that has no formal governing documents—during which the attendees conduct business and may attempt to form a permanent organization. These gatherings generally do not have an established order of business or parliamentary authority; however, both could be adopted by the attendees.

REGULAR MEETINGS

18.5 A regular meeting of an organization or board is one of a series of meetings for which the dates—and sometimes location—are established in the bylaws or set by adoption of a motion. The location can be either a physical place or a virtual setting or a combination thereof, which is commonly referred to as a *hybrid meeting*. At a regular meeting, the usual business of the organization is conducted. Since members are presumed to be familiar with the bylaws and standing rules of order, when meetings are specified therein, no additional notice of regular meetings is required unless the bylaws or standing rules of order provide for further notice or unless notice of regular meetings is customary.

18.6 The regular time and place for meetings that have been established by rule cannot legally be changed without giving notice to all members or amending the rule. The regular time and place of a meeting that are established in the bylaws cannot be altered without amending the bylaws.

18.7 At a regular meeting, any business can be conducted that comes within the scope of the organization's purposes unless otherwise restricted by the governing documents. The organization should be cautious in choosing to restrict items of business to a particular meeting as this may limit flexibility to accomplish necessary business.

18.8 No meeting may begin before the time stated in the notice or set by custom unless all members are present and consent.

SPECIAL MEETINGS

18.9 A special meeting, also known as a *called meeting*, is a meeting that is not regularly scheduled and is held to conduct specified business as stated in the *call of the meeting*. Any special meetings of an organization or a board must be called in accordance with the bylaw provisions governing special meetings or in accordance with applicable statutory requirements. If special meetings are not authorized in the bylaws or statute, a special meeting cannot be held. If special meetings are to be authorized, the organization's documents must provide the method by which special meetings may be called, who may call the special meeting, the notice required, and specific requirements for what business may be conducted at a special meeting. For example, the bylaws may provide that special meetings may be called by the board or must be called upon petition by 10 percent of the membership with no less than a one-week notice via email to consider the items listed in the call of the meeting.

18.10 If the bylaws are silent or do not explicitly provide for other business to be conducted, only items of business specifically stated in the call of the meeting may be acted upon.

18.11 All members must be notified of a special meeting, and the call or notice must state the items of business that will be considered and voted on.[59] A copy of the call for the special meeting must be inserted in, or attached to, the minutes of the meeting. Only those items of business stated in the call for a special meeting may be considered unless the governing documents specifically authorize other business. No new items of business may be added to the agenda or may be acted upon after the notice period has expired. The special meeting is conducted in the same manner as any other business meeting, but business is limited to the items provided in the notice. The statement of business to be considered must be specific, and if action is to be considered at the meeting, this fact must be stated in the notice. If a notice states that one of the purposes of a special meeting is "to hear a report of the land purchase committee," the report can be read, but no action can be taken on recommendations of the committee unless the recommendations are stated in the notice and it is clear that they are to be voted on at the meeting. Similarly, if a notice states that the purpose of the special meeting is "to adopt a motion that the vice president be censured and requested to resign," the body cannot adopt a motion to remove the vice president. However, conditional notice is acceptable; for example, the notice could provide that "should the vice president resign, a replacement will be elected." General broad statements describing business to be conducted, such as "any other proper business that may come before the meeting," do not give valid notice.

18.12   Minutes of previous meetings are not reviewed or approved at a special meeting unless included in the meeting notice as items of business to be considered, but any section that applies to items under consideration may be read for reference at the time of discussion on that item. The minutes of the special meeting are approved at the next regular meeting.

18.13   In large state/provincial, national, or international organizations, provisions in the bylaws for special meetings of the whole membership are often unrealistic. The governing board of such organizations should be empowered to handle most emergency or urgent organizational business. The bylaws section on special meetings should be limited to extreme situations, contain high requirements for holding the meeting, and include specific details on member notification.

CANCELING OR CHANGING A SCHEDULED MEETING

18.14   Sometimes unanticipated circumstances may preclude the ability to hold a meeting as scheduled. If the meeting was originally established by a motion and there is an intervening meeting, this can be changed by use of the Motion to Amend a Previous Action.

18.15 Otherwise, if a regular or special meeting has to be canceled or postponed, or the date, time, or location must be changed, the authority to do so and the process to do so must be stated in the bylaws. If the bylaws are silent on such provisions, the decision to cancel, postpone, or change the time or location of the meeting may be made by the body or person that originally called the meeting. If this is not possible, the board may make the decision, and if there is no board, a majority of the elected officers may do so. At least 24 hours written or electronic notice must be given of such changes. If emergency circumstances preclude such notice, the same provisions to make the change apply, with a one hour written or electronic notice AND a posting at the original location as long as the locations are in very close proximity as to time and place.

CONTINUED MEETINGS

18.16 When members wish to continue a regular or a special meeting at a later time, a Motion to Adjourn the meeting and to continue it at a definite later time makes the second meeting a continued meeting, which is legally a continuation of the original meeting. For more information on the use of the Motion to Adjourn to establish a continued meeting, see Chapter 15. The meeting is continued on the date, time, and at the location as set forth in the adopted Motion to Adjourn. The interval between the two meetings is like a recess, which may last for days or even weeks but must not extend past the start of the next regular scheduled meeting. A continued meeting is sometimes referred to as an adjourned meeting, but the term *continued meeting* is recommended because it is less confusing as to the intent of the action taken.

18.17 The continued meeting is called to order, and a quorum is established to open the meeting. From that point on, the meeting follows the previous agenda from the original meeting, beginning exactly where the prior meeting finished. If a question was pending when the meeting adjourned, that question is still pending, as recorded in the secretary's notes, when the continued meeting is called to order. An organization can conduct any business at a continued meeting that it might have conducted in the original meeting, and any limitations, such as debate limits that might have been imposed at the original meeting, remain in force at a continued meeting. A continued special meeting can conduct only such business as could have been conducted at the original special meeting.

18.18   The minutes of both the original meeting and any continued meetings comprise one set of minutes and are considered at the next regular meeting.

18.19   Special notice is not required for a continued meeting because it is legally a resumption of the original meeting, but it is a good practice to notify all members of continued meetings when possible, and organizations would be wise to adopt rules regarding notice requirements for continued meetings that would meet their needs. For more information on notices of meetings and proposals, see Chapter 20.

18.20   A continued meeting may be again continued to a later date as long as the continuation occurs prior to the next regular scheduled meeting.

CLOSED MEETING

18.21   A closed meeting, sometimes referred to as an *executive session*, is a meeting open only to current members of the body that is meeting and is a meeting in which sensitive or confidential matters may be discussed and acted upon. Any discussion held or actions taken are legally considered as confidential, and all information must remain within the confines of the meeting unless the body that is holding a closed meeting directs otherwise by formal motion.[60] A motion to go into a closed meeting is privileged, is not debatable but is amendable as to who may attend in addition to members and is adopted by majority vote.

18.22   Boards and committees are normally considered to operate in a closed meeting unless the organization documents state otherwise. Boards and committees may invite members of the organization, staff, or others to attend as observers or to obtain information.

18.23   In a closed meeting, only those who are members of the body that is meeting are allowed to attend; for a board or committee, that means only the members of the board or committee rather than all members of the organization. In a membership meeting, only members of the organization have a right to attend the closed meeting. Guests, such as witnesses, advisors, or staff, may attend only by invitation of the body that is in a closed meeting.

18.24   Personnel matters, such as discussion of salaries and evaluation of employees, should be handled in a closed meeting, as should discussions of pending legal problems, legal or financial advice, negotiation strategies, and other matters of a highly sensitive nature that may cause harm to the organization if not held in a closed meeting. Disciplinary actions against a member of an organization must be handled in a closed meeting.

18.25 Some states have *sunshine laws* or *open meeting laws* that restrict the use of closed meetings. These laws may apply to such organizations as corporations, charities, not-for-profit groups, municipalities, and school boards. Closed meetings cannot be used to conceal matters that members or, if applicable, the public have a right to know, such as financial information, or any matters that may be required by law to be conducted in open meetings.

18.26 The minutes of a closed meeting are available only to current members of the body holding the meeting unless the law or the bylaws require otherwise or the body holding the closed meeting votes to make its minutes available to others.

18.27 Any action taken in a closed meeting may have the confidential nature of the meeting and its protections removed by a majority vote. This vote to remove confidentiality or to report the motion must also be taken in a closed portion of the meeting.

18.28 Members who violate the confidentiality of a closed meeting are subject to disciplinary action. Staff and other nonmembers who violate the confidentiality of a closed meeting may be subject to penalties as well.

ELECTRONIC MEETINGS

18.29 Unless prohibited by the bylaws or any applicable statute, any meeting may be held as an electronic meeting, that is by telephonic or electronic means, or as a hybrid meeting, with some members grouped together in specific location(s) and with other members participating by telephonic or electronic means. Electronic or hybrid meetings must have the same protections for the rights of members as other meetings although the procedural rules associated with such meetings may differ.

18.30 See Chapter 19 for additional information on electronic meetings.

ACTIONS WITHOUT A MEETING

18.31 Communications by postal mail, fax, email, and other means in which members are unable to have simultaneous aural communication with all other members cannot be substituted for traditional meetings and are not meetings in the true sense. Decisions may be made outside a meeting by these means only if the law permits, and the procedures are developed within the organization's governing documents. Unless there is a provision allowing this type of action in either the governing documents or statute, such action is prohibited. Note that most state codes prohibit action without a meeting except by *unanimous written consent*.[61]

18.32 Unanimous written consent is an alternative method for a body to act without a meeting. The exact action to be taken must be provided in the form of a motion that is complete, clear, and unambiguous. In this case, express written consent of every one of the members must be received, including via email or other electronic means, with the possible exception of members who have a conflict of interest. The action has not been approved if even one member has failed to respond in the affirmative. Action by unanimous written or electronic consent, instead of at a meeting, must be allowed by statute or the bylaws.

18.33 This alternative method of action has become more common with the availability of electronic consent. Because it is convenient, particularly in small bodies, this method can be easily abused to negate the intentionally deliberative decision-making process of a formal meeting. It should be reserved for situations when there is insufficient time to provide meeting notice and an action is widely supported and clearly necessary.

FAILURE TO CALL MEETINGS

18.34 If officers or directors fail to call a meeting in accordance with the organization's governing documents, members may demand that they send a call to the membership. This is especially critical if there is a significant action, such as an election, to be taken by the assembly. If the leadership fails to perform its duty to issue the call, statutes or the bylaws may provide that a group of members or a single member may call the meeting and designate the time and location. In such cases, the requirements of any applicable statute should be strictly met. In the absence of guidance in the governing documents or applicable statute, this parliamentary authority provides that a group representing 10 percent of the membership or any two officers are allowed to call the meeting and designate the time and location if it can be demonstrated that those who are responsible have failed to call a meeting.

CHAPTER 19. Electronic Meetings

19.1 *Electronic meetings* are not a new aspect of parliamentary procedure; however, advancing technology is making these types of meetings both more accessible and a more convenient method for people to gather and make decisions. This advancement makes meetings more readily available to members and changes the dynamics of what meeting organizers and attendees must consider to have an efficient meeting that also upholds the fundamental principles of parliamentary procedure. As the use of electronic meetings continues to expand, having clear rules and methods to conduct these meetings in a fair and effective manner is important.

19.2 The terminology related to meetings with a virtual component requires an initial understanding and definitions. A *virtual meeting* or an electronic meeting is an official assembly of the members of an organization or board during which the members participate entirely electronically. A hybrid meeting is an official assembly of the members of an organization or board during which some members meet in one or more physical locations, and some members participate virtually. Each of these meeting methods presents different challenges that must be considered.

19.3 In a meeting in which the participants do not all meet in a physical location but communicate through various technologies, the rights of absentees must be carefully protected through rules developed for this type of meeting.

19.4 Additionally, different types of rules are needed to protect the rights of those in attendance at meetings held electronically. Examples of these rules are recognizing members to speak; for taking a vote; and for ensuring that only members attend the meeting. As with any meeting, minutes must be produced. Organizations may need to develop procedures by which members can confirm their identities in cases where visual or voice identification of each participant is not possible. The rigidity of such procedures will depend on the technology available and the level of identification that meets the needs of the organization.

19.5 Nine broad topics must be addressed when considering and planning for a meeting with a virtual component:

1. characteristics of an electronic meeting;

2. notice;

3. quorum;

4. fairness in seeking and obtaining recognition;

5. making motions;

6. points of order and appeals;

7. debate;

8. voting; and

9. legal requirements.

19.6 Sample rules for convention rules for hybrid meetings are included in Appendix D.

CHARACTERISTICS OF AN ELECTRONIC MEETING

19.7 Electronic meetings are allowed unless the governing documents of an organization or applicable law specifically prohibits their use. However, electronic meetings must facilitate the exercise of the fundamental rights discussed in this parliamentary authority. These fundamental rights have been developed, refined, and vetted at in-person meetings over centuries, whereas electronic meetings have only been possible for the past few decades and have only been broadly accessible more recently.

19.8 The goal of any electronic meeting, other than to conduct the society's business, is to support group decision-making while complying with the fundamental principles of parliamentary procedure. This is best done by operating as closely to an in-person meeting as possible.

19.9 Any requirement in this parliamentary authority that would apply in an exclusively in-person meeting also applies to meetings with a virtual component. Any exceptions are expressly noted. Electronic meetings will inherently derive most of the rules governing their procedure from many other chapters in this book, such as Chapter 1, "Parliamentary Law," Chapter 2, "Fundamental Principles of Parliamentary Procedure," Chapter 3, "Rights of Members and Organizations," Chapter 18, "Types of Meetings," and Chapter 20, "Notice of Meetings and Proposals." However, this list should not be considered exhaustive. Consultation with a professional parliamentarian familiar with electronic meetings will help to identify essential meeting characteristics that should be incorporated into electronic meetings, and to evaluate the available technologies and vendors that are considered.

19.10 With advancing technology, organizations often desire to find a platform or service that attempts to solve all the concerns related to electronic deliberative assemblies, such as hosting the meeting, voting, registration, etc. It is unrealistic to expect that a single meeting platform will meet all needs or is the best option to do everything. Organizations should compile the technical tools and rules that satisfy the needs of their members instead of trying to change the organization's culture to match the available tools. For example, using one service to host the meeting and a separate service as a voting platform is usually advisable since each tool will be utilized for a specific purpose, and in some cases, the two purposes may be incompatible. Some organizations attempt to vote on the meeting platform but then realize that there are multiple voting members in a single location, many of whom are now disenfranchised by the single connection to the meeting. Additionally, any nonmembers attending may be permitted to vote improperly. Expecting a single platform to meet all the organization's needs would be comparable to expecting an in-person venue to provide ballots and election tellers as part of their meeting service.

NOTICE

19.11 The principles and rules established in Chapter 20, "Notice of Meetings and Proposals," remain in full force for meetings with a virtual component, except distinctions discussed below; however, if a meeting is to have a virtual component, the method by which members attend and participate must be made available to members prior to the start of the meeting.

19.12 Technical requirements may require that members preregister in advance of the meeting to be eligible to participate and vote at the meeting. For example, there may be a need to enter participants' information into the voting system. If such preregistration is required, it is incumbent upon meeting organizers to make information about this preregistration requirement available to all members as a part of the call to the meeting, and to minimize the time between this advance registration deadline and the beginning of the meeting.

19.13 A second distinction in notice requirements for electronic meetings is that a previously noticed in-person meeting can be changed to an electronic meeting if members receive the change in meeting method in a reasonable time frame. This rule allows meeting organizers the flexibility to alter a method of a meeting if circumstances require a change. For example, a meeting organizer may recognize that a quorum may not be achieved with a previously noticed in-person meeting, but if a virtual or hybrid meeting were an option, a quorum might be more easily obtained. Additionally, if the venue where the meeting is to take place is no longer available, this would not prevent the organization from conducting its business. If the meeting is noticed as an in-person meeting, there is no right to attend the meeting electronically; just as if the meeting is noticed as an electronic meeting, a member does not have the right to attend in person. The authority to call a meeting also includes the ability to determine or modify the method of meeting.

QUORUM

19.14 In addition to notice requirements, any organization must handle the challenges of determining quorum when conducting meetings with a virtual component. In some instances, it may be necessary to conduct a roll call that may be burdensome if the assembly is of any significant size. Instead, the assembly may conduct an electronic roll call using an electronic balloting system if the system can be set up so that only members entitled to participate in the roll call receive the electronic roll call or are able to cast ballots. This method can quickly determine the quorum for both virtual and hybrid meetings.

19.15 It is also important to note that in many cases, the number of people attending on a virtual platform may differ from the number of people entitled to vote. Staff, speakers, sign language interpreters, a parliamentarian, and technical support are all groups that may be online in the meeting but may not be entitled to vote. Often the total number of votes cast will be less than the total number of those attending the meeting, and, in some instances, this difference may give an impression of more members being present than are counted in determining a quorum.

FAIRNESS IN SEEKING AND OBTAINING RECOGNITION

19.16 One of the biggest hurdles any organization will need to solve to have a successful meeting with a virtual component is how to treat members fairly and equitably when attempting to seek and obtain recognition. Members should be recognized in the order in which they attempt to gain recognition, except for any circumstances that require preference in recognition. Additionally, if alternating speakers between pro and con is desired, methods for determining the view of the speaker must be determined and communicated.

19.17 Meeting organizers should use a digital recognition system for virtual and hybrid meetings. For virtual meetings, the system will be the same for each participating member. Hybrid meetings present a more substantial challenge since the members attending virtually will not be physically in front of the presiding officer, and the members attending in person may not have access to the same digital tools. One solution that an organization may consider is to have all members seek recognition in the same manner whether attending in person or virtually. An example of this is the use of a digital system accessible to each member, whether attending virtually or in person, by entering their information either on their own separate device or through a central monitoring station or as simple as a group text message. This would create a level playing field for those attending in different formats and ensure the presiding officer recognizes members in the order in which the electronic recognition system received the request for recognition. This method requires building a queue of members seeking recognition, like a line forming at a microphone in a fully in-person meeting.

19.18 A simpler, yet somewhat less fair, method is for the presiding officer to alternate calling on an in-person attendee followed by a virtual attendee. Whatever method is used must be clearly explained to all attending, so that every member present understands how to seek and obtain recognition.

19.19 Meeting organizers should develop processes to allow members to separately seek priority recognition for motions that are allowed to interrupt, such as Points of Order or Appeals. Some organizations allow the "raise hand" feature of the meeting platform to be used for interrupting motions; others may have a separate text list for priority recognition while still others may find it appropriate to allow for all interrupting motions to be made verbally without recognition. These same methods could be used for any other motions that the assembly allows to interrupt the proceedings.

19.20 The presiding officer should not allow this system to be abused or manipulated by members using the process to raise a point of order or other interrupting motion and then, once obtaining recognition, attempting to make a different motion or speak in debate. This should immediately be ruled out of order, just as it would be at an in-person meeting.

MAKING MOTIONS

19.21 Processing motions can be more cumbersome in meetings with a virtual component. Therefore, submitting and stating motions should be handled as designated by an adopted standing rule of order or a temporary rule. If no rule exists, the presiding officer may determine how motions are submitted; however, motions should be submitted in writing prior to the member seeking recognition. The motion must then be stated by the presiding officer and, if feasible, should be displayed for members to read.

19.22   Members making motions must still be recognized and move the adoption of the motion, even if there is a requirement that a written motion be submitted in advance of seeking recognition. Submitting a motion in a chat feature or to an email account does not replace the requirement of a member being recognized and formally making a motion at any meeting—whether in person, virtual, or hybrid.

POINTS OF ORDER AND APPEALS

19.23   Members must retain the ability to raise a point of order and to appeal in meetings with a virtual component. The requirement that a point of order be raised in a timely manner is not waived in these types of meetings; however, if the technology or the administration of the meeting prevents a member from being able to raise a timely point of order or an appeal, then the timeliness requirement should be relaxed subject to the discretion of the presiding officer, with that judgment subject to appeal.

DEBATE

19.24   Debate in meetings with a virtual component must be limited to the oral presentation of debate, meaning that written communications in a virtual meeting platform do not constitute a valid method of facilitating debate. In addition, digital recognition software should be structured to allow members to identify themselves, whether they are debating for or against a motion.

19.25   This system should work with the processes described in the Fairness in Seeking and Obtaining Recognition section mentioned above so that members attending virtually are treated fairly and equitably when participating in the discussion.

19.26   Allowing members to communicate in writing to all members, such as in a chat open to all attendees, violates rules related to fairness and decorum whether the meeting is entirely virtual or hybrid. In a virtual meeting, open chat can lead to abuses of decorum and presents a distraction from the speaker. In a hybrid assembly, the virtual attendees may have access to this feature and the in-person attendees may not, thus making this even more disparate. Just as verbal discussions among members who are not recognized would be a breach of decorum and not in order in a completely in-person meeting, nonverbal discussions constitute a similar breach, whether the meeting is in person, virtual, or hybrid.

VOTING

19.27 One of the most important aspects of any meeting is conducting the vote; however, the validity of votes is even more crucial when participants cannot observe the physical voting process. In addition, when voters are not participating in meetings by the same method, voting becomes even more of a challenge. Members should vote in the same method regardless of how they participate in the meeting. For example, it is improper for in-person members to vote with roll call, voice, or counted votes while members attending virtually vote electronically, and then for the organization to try to reconcile the different voting methods.

19.28 The use of general consent is a useful tool in these types of meetings if members can verbally object and they are given adequate time to object. If an objection is noted within a reasonable time frame after the presiding officer asks for objections, or announces that there is general consent, it is necessary for a formal vote to be taken.

19.29 Many meeting platforms have built-in polling features that may appear to satisfy the requirements for voting. However, it should be noted that in-person attendees may not have access to those platform tools, and would be disenfranchised in those instances. Additionally, some members entitled to vote may not be able to vote depending on their meeting software access. Some platforms restrict the polling platform to attendees only, and platform administrators may not be able to vote. Any polling system that does not allow all members to vote in an identical manner is not sufficient. Likewise, any voting system must preclude nonmembers from voting.

Balloting in a Virtual or Hybrid Meeting

19.30 Special care must be utilized when ballot votes are required or anticipated during a virtual or hybrid meeting. The polling feature of some meeting platforms may not meet the requirement for a ballot vote. There are three primary reasons for this:

1. The polling feature may allow voting by attendees who are not authorized to vote because it allows all meeting participants to participate in the poll, even those who are not entitled to vote, such as guests or staff.
2. The polling feature may not allow all voters to vote by limiting the role of hosts or cohosts, or not permitting individual votes for all participants on a single connection.
3. The polling feature may not ensure the confidentiality of individual member's votes. To be a satisfactory method of conducting a ballot vote in this environment, the platform must assure or guarantee the confidentiality of how a member voted. It must also ensure that no member or official of the organization conducting the meeting could uncover such information.

19.31 All the fundamental steps of ballot voting must still be followed and not every platform is capable of satisfying these requirements. For example:

1. An election ballot must allow for all the nominated candidates plus a spot for write-in candidates.
2. The electronic ballot may also require an option for abstentions if there are to be multiple races balloted on the same ballot. Some voting platforms do not allow a voter to move to the next race unless a selection is made in a prior race.
3. The platform must ensure that only those members allowed to vote are permitted to do so. One method of ensuring that the members permitted to vote are still in the virtual room is to announce that the polls are open and closed only to the participants viewing the meeting and not via email for each vote. Some systems use QR codes, which must be scanned to access the ballot.
4. In any hybrid meeting, it is important that all members vote via the same method. It is improper to vote by electronic ballot for part of the members and paper ballots by another portion of the members.

LEGAL REQUIREMENTS

19.32 Many state nonprofit codes have differing requirements for organizations conducting electronic or virtual meetings. While most states will defer to the bylaws to authorize or prohibit electronic meetings, an increasing trend among states is to allow the use of electronic meetings unless prohibited in the bylaws, or in the case of general membership meetings, they can be authorized by the board of directors.

19.33 There is a difference between electronic meetings and action outside a meeting. There are usually statutory provisions that cover both situations; however, the authorization of one does not mean the authorization of the other. Electronic meetings are intended to be deliberative assemblies conducted without being entirely in person and should retain the fundamental characteristics of in-person meetings.

OTHER CONSIDERATIONS

19.34 There are many procedural aspects to consider when it comes to electronic meetings. Logistic concerns may also impact an attendee's right to an efficient meeting. Any time there is a change as to how a meeting is conducted, the implications of the change must be explored, and the consequences must be addressed and resolved, preferably well in advance of the meeting. In general, virtual or hybrid meetings may take longer to accomplish the same amount of business because of the technical and logistical considerations. This section does not contain any specific rules that must be followed but is an attempt to lessen the learning curve for organizations attempting electronic meetings for the first time.

19.35 Electronic meetings offer many benefits, including greater participation and financial savings for the organization and members, but there may be notable downsides to the member experience. In part, this can be attributed to the lack of in-person interaction during recesses, breaks, or meals. Other downsides to the member experience can be caused by audio problems, including audio "breaking up," lack of synchronization between audio and video, and inability to hear because a speaker does not know how to unmute. Finally, the ready availability of distractions may tempt members, preventing them from remaining fully engaged and attentive during the entire meeting, which may reduce the quality of decision-making.

Accommodations

19.36 While it is not a procedural issue to provide accommodation, there may be legal or policy requirements. Many organizations offer sign language or on-screen transcription or translation services as part of their electronic meetings. This is like the situation at in-person meetings and may, at times, be of benefit to all members. In addition, it is important to note that a sign language interpreter may need to be highlighted or positioned so to be visible to attendees at all times.

19.37   On-screen transcription services often provide a valuable tool for attendees and the secretary after the meeting. However, these transcriptions do not constitute minutes and are often unreliable as they are automatically generated. Additionally, these services may be automatically enabled and start immediately. If there are times when the meeting has not been convened, this service should be disabled to ensure that conversations are not preserved when they would otherwise be confidential. This is especially the case during closed meetings.

19.38   Sign language and on-screen transcription are examples of accommodations but are not an exhaustive list. Discussion on the accommodations that may be needed by attending members should take place well in advance of the meeting.

Scheduling Concerns

19.39   One aspect for meeting organizers to consider is the amount of time members are at their electronic devices participating. Meeting organizers should build breaks into the schedule to allow attendees to participate fully in the business without experiencing electronic meeting fatigue.

19.40   Organizers should also be aware that members attending virtually may be in different time zones and this should be considered when setting meeting times to accommodate all participants as well as possible.

19.41   In compensation for the downsides of virtual meetings, where an in-person meeting might be scheduled for a single day, a virtual meeting may be divided into several shorter sessions, reducing meeting fatigue and allowing broader member participation.

Practice Makes Perfect

19.42   The most practical advice regarding electronic meetings is to practice. The platform, new voting methods, the process of seeking recognition, and displaying motions may be new concepts for some members attending, whether in person or virtually. Even when organizations and members are experienced with holding virtual meetings, technological changes will inevitably occur, perhaps without notice to the users. Many organizations may find it helpful to offer a technical session before the start of each meeting or convention to allow for greater comfort for those in attendance. Additionally, it will allow the processes to be tested and modified before the meeting. Working out any technical issues before substantive discussion or votes are taken in the meeting is ideal.

19.43 Practicing will not only make the presiding officer and meeting organizers more confident in the technology and planning of the meeting, but it may also expose weaknesses and deficiencies in the system. It will also allow the members to feel more confident in the systems put in place to support their meeting.

Technology Support Staff

19.44 Organizations that use electronic methods to distribute essential information pertaining to a meeting, conduct meetings, or take votes should consider hiring a technology consultant or consulting firm or using existing information technology staff to assist with these tasks. The technology staff should be prepared to address any technological problems that may arise and work with the officers, executive director, and the parliamentarian to ensure that the organization's electronic meetings and voting are conducted properly.

CHAPTER 20. **Notice of Meetings and Proposals**

IMPORTANCE OF NOTICE

20.1 Meetings, conventions, and certain important proposals that will come before the members for decision require advance notice to members. The courts will not uphold the decisions of a meeting if the notice requirements for the meeting, or for any action that requires notice, have not been met. If there is proof that notice of a meeting is purposely or negligently withheld from any member, actions taken at that meeting are not valid.[62,63] Such actions would still be invalid even when that member's vote would not have affected the result, as the member's participation in debate could have persuaded other members to change their votes. The only variation from this rule is that an affirmative vote of all the members may waive the lack of proper notice. For more information on this rule, see the section, Waiver of Notice, at the end of this chapter.

NOTICE PROTECTS MEMBERS

20.2 Common parliamentary law provides for the full protection of every member by strict enforcement of notice requirements before a meeting. It does not protect absentees who have had notice but who fail to attend, or members who come late or leave early. A member who has been sent notice of a meeting or a convention, or of an action that requires notice, and who does not attend, relinquishes the right of decision to those who are present. When proper notice has been given and a quorum is present, it cannot be contended that those members present are "not representative" or that the meeting is "not representative," since legally all members are equal.[64]

NOTICE OF MEETINGS

20.3 Notice of a meeting must be sent to all members unless notice is not required in accordance with the provisions in Chapter 18, the section on Regular Meetings. Unless prohibited by statute or the bylaws, organizations may provide notice through email. Statutory requirements for notice in the appropriate jurisdiction should be checked carefully prior to adopting rules authorizing notice via email or other means. Organizations need procedures for keeping relevant contact information current, as well as methods for providing notice to members without email addresses and/or internet access.

20.4 The notice must clearly indicate the date, the time, and the place of the meeting. For these purposes, a meeting held entirely telephonically or electronically is considered to be held in a separate place from any physical location, and complete instructions on how to attend the meeting, or how to register with the electronic system to be permitted to attend the meeting, must be included in the notice of such a meeting. A change in physical location of a meeting to a location within close proximity does not invalidate the notice of the meeting, provided that attendees arriving at the first location are directed to the second location. A change in an electronic meeting link or a change from an in-person meeting to an electronic meeting does not invalidate the notice of the meeting, provided that all members are notified of the change. Notice of any meeting sent so late that a substantial percentage of the members cannot attend is not a valid notice, even if all other requirements have been fulfilled.

20.5 Provisions for notice in the governing documents should include the acceptable methods for giving notice, including the timing of such notice, as it applies to special meetings, the annual meeting, and regular meetings if notice is required for such meetings. If the time of notice is not specified, notice should be given a reasonable time in advance, considering all the circumstances. Notices sent to the membership must state the following basic information:

1. the exact date and time of the meeting; and

2. the exact place of the meeting or that the meeting will be held virtually.

20.6 Additionally, any information that would assist a member in preparing for the meeting should be included.

20.7 *Convention notices* may also be referred to as a *call to the convention*. The notice must give the exact time and place of the convention and usually includes the method of accrediting delegates and directions for submitting resolutions, reports of officers and committees, and proposed amendments to the bylaws. The notice by the organization is given as provided in the bylaws or rules. A notice can be in the form of a greeting, or in any form that makes it clear that a convention is being held and provides the date, time, and location of that convention.

20.8 An annual meeting or a convention requires notice. Such meetings are usually held annually at the termination of the organizational year to elect or install officers and to hear reports. Annual meetings require notice to all members of the time and place of the meeting and of any business to be conducted that is unique to the annual meeting, such as election of officers. Conventions require notice to all delegates including the same information. The organization's governing documents may indicate the items of business to be covered at an annual meeting or convention, and if so, specific business need not be included in the notice unless it is a variation from the expected items.

20.9 Regular meetings require notice as designated in the organization's governing documents, and no notice is required if the governing documents of the organization provide for meetings to be held on specific regular dates—for example, the third Wednesday of each month. Regular meetings may also be established by resolution. Any regular meeting of an organization may transact any business not requiring advance notice. If, however, the officers responsible for giving notice know that a proposal of great importance, which may not require advance notice, will be brought up at a regular meeting, they should, as a matter of good faith, give notice of the proposal.

20.10 Special meetings require notice of date, time, and place of meetings, of specific proposals to be considered and decided, and of subjects to be reported on. At the meeting, the members may amend the proposals stated in the notice but cannot consider any business that is not stated or reasonably implied in the notice. For example, the motion stated in the notice, "to purchase a new car for the executive director," reasonably implies that if the noticed motion is adopted, the current system of renting a car for the executive director's use will be ended, and a motion to do so would be in order. Under this statement of purpose, however, the meeting cannot consider the employment of a consultant. For more information on special meetings, see Chapter 18.*

20.11 Continued meetings, that is, meetings that are a resumption of meetings that were adjourned to a particular hour or date, do not require notice. If either a regular or a special meeting that has been properly called votes

---

* For information on alternative notice options when the secretary neglects to send notice, see *Parliamentary Journal* Opinion 2008-527. For information on who calls the meeting when the board is recalcitrant, see Opinion 2013-582.

to adjourn to a later time to continue the meeting, this is sufficient notice. Good organizational practice, however, suggests that a notice of the continued meeting be sent to all members, at least electronically. The exception to this practice would be when notice would be futile, such as an additional day for a convention.

20.12 Notice of board and committee meetings must be sent as specified by the governing documents of the organization. If none is specified, reasonable notice must be sent to all members of the body that is meeting. Notice of meetings must be given for the first meeting of a special committee and the first meeting of a standing committee after any change in its membership, or after a change in the organizational year. All subsequent meetings of committees are considered continued meetings and do not require notice.

20.13 Special attention needs to be given to electronic meetings. The notice for such meetings must contain instructions on how members may attend and participate in the meeting. Some organizations require members to register for a meeting in advance, providing relevant information for verification. If this is the case, instructions relating to registration, including deadlines and contact information for any registration difficulties, must be clear. In any case, instructions must be provided in advance of every electronic meeting, even if the organization has held electronic meetings in the past. Due to security concerns, the link or meeting code may be sent to members shortly before the meeting. Current and accurate contact information for technological support should also be provided.

NOTICE OF PROPOSED ACTIONS AND SCOPE OF NOTICE

20.14 A proposal that according to the organization's governing documents requires advance notice cannot be considered at any meeting unless proper notice of the proposed action has been sent. Even with unanimous approval of the members present at a meeting, a proposal that was not noticed properly is invalid, with one exception as noted in the next section. Amendments to the bylaws or charter, sale of property, large and unusual expenditures, election of officers, and other items of similar importance require whatever notice is specified by the bylaws or rules of the organization. The proposals to be voted on must be stated specifically; this does not mean exactly verbatim but rather with sufficient information that a member receiving the notice will understand the purpose and intent of the proposal with sufficient clarity to come to the meeting prepared to discuss the question knowledgeably.[65]

20.15 Amendments to motions must fall within the scope of the notice given.[66] For example, if an organization's bylaws set the number of members of the board at 13 and notice was given to reduce the board to nine members, any amendment specifying a figure between nine and 13 would be in order, but an amendment increasing the number of members above 13, or reducing the number of board members below nine, would be out of order. The scope of notice relates to actions that can reasonably be expected to be adopted at the meeting. Actions that are between the status quo and the proposed action for which notice was given and amendments that are reasonably foreseeable are within the scope of notice.

20.16 When an action that required advance notice has been taken, any motion having the effect of voiding or changing the original action requires the same notice. For example, if a motion to lease property belonging to an organization originally required notice for its adoption, a motion to cancel the lease requires the same notice.

WAIVER OF NOTICE

20.17 If there was a mistake in a notice or a failure to send notice to every member and yet at the time the matter is introduced, every member is present at the meeting, and no one objects to the lack of notice, the members waive notice by the fact of their attendance and their participation in the meeting. Members may also waive notice by signing a written *waiver of notice* before, during, or after the meeting.

CHAPTER 21. Order of Business and Agenda

USUAL ORDER OF BUSINESS

21.1 An order of business is a blueprint for meetings. It is a defined sequence of the different categories of business in the order in which each will be called up during business meetings. Its purpose is to provide a systematic plan for the conduct of business. The agenda is not the order of business but is a specific list of items to be brought before the meeting and may be based on the order of business. An organization may wish to adopt, as a standing rule, a particular order of business that works best for itself. This should not be adopted as part of the bylaws because the bylaws cannot be suspended.

21.2 If the bylaws or standing rules of order do not include an order of business, parliamentary law has established the following pattern:

1. call to order;
2. disposition of previous meeting minutes;
3. *reports of officers*;
4. reports of governing board, standing committees, and special committees;
5. unfinished business;
6. new business;
7. announcements; and
8. adjournment.

21.3 When there is an invocation, an opening ceremony, preliminary remarks, a roll call, the formal establishment of a quorum, or approval of the agenda, these follow the call to order in the listed sequence. Some organizations include an informal item called the *good of the order*, or something similar, just before adjournment. This is an informal agenda item in which members may make suggestions for the improvement of the organization or suggest how the meeting's processes may be improved. No business may be conducted, and no motions may be proposed under this category.

21.4 Some organizations also include a program, such as a guest speaker or entertainment. The more common practice is to recess the business meeting prior to the program or activities of a social nature and adjourn afterward (to allow resumption of business for motions arising out of the program and courtesy motions) rather than to adjourn before the start of the program. It is incumbent on an organization to define an order of business that best meets the needs of the assembly. For example, a board of directors may have a different order of business than a general meeting of members. While most organizations use the traditional order of business shown above, or a variation thereof, some organizations structure the form around different segments of the organization's business. Others may opt for a structure based on the organization's strategic plan.

21.5 The order of business for a special meeting consists only of the call to order, consideration of the items of business stated in the notice of the meeting, and adjournment.

21.6 The order of business of a convention or annual meeting should be prepared to fulfill the needs of the organization and its members. When a program or schedule for a business meeting has been adopted by a convention or annual meeting and a time has been fixed for considering certain items of business, the following rules apply as they do in any meeting:

21.7 Timed Items and Scheduled Orders on the Agenda

Intention of the Body	Vote Required to Adopt Agenda	Rescheduling Rules
Timed items are to be considered scheduled orders	Two-thirds	Scheduled orders cannot be taken up ahead of the scheduled times
Timed items are estimates	Majority	Estimated times can be deviated from by general consent or majority vote
Some items are estimates; others are scheduled orders	Two-thirds	Those items marked as scheduled orders cannot be taken up ahead of the scheduled time; however, other items may be taken up at a different time by general consent or majority vote

AGENDA

21.8 An adopted agenda is a list of the specific items under each division of the order of business that the members agree to consider in the meeting.

Some organizations follow the practice of including in the agenda time frames or specific start times for each category of business or even for each agenda item. Each organization has its own needs, and, for some that have much business to accomplish in a limited time, that level of detail may be useful. Other organizations may find that such details remove needed flexibility.

21.9   The list under reports of officers, for example, would include the treasurer's report.

21.10   An agenda is usually prepared by the president in consultation with the secretary, with the assistance of staff, and is usually sent to the members before the meeting with additional meeting materials. This agenda is open to changes by the members by majority vote. An organization may, in its standard order of business, include a consent agenda or a *priority agenda* as defined later in this chapter. Either could also be included on the agenda for a particular meeting.

21.11   A proposed agenda is circulated before or at the meeting, and may be amended, before being adopted by majority vote or by general consent. The adoption of the agenda occurs after the meeting is called to order and a quorum is established. If the circulated agenda is not adopted, it is merely a guide and does not restrict the assembly from deviating from or adding to it.

21.12   Organizations that do not formally adopt a specific agenda are presumed to proceed under the standard order of business. Changes may be made to the standard order of business by majority vote.

FLEXIBILITY IN THE AGENDA

21.13   Unless the organization has a rule to the contrary, the use of an adopted agenda does not preclude other items of business from being added, deleted, or moved around on the agenda during the meeting. The presiding officer may suggest changes in the agenda but may not unilaterally make such changes. Except for special meetings, an agenda is flexible and may be changed by general consent or by a majority vote. For example, if a committee chair is absent but will be present later, the presiding officer may state, "The chair of the committee on finance is absent but will arrive later. Is there any objection to taking up the report of the special committee on offshore opportunities? There being no objection, the chair of the special committee will report." If any one member objects, a vote must be taken to authorize the variation from the agenda.

21.14 Items may be designated for a specific time by a two-thirds vote; in such cases, these scheduled orders take priority over any business currently pending at the designated time. Additionally, events such as elections or selection of a nominating committee may be required to occur at a specific meeting by the bylaws and should be included in the agenda as appropriate.

21.15 While an agenda for a special meeting may not be added to, the agenda items may be taken up in a different order either by general consent or a majority vote.

21.16 A continued meeting uses the same agenda as was in force at the meeting that created the continued meeting. See Chapter 15 and Chapter 18.

CONSENT AGENDA

21.17 Organizations with many routine or noncontroversial matters to approve can save time by use of a consent agenda, also called a consent calendar. This is a part of the printed agenda listing matters that are routine or expected to be noncontroversial and on which there are likely to be no questions, amendments, or debate.

21.18 Before taking action, the presiding officer allows time for the members to read the consent agenda to determine if it includes any matters on which a member may have a question, or which they would like to discuss or vote against. A single member has the right to remove any item from the consent agenda with no explanation required, in which case it is transferred to the regular agenda for separate consideration. A member may ask a question to clarify a consent agenda item without removing it from the consent agenda, but if this proves to be more than a clarification, the presiding officer can remove it and place it on the regular agenda. General consent to approve all remaining items is assumed when no one else rises to remove an item from the list. The presiding officer then announces that the remaining items are approved *en bloc*, saving the time that would be required for individual consideration and votes.

Presiding Officer:	The next business in order is the consideration of the consent agenda. Please review the consent agenda, and let the chair know if there are any items you would like removed for separate consideration, or any items for which you have a clarifying question. (pause) There being no items to be removed from the consent agenda, the items on the consent agenda are adopted.

21.19 An organization that includes a consent agenda in its standard order of business may adopt a standing rule of order to determine who shall establish the consent agenda. If there is no standing rule of order, it is prepared by the presiding officer in consultation with the secretary. Additionally, if the presiding officer or any member senses that the assembly could dispose of many items en bloc, such as multiple recommendations from a committee, the presiding officer or the member can propose that they be considered as a consent agenda. When this is proposed, any member may remove any item from the group of items for individual consideration, and the remainder are approved en bloc as outlined above.

21.20 See Chapter 25 for an extensive description of the use of the consent agenda by convention reference committees, which may differ in some ways from the discussion above.

PRIORITY AGENDA

21.21 A priority agenda allows a meeting to take up important agenda items, or business of significant consequence, early in the meeting. This is useful when there are many items of business and limited time for their consideration. The priority agenda permits these important items to be deliberated thoroughly and ensures that the most important decisions are reached in the meeting. The priority agenda is usually taken up after the consent agenda is disposed of.

21.22 An organization that includes a priority agenda in its standard order of business can adopt a standing rule of order to determine who decides the business items to be placed on a proposed priority agenda and their sequence. It could be, for example, the president of the organization alone, the officers, the executive committee, a reference committee, or a special committee. If not otherwise provided, it is the presiding officer in consultation with the secretary. The assembly has final say on the priority items and can amend the priority agenda by majority vote or by general consent.

ITEMS ON THE USUAL ORDER OF BUSINESS

Call to Order

21.23   The presiding officer, after ascertaining the presence of a quorum, calls the meeting to order at the scheduled time by rapping the gavel and announcing, "The meeting will come to order," or "The Annual Meeting of the American Institute of Parliamentarians is called to order." If a quorum is not present, see Chapter 22.

Disposition of Previous Meeting Minutes

21.24   Unless there is an invocation, an opening ceremony, a roll call, the formal establishment of a quorum, adoption of convention rules of order, or approval of the agenda, the first item of business is the review, correction, and approval of the minutes of the previous meetings. If minutes have been sent to each member by mail or electronically, they usually are not read. The presiding officer must, however, call for corrections to any minutes to be approved by the assembly. Corrections can be handled by general consent, but, in the case of a dispute, debate is permitted, and a majority vote is required to adopt a correction. After corrections, if any, the minutes can be adopted by general consent, or if in dispute, by a majority vote.

21.25   If a minutes approval committee has approved the minutes, the approval is announced and no further action is required, but corrections may still be offered by the Motion to Amend Something Previously Adopted.

Postponement of Disposition of Minutes

21.26   The approval of any unapproved minutes may be postponed to a certain time, including to a subsequent meeting, by general consent or by majority vote although this is generally not advisable. If the review of unapproved minutes has been postponed to the current meeting, the agenda lists them in chronological order for approval. For more information on minutes, see Chapter 23.

Reports of Officers

21.27   Other than the president and the treasurer, officers only report if responsible for an area of the organization that has been active since the previous meeting. If not otherwise provided in the organization's standard order of business, officers usually report in the order listed in the bylaws. The president typically reports on the state of the organization since the previous meeting, although this may be done by the *executive director* in organizations with professional staff.

21.28 The treasurer typically gives a brief report. This may consist simply of a verbal report of the cash on hand. The report may also include additional items such as outstanding obligations, or it may include a summary of income and expenditures since the previous meeting, with mention of any unusual items. Organizations should adopt a procedure specifying the intended level of detail. The presiding officer inquires whether there are any questions on the report for the treasurer. After any questions are answered, the presiding officer then states that the report of the treasurer will be filed. No action by the assembly is appropriate to be taken on such a report. Instead, only an audited financial report, typically prepared annually, is adopted by an assembly. For more information on financial reporting, see Chapter 32.

21.29 The secretary's report, if any, is usually limited to summarizing official correspondence. Significant correspondence, particularly from a parent organization, may be read in full.

Reports of Governing Board, Standing Committees, and Special Committees

21.30 When there is a report of the board of directors or governing board, this report comes first. The presiding officer calls on the chair of the board, then standing committees, and then special committees to report. Committees are called on in an order determined by the presiding officer when setting the agenda, subject to amendment by the assembly. The vice president or secretary often presents for the board when the president also serves as chair of the board. Written reports of committees are filed but not voted on, except when the organization's rules require specific reports to be approved by vote.

21.31 In constructing the proposed agenda, the presiding officer takes note of which committees, standing or special, are prepared to report or have been ordered to report at that specific meeting. Only those prepared or required to report are called upon. The reports are subject to late additions.

21.32 Unless otherwise provided by a standing rule of order, if an officer or committee also presents recommendations, these are considered and voted on immediately after the relevant report. Some organizations, however, adopt a rule requiring such items to be considered under new business. In organizations receiving reports from staff, customs or rules will determine the point in the order of business for such reports.

Unfinished Business

21.33 If there is any unfinished business, the presiding officer announces, "The next order of business is unfinished business," and introduces the first item of business under this section.

21.34 Unfinished business includes only two types of items:

1. any motion or report that was being considered and was interrupted when the previous meeting adjourned; and
2. any motion or report that was postponed to the current meeting but not set as an order for a particular hour.

21.35 The presiding officer presents an item of unfinished business to the assembly by stating, for example, "The resolution concerning the use of social media was pending at the time of adjournment of the last meeting and is now before the assembly for consideration. The secretary will read that motion." After the motion is read, the presiding officer continues, "Discussion is now in order on the motion as read by the secretary."

21.36 The fact that a subject has been discussed previously does not make it unfinished business. Items of business that were referred to a committee are not unfinished business. In addition, an item of business on the agenda that is never introduced because of adjournment is not unfinished business but may be placed on the next meeting's agenda as new business. With the assistance of the secretary or parliamentarian, the presiding officer determines whether there is any unfinished business for consideration and, if there is none, announces this fact and immediately proceeds to new business. If there is unfinished business, the presiding officer takes up the item interrupted by adjournment first, and then the postponed items in the order in which they were postponed.

21.37 The presiding officer should not ask for unfinished business but instead call up the item of business directly as follows:

Presiding Officer:	When the last meeting adjourned, the motion to plant a garden was on the floor. Is there any discussion on the motion to plant a garden?

21.38   An annual meeting of an organization with no other regular meetings has no unfinished business when it is called to order, although items may be postponed to this category of business during the meeting. Similarly, the first meeting of a board with a bylaws-mandated change in membership or the first day of a convention would not have unfinished business. See the rules on postponement discussed in Chapter 14.

New Business

21.39   The presiding officer opens new business by declaring, "New business is now in order."

21.40   New business includes any proposal that any member may wish to present to the assembly. If an agenda was adopted and items of business were placed under new business at that time, these items are automatically taken up in the designated sequence unless the assembly orders otherwise. The opportunity to present new proposals and business items assigned to other categories but inadvertently overlooked earlier continues until the meeting is declared adjourned.

21.41   New Business is in order, even if not included as a category on an adopted agenda.

Announcements

21.42   A meeting is expedited by having a regular place in the order of business for announcements. The presiding officer may make announcements and then call for announcements from members.

Adjournment

21.43   When a Motion to Adjourn has been made, seconded, and adopted, the presiding officer formally ends the meeting by declaring it adjourned. Alternatively, after asking, "Is there any further business?" and getting no response, the presiding officer assumes general consent and says, "There being no further business, the meeting is adjourned."

21.44 Unless there is no quorum present, the presiding officer cannot declare the meeting adjourned without a formal vote or general consent if any member wishes to bring up additional business. The decision on whether to adjourn is made by the members, not by the presiding officer.

21.45 If a Motion to Adjourn is adopted and announcements have not already been made, they are usually permitted by the presiding officer before the actual declaration of adjournment.

CHAPTER 22. Quorum

REQUIREMENT FOR A QUORUM

22.1 A quorum is the minimum number or proportion of the members of an organization that must be present at a meeting to transact business legally. If a quorum is not present, the presiding officer may call the meeting to order to establish that a meeting was held, but the organization may not transact business. However, agenda items that do not require a vote may be dealt with, such as hearing informational reports, hearing speeches by guests, and conducting programs. For meetings that are called to order and no quorum is established, voting on the Motions to Recess and to Adjourn is in order.

22.2 Urgent or emergency business can be conducted at the discretion of those in attendance. However, if not subsequently ratified at a meeting with a quorum present, all such actions are the responsibility of the individuals who voted in favor of the action at the inquorate meeting, not of the organization. In this instance, a member has a right to have their negative vote recorded in the minutes on demand. See Chapter 13 for information on the Motion to Ratify.

22.3 The minutes of an inquorate meeting will document that a meeting occurred, noting the absence of a quorum, and briefly describing the activities that were conducted.

QUORUM REQUIREMENTS

22.4 The bylaws of an organization should state the number or proportion of members that constitutes the quorum at membership meetings, board meetings, and committee meetings. In the absence of such a bylaw clause or applicable statutory provision, under parliamentary law:

1. in the case of membership organizations with a verifiable roll of members, the quorum is fixed at a majority of the voting members;[67] and
2. in the case of organizations with an indefinite number of members, such as some churches or neighborhood groups that do not charge dues, the voting members who attend a meeting, however few in number, constitute a quorum.[68]

22.5 A quorum requirement specifying either a proportion or a minimum number is also acceptable, for example, a quorum of "either 20 percent of the membership or seven people, whichever is lower." Quorum requirements should be clearly written so as not to be interpreted in more than one way.

22.6 At membership meetings, the quorum requirement of a majority is often too high, and most groups have a more realistic provision. The number required for a quorum should be small enough to ensure that a quorum will usually be present but large enough to protect the organization against decisions being made by a small minority of the members. A mass meeting or an organization without a definite membership counts the members present, no matter what their number, as a quorum. In organizations with a fluctuating membership, it may be wise to select a *proportion of the membership* as a quorum, so the quorum will vary as the membership varies. An organization might provide, for example, that one-eighth or one-tenth of the members constitutes a quorum.

22.7 However, using a proportion of the membership as the quorum may cause disputes when the membership number is not easily known at any instant in time. When a fixed number is required for a quorum, a reduction or increase in the number of members of the organization does not alter the number constituting a quorum. Applicable corporate law may impact an incorporated organization's decision on establishing a minimum quorum provision.

22.8 In conventions where the business of the organization is conducted by delegates who are expected to be present at all business meetings, the required quorum should be a majority of the delegates registered at the convention. For more information about the definition of a delegate or a quorum at a convention, see Chapter 24.

22.9 In some organizations, a quorum is defined as a proportion of members present and a proportion of constituencies present. For example, a quorum can be defined as 200 members present, representing at least 25 member clubs. This type of quorum is called a *qualified quorum*. It is useful when an organization requires a balance of representation from constituencies, or geographic regions, and members.

22.10 In boards and committees, the quorum is a majority of the current members of the board or committee then in office unless set at a different level in the organization's governing documents or by statute. Neither a board nor a committee can set its own quorum unless expressly granted this authority by the organization's rules.

COMPUTING A QUORUM

22.11   A quorum always refers to the number of members present, not to the number voting. If a quorum is present, a vote is valid even though fewer members than the number specified as the quorum vote.

22.12   In computing a quorum, only members in good standing are counted. The meaning of the phrase *in good standing* varies with different organizations according to their bylaws. (See the default definition of this term in the *Glossary of Parliamentary Terms*, and further explanations in Chapters 3 and 5.) The presiding officer, if a member, is counted in computing a quorum.

22.13   Other members who are *ex officio members* are counted in determining the number required for a quorum unless the governing documents or statute direct otherwise. These individuals may be designated as consultants or otherwise excluded from the computation of or presence of a quorum in the governing documents if the organization wishes.

22.14   If a quorum is present, a majority of those voting, which is often a small proportion of the total membership, has the right to make decisions for the organization. This fact suggests that rigorous and exacting requirements for notifying all members of meetings must be observed so that all members will have an opportunity to attend and vote.

22.15   A member of the board may be disqualified from voting on a particular question because of personal interest or benefit in it. Organizations should look to applicable law in their jurisdiction to ensure compliance with the quorum requirements and specifically where a member has declared a personal interest in a question currently before the body. For organizations adopting this parliamentary authority, a board member with a personal interest may not vote or debate on the matter but, if present, is counted toward the quorum unless the bylaws of the organization or applicable law requires otherwise.

RAISING A QUESTION ON QUORUM

22.16   It is the duty of the presiding officer to notify the assembly whenever it becomes apparent that a quorum is not present. If the presiding officer fails to do so, any member who doubts that a quorum is present at a particular time during a meeting has the right to rise to a point of order and request that the members be counted, known as a *quorum call*. A member may also rise to a Parliamentary Inquiry to inquire whether a quorum is present.

22.17   In either instance, if there is a possibility of achieving a quorum by gathering members from outside the meeting hall, such steps are permissible to achieve a quorum and continue the meeting.

22.18   The presence of a quorum is determined by counting the members present or by calling the roll. The presence or absence of a quorum at any time can be established by entering the number present in the minutes. Repeatedly questioning the presence of a quorum cannot be used for the purpose of delay.

PRESUMPTION OF A QUORUM

22.19   If the presence of a quorum is to be questioned, it must be raised at the time of voting on a particular motion or before the next item of business has begun. It cannot be raised later.

22.20   Unless the minutes document that a quorum was not present at the time of voting on a motion, it is presumed that since the minutes show that a quorum was present when the meeting began, a quorum continued to be present until recess or adjournment. It is not permissible at some later time to question the validity of an action on the grounds that there was not a quorum present at the time the vote was taken.[69]

22.21   Some organizations, by custom, will reestablish the presence of a quorum after a substantial break in the proceedings or after an overnight recess.

CHAPTER 23. Minutes

IMPORTANCE OF MINUTES

23.1 Minutes are the legal history and record of official actions of an organization. Minutes are the formal record of a *deliberative assembly*'s proceedings, approved (as corrected, if necessary) by the assembly.[70] Minutes are not a substitute for attendance at meetings but, instead, provide a record of reports and decisions made at a meeting on behalf of the entire membership. The accuracy of minutes is essential. The documents are used by auditors as proof of financial actions authorized by the organization and by courts as evidence of actions taken.

RESPONSIBILITY FOR ACCURATE MINUTES

23.2 The secretary is responsible for recording all actions taken at business meetings, preparing proposed or draft minutes, recording any corrections, and certifying the official minutes by signing them when approved by the organization. If the approved minutes are in an electronic format, a digital signature must be affixed when they are approved. The members of the body that held a meeting bear the final responsibility for identifying errors and approving the minutes of that meeting.

23.3 A verbatim record or recording of the meeting is not the official record. A verbatim record or recording contains elements, such as debate, that should not be included in the formal minutes. These transcripts or recordings may be used by the secretary as an aid in preparing the proposed minutes, but do not take the place of the minutes document.

23.4 The secretary is responsible for the completeness and accuracy of the proposed minutes. If the secretary is absent from a meeting, the assembly elects a temporary secretary for that meeting. The notes taken by the secretary during a meeting are not an official document but are considered to be informal notes; once the proposed minutes are approved, the informal notes are no longer required and can be discarded.

MINUTES FORMAT

23.5 The format of minutes should meet several specific objectives: The minutes should be easy to review for pertinent actions and contain the essential information required by the organization. The use of a template allows an organization to establish a consistent format that is easily duplicated from meeting to meeting and that meets the basic requirements in an easy to read form.

23.6 There are several formats that may be used, and each organization should develop the one that works for it. The complexity of the organization's meetings may determine the format chosen. For an example of model minutes using the subject format, see Appendix E. Two other possible formats for minutes are available online at www.aipstandardcode.com.

MINUTES PREPARATION

23.7 The secretary should prepare the minutes as soon as possible after a meeting while the notes are still meaningful. A delay in preparing the minutes may result in misinterpretation of the notes taken during the meeting. In some instances, an employee or other third party may prepare the minutes under the secretary's direction, but only the elected secretary or the temporary secretary may sign them.

ACCESS TO MINUTES

23.8 The secretary is the custodian of the official minutes. The minutes of a general membership meeting or convention are open to inspection by members of the organization.[71] Except when the law or bylaws indicate otherwise, minutes of a board or committee meeting are available only to current members of the board or committee, although the board or committee may vote to make them more widely available for appropriate purposes. In the case of some incorporated organizations or public bodies, the law may require that the minutes of open sessions be available to members or to the public.

23.9 Current members have access to all minutes of that body; however, once a member leaves the body, that individual no longer has the right to access the minutes, even of the meetings that the member attended.

23.10   The requirements for a member to maintain confidentiality of closed meeting actions, including closed meeting minutes, remain even after the member has left the body.

CONTENT OF MINUTES

23.11   Minutes are generally a record of all actions and proceedings but are not a record of discussion. The opening paragraph contains the following information:

1. the date, hour, and place at which the meeting was called to order;
2. the type of meeting—regular, special, or continued;
3. the name of the presiding officer; and
4. the name of the person responsible for preparing the minutes—secretary or temporary secretary.

23.12   A subsequent paragraph should indicate that a quorum was present either by declaration of the chair, by recording the number of members present, by listing a roll call of members, or by noting that the credentials report was adopted.

23.13   A copy of the notice or call to the meeting should be included or attached to the minutes of a special meeting.

23.14   Each action of the assembly should be recorded in a separate paragraph. The minutes record all main motions or resolutions that were stated by the presiding officer and the way in which the assembly disposed of each such motion, whether temporarily or permanently. The minutes record the wording of the motion as it was disposed of.

23.15   Some organizations do not include the name of the maker of the motion, as this may lead to confusion when the motion has been substantially modified and no longer is the same proposal the member originally presented. If the mover of the motion is indicated in the minutes, it is good practice to record both the original motion and the motion in its final form. In any event, the name of the seconder is not included in the minutes.

23.16   When a vote is counted, the number voting on each side is recorded. In a roll call vote, each member's vote is recorded in the minutes or an attachment. Remarks of a member wishing to state a dissent or position on a motion, or a record of an individual member's vote other than as part of a roll call vote, are not recorded unless a motion permitting such action is adopted by majority vote or such action is required by law. An exception for action taken in inquorate meetings is discussed in Chapter 22. If a director or officer has declared a conflict of interest and therefore has not voted on a motion, the declaration and abstention are both recorded. A motion withdrawn after being stated by the presiding officer is recorded in the minutes. If a motion is withdrawn before it is stated by the presiding officer, it is regarded as never having been made and is not recorded in the minutes.

23.17 Notices given at a meeting are recorded in the minutes if they affect a future action at a later meeting. For example, if notice of a bylaw amendment must be given prior to its consideration, and such notice is given at the current meeting, that notice is included in the minutes of the current meeting.

23.18 Each report given is listed with the name of the member presenting the report, and any action that was taken. A summary of the report, however, is not included. Copies of the complete report may be attached to the official minutes but are not approved as part of those minutes. If the report is filed separately, the minutes include a reference to where the report may be found. Reports that are attached to the minutes are available to members who have the authority to access those minutes.

23.19 Points of order and appeals are included in the minutes, along with the presiding officer's ruling and the reasons for it. Such rulings, appeals, and reasons for the rulings are important as persuasive precedents for the organization. They can be used as references for future presiding officers and assemblies.

ITEMS THAT SHOULD NOT BE INCLUDED IN MINUTES

23.20 Minutes do not contain procedural motions that are handled during deliberation of the main motion, except when they affect future action, as when a meeting votes to adjourn with a main motion pending or a Motion to Refer to a Committee or a Motion to Postpone to a Certain Time carries a main motion and any pending amendments forward to a subsequent meeting. For example, primary amendments are not included unless they are adopted, in which case they are reflected in the wording of the main motion as finally disposed of. Likewise, when a Motion to Limit or Extend Debate or to Close Debate and Vote Immediately is adopted, it is not included in the minutes. Motions to Recess, unless needed for clarity, are also not included.

23.21 The names of seconders are not included in the minutes unless required by the governing documents of the organization.

23.22 Minutes never contain personal opinions, personal interpretations, or comments. Descriptive or judgmental phrases, such as "a heated discussion," have no place in a factual record of business and may lead to disputes and even legal consequences. Neither debate, nor points made in debate, nor the names of those speaking in debate are included in the minutes unless the body directs any such inclusions by majority vote. Programs are referred to by title, subject, or description and do not include any summaries or personal impressions.

23.23 Criticism of members is never included except when action on a motion to censure or reprimand a member has been stated.

CLOSED MEETING MINUTES

23.24 Minutes of a closed meeting or the closed portions of a meeting should be prepared by the secretary and maintained separately from the regular minutes of the organization. These minutes are prepared in the same format as regular meeting minutes. Minutes of a closed meeting must be approved only in a closed meeting. Some or all of the final actions taken during the closed meeting may be disclosed by adopting a motion in the closed meeting authorizing such a report. Those final actions are then recorded in the minutes of the regular meeting of the organization as well as in the minutes of the closed meeting.

23.25 The minutes of the regular meeting may contain a note such as: "The assembly, joined by legal counsel and the parliamentarian, entered closed session at 11:15 a.m." and "The assembly returned to open session at 12:10 p.m.," along with any reports authorized in the closed session for inclusion in the regular meeting minutes.

DISPOSITION OF MINUTES

23.26 Before the assembly approves the minutes, they are merely the secretary's draft of what happened at the meeting. Minutes become the official record of the organization only after approval. The correction and approval of the minutes at the next regular meeting are the duty of the assembly unless that authority has been given to a minutes approval committee as described in the next section, Approval of Minutes by a Minutes Approval Committee.

23.27 At the appropriate place in the order of business, the presiding officer calls on the secretary to present the proposed minutes. It is common practice for organizations to distribute these draft minutes to the membership in electronic or written form prior to the meeting, and they are only read aloud in full if no copies are available to the assembly. Draft or proposed minutes should be clearly identified as such until approved.

23.28 The presiding officer asks, "Are there any corrections to the minutes?" If no corrections are suggested, the presiding officer declares the minutes approved as presented.

23.29 When corrections are suggested, the presiding officer may seek general consent by saying, "If there is no objection, the correction pointed out by Member A will be made." If there is an objection to a proposed correction, the presiding officer assumes the motion to approve the correction, which requires a majority vote to adopt. Corrections are incorporated directly into the draft minutes of the meeting for which the corrections were made.

23.30 When no further corrections are suggested, the presiding officer declares the minutes approved as corrected. The secretary certifies them as the officially approved minutes, perhaps by writing the word *Approved* at the end of the document, entering the date of approval, and signing the document.

23.31 The only changes that may be made to the minutes are to add or correct them to accurately reflect the actions that took place during the original meeting, or to remove language that should not be included in the minutes. Additional information or actions that were taken after the close of the meeting may not be added to the pending minutes. It is not in order to change the proposed minutes to remove motions adopted or actions taken to pretend that it did not occur.

23.32 If an error in the minutes is discovered after the minutes have been approved, the error may be corrected by the assembly, regardless of the lapse of time, by a majority vote on a Motion to Amend a Previous Action.

23.33 The presentation of the proposed minutes may be postponed. However, organizations should not make a practice of postponing the review and *approval of minutes* since delay makes it more difficult for members to detect errors. Until the minutes are approved by the assembly or its designated minutes approval committee, they are not official, and they should not be approved until they have been reviewed by the assembly or by a designated committee.

APPROVAL OF MINUTES BY A MINUTES APPROVAL COMMITTEE

23.34 Often, organizations appoint a committee that has the authority to approve the minutes. Such a committee may be appointed to relieve the full body of the time required to approve minutes, to ensure that approved minutes are available more promptly, or to ensure that those organizations that do not meet frequently have a method for timely correction and approval of minutes. Because the assembly has the authority to approve its own minutes, the authority for a minutes approval committee should be included in the organization's governing documents or granted by adoption of a motion. Usually, the committee is given complete authority to approve the final minutes and report to the assembly. The minutes may be corrected by the assembly if an error is found in the future. The minutes approval committee may be a standing committee, a special committee appointed at the beginning of the meeting, or the executive committee or governing board that is given this responsibility.

23.35 To carry out their responsibilities, members of the minutes approval committee will likely find it necessary to take their own notes at the meeting in the same way that the secretary must take such notes, and therefore should be appointed as early as possible.

23.36 The secretary's draft of the minutes is sent to the minutes approval committee. The committee members are expected to respond to the secretary with corrections in a timely manner. The secretary will then compose the final draft based on the editing from the committee and obtain the committee's approval before submitting it to the organization.

23.37 The minutes approval committee is the delegated authority over the content of the document. The secretary's notes of the meeting are only a draft until approved by the committee. The secretary, if in disagreement with the approved minutes, may offer a motion with a proposed correction, as may any member of the assembly. If there is such a proposed correction, the assembly will determine the final text by majority vote.

PUBLISHED MEETING REPORTS

23.38 Some organizations provide members with a record of their activities in published meeting reports. Such reports may be distributed to all members of the organization or selected subgroups. While minutes are generally limited to the substantive action items taken at a meeting, published meeting reports may contain additional information.

23.39 Documents published on the website, in newsletters, or in other organizational communications are often a summary of actions taken at a meeting. The intent is to keep members aware, in a simplified format, of actions taken. While these various types of meeting reports may be a useful practice, they do not replace the need for a formal set of official minutes with proper content.

RETENTION OF MINUTES

23.40 An exact copy of the official, approved minutes should be entered in a suitable record format and kept in a safe place. If minutes of the organization are in digital form, it is important that secure backup copies are made and can be made readily available when needed.

23.41 Signed minutes should be maintained with the same security measures as other legal documents of the organization.[72]

23.42 Electronic archiving is the standard for most organizations. Most states recognize legal documents as those that may be retrieved into hard copy. If various versions of electronic files of minutes occur due to corrections, the versions should be clearly identified and dated, with the currently correct version always identified as official in some way and with draft or prior versions deleted as appropriate. At the close of a term, a hard copy or a retrievable electronic copy of the approved minutes and all legal documents of the organization for that term should be kept in a safe location for legal and historical purposes.

"DISPENSING WITH THE READING OF THE MINUTES"

23.43 Members sometimes make a motion to dispense with the reading of the minutes. However, this creates problems because of the uncertainty of the meaning of this motion. This parliamentary authority does not require formal reading of the minutes although members need to be able to review them prior to approval as discussed above.

23.44 A motion to delay the review until later in the meeting should be worded as "that the approval of the minutes be postponed to (time)." If approval of the minutes is postponed to a later meeting, they are taken up in the order of the oldest to the most current meeting and the minutes are approved individually, although they may be approved en bloc if there is no objection. Postponement of approval of minutes to a future meeting does not place that approval under unfinished business; the postponed approvals are considered in the order of business designated for approval of minutes.

23.45 Using a motion to "dispense with the review of the minutes" to avoid considering the minutes at all is not in order. The minutes are the official document and must be approved to provide a legal record of the meeting.

COMMITTEE MINUTES

23.46 Minutes, if kept during committee meetings, should have sufficient content to support the work of the committee and are usually less formal than minutes of a board or assembly. In committees, minutes may be kept by the committee chair or a secretary. Committee minutes are generally brief, but in some cases, may include summaries of the discussion to be referenced to prepare the committee's report; however, the minutes are not the committee report and should not be offered as such.

23.47 Committee minutes are open only to the members of the committee unless ordered to be produced by the entity establishing the committee.

CHAPTER 24. Conventions and Their Committees

24.1 A convention of an organization is a scheduled single meeting or a series of meetings that follow in close succession. Regardless of the number of meetings comprising the convention, it is regarded as a single meeting. A convention must be provided for in the bylaws. Organizations that hold their business meetings in convention format operate through a body of delegates, selected in accordance with the governing documents, to represent the general membership. In addition to delegates, a convention often provides an opportunity for all members from geographically diverse areas, often at the state/provincial, national, or international level, to come together. Organizations most commonly hold a yearly convention, although it may be held more or less frequently.

24.2 During the convention, the voting members assemble to transact important business. In addition to the conduct of business, the convention may offer educational sessions, social gatherings, and updates in the organization's particular field, as well as opportunities to exchange ideas and experiences and to enjoy the fellowship of others who share a common interest.

24.3 While every member of an organization is ordinarily allowed to attend the convention, in larger organizations the business is commonly conducted by a smaller legislative body provided for in the bylaws, such as a house of delegates or other representative delegate assembly.

24.4 Business conducted by the assembly may include election of officers, consideration of informational reports, and action on resolutions. The assembly often carries out much of its preparatory and deliberative work through standing or special committees of the organization or convention committees in advance of the convention itself. These committees, while they are officially created by the convention itself, are, in reality, formed by the body authorized to call the convention.

DELEGATES AND ALTERNATES

24.5 The bylaws will provide for the composition of a delegate assembly and its powers. Delegates are usually selected by the various constituent, component, and affiliate groups, or chapters or branches of the parent organization to represent the constituency that selected the delegate. The applicable governing documents may also provide for at-large delegates, who typically do not represent a single constituent unit. Some or all officers, committee chairs, or other members designated in the bylaws may serve as members of the convention with full rights unless specified otherwise. Usually, each convention has its own body of delegates whose status as delegates ends with the final adjournment of the assembly.

24.6 It is the responsibility of delegates (or other voting members) to become educated about the business to be conducted by the assembly, both before and during the convention, and to act in the best interests of the organization as a whole. The actions of the assembly determine the fundamental direction of the entire organization until the next convention, providing for its policies, programs, and use of resources. Actions of the assembly may facilitate or block the ability of the organization's leadership to move the organization in a particular direction in the immediate future.

24.7 While delegates should attempt to communicate with their constituents and to learn their opinions, values, and concerns, it is usually not wise for delegates to be instructed by their constituents to take specific actions on items of business. The delegates need to be free to listen to the discussion, weigh the pros and cons, and vote according to what appears to be the wisest course for the organization. The members whom the delegates represent may be unaware of the full range of arguments and information to be presented at the convention and cannot know the final wording of the proposed action if it is amended.

24.8 Delegates also have a responsibility to report to their constituencies on the actions taken and to explain the facts and arguments that resulted in the decisions that were made.

24.9 The bodies selecting delegates are often authorized to select alternates as well. The duties of alternates may include but are not limited to:

1. serving in place of a delegate who is unable to attend all or part of the meetings;

2. learning about the operation of the organization and its convention and becoming educated in the matters of concern to the assembly; and

3. assisting in communicating the concerns of constituents to the assembly's members and communicating the business of the assembly to their constituents. In many organizations, alternates have virtually identical responsibilities as the delegates but without the right to vote.

DELEGATE NOMINEES

24.10 A person designated by a constituent unit as a delegate is a *delegate nominee*. For the purposes of determining a quorum at a convention, a delegate nominee does not become a delegate until the individual has registered for the convention, paid the required fee if any, appeared at the convention, either in person or virtually, and been at least preliminarily seated as a delegate by the credentials committee unless otherwise stated in the organization's governing documents. This fact does not prevent the convention committees from completing their duties prior to the convention as if they were delegates.

24.11 Unless otherwise specified in the governing documents, a quorum for a convention is a majority of the delegates as defined above.

CONVENTION COMMITTEES

24.12 Committees common to most conventions are the credentials committee, convention rules committee, and the program committee. Other committees described below, such as the tellers committee and bylaws or governance committee, may be committees of the organization that are also assigned convention-related duties or can be convention-only committees that only exist in anticipation of the convention and dissolve when the convention finally adjourns.

24.13 Adoption of the credentials committee's report establishes the voting body and is followed immediately by consideration and adoption of the reports of the convention rules committee and the program committee.

24.14 Organizations with a high volume of resolutions to consider often provide for one or more reference committees, sometimes referred to as resolutions committees. The ultimate role of these committees is to assist delegates in their decision-making by summarizing facts and arguments and recommending actions on resolutions. These committees often conduct hearings to aid in their duties. For more information on reference committees, see Chapter 25.

CREDENTIALS COMMITTEE

Duties of the Credentials Committee

24.15 A convention credential consists of documents and/or other items such as lanyards or badges identifying members who may be admitted to the business sessions and who are entitled to vote. Convention credentials are issued by the credentials committee, which may be either a standing committee of the organization or a committee of the convention. This committee has duties specific to the convention for which it is created, which are performed ahead of and during the convention, even though the convention hasn't been officially constituted. The credentials committee examines the records submitted by the organization or constituent units identifying delegate nominees or alternate nominees and authorizes the issuance of convention credentials to voting members.

24.16 The credentials committee maintains a continuously updated count and roster of the members in attendance, to assist the presiding officer in determining the presence of a quorum or to assist in the conduct of a roll call vote.

24.17 The bylaws, convention rules, or a vote of the assembly may assign duties related to supervision of voting and election procedure to the credentials committee.

The Credentials Committee Report

24.18 The credentials committee must report before any item of business can be presented to the voting body for decision at the first meeting of the assembly, including challenges to the actual holding or validity of the convention. The initial report of the credentials committee must include, at a minimum, the list of the members entitled to vote. When adopted by those members on the list, this report becomes the official roll of the voting members, who may then vote on any supplemental reports, as well as all other business of the assembly. The credentials committee's report is adopted by a majority vote.

24.19 Language similar to the following is used for the adoption of the credentials report:

Presiding Officer:	The credentials committee is responsible for recommending the roll of delegates and alternates who will serve for the remainder of this convention and hears challenges concerning the seating of delegates and alternates, if any are made. Will the chair of the credentials committee please report?
Credentialing Chair:	The credentials committee submits the roll of delegates who have been registered up until (state time) and recommends that these delegates be seated at this convention. By direction of the committee, I move adoption of the credentials committee report.

Challenging the Seating of Delegates

24.20   If the committee has a question regarding the eligibility of a member to serve as a delegate, this committee brings the question to the seated delegates during adoption of the credentials report and may make recommendations on whether the member should serve in the assembly. If the committee's recommendation is that the delegate not be seated, the challenged delegate may not vote on any other challenged delegates until seated by the assembly.

24.21   Alternatively, there may be a challenge to a member's right, or even a delegation's right, to be seated. Only delegates listed on the credentials report, or who have been added to the report via an adopted amendment, may challenge the credentials of other delegates on the credentials committee report. Such a challenge is presented while the motion to adopt the credentials report is pending.

24.22   No challenge of delegates or delegations may involve more than one delegation at a time. A challenge to a delegate or delegation is a primary amendment to the credentials committee's report and only one primary amendment can be considered at one time. Delegates challenged from the floor during the credentials report may not vote on the challenge against themselves but may vote on other challenges.

Presiding Officer:	It has been moved that the credentials report be adopted. Is there any discussion?
Member: (after gaining recognition)	I move to amend the report by striking out "John Smith" and inserting "Alice Sturgis." (Another member seconds.)

24.23   Only those delegates on the credentials report are counted in establishing the number of delegates required for a quorum (if a percentage of the delegates), and only delegates currently on the credentials report are counted to determine if that quorum is present. Those currently involved in a challenge cannot be considered in the determination of a quorum. This is true no matter how large the delegation is. This also means that the quorum may change while a motion to adopt the credentials report is being considered as delegates or delegations are added.

24.24   The following table compares the voting rights of potential delegates on the initial credentials committee report and on any challenges.

Who	Vote on Challenged Credentials?	Vote on Final Report?
Delegates on the Roll from the Credentials Committee		
Not subject to a challenge	Yes	Yes
Who become challenged	Yes, on all challenges but their own. If removed from the report, the individual loses all delegate rights.	Yes, if seated
Delegates NOT on the Roll from the Credentials Committee		
Who are presented by the credentials committee as part of a challenge	No, unless seated by the convention, then they can vote on subsequent challenges.	Yes, if seated
Who are the subject of an amendment to the report	No, unless added to the report, then they can vote on subsequent challenges.	Yes, if seated

Transferring Credentials

24.25   The execution of the credentialing committee's duties obviously requires the cooperation of delegates in observing rules regarding entering and exiting the meeting room. Unless the convention rules state otherwise, delegates may only transfer their credentials, voting cards, ballot books, voting keypads, or other indicators of voting privileges to an alternate through the credentials committee.

24.26   Some organizations may have rules authorizing individual delegates to transfer all, or some, of the privileges of assembly membership to alternates, but to do so with less involvement of the credentials committee, which may simply provide documentation to facilitate the transfer. Such rules may be useful in large assemblies, in which the more frequent, but temporary, substitution of alternates is desired to permit any special knowledge or expertise of alternates to be applied to the consideration of particular issues.

24.27   A supplemental report is usually made at least daily since new delegates and members arrive and are credentialed as eligible to vote or alternates are substituted for the delegates. Supplemental reports may be requested before critical votes or elections to document the continued presence of a quorum and to determine the number of delegates. Unless otherwise provided in the bylaws or convention rules, newly registered delegates may participate and vote immediately upon receipt of credentials from the committee and do not have to await the approval of the next supplemental report. The credentials committee stays on duty during the business meetings.

Registration Report

24.28   Although various types of reports may be presented, it is important to understand that only the roll of delegates is adopted. In many organizations it is also customary, if there are various classes of membership in attendance at the convention, for the credentials committee to include a delegate breakdown such as the number of officers, state presidents, and delegates.

24.29   In some organizations, a separate registration report, listing those who are alternates, non-voting members, and guests, is also produced for informational purposes. Sometimes the report will include information on which components and geographical areas are represented and in what strength. This demographic information may be interesting and useful but is not essential to the most important purpose of the credentials report, which is establishing and maintaining the roster and count of voting members of the assembly.

CONVENTION RULES COMMITTEE

24.30   The convention rules committee recommends to the assembly a set of convention rules that define the operating procedure that will be followed during the convention when it is desired to vary from, or add to, the provisions of the parliamentary authority. These rules govern how the assembly conducts its business and must, of course, not conflict with any convention procedures found in the bylaws or other higher-ranking documents of authority.

24.31   The convention rules committee's report is submitted immediately after the credentials committee's report. The convention rules often are the same from convention to convention and are usually published and distributed to the voting members in advance of the convention, identifying any proposed changes from previously adopted rules. Unless otherwise provided in statute, the bylaws, or standing rules of order, the convention rules are adopted by a majority vote and, once adopted, may be amended, repealed, or suspended by a two-thirds vote. When a convention rule is repealed, it defaults to the rule in the adopted parliamentary authority. When a rule is suspended, it is to permit a certain action to be taken that otherwise could not be taken under the rules. For more information on the Motion to Suspend the Rules, see Chapter 16.

24.32   The rules of one convention do not carry forward to subsequent conventions unless the organization's governing documents state otherwise. If the organization's governing documents provide for the convention rules to continue from year to year, each convention does not need to adopt the rules; instead, changing these rules would require a two-thirds vote unless the governing documents set a different threshold.

24.33   The convention rules ordinarily cover subjects such as:

1. seating of delegates and others;
2. recognition for speaking;
3. limits on debate; and
4. privileges of nonvoting members.

24.34   Some assemblies may designate special microphones and other ways of obtaining recognition for debate and other purposes.

24.35   Supplemental rules on election procedures and reference committees not provided for in the bylaws may be included in the convention rules or other governing documents.

PROGRAM COMMITTEE

24.36   The program committee of a convention is responsible for planning the schedule of meetings, activities, and special events of the convention. This is the last of the reports usually required for the official organization of the convention. The proposed schedule is submitted to the convention. After approval, it becomes the agenda for the convention and establishes the nonbusiness schedule as well.

24.37 Once the agenda has been adopted, it is no longer under the control of the program committee and any subsequent changes must be made by the assembly itself, either by majority vote or general consent. However, it is often the program committee that will have information regarding necessary changes and that will therefore propose any such changes.

TELLERS COMMITTEE

24.38 Many conventions have a tellers committee, which helps the presiding officer tally counted votes and which usually counts ballots as well. The committee may be responsible for preparing ballots, which includes designating the use of alternate colors or another method to maintain ballot security and avoid confusion.

24.39 Not all organizations have a separate tellers committee; some provide for an election committee to assist with elections, including tellers' duties. Since the credentials committee identifies who is qualified to vote, its members may also be assigned responsibility for distribution of ballots.

24.40 Whichever committee is responsible, systems should be in place to ensure ballot security: that no one receives ballots unless qualified to vote; that no one transfers his or her ballot(s) to another member; that no one receives a duplicate set of ballots; and that no two ballots in a set are identical to prevent a member from voting more than once on a given proposal or election. Voting members are not allowed to complete their ballots before instructed to do so and are not allowed to submit their ballots after the chair has announced that the time for voting has expired.

24.41 The tellers committee issues a report for all counted and ballot votes. The tellers' report is read to the assembly and repeated by the presiding officer who then announces the results, the outcome of the vote, and the effect of the vote to the assembly. See Appendix H for a sample tellers' report for elections.

BYLAWS OR GOVERNANCE COMMITTEE

24.42 As a standing committee of the organization, the bylaws or governance committee will have duties as described in the bylaws and standing rules of order, which may include duties at the convention, or the convention may assign convention-related duties to this standing committee. Some organizations may choose to appoint a convention bylaws committee to perform those convention-related duties although this may lead to confusion of responsibility if there is a standing bylaws committee.

24.43 Such duties may include receiving and reviewing, in advance of the convention, the wording of all proposed amendments to the bylaws and other governing documents that have been submitted for consideration by the convention. The documents of authority may require the bylaws committee to review the wording of any new amendment to the bylaws or other governing documents proposed by a reference committee during the convention.

24.44 Having extensive familiarity with the entire bylaws, the members of this committee can provide proper wording of proposed bylaw amendments to accomplish the intent without ambiguity. This committee may also be able to prevent the occurrence of conflicting bylaw provisions resulting from amendments, assist with consistent formatting, and ensure the inclusion of additional amendments that may be needed as a consequence of adopting a proposed amendment.

24.45 The bylaws or governance committee has only the power to comment on and make recommendations regarding the proposed amendments unless more authority is granted, as described below. The committee needs to be specifically empowered if it is to have any of the following powers:

1. approve the text of the amendment as written for submission to the assembly;
2. reword the amendment to accomplish the intent of the maker in proper form used by the organization; and
3. combine several similar amendments with the permission of their proposers.

24.46 The committee is not empowered to prevent the adoption of any proposed amendment by declining to report it to the voting body unless such authority is included in the bylaws, other governing documents, or convention rules. If the committee were given the power to decide to present some amendments and not others, it would have the power to control amendments to the bylaws; this power is exclusive to the full assembly.

CHAPTER 25. Reference Committees

25.1 When an organization has a very extensive or complex agenda, it may establish reference committees, sometimes called resolutions committees, to assist in the timely conduct of its business and to optimize the decision-making process within the time constraints that exist. Such a system usually provides for the referral of all motions and reports to one or more reference committees.

25.2 These committees consider the items referred to them and provide recommendations for action by the full assembly. The following discussions assume that the reference committee system used will include open hearings, which the delegates attend to ask questions, receive information, and provide their own opinions and testimony on the resolutions; however, different procedures may be authorized to fit the needs of the organization.

25.3 More recently, some organizations are providing mechanisms for online submission of testimony or virtual hearings in addition to, or occasionally instead of, in-person testimony, with such testimony available for review by all delegates in advance of the meeting.

25.4 A reference committee system is usually provided for in the bylaws of the organization with the duties defined in the organization's convention rules. The purpose of the reference committee is to arrive at recommendations for action on the items of business referred to it. This is usually done by studying the resolutions and background information before the convention and then hearing testimony from the membership.

25.5 The size of the organization and its assembly, the number and complexity of resolutions, and the time available during the convention for consideration of business will determine the number, structure, and operation of the reference committees. Some organizations may find it helpful to have multiple reference committees and to assign one or more related areas of concern to a single committee such as budget and finances, membership, education, legal, bylaws, administrative, and legislative/governmental.

25.6 The use of reference committees may divide the work of conducting hearings, investigating, and making recommendations on proposals among several smaller representative groups. The full assembly can dispose of an extensive agenda, doing so with a thorough consideration of the facts about each proposal but with greater efficiency than would occur if the entire voting body conducted the full debate and consideration necessary to decide the best final action on every item of business.

25.7 There are a wide variety of ways to implement a reference committee system, and many, but not all, of the options are described in this chapter. Each organization should adopt procedures that best meet its needs.

COMPOSITION AND APPOINTMENT

25.8 Reference committees should be large enough to provide a reasonable cross section of the membership or convention delegates without becoming unwieldy in size. If the composition of the committees is not specifically defined in the bylaws, the bylaws should designate how committee members will be appointed. Appointment by the president is customary in some organizations. Those organizations that elect another officer specifically to preside at the assembly's meeting, for example, a Speaker of the House of Delegates, often designate that officer to appoint the members of the reference committees.

25.9 Members of a reference committee should have knowledge and experience in the assigned subject matter and have no likely conflicts of interest. Members must be willing to do the work that will be needed in advance of the convention, and attend the convention, including all meetings and hearings of the reference committee. Appointment should occur well in advance of the start of the committee's work to ensure that the composition of the committees is established when the work begins.

25.10 An organization may provide for one or more non-voting committee advisors to be included in a reference committee for various purposes. If available, staff members of the organization are often assigned to reference committees to provide relevant background information and facts, as well as to assist in the mechanics of each committee's operations and writing reports.

25.11 The advantages of using a reference committee system include:

1. The assembly is able to deal with many business items without having to spend the time that might be needed to hear the full debate on every item.

2. Each item of business may receive more in-depth consideration than it might receive in the full assembly.
3. The usual limits on length and number of speeches may be relaxed to allow more input from members than might occur in a formal session.
4. The rules often allow members of the organization who are not voting members of the assembly to provide testimony. Sometimes even those who are not members of the organization are permitted to testify. This provides the assembly with a broader perspective on issues than the voting members alone might have.

INTRODUCTION OF RESOLUTIONS AND REFERRAL

25.12 Many organizations with conventions require that all proposals for consideration by the voting body be submitted by a certain date prior to the convention. Convention rules should provide a mechanism for the assembly to permit the late introduction of resolutions since business may arise that cannot be anticipated before the designated deadline. Such rules may provide for the full assembly to determine if such late resolutions are to be considered or may assign that decision to a committee.

25.13 Depending on the bylaws or rules, proposals in the form of motions or resolutions may be submitted by constituent or component organizations, committees or boards of the organization, officers, delegates, and in some organizations by individual members. Standing and special committee reports with recommendations for action should also be referred to appropriate reference committees. Informational reports without recommendations for action may be referred to reference committees, or filed without such referral, as the organization wishes.

25.14 The rules of the organization should identify how referral of resolutions to the various reference committees should be made; the most common practice is for the presiding officer to make the referrals. If there is no provision, the presiding officer is authorized to make those referrals.

25.15 The resolutions should be referred and thus assigned to a reference committee within a few days after the deadline for their submission. Because these assignments are made in accordance with the adopted rules, the resolutions do not need to be introduced on the floor of the assembly prior to their referral.

25.16 Resolutions submitted after the deadline, sometimes known as "late" resolutions, may be subject to additional procedures to determine if they will be considered. Those resolutions accepted for consideration are referred to reference committees as well.

25.17 Each delegate should be provided with the full text of all reports and resolutions well in advance of the convention, including background material in accordance with the customs and rules of the organization; a list of which reference committee has received each resolution for consideration; and the assigned time and place for each committee's open hearings. Delegates are expected to prepare for the meeting by reading these materials in advance of the meeting. In organizations with particularly large agendas, constituent organizations such as state associations may divide the work of preparation among its delegates, who then report to the full constituent delegation.

25.18 In a reference committee system, every submitted resolution is referred to a committee and must be reported out unless the rules provide otherwise.

25.19 Some organizations may provide a mechanism for the assembly to meet before hearings begin, without debate and usually by two-thirds vote, to reject the consideration of a resolution. Some may authorize the reference committee to reject a resolution although the full assembly should have a mechanism to bring a rejected resolution to the floor. Rejected resolutions are no longer part of the reference committee's agenda and will not be considered in hearings or in the full assembly.

25.20 The rules may provide a method for a resolution to be withdrawn by the submitting body with majority approval by the assembly. In every instance, once a motion has been distributed to the delegates, it can only be withdrawn by the submitting body, with a majority vote, through a vote on the floor.

HEARINGS

25.21 The primary duties of a reference committee are to obtain and study the relevant background information; to hold open hearings to receive additional information, opinions, and testimony on all matters referred to the committee; and to recommend the most appropriate actions to be taken by the full assembly.

25.22 The success of a reference committee system depends on the willingness of the delegates to accept such a system with recognition and acceptance of its purpose, which is to expedite decision-making while also ensuring a deliberative process. It also depends on an understanding that members wishing to participate in debate should begin by presenting their information and opinions during the hearings, which are, in such a system, the preferred and primary opportunity to do so, rather than requiring the entire assembly to invest the time necessary to hear such presentations.

25.23 Reference committee hearings can be scheduled sequentially, allowing attendance by all who are interested. They may also be scheduled simultaneously, which will preclude all members from hearing all testimony. With simultaneous, or even overlapping hearings, members must sometimes be willing to rely on others to present their points of view, and to report to them on testimony that was not directly experienced.

25.24 Hearings are most commonly open to all members of the organization, whether or not voting members of the full assembly, though some organizations restrict testimony to voting members. Some organizations allow testimony from those who are not members of the organization.

25.25 Testimony should be directed to the committee, not to others in attendance.

25.26 It is frequently necessary to place some limitations on the time available for testimony, on the duration of testimony by any given person, on the number of times any person may testify, or some combination of these. Such limitations may be established by rule or may be placed at the discretion of the committee. However, if limits on testimony are too restrictive, delegates whose views can't be adequately presented may decide to do so in the full assembly, reducing the efficiency that is one of the purposes of the reference committee system.

25.27 Usually, an individual may not testify a second time on the same issue until those wishing to testify have had an opportunity to do so once. This limitation may sometimes be relaxed for the author of the resolution or for others with relevant information on a specific issue. The committee chair must conduct the hearing with a careful balance of the members' right to testify against the need to complete the hearings in a timely manner.

25.28 If time constraints prevent the opportunity for every member who wishes to speak, consideration should be given to extending the duration of the hearing if possible. All members should have the right to be heard, and no member should be denied the right to testify. However, to conserve time, those testifying should refrain from repetitive testimony or from expressions of support for opinions already expressed by others.

25.29 While testimony in the reference committees may be somewhat informal, decorum must be maintained, as described in Chapter 11. The committee chair is empowered to exclude any nonmember of the committee who is disruptive from the hearing room. The committee is empowered, by majority vote, to exclude any committee member who is disruptive from the hearing room.

25.30 Motions are not in order during reference committee hearings. A member wishing to amend a resolution may, however, provide the reference committee with the language of the proposed amendment and urge the committee to recommend such an amendment, but the amendment is never moved or formally considered at the hearing. In the same manner, testimony may urge the committee to recommend a referral of the resolution.

25.31 Because attendance at the reference committee hearing may not be representative of the full voting body, votes, including nonbinding "straw votes," are not taken in reference committee hearings. It is not the role of those providing testimony to take actions that might bind the reference committee in its closed meeting deliberations. The reference committee will be making recommendations for action as described below, and the number of those in favor of and opposed to a resolution during the hearing should not be a dominant factor in the committee's decision-making process.

25.32 The members of the reference committee should take care to conduct themselves as impartial recipients of the testimony provided. Reference committee members may not provide testimony, either while seated as a member of the committee or by temporarily relinquishing committee membership and testifying with the others in attendance. Such testimony by a reference committee member might create the perception that the committee members are not hearing testimony with an open mind but have instead decided their position on the issue before hearing all points of view.

25.33 Reference committee members are permitted to ask questions to clarify the testimony of a member or to obtain additional information on the matter at hand. Such questions should be carefully worded to ensure that they do not reveal any bias of the committee member on the issue.

Often all questions from committee members are provided to the committee chair who will ask them as appropriate.

25.34   Reference committee members who have important information on the issue, or who have strong opinions on it, will have the opportunity to share that information or opinion with other committee members during the committee's deliberations.

25.35   While resolutions are usually considered in sequence by resolution number, the reference committee is often authorized to group those that have a common topic.

25.36   The reference committee may be authorized to consider written testimony as well as that provided at the hearing. Some organizations are using technology to allow the submission of such testimony, and to allow responses to it, in advance of the meeting. Reference committee members and delegates are expected to familiarize themselves with such submissions. Limits may be imposed on the length of testimony submitted, in writing or electronically, to increase the likelihood that these submissions can be read and considered with a reasonable investment of time.

25.37   If the assembly fails to provide appropriate meeting procedures, the committee is responsible for developing any rules that may be beneficial to the efficient conduct of their work during the hearings.

DEVELOPMENT OF RECOMMENDATIONS

25.38   After hearings have been concluded, the reference committee deliberates, usually in a closed meeting, on its recommendations for action on each item of business that has been referred to it.

25.39   The committee decides what action will be recommended to the assembly, usually a recommendation to adopt, adopt as amended, Adopt in Lieu of, or defeat. Appropriate employed staff, the parliamentarian, and officers can then assist the committee in determining the actual wording of the recommendations. Specific recommendations are selected to ensure the least procedural confusion, and clarity of what is proposed, while expediting final action by the assembly.

25.40   The committee recommends what it believes will be best for the organization based on facts available and the strength of testimony provided. The persuasiveness of facts is far more important than the quantity of testimony.

25.41 All items referred to the reference committee must be reported back to the full assembly for action unless otherwise provided for in the rules. The reference committee should make every effort to avoid reporting on an item of business without making a recommendation. If an item of business is omitted from the reference committee's written report, the presiding officer should nevertheless place that item of business before the assembly at the appropriate time, and the item will then be considered and disposed of by the assembly acting without a committee recommendation.

REFERENCE COMMITTEE REPORTS

25.42 Typically, the reference committee develops a written report with its recommendations on each item of business referred to it.

25.43 The format of the written report will vary from organization to organization but should provide some orderly presentation of the recommendations, including the text of the original resolution, for easy consideration by the full assembly. Often all resolutions are presented in numerical order unless another logical grouping is more useful.

25.44 Each organization should adopt a standard format for its reference committee reports. This will provide year-to-year consistency in the appearance of the reports of reference committees.

25.45 However organized, the reference committee report should contain a clearly stated recommendation for action on every item of business. The recommendations may include actions like those available to an ordinary assembly, except that postponements are not ordinarily permitted. See Chapter 14 for limitations that would affect postponements in an annual meeting or convention. Recommendations include:

1. Adoption: The committee recommends that the resolution be adopted as submitted.
2. Defeat: The committee recommends that the resolution be defeated. Some organizations choose to word this recommendation as "rejection," "do not adopt," or "the reference committee recommends a 'no' vote."
3. Amendment and approval as amended.
4. The committee offers a motion for one or more primary amendments to insert, strike, or strike and insert and, if the amendment is adopted, recommends adoption of the amended resolution.

5. When a reference committee offers a new resolution to replace one or more of the submitted resolutions, it may offer a Motion to Adopt in Lieu of the other resolutions (see the section, Motion to Adopt in Lieu of, later in this chapter). Adopt in Lieu of may also be used when two or more of the submitted resolutions are combined, in full or in part, into a single resolution by the reference committee.

6. Referral: The committee offers a motion for referral, which may include details such as the body to which the referral should be made, instructions for studying the referred matter, and instructions on reporting. The assembly may empower the body to which the referral is made to take final action on the referred item instead of bringing it back to the full assembly. This is accomplished by a Motion to Refer with power to act.

7. Table: The committee offers a Motion to Table, which has the effect of killing the resolution by a two-thirds vote without debate or amendment.

25.46 Sometimes one or more of the reference committees are permitted, or even expected, to originate motions or courtesy resolutions to express appreciation for service by officers, convention committees, retiring members of boards of directors, or other similar honorary matters.

25.47 The reference committee recommendations should result in resolutions that are worded in the affirmative and that are clear and unambiguous in their meaning; this is an important duty of the reference committee if the originally submitted resolution does not have these features. The resolved clauses represent the action to be taken and should be complete in themselves while the whereas clauses provide rationale for the action.

25.48 Reference committee reports may include reasons for the committee's recommendations. This is particularly important when the recommendations are based on information that was not presented in the open hearings because members were not exposed to that information; an example might be advice from subject matter experts during the committee's closed meeting. When there are no other well-functioning mechanisms for voting members to obtain such information, the explanations may include the relevant facts, arguments, and testimony that were considered so that members who did not attend the hearings may more fully understand the committee's rationale.

25.49 It is best practice that the financial impact of adopting a resolution be included in the reference committee report.

25.50 In a closed meeting, the full committee approves its recommendations. The committee chair often drafts any explanatory language. When this is done, the committee should reconvene to approve the final wording of explanations. The report should then be signed by all members of the reference committee. On rare occasions, a minority report may be necessary and is handled in the same manner as minority reports from other committees.

CONSENT AGENDA IN CONVENTIONS

25.51 In a convention, the consent agenda, sometimes called a consent calendar, is usually composed of all items on which the reference committee feels its recommendations are likely to be accepted by the assembly without objection. This conclusion by the reference committee may be based on a lack of testimony on an item or on testimony being heavily in support of the committee's recommendation. Items on which there is likely to be difference of opinion or debate are usually not included on the consent agenda.

25.52 Most organizations allow any noncontroversial items to be included on a consent agenda, no matter what the reference committee's recommendation for action may be. Any item(s) may be removed from the consent agenda on the demand of an individual member. After calling for the removal of items from the consent agenda, the adoption of the consent agenda enacts the recommendation or the proposal of the reference committee on each remaining item. For example, should the recommendation be to "adopt" the main motion, the main motion would be adopted. Conversely, if the recommendation is to "defeat" the main motion, the main motion would be defeated. If the recommendation is to amend the main motion and adopt as amended, both of those motions would be enacted. The en bloc action on a variety of parliamentary actions in one step is a unique feature of the consent agenda. Those items removed from the consent agenda will receive separate consideration at a later point in the meeting.

25.53 In its most expansive application, all items of business are placed on the consent agenda, without regard to the likelihood of removal, and only those items that are removed and placed on the regular agenda are given individual consideration.

25.54 A consent agenda that is proposed with the inclusion of all items of business is most appropriate in organizations where:

1. There is a very extensive agenda.

2. Most members are willing, in the interest of time, to allow items to be disposed of as recommended, recognizing that one individual's opposition to the recommendation is not likely to prevail if the item is removed.

3. The reference committee accurately anticipates the will of the full assembly in most cases, providing recommendations that are acceptable to the assembly on most items of business.

4. The members fully understand and are willing to exercise their right to remove items with belief that it is important to do so or that it will be a productive effort.

5. Members recognize that the use of a consent agenda that includes all items of business is helpful to the timely disposition of the extensive agenda.

25.55 The consent agenda is adopted as shown below. Once all members have an opportunity to remove items, the presiding officer then states, "There being no further requests to remove items from the consent agenda, the balance of the consent agenda is approved."

25.56 Bylaw amendments and other actions that require a vote that is higher than a majority may be included in the consent agenda. Since the consent agenda is adopted by general consent, it is presumed that the assembly has acted with the necessary vote threshold.

25.57 Ordinarily, if the assembly must act on a budget, that item should not be placed on the consent agenda. Action on other items of business may require that the budget be amended to reflect the other decisions before it is adopted.

25.58 In some cases, a member or constituent unit that proposed a resolution may wish to withdraw that resolution from consideration by the assembly, and if there is no objection from the assembly or the request to withdraw the resolution is approved by the assembly by majority vote, the resolution is withdrawn from consideration as any other withdrawn motion or resolution. It will not be considered during the meeting but will be recorded in the minutes as withdrawn.

PRIORITY AGENDA

25.59 In some organizations, and particularly in conventions, if the available meeting time is less than the time required, a priority agenda may be employed. This is a method of considering important items of business before the remainder of the agenda is considered. The priority agenda is explained in more detail in Chapter 21.

25.60 Using a combination of the consent agenda and the priority agenda allows the meeting to focus on the most important items while still being purposeful and efficient.

25.61 The presiding officer, with the assistance of the reference committee chair, might deal with business in the following order:

1. Items or resolutions to be withdrawn and not considered by the assembly are identified.
2. Reference committee reports are distributed in advance or read, and as each is presented, a request is made for delegates to identify items or resolutions for removal from the consent agenda and placement on the regular agenda for individual consideration and action.
3. Adoption of the remainder of the consent agenda is accomplished by general consent.
4. Items on the priority agenda are considered and disposed of.
5. Recommendations that were not included on the consent agenda, along with items or resolutions removed from the consent agenda but now on the regular agenda, are considered.

25.62 Although this sequence of business is one used by many organizations, other orders of considering consent agendas and priority agendas may be used.

ACTION ON REPORTS

Consent Agenda

25.63 Should both a consent agenda and a priority agenda be utilized, reference committees submit items for inclusion on the consent agenda. The report of the reference committee can be read or distributed in advance. The presiding officer first processes the consent agenda of the reporting committee.

25.64 Removal of items from the consent agenda is requested, and then members may obtain recognition and identify the item to be removed. A single member may request, without explanation, that an item be removed from the consent agenda. Sometimes a brief question on an item may be permitted without requiring its removal, but if the question can't be asked and answered quickly, the item should be removed from the consent agenda.

25.65 The remainder of the consent agenda is then adopted, without debate, by general consent. The presiding officer announces that the consent agenda is adopted but does not need to announce the disposition of the individual items on the consent agenda.

Priority Agenda

25.66 If a priority agenda is utilized, after providing an opportunity for the assembly to modify it, the presiding officer should present the items on the priority agenda for consideration by the assembly in the order designated unless there are provisions on the regular agenda for other time-sensitive items, such as elections, to be disposed of first.

25.67 If a priority agenda is used, the items on the priority agenda are considered immediately after adoption of the consent agenda.

25.68 After disposition of all items on the priority agenda, reference committee reports are heard if they were not heard during consideration of the consent agenda. In some organizations, the sequence in which these reports are taken up is designated, but in most, the presiding officer may determine the sequence that is felt to be most conducive to the assembly's decision-making process. Sometimes the effect of various resolutions demands that some be considered and disposed of before others are taken up.

25.69 Once the consent agenda and the priority agenda have been disposed of, the presiding officer then deals with reports and recommendations from the reference committees, along with any items removed from the consent agenda.

Reference Committee Report

25.70 When considering each item, the reference committee's recommendation is read. Since delegates typically have the written report, it is not customary to read the entire resolution to the assembly. Custom will direct whether the reference committee's rationale will be read aloud. Any member can demand that an item be read unless the organization's rules prevent such a demand, or the demand is dilatory.

Reference Committee Recommendations

25.71 Items removed from the consent agenda are considered during the report of the reference committee that submitted the recommendation to the consent agenda.

25.72 Once an item is removed from the consent agenda and is considered independently, the assembly votes on the original resolution along with other subsidiary motions reported back by the reference committee. Specifically, if the reference committee recommendation is to defeat the motion, the assembly still votes on the motion, with the reference committee recommendation to defeat treated as a suggestion to vote "No."

25.73 If the committee recommends an amendment in any form, or that the motion be referred, that motion is considered immediately. If the Motion to Amend or the Motion to Refer is defeated, the original resolution is still before the assembly for action without a recommendation from the reference committee.

25.74 After those items are disposed of, individual resolutions that were never on the consent agenda are dealt with. As opposed to the constraint during hearings, members of the reference committees may fully participate in debate in the full assembly if voting members of the assembly.

25.75 The presiding officer maintains control of the meeting while the chair of the reference committee is reporting and presenting the recommendations of the committee. It is not in order for the chair of the committee to control the debate and take the vote. The reference committee chair should be stationed at a secondary lectern to introduce the committee's motions, if necessary, and to explain the committee's reasoning in debate, if required.

MOTION TO ADOPT IN LIEU OF

25.76 In ordinary assemblies, that is, those that are not conventions of delegates, it is rare for more than one motion or resolution on a subject to be submitted in advance, and therefore only one main motion will be considered at a time.

25.77 In a convention, in contrast, motions and resolutions are usually required to be submitted in advance. Multiple resolutions on similar subject matter are commonly received and referred to the reference committee, which may wish to propose a single replacement that takes the best features of each of these multiple resolutions, based on testimony and other background material, and to recommend its adoption rather than make recommendations on each underlying resolution.

25.78 Since the purpose of the reference committee system is to expedite business, and since there is a presumption that the reference committee usually provides a recommendation that is most likely acceptable to the assembly, a mechanism to arrive at that final action with fewer procedural steps and votes is appropriate.

25.79 That mechanism is the use of an Motion to Adopt in Lieu of. The reference committee recommends that its motion or one of the underlying motions be adopted in place of the other resolution or resolutions, specifically identifying those to be replaced, usually by resolution number or another assigned identifier.

25.80 If the recommendation is adopted as part of the consent agenda, the reference committee motion is adopted, and the other resolutions are not acted on directly but are defeated.

25.81 If the recommendation is removed from the consent agenda and placed on the regular agenda, all the underlying resolutions are automatically removed with it. In this case, the reference committee's Motion to Adopt in Lieu of is taken up first. The reference committee's Motion to Adopt in Lieu of, when pending, may be perfected by amendments, and if it is then adopted, it is enacted. With the adoption of the Motion to Adopt in Lieu of, the underlying resolutions are defeated.

25.82 When the vote is taken on the Motion to Adopt in Lieu of, an affirmative vote adopts it and that is the only vote needed. If the Motion to Adopt in Lieu of fails, the proposed motion has been eliminated.

25.83 If the Motion to Adopt in Lieu of proposed by the reference committee is defeated, the presiding officer announces this, and that any member may propose the adoption of any one of the underlying resolutions in lieu of the other remaining underlying resolutions. Again, if the proposed Adopt in Lieu of resolution is adopted, the remaining underlying resolutions are defeated. This process may be repeated until one of the resolutions is adopted in lieu of the others or until none of them are adopted.

25.84 In summary, the Motion to Adopt in Lieu of would be used to bring a single resolution before the assembly for its consideration in disposing of an issue for which there were multiple resolutions. By adopting that motion after usual debate and amendments, the assembly disposes of the issue with one vote instead of two or more votes without having to repeat debate. If an Motion to Adopt in Lieu of fails, any member may move adoption of one of the underlying motions in lieu of the other remaining motions. See Appendix I for a flowchart of this process.

Example

Reference Committee Chair:	The committee moves adoption of resolution A in lieu of resolutions B, C, and D.
Presiding Officer:	The question is on the motion to adopt resolution A in lieu of resolutions B, C, and D. Discussion is now in order on resolution A. (Processes debate and amendments.)
Presiding Officer: (continues)	Those in favor of adopting resolution A in lieu of resolutions B, C, and D, raise your voting cards. Cards down. Those opposed, raise your cards. Cards down.
Presiding Officer: (continues if motion is adopted)	There is a majority in favor, and you have adopted resolution A in lieu of resolutions B, C, and D.
Presiding Officer: (continues if motion is defeated)	There is not a majority in favor. The motion to adopt resolution A in lieu of resolutions B, C, and D is defeated. A member may now move adoption of resolution B, C, or D. The delegate at microphone 1 is recognized.
Delegate:	I move to adopt resolution D in lieu of resolutions B and C. (Another member seconds the motion.)

25.85 Debate, amendments, and votes would continue until resolution D is in the form the assembly prefers. The assembly would then vote on the Adopt in Lieu of resolution, disposing of it in the same manner as occurred with resolution A above, with the same consequences. The process would continue until a resolution is adopted, or all are defeated, or no member approaches the microphone to move any further motions on the matter.

REFERENCE COMMITTEE INFLUENCE

25.86 The reference committee's recommendation is often persuasive in determining the decision of the assembly. The great influence exercised by the committee, however, is advisory.

25.87 It is important that the assembly fully understands that it may consider all proposals submitted to it and make the final decision on them. If the voting body does not agree with the reference committee's recommendation about a resolution, the resolution may be removed from the consent agenda and disposed of in any manner the assembly finds appropriate. The assembly retains the power and responsibility of final decision on every item of business.

25.88 Every member must be vigilant, knowledgeable of each item of business, and prepared to lead the assembly in the decision-making process. If there is disagreement with the reference committee's recommendation, the assembly may concur with the member.

ORGANIZATION LEADERSHIP

CHAPTER 26. Nominations and Elections

CHOOSING ORGANIZATION LEADERS

26.1 The process of nominating and electing officers is vital to every organization because the abilities and talents of its leaders largely determine the organization's achievements.

26.2 Parliamentary law permits wide latitude of choice in each step of the nominating and electing process. There is no one perfect method, but there are certain procedures that experience has proven to be better than others for obtaining good leaders.

BYLAW PROVISIONS ON NOMINATIONS AND ELECTIONS

26.3 The bylaw provisions on nominations should include the offices to be filled, the eligibility and qualifications of candidates, the person or group who may nominate, and the method and time of nominating. If a nominating committee is to be used, provisions for selecting its members and determining their qualifications, instructions, duties, and reporting should also be included. The bylaw provisions on elections should include the time, place, and method of voting; the notice required; a statement of who is eligible to vote; the vote required to elect; the method of conducting the election; and the time when the new officers take office. If no time is designated for taking office, those elected take office at the adjournment of the meeting or convention at which elections occur.

26.4 Provisions related to filling a vacancy in office should also be included and may include a provision for a special election.

26.5 Some organizations have certain procedural requirements, such as advance announcement of candidacy, certification of eligibility, statement of willingness to serve, submission of conflict-of-interest statements, or compliance with submission deadlines. Such restrictions might limit the organization's choices and therefore prevent the election of a member who might otherwise be the best-qualified candidate or result in there being no eligible candidate; therefore, such restrictions should be carefully considered before being put in place.

26.6 Care should be taken to provide sufficient flexibility in the overall nomination and election processes to allow the organization to address unanticipated circumstances; often a provision authorizing the board or a standing committee to resolve such issues is sufficient.

NOMINATIONS FROM THE FLOOR

26.7 A nomination is the formal presentation to an assembly of the name of a member as a candidate for a particular office. If the bylaws do not provide the method for nominating officers or directors, any member may propose a motion determining how nominations are to be made.

26.8 Unless the bylaws provide otherwise, nominations from the floor are always permitted, even if the initial nominations are made by a nominating committee.[73] To open nominations, the presiding officer may ask, "Are there nominations (or further nominations) for the office of president?" Any member may then rise and say, for example, "I nominate Alice Sturgis."

26.9 Relying solely on nominations from the floor may not be the most effective method for securing the best candidates. The lack of time for considering qualifications may impair the determination of the best candidates. A nominating committee will usually select good candidates, but nominations from the floor should always be provided as a safeguard.

CLOSING NOMINATIONS

26.10 The presiding officer should repeat the request for further nominations and should pause to allow ample opportunity for members to present nominees. When there appears to be no further nominations for a particular office, the presiding officer declares nominations for that office closed. A Motion to Close Nominations is not required but, if made, cannot interrupt, is not amendable and not debatable, requires a second, and requires a two-thirds vote for adoption. The presiding officer must not recognize a Motion to Close Nominations or declare them closed if any member is rising for the purpose of making a nomination.

26.11 If nominations have been closed, they may be reopened by a motion to this effect until voting has begun. The Motion to Reopen Nominations cannot interrupt, is not amendable, not debatable, requires a second, and requires a majority vote for adoption.

DEBATING NOMINATIONS

26.12   It is best practice for organizations to adopt rules in advance that govern speeches and debate related to nominations and candidates. Although nominations do not require seconds, limited debate in support of a candidate may be permitted by the rules governing speeches. If the report of a nominating committee states the qualifications and abilities of its nominees, a member who nominates from the floor may also state the qualifications and abilities of the candidate.

26.13   If no other rules are provided, nominations are debatable by members, and candidates are allowed to speak on their own behalf, even if not otherwise members of the body. The rules of decorum in debate apply and must be strictly enforced. (See the section, Rules of Decorum and Conduct in Debate, in Chapter 11.)

VOTING FOR CANDIDATES NOT NOMINATED

26.14   A member need not be nominated for an office, either from the floor or by a committee, when the vote for election is taken by ballot or by roll call. Unless the bylaws require a nomination to be eligible for election, members may vote for anyone who is eligible, regardless of whether the person has been nominated, by writing in the name of their choice on the ballot or voting for that person on roll call. These are referred to as write-in votes. Unless the bylaws require that a candidate must have been nominated to be eligible, then whatever voting system is used must allow for write-in votes.

26.15   Unless clearly provided otherwise in the bylaws, any member receiving the necessary vote and meeting the other requirements for office as required in the governing documents is elected, whether nominated or not.[74] While nominations are not needed, they provide guidance to members on whom to vote for. A member may decline a nomination and, if elected, also has the right to decline the office.[75]

SELECTING A NOMINATING COMMITTEE

26.16   A nominating committee is one of the most important committees of an organization because it can help secure the best leaders. Nomination of candidates by a committee has advantages. A committee has the time to study the current leadership needs of the organization and to select candidates to meet these needs. The committee can interview prospective nominees; investigate their experience, qualifications, and abilities; persuade them to become candidates; and secure their consent to serve if elected. The committee is also able to consider other criteria that the organization deems important, such as equitable representation among different groups or different geographical areas.

26.17 A nominating committee should be a representative committee. Some organizations provide, for example, that if the nominating committee consists of five members, three of the members are elected by the membership, and the chair and the fifth member are appointed by the governing board. The members chosen by the board are usually current or recent members of the board who, by reason of their service, have a broad and up-to-date knowledge of the needs of the organization and of the leadership abilities of its members. The members of the committee elected by the membership usually reflect the viewpoint of the general membership.

26.18 When possible, the committee should reflect the whole organization. Any plan by which experienced leaders choose some of the members of the nominating committee and the membership chooses the other members is usually effective in securing a committee that is both representative and knowledgeable.

26.19 The president, president-elect, and immediate past president should not appoint any members of the nominating committee, serve on the committee, give the committee instructions, or take any part in its deliberations, although they may provide information upon request. This requirement protects both the officer and the committee from accusations of favoritism or self-perpetuation.

26.20 When a nominating committee is used, it is essential that the members be chosen wisely and democratically and that both the committee and the membership be protected by permitting nominations from the floor or by petition.

DUTIES OF A NOMINATING COMMITTEE

26.21 A carefully chosen nominating committee should be permitted to use its judgment in selecting the candidates who will give the best service to the organization. It should choose the candidates on the basis of what is best for the organization as a whole and not on the basis that an office is a reward to be given to a deserving member. The committee may invite suggestions but is not limited by them.

26.22 A few organizations use the nominating committee as a data gathering group to which names are sent. This type of committee does little more than compile a list of nominees based on suggestions received and verify their eligibility for, and consent to accept, office.

26.23 However, many organizations believe that the best leaders are secured by delegating to the nominating committee the duty to find and nominate the best candidates. The duties usually assigned to such a nominating committee are:

1. to select nominees whose experience and qualities meet the needs of the organization;
2. to contact prospective nominees and obtain their consent to serve if elected;
3. to prepare and submit a report, which may include the reasons for the selection of the nominees; and
4. to nominate their chosen nominees.

26.24 An organization should state clearly in the bylaws the duties of the nominating committee. Otherwise, it is up to the nominating committee to determine whether it will simply nominate all candidates found qualified or nominate only the candidate or candidates who it determines are best suited for each position.

QUALIFICATIONS OF NOMINEES

26.25 Qualifications for each office, to be enforceable, must be stated in the bylaws, a document of higher authority—such as a charter or constitution, or a document designated in the bylaws. No member who lacks the qualifications specified in the documents described above can be a candidate for, or be elected to, an office. The nomination of an unqualified member must be ruled out of order.

NOMINATION TO MORE THAN ONE OFFICE

26.26 No member can hold two incompatible offices. Incompatibility not only consists of practical impossibility to perform the duties of both offices but also includes a conflict between the duties of the two offices. Offices with the inherent duty of substituting for a higher ranking officer in that officer's absence or inability, such as a vice president for the president, or assistant treasurer for the treasurer, are inherently incompatible with the higher office because the bylaws clearly intend to provide an alternative.

26.27   In their bylaws, some organizations combine two offices, thus, in effect, declaring them compatible. For example, the offices of secretary and treasurer are sometimes combined as secretary-treasurer. Membership on the governing board is usually compatible with other officer positions. Officers in local units might also be elected as delegates to the assembly of the parent organization.

26.28   If it is not clear whether certain offices are incompatible, the organization should clarify the compatibility or lack thereof in its bylaws.

26.29   A member may be nominated for two incompatible offices at the same election. If, however, the member is elected to both positions, the member must immediately choose which office to fill and forfeit the other. This would result in an *incomplete election* for the forfeited office, and the election meeting could then complete that election.

26.30   Unless the bylaws provide otherwise, a member who holds an office may be a candidate for another office without first giving up the current office, but if the member is elected to and accepts an incompatible office, the former office is forfeited.

NOMINATING COMMITTEE MEMBERS AS CANDIDATES

26.31   Members who are likely to become candidates should not serve on a nominating committee, but members of the committee can become candidates. If a member of the nominating committee wishes to be considered as a nominee or declares candidacy for a position, the member must resign from the committee.

SINGLE AND MULTIPLE NOMINEES FOR A POSITION

26.32   If an organization chooses a representative nominating committee carefully and democratically, it is desirable to nominate a single candidate for each office. A *single slate*, meaning one nominee for each office, frequently offers certain advantages provided that nominations may also be made from the floor or by petition and that election by write-in votes is not forbidden.

26.33 In some organizations the belief persists that it is more democratic to have two or more nominees for each office in order that there may be a contested election *(a multiple slate)*. For a number of reasons, it is usually not best practice to require the nominating committee to submit more nominations than there are positions to be filled. A nomination process that requires the nominating committee to select two nominees for a single position is inefficient in terms of time, energy, and possibly money. If a fully qualified candidate is selected, but the governing documents of the organization require two nominees, the committee may find itself in the position of insincerely nominating a second candidate. A member nominated only to fulfill the requirement may be unwilling to run in the future after having been defeated once.

26.34 If the nominating committee fails to express the will of the majority of the membership in its selection of nominees, this is most readily corrected by nominating candidates from the floor to provide a contested election.

ELECTION COMMITTEE

26.35 Organizations usually appoint an election committee that conducts the election. The members of this committee should be well respected in the organization, not be openly supportive of any one candidate, be detail oriented, be knowledgeable of election rules, and, if possible and important to the organization, be selected from different constituencies or geographic regions.

26.36 The committee supervises preparing and printing ballots and distributing them to voting members either at a meeting or convention or by mail, collecting and counting the ballots, and preparing the report showing the results of the election. Those who count the ballots are typically called tellers in nonprofit membership organizations and *inspectors of elections* in business corporations. Tellers also frequently distribute and collect the ballots. In organizations with an election committee, the tellers are usually members of the election committee or a subcommittee of the election committee. If the rules are silent on a tellers committee, the presiding officer has the authority to appoint a tellers committee.

26.37 An organization should define ahead of time the method and the procedures by which it elects its leaders. It is incumbent upon the organization, however, to define the method and procedure that will best meet the organization's needs.

26.38 Procedural details related to the election need not be in the bylaws but should be proposed by the election committee and adopted prior to the election.

26.39 See the section, Vote Necessary to Elect, when the bylaws are silent on the rules for electing leaders.

COUNTING BALLOTS

26.40 The election committee or the tellers are generally responsible for seeing that ballots are counted accurately. Many organizations have developed effective ballot-counting methods that meet their own needs. Any method is appropriate if it is accurate and efficient. In many organizations, a form of electronic voting is often used. Testing any system prior to use is an important step in ensuring election confidence and integrity.

26.41 If counted by hand, the paper ballots may be divided among teams of readers, recorders, and checkers and counted in the same way by each team. Announced candidates or their designees have a right to attend and unobtrusively observe the vote count. If there is a possible error, a teller or observer says, "Stop," and the vote is verified before proceeding.

SECURITY AND PRIVACY OF BALLOTING

26.42 It is of critical importance to implement and strictly adhere to procedures and safeguards that ensure ballot security and a correct report of the vote count, particularly in elections. Ballot security measures include provisions to ensure that only an eligible member is able to obtain a ballot and cast a vote, no one may cast another member's ballot without authorization of proxies, and no one may vote more than once.

26.43 Because the intent of voting by ballot is secrecy, procedures should be in place to protect the privacy of members casting their votes, and to ensure that no one can identify a member's ballot. If limited disclosure is required by the voting technology, those who have access to the information should understand the responsibility to maintain the secrecy of the votes of individual voters. In fact, the term *secret ballot* is often used to emphasize this principle although any reference to a ballot vote is presumed to be secret unless specified otherwise.

DETERMINING VALIDITY OF BALLOTS

26.44 *Invalid ballots* are classified on the tellers' report as "illegal ballots." The way that votes are counted is determined by the following rules:

1. A mistake in voting for a candidate for one office does not invalidate the vote for candidates for other offices on the same ballot. The mistaken vote is counted as an illegal vote, and the remaining votes are credited to the appropriate candidate.

2. A technical error, such as a misspelling or using a cross instead of a check, does not invalidate a ballot if the intent of the voter is clear.

3. A torn or defaced ballot is counted if the intent of the voter is clear.

4. Votes for ineligible persons are reported as illegal votes, which may not invalidate a complete ballot.

5. Blank ballots are ignored; they are not counted and do not affect the number necessary to elect a candidate or to adopt a proposal.

6. If several nominees for equal offices, such as members of a governing board, are voted for in a group, a ballot containing fewer votes than the number of positions to be filled is valid. But a ballot containing votes for more than the number of positions to be filled is reported as an illegal ballot, and no votes are credited to any candidate.

7. Two marked ballots folded together are each reported as illegal ballots. A marked ballot folded with a blank ballot is credited to the candidate, and the blank ballot is ignored.

26.45 If the results of the count by the committee appear to be incorrect, a recount must be done. If more ballots have been cast than there are members entitled to vote, or if there has been any violation of the right of members to vote, and the result of the election could have been affected by the error, the vote must be retaken. If there are errors that could not change the result of the election, a vote need not be retaken.[76]

REPORT OF ELECTION COMMITTEE OR TELLERS

26.46 The following example shows the essential requirements of a report of an election committee or tellers committee:

REPORT OF ELECTION COMMITTEE April 7, 20XX CARTER COUNTY LITERARY SOCIETY	
Eligible voters	205
Total ballots cast	201
President	
Legal votes cast for president	195
Illegal votes (cast for ineligible person)	2
Blank ballots for position	4
Number of votes necessary to elect	98
Candidate A received	128
Candidate B received (write-in votes)	67
Secretary	
Legal votes cast for secretary	201
Number necessary to elect	101
Candidate D received	198
Candidate E received (write-in votes)	3
Legal ballots cast for trustees	197
Illegal votes (overvote–voted for more than 3 candidates)	1
Blank ballots for position	3
Number necessary to elect	99
Candidate F received	190
Candidate G received	181
Candidate H received	153
Candidate I received (write-in votes)	6
Signatures of Committee	

26.47 In the preceding tellers' report, three elections are reported on the one form. See Appendix H, Tellers' Report—Election, for a typical tellers' report for the election of a single office. The report must account for all ballots cast, both valid and invalid. Blank ballots need not be reported but can be useful in determining how the majority vote was determined, as above when there are multiple positions on a single ballot. If any ballots or votes are rejected as illegal, the number must be reported and the reasons for rejection must be given. Illegal votes and blank ballots for that position are not counted toward determining the majority. The number of votes received by each candidate and the number of write-in votes for any member, qualified or unqualified, must be included in the report and must be read.

26.48 The chair of the tellers committee reads the report without stating who is elected and delivers it to the presiding officer. The presiding officer repeats the report and then declares who is elected.

26.49 The report is signed by all members of the tellers committee. Tally sheets are signed by those who marked them. All ballots, tally sheets, and records are delivered to the secretary of the organization, who keeps them sealed until directed by the governing board or the assembly to destroy them. If there is no direction to the contrary, election materials may be discarded after the time in which the election could be challenged.

VOTE NECESSARY TO ELECT

26.50 Unless specified otherwise in the bylaws or a higher-level governing document, elections are conducted by ballot, except as provided in the next section, and require a majority vote for election. Specifically:

1. A candidate who receives a majority of the legal votes cast for a single office is elected.

2. A candidate who receives a plurality of the legal votes cast, but not a majority, is not elected unless there is a provision in the bylaws for election by plurality.

3. When election to an office requires a majority vote, the requirement for a majority vote cannot be waived.[77] In this situation repeated rounds of voting occur with all candidates remaining on each ballot until a candidate receives a majority of the legal votes cast or a candidate withdraws. The assembly may adopt motions to enable it to complete the election within a reasonable time. Such rules are best adopted prior to the election but may be adopted immediately prior to subsequent ballots. For

instance, members in a meeting may vote to drop the candidate with the lowest number of votes either before or between any rounds of voting unless prohibited in the bylaws. In cases of mail balloting, the organization can seek informal consent from the candidates that the one receiving the lowest number of votes will be dropped. Such consent should be sought in advance.

26.51 For more information on adopting rules for conducting an election, see the section, Supplementing Procedural Rules by Motions, in Chapter 4.

ALTERNATIVES TO A BALLOT VOTE ELECTION

26.52 When the bylaws require a ballot vote for election, then the election must be conducted by that method unless the bylaws also provide exceptions. Such an exception would be useful when there is a single nominee for an office or the number of candidates for a specific office is equal to or less than the number of positions to be filled. For example, using the single nominee example, the bylaw exception might be as simple as declaring the single nominee elected.

26.53 This parliamentary authority provides that if there is only one nominee, or the number of nominees is equal to or less than the number of positions open for an office, the presiding officer may conduct the election by general consent, or *acclamation*, unless a single member objects. If there is an objection, the presiding officer calls for the ballots to be distributed.

26.54 Some organizations use electronic keypad voting or voting software at their meetings. This method of voting is a form of ballot voting, and therefore must preserve the security and secrecy of the ballot vote. If such a keypad or software system does not provide a mechanism for write-in votes, the use of the system should be formally authorized by the assembly, and such authorization prohibits write-in votes.

26.55 Elections may only be conducted by roll call if the organization's bylaws authorize this. Roll call voting may be useful in elections conducted in *telephonic meetings*, as it ensures that each vote is made by a voting member.

26.56 Contested elections may not be conducted by voice vote if this parliamentary authority is used. Elections may only be conducted by show of hands or rising if the organization's bylaws authorize this. Should an organization choose to conduct elections by any of these methods, neither of which are recommended, the election should be conducted as follows:

Presiding Officer:	Voting will be conducted for the candidates in order. Those in favor of candidate A, please rise. Be seated. Those in favor of candidate B, please rise. Be seated. (Continue for each candidate.) Candidate B is elected.

26.57   Tellers may be utilized to count votes.

MOTION TO MAKE A VOTE UNANIMOUS

26.58   A unanimous vote means that all the legal votes cast were cast on one side and that there were no votes cast on the other side. One misunderstanding is that a vote that is not unanimous can be made unanimous by adopting a motion to that effect by majority vote; however, such a motion is not in order. Sometimes the candidate receiving the second highest number of votes, or one of that candidate's supporters, proposes a motion to make or declare the vote unanimous for the elected candidate. This should be recognized as a gesture of support for the successful candidate; no actual vote should be taken, and this does not change the legal vote.

WHEN ELECTIONS BECOME EFFECTIVE

26.59   An election becomes effective upon adjournment of the meeting or convention at which the election takes place unless some other time is specified in the bylaws. Those candidates who are present are declared elected if they do not immediately decline at the time of the election. The election of a candidate who is absent becomes final after the election and as soon as the person is notified and agrees to serve.

26.60   The ceremony of installing officers does not determine the time at which they assume office unless the bylaws contain a provision that the new officers take office at the time of their installation, which is not recommended. If for any reason, the installation is delayed or prevented from occurring, the scheduled time of the installation is deemed to be the time at which the newly-elected assume office.

CHALLENGING THE RIGHT TO VOTE

26.61   In meetings of the membership, a member may *challenge the right of another member or members to vote*, or the validity of a proxy,* by presenting

---

* See Chapter 6 for information on voting by proxy.

the challenge to the election committee. If there is no election committee, the challenge is decided by the assembly. If the right of a member to vote is challenged, the assembly may decide the matter or may refer the question to a committee for a hearing.

26.62 In a convention, a delegate, whose credentials have been accepted by being included in a report of the credentials committee that has been adopted, may not have their right to vote challenged later. It is best practice to have an updated credentials report prior to elections or any other important vote and this would be the mechanism to challenge those delegates. See Chapter 24 for credentials challenges in a convention.

CHALLENGING AN ELECTION

26.63 An election may be challenged only during the time that it is taking place or within a reasonably brief time thereafter. Elections that occur during a meeting may not be challenged after the adjournment of the election meeting or convention unless an organization provides special procedures for *challenging an election*, or the challenge alleges fraudulent activity or that sufficient ballots were cast by those ineligible to vote to affect the result. Once brought forward, election challenges should be resolved, if at all possible, by the assembly at the same meeting or convention as the election. If resolution of the challenge by the assembly is not possible, this parliamentary authority authorizes the board to resolve the matter shortly after the meeting.

26.64 In the case where an election may have been based on election fraud, criminality, or ballots cast by ineligible voters and such activity is discovered after the meeting has adjourned, it should be promptly reported upon discovery and appropriate action should be taken. Such a challenge cannot be raised, however, after the *term of office* of the individual challenged has expired.

26.65 In situations where elections take place outside a meeting, for example, electronically or by mail ballot, or where the announcement of the election results takes place after the adjournment of the meeting or convention, the bylaws should specify who resolves an election challenge and within what time limits the challenge may be made. If the bylaws are silent and the conditions of the previous paragraph do not apply, this parliamentary authority specifies a time limit of seven calendar days to register an election challenge after the results have been announced or officially posted to the membership, and that the challenge is to be resolved by the governing board of the organization in office at the time of the challenge. No member of the governing board can vote on a challenge that has the potential of directly affecting an office held by that member. If this results in the governing board being unable to resolve the challenge, then it must be resolved at the next meeting of the membership, either a regular or special meeting called for that purpose.

26.66 The valid grounds for challenging an election are both:

1. that persons who are ineligible have voted, that procedures or actions during the election were unauthorized or illegal, that there was negligence in conducting the election, or that the election requirements in the bylaws or adopted rules were not correctly interpreted or followed, or, in their absence, procedures required for carrying out a fair election were not observed; and

2. that these violations could have changed the result of the election.

26.67 If a bylaw provision or the assembly authorizes a voting system, its reported outcome is presumed to be accurate and may not be challenged solely based on the system or technology that was used. For example, if a keypad voting system reports fewer total votes cast than the number of members eligible to vote, in the absence of clear evidence that some members cast votes that were not counted, the reported votes are presumed to be complete and correct.

26.68 It is always good practice to be prepared to conduct a paper ballot vote in case there are technical problems with electronic voting systems that cannot be resolved in a timely manner, or in case a challenge to such a system results in the assembly ordering a paper ballot vote.

26.69 It is recommended that the organization adopt its own procedures and rules for challenges of elections, for resolution of such challenges, and for addressing its particular voting procedures, customs, and associated (real or potential) election problems. Such procedures should carefully balance the fair treatment of all parties involved and the need for a correct election outcome against the need to resolve any disputes with finality and as promptly as possible.

INCOMPLETE ELECTIONS

26.70 If the assembly is for any reason unable to elect a member to fill a position, the resulting situation is called an incomplete election. Such a situation might occur if no candidate achieves a majority and a majority is required for election, or if there are no members willing to seek an open position, or if a member is elected to more than one office and must choose between them, leaving the position not chosen unfilled.

26.71 An incomplete election is not the same as a vacancy in a position; a vacancy exists if a person who holds a position resigns, dies, is removed, or in some other way no longer holds the position.

26.72 Ordinarily, if an incomplete election occurs during a meeting, those present take one or more of the steps noted in the section, Vote Necessary to Elect. If such steps do not result in completing the election, ideally, before the meeting adjourns, a continued meeting will be established for the completion of the election. If this does not occur, a special meeting can be called to complete the election. If neither of these meetings occur, the election is taken up at each successive regular meeting until it is completed.

26.73 Organizations should adopt procedures, ideally in advance, to address incomplete elections, especially for those organizations that conduct elections separate from a meeting, for example, online elections or elections by mail.

26.74 Some possible procedures might be to adopt bylaw provisions that either permit the governing board to complete the election, to treat the incomplete election as a vacancy, or to determine the election by lot, such as cutting cards or tossing a coin. In the absence of bylaw procedures, however, none of these solutions can be applied to resolve an incomplete election.

26.75 The incumbent remains in office until the election is completed. If there is no incumbent or the incumbent is unable or unwilling to continue, the president or the board may assign the duties associated with that position to other members on an interim basis.

CHAPTER 27. Officers

27.1 The officers of an organization are members who are usually given important responsibilities, duties, and powers because of their designated positions. Without officers to carry out these responsibilities and duties, much of an organization's work might go undone, and the ability of the organization to make necessary decisions so it may function fully between meetings might be significantly hampered.

27.2 The officers in an organization are designated by the organization's bylaws, and officers have few, if any, inherent powers beyond those described in the bylaws or statute. The following discussions explain customary officers and duties, but any differing provisions in governing documents would prevail.

THE PRESIDENT

27.3 The president or the head of an organization, whatever the title may be, usually has three roles: leader, administrator, and presiding officer. Each role calls for different abilities. There are many texts available on leadership, and that topic is outside the scope of parliamentary procedure.

The President as Administrator

27.4 The following are important duties usually performed by the president as an administrator although, depending on the organization, some or all of these may be delegated or assigned to others:

1. act as chief administrative officer and official representative of the organization;
2. exercise supervision over the organization and all its activities and senior employees;
3. represent and speak for the organization in accordance with adopted policies;
4. appoint committees as directed by the bylaws or the assembly;
5. ensure the implementation of adopted actions; and
6. sign letters or documents necessary to carry out the will of the organization.

The Presiding Officer

27.5 As presiding officer, the president is the leader and representative of the entire assembly. The presiding officer must maintain control of meetings yet must always act primarily to assure that the members are able to make collective decisions in a respectful and thoughtful manner.

27.6 In some organizations, especially those with delegate assemblies, the bylaws may assign the duty to preside to another individual instead of the president and that individual would serve in most, if not all, of the roles described here for the presiding officer.

27.7 The presiding officer must meet each situation with flexibility of judgment, common sense, and fairness to all members—always acting impartially and in good faith, instead of being limited to mechanical responses. For example, if a member moves to adjourn, and the presiding officer knows that there is important business that needs consideration, this should be explained to the member, who may then withdraw the motion. If the member declines, the presiding officer should explain this business before the vote on adjournment is taken. The presiding officer should exercise wide discretion in a meeting, always for the benefit of the assembly.

27.8 The presiding officer may modify the formality of the procedure employed, depending on the group's size and the complexity and contentiousness of the issues involved. A degree of informality can often facilitate the conduct of business, but the presiding officer must be prepared to return to greater formality at the first suggestion of difficulty and may wish to use this approach with larger assemblies as well.

27.9 The presiding officer may be flexible in assisting members to exercise their rights and privileges during discussion. Although the presiding officer should remain impartial, it is appropriate to state facts of which members may not be aware, as long as this is done in an unbiased manner. The presiding officer should encourage discussion and should see that all sides of a controversial question are examined by inviting members who wish to present different viewpoints and by alternating the discussion opportunities between those in favor of and those opposed to the question.

27.10 The presiding officer should make sure that members understand all proposals and what their effect will be if adopted or defeated. The presiding officer must make certain that members understand what business is pending and limit discussion to the question that is immediately pending.

27.11   A presiding officer works to protect the group from improper conduct and should act against those who are using dilatory tactics, including denying recognition to those who persist in such behavior. The presiding officer encourages thoughtful decision-making, exposes attempts to take advantage of members' lack of parliamentary knowledge, and promptly rules discussion of personalities out of order.

27.12   A presiding officer, while not being dictatorial, must be firm and decisive, courteous, patient, and alert to ensure progress.

27.13   Presiding is an art that cannot be learned entirely from a book. The skillful presiding officer knows how to discourage tactfully the member who talks too much or too often and how to encourage the shy member. When an assembly grows impatient, a good presiding officer knows how to shorten discussion and how to move business along but also senses when members are confused and when the business should move more slowly. A fundamental factor that will distinguish a skillful presiding officer is having a particularly good working knowledge of parliamentary procedure and how to apply it with authority.

27.14   Associate Justice Felix Frankfurter described the ideal presiding officer when he wrote of Chief Justice Charles Evans Hughes:

> *He presided with great courtesy and with a quiet authority ... with great but gentle firmness. You couldn't but catch his own mood of courtesy.*
>
> *He never checked free debate, but the atmosphere which he created, the moral authority which he exerted, inhibited irrelevance, repetition, and fruitless discussion.*
>
> *He was a master of timing: he knew when discussion should be deferred and when brought to an issue. He also showed uncommon resourcefulness in drawing elements of agreement out of differences, and thereby narrowing, if not always escaping, conflicts.*[78]

27.15   See Chapter 28 for additional tips for presiding officers.

When the President Presides

27.16   The president presides at all meetings at which business may be conducted unless another individual has been designated as the presiding officer. If no officers are present at a meeting, any member may call the meeting to order and preside over the election of a temporary presiding officer (or *chair pro tem*). At social or program meetings, the program chair or another member may conduct the proceedings if no business is conducted. At business meetings, the presiding officer designated in the governing documents, if present, presides and cannot delegate this duty without permission from the assembly, except as noted below.

27.17 The presiding officer does not usually participate in debate; however, should the presiding officer wish to do so, the chair should be handed over to an individual who has not expressed an opinion in debate. This is usually the individual designated in the governing documents to act in the absence of the presiding officer but may be another impartial officer, member, or even the parliamentarian. If there is an objection to the person designated to serve as temporary chair, the assembly decides by majority vote without debate. Once a temporary occupant has assumed the chair, that responsibility is retained until the main motion is disposed of, and then it is returned to the presiding officer.

27.18 The presiding officer does not leave the chair merely to provide important facts of which the assembly may not be aware, although great care must be taken to do so in an impartial manner. However, if a motion applies to the president solely, the president-elect, if there is one, or the vice president is asked to take the chair until action on the motion has been completed. This is true whether the motion affects the president favorably—such as, for example, to award a life membership—or adversely, as in a vote of censure. The president does preside during an election even when he or she is a candidate for office.

27.19 Although there is a general principle that a person does not give up any basic rights of membership by becoming an officer, the presiding officer of an assembly should not propose or second a motion or nominate a candidate. The presiding officer retains any voting rights that would otherwise be held but usually does not exercise the right to vote, except when voting by ballot or to change the outcome of a vote.

THE PRESIDENT-ELECT

27.20 Some organizations elect an officer who will move into the office of president automatically at the end of a term as president-elect. The president-elect often has specific duties intended to increase that person's familiarity with the workings of the organization. The president-elect is in preparation for the office of president and automatically becomes the president when the latter's term of office expires.

27.21 The president-elect assumes the duties of the president in case of the absence or temporary incapacity of the president and becomes president on the death, resignation, removal, or permanent incapacity of the president unless the bylaws provide differently. This succession cannot be declined. Following completion of that term, that person serves the term as president as originally elected.

27.22 The president-elect also presides when the president is absent from a meeting, or it is necessary for the president to leave the chair temporarily. When acting in the place of the president at a meeting, the president-elect has all the procedural powers, duties, responsibilities, and privileges that the president may exercise at a meeting, but this does not entitle the president-elect to exercise other powers of the president designated for use outside the meeting, such as making appointments.

THE VICE PRESIDENT

27.23 When there is no president-elect, the vice president assumes the duties of the president in case of the absence or temporary incapacity of the president and becomes president on the death, resignation, removal, or permanent incapacity of the president unless the bylaws provide differently. This succession cannot be declined.

27.24 If the bylaws provide for filling a vacancy in the office of president that is not automatic, the vice president assumes all the duties of the president until the vacancy is filled, doing so without vacating the office of vice president.

27.25 When acting in the place of the president at a meeting, the vice president has all the procedural powers, duties, responsibilities, and privileges that the president may exercise at a meeting, but this does not entitle the vice president to exercise other powers of the president designated for use outside the meeting, such as making appointments.[79,80]

27.26 The vice president has only a few responsibilities established by parliamentary law but is often assigned other duties by the bylaws. Vice presidents frequently direct departments of work or study; head important committees, such as the finance or strategic planning committee; serve on the governing board; and perform other assigned duties.

27.27 When there are ranking vice presidents, the first vice president presides in the absence of the president and becomes president if that office is vacated unless the bylaws provide otherwise. If any vice president becomes president or otherwise vacates his or her office, the lower-ranking vice presidents move up in rank, and the vacancy in the lowest ranking office of vice president is filled by the body assigned to fill vacancies in office unless otherwise directed in the bylaws of the organization.[81,82]

THE SECRETARY

27.28 The president and the secretary are the minimum required officers of the organization. The secretary has extensive duties, serving as the chief recording and corresponding officer and the custodian of the records of the organization.[83] In some organizations, employees perform these functions, and the bylaws may permit the organization to designate an employee to be the secretary. Most membership organizations, however, elect a member as secretary, who is responsible for ensuring that the secretarial duties are performed properly, either by performing them personally or by overseeing the appropriate staff in those duties. The secretary works closely with the president.

27.29 The chief duties of a secretary are to:

1. oversee, or prepare, and submit for approval the minutes of the meetings, and enter any subsequent corrections (see Chapter 23 for more information on minutes);

2. provide the presiding officer or the assembly with the exact wording of a pending motion or of one previously acted on;

3. maintain an accurate list of members and call the roll when directed by the presiding officer;

4. read all papers, documents, or communications as directed by the presiding officer;

5. bring to each meeting a record of past minutes; a copy of the bylaws, rules, and policies; a list of the members; a list of standing and special committees; and a copy of the parliamentary authority adopted by the organization;

6. provide information located in the minutes reasonably requested by officers or members;

7. assist the presiding officer before each meeting in preparing a detailed agenda;
8. preserve all records, reports, and official documents of the organization except those specifically assigned to the custody of others;
9. prepare and send required notices of meetings and proposals;
10. provide the chair of each committee with a list of the committee members, a copy of all proposals referred to the committee, or the motion referring a subject to the committee, instructions, and other materials that may be useful;
11. sign official documents to attest to their authenticity;
12. carry on the official correspondence of the organization as directed, except correspondence assigned to other officers; and
13. perform any additional duties required by the bylaws or applicable statutes.

27.30 In addition to these duties, the secretary performs many other tasks, such as calling attention to actions in the minutes that have not been carried out and keeping a report book or file of all reports submitted, a correspondence file, and a book of adopted policies and procedures. The secretary is responsible for calling attention to deadlines and the dates for taking certain actions.

27.31 If the secretary resigns, is unable to act, or neglects to carry out the secretarial duties, the senior officer then in office may send out any necessary notices or may assign the duties of the secretary to one or more other members until the vacancy in the office of secretary is filled or the secretary resumes the duties of the office.

27.32 The elected secretary does not forfeit any rights of membership by reason of holding office and may propose motions, debate, and vote on all measures.

27.33 Some organizations divide the secretarial duties between a recording secretary and a corresponding secretary. The corresponding secretary may be assigned specific duties to monitor electronic communications, websites, and social media and to respond to members and nonmembers as appropriate, along with other duties.

THE TREASURER

27.34 The treasurer is responsible for the collection, safekeeping, and expenditure of all funds of the organization and for keeping accurate financial records. In many jurisdictions, the treasurer of a corporation may have additional duties prescribed by statute.

27.35 In organizations that delegate to employees the work of collecting, disbursing, and accounting for funds, the treasurer, whether an elected member or an appointed employee, is ultimately responsible for the performance of these duties and for the accuracy of the treasurer's reports.

27.36 The treasurer collects and disburses funds only as directed by law, the bylaws, the membership, the board of directors, or other authority provided for in the bylaws. The treasurer does not have the power to borrow money or disburse funds except as authorized. The treasurer usually helps prepare the budget and serves on the finance committee.

27.37 The treasurer reports on the finances of the organization at each membership and board meeting in appropriate detail, answers any questions on financial matters, and submits a full report to the membership annually. For more information on the report of the treasurer, see Chapter 32.

APPOINTED OFFICERS

27.38 If the bylaws authorize it, the president or board may appoint additional officers. Unless otherwise provided, appointed officers have no powers or rights as such, and only carry out duties as directed.

The Parliamentarian

27.39 There are two types of parliamentarians.

27.40 The first type of parliamentarian is the employed consultant who has had training and professional experience in parliamentary law and who is not a member of the organization. Professional parliamentarians are credentialed by either the American Institute of Parliamentarians or the National Association of Parliamentarians, or both. For more information on the role of the parliamentarian, see Chapter 29.

27.41 The second type of parliamentarian is the member parliamentarian elected by the members or appointed from the membership by the presiding officer. The choice of a member parliamentarian should be based primarily on the member's knowledge of parliamentary procedure. A member parliamentarian may also be intimately familiar with the rules, customs, and culture of the organization, and bring institutional and historical knowledge to the presiding officer.

27.42   However, a member parliamentarian likely does not possess the same expertise as a professional. Additionally, the member parliamentarian may hold—or be perceived to hold—an interest or bias in the outcome of some items of business.

27.43   In any case, the member parliamentarian provides advice to the presiding officer and does not make or offer rulings. This member is required to refrain from voting and participating in debate and should only address the assembly on parliamentary matters when expressly requested to do so, as with any credentialed parliamentarian.

27.44   Like the president, the member parliamentarian maintains neutrality during the meeting and refrains from voting, except by ballot, and refrains from making motions and participating in debate.

The Sergeant at Arms

27.45   The sergeant at arms, under the direction of the presiding officer, helps to maintain order and decorum at meetings. The sergeant at arms controls access to the meeting, directs the ushers, and is responsible for the comfort and convenience of the assembly. In a small organization, these duties may be performed by one person, but in a large one, there may be a staff of assistant sergeants at arms.

HONORARY OFFICERS

27.46   Some organizations provide in their bylaws for honorary officers. Honorary titles are created as a compliment to those on whom they are conferred; such honorary titles generally carry with them the right to attend meetings and to speak but not to propose motions, vote, or preside. If there are to be honorary officers, the bylaws of the organization must specify the office and its rights and privileges. Holding an honorary office does not prevent a person who is a member from exercising any rights as a member or from holding a regular office.

IMMEDIATE PAST PRESIDENT

27.47 Some organizations provide for an officer position of immediate past president, which is then filled by the outgoing president when that term is completed. This may be an honorary position or may include powers and duties defined in the bylaws. The outgoing president is the immediate past president unless the outgoing president did not complete their term as president. However, without a bylaw provision, this is not an officer position but is merely a statement of fact. If such an office is described in the bylaws, provisions should also address whether and how a vacancy is filled, any circumstances that would prevent holding the office, and other considerations.

POWERS OF OFFICERS

27.48 The actual powers and duties of officers are stated in the bylaws and sometimes in statutes and charters. In addition, officers have the implied power to do whatever is necessary to carry out the functions and duties of their office. For example, a president who has the duty of appointing a committee has the implied power to fill a vacancy on the committee or to remove and replace a committee member who fails to perform prescribed duties. However, when an officer's powers and duties are listed in the organization's governing documents, the officer generally has no additional powers or duties except those that arise directly from those listed or are otherwise granted by the assembly.

DELEGATION OF AUTHORITY BY OFFICERS, BOARDS, AND COMMITTEES

27.49 Both officers and members should understand their responsibilities in delegating to other members or employees the powers, duties, and responsibilities assigned to them by the law or the bylaws.

27.50 The basic principle of delegation is that the members, officers, boards, or committees delegating authority retain full responsibility for the performance or exercise of the powers, duties, and responsibilities that have been delegated.[84] They also are responsible for negligence and its consequences in the exercise of the delegated authority.

27.51 There are two general types of powers, duties, and responsibilities: legislative and administrative. Legislative powers and duties are those intended to have a long-term effect on the organization, and that are provided for in the law or bylaws, either expressly or by implication. These powers and duties cannot be delegated, except in profit-making corporations where most duties are delegated to the board. For example, if the bylaws provide that an organization's officers are elected by the membership at the annual meeting, the members cannot delegate this duty to the board of directors.

27.52 Administrative powers and duties are of two kinds: discretionary and ministerial. Discretionary powers and duties depend on a special trust in the officer, board, or committee member and involve personal reliance on that person's wisdom, integrity, and discretion. An example of a discretionary duty is the appointment of committees by the president or the certification of minutes by the secretary.

27.53 Discretionary powers and duties assigned to a particular officer or board by statute, charter, or bylaws can never be delegated. For example, a board of directors of a nonprofit corporation cannot delegate its power to borrow money. The board of directors can authorize a committee or an employee to investigate and recommend the best rates and sources for borrowing money, but the final decision must be made by the board.

27.54 Ministerial powers or duties do not call for the use of discretion but involve only the faithful performance of a mechanical or clerical function. Ministerial powers and duties can be delegated freely to members or employees. For example, a secretary has the ministerial duty of sending out notices of a meeting already authorized and can delegate this duty to other members or employees.

27.55 A committee may delegate some of its powers and duties to a subcommittee, but the committee remains responsible for all actions of its subcommittees.

27.56 Powers and duties should be delegated carefully and with the knowledge that the responsibility for supervising their exercise and execution remains with those delegating the duties.

TERM OF OFFICE

27.57 The bylaws should define the term of office of all officers, directors, and committees. Bylaws sometimes limit the number of consecutive terms that a member may hold an office, and in some cases the total number of terms permitted to be served. This provision is intended to prevent domination of the organization by a few members. However, a limitation on terms is a limitation on the right of members to elect whom they please. The deciding principle should be the overall good of the organization.

27.58 Many organizations favor a short term of office, which brings officers up for review by election frequently. If the members are alert and interested, it is often unnecessary to limit the number of terms to which a member may be elected. One term may be too long for a poor officer and three terms may be too short for a good officer.

27.59 When term limits are provided for in the bylaws for a particular office, service in office for a partial term is not counted as a term served for the purposes of term limits.

27.60 In contrast, when eligibility to hold a certain office includes a requirement that a member must have served a term in another office, serving for half or more of a term fulfills the requirement.

27.61 Officers are not always elected with regularity or at the precise time prescribed by law or the bylaws. The incumbents continue to hold office until their successors are elected or appointed.

27.62 It is generally not good practice to limit the total number of years a member can serve on a board without regard to which positions are held. The restriction can cause unanticipated problems as members move through the officer positions and use up their limited time on the board.

VACANCIES

27.63 The bylaws should include the procedure for filling vacancies. A vacancy in an office or a board position usually occurs because of the death, resignation, or removal of the officeholder, or a finding that the officeholder is ineligible. In these instances, there is no question that a vacancy exists. Such vacancies shall be recorded in the minutes.

27.64 There is sometimes uncertainty whether a vacancy has occurred, such as when there has been an abandonment of the office, an implied resignation, prolonged neglect, or an inability to act. If there is a question as to whether an office is vacant, the board declares the office vacant before a member is chosen to fill the vacancy.

27.65 Declaring a vacancy is not a means of removing an officer or a board member. These positions cannot be declared vacant when there is an eligible incumbent willing and able to continue in the office. The removal of such an incumbent would require the disciplinary procedures defined in Chapter 33.

27.66 A vacancy is filled by the same authority that selected the officer, or director, unless the bylaws provide otherwise. A special election may be called to enable the members to fill a vacancy. In such a situation, the president or the board is authorized to assign the duties of the vacant office to others until the vacancy is filled.

27.67 Some bylaws provide that the officer who is next in rank automatically moves up to fill a vacancy. Other bylaws require the board of directors to fill vacancies not otherwise provided for. If this duty is delegated to the directors or to any other group except the membership, unless the bylaws provide otherwise, the member chosen to fill the vacancy serves only on an interim basis until the next regular or special meeting at which the vacancy can be filled for the remainder of the term by the membership.

27.68 Vacancies in elective positions must not be ignored or concealed. Members should be informed promptly of a vacancy, and the vacancy should be filled as soon as possible. If the board of directors or the president knows that there is, or is about to be, a vacancy, this knowledge cannot properly be withheld until after a meeting, convention, or election at which the members could have elected someone to fill the vacancy.

27.69 Neither officers nor members should try to outwit the provisions of the bylaws by maneuvering to fill vacancies in elective positions by appointment. No member should accept any position with the intention of resigning to create a vacancy and thereby permit the appointment of another member.

27.70 The president, with the approval of the board, may assign the duties of a vacant officer position to one or more qualified members or to non-member staff on an interim basis. A vacancy in an officer or board position should never be allowed to prevent the organization from operating at any level.

THE EXECUTIVE DIRECTOR

27.71 While many small organizations operate solely through volunteers or a governing board or with some part-time staff, other organizations employ a chief administrator who is called by various titles, frequently the executive director. This person is usually chosen by the governing board or executive committee and is responsible to the selecting body.

27.72 The executive director, usually under supervision of the governing board, directs the administration of the organization, employs staff members, and performs any other duties assigned in accordance with the governing documents and the contract.

27.73 Typically, the executive director is the supervisor of all employed staff and the primary liaison between the staff and the board.

CHAPTER 28. The Skill and Art of Presiding

SKILL AND ART

28.1 Presiding is both a skill and an art. The skill is the what—knowing all the rules in your parliamentary authority, as well as the organization's bylaws and any temporary and standing rules of order it may have. The art is the how, why, and when to apply them.

FOUNDATIONS

28.2 The items in this list, when performed well, will build the trust of the assembly in the presiding officer. When trust is established, the presiding officer will be able to keep the meeting moving smoothly and efficiently with fewer interruptions:

1. demonstrate impartiality;
2. be helpful;
3. lead competently;
4. process motions efficiently;
5. understand meeting structure; and
6. manage decorum.

Demonstrate Impartiality

28.3 The presiding officer must project impartiality and treat all members fairly and does this by treating all members equally and with respect, avoiding actions that may be seen as attempts to influence the outcome, and refraining from speaking in debate on the merits of the issue. The effective presiding officer always remembers that it is the assembly that makes the decisions. The presiding officer rarely has no opinion on an issue but must conduct the business of the meeting impartially.

Be Helpful

28.4 Members appreciate and respect a presiding officer who is helpful and assists members in achieving their goals. New members may require such assistance, but experienced members may also request help through

Parliamentary or Factual Inquiries. Help should be provided gracefully. The presiding officer continues to build the goodwill and trust of the assembly with behavior that is helpful rather than impatient, unsympathetic, or condescending. Other members will appreciate the instruction and guidance that may, in fact, save time as others may have the same issue. Good answers to questions from a member or delegate are instructive and helpful to all.

28.5   Such learning opportunities can arise spontaneously or be anticipated by the presiding officer. If anticipated, the presiding officer may solicit a member in advance to make a Factual or Parliamentary Inquiry to illustrate the point. Such inquiries require priority recognition and can set the stage for a smoother-running meeting.

28.6   Alternatively, the presiding officer may provide a short explanation of a parliamentary or factual issue before the assembly if it does not become debate or an attempt to influence the decision.[85],[86]

Lead Competently

28.7   Projecting competence is essential as presiding officers present themselves to the assembly. It assures the members that the presiding officer knows the rules and applies them correctly to facilitate the conduct of the meeting. Presiding officers project competence so that members believe the presiding officer has the correct information to make the ruling, to make the right ruling, and to convince the members that the ruling is correct.

28.8   Competence is projected by consistently using the right language and a deliberate approach. This can be accomplished by overtly demonstrating fairness and explicitly taking the time to ensure that everyone understands the proceedings.

28.9   When presiding, a presiding officer projects both a nonverbal image and a verbal image. The nonverbal image indicates a sense of professionalism and their respect for the assembly. Generally, business attire and a confident posture present an image of professionalism. Maintaining eye contact conveys to the members that the presiding officer is paying attention to the assembly. The competent presiding officer is aware of their own facial expressions and maintains a pleasant demeanor throughout the meeting, even during contention or procedural confusion.

28.10   The verbal image is both what you say and how you say it. Establishing a cadence when processing motions and taking the votes, speaking deliberately and unhurriedly but without hesitations, and speaking with confidence all help to establish your verbal image.

28.11   Here are some acts that help demonstrate early in the meeting that the presiding officer can competently lead the meeting:

1. Prepare the members by letting them know that the meeting will be starting soon. The presiding officer should announce that the meeting will be called to order shortly, and that members should take their seats.
2. Start the meeting on time. Delaying the start penalizes those who are punctual and encourages a culture of inefficiency. The call to order should be preceded by a clear signal to obtain the attendees' attention, such as a vocal call or a single strike of the gavel.
3. Take your time early in the meeting. Be patient with members as the meeting begins. Be deliberate about going through each of the steps in processing motions using a practiced and repeatable cadence. Be sure everyone is clear on the effect of their vote prior to voting. Repeat each of the steps when announcing the result of a vote. Taking the time to explicitly repeat steps early in the meeting builds confidence in the impartiality and fairness of the presiding officer. Taking this time also allows members to demand a division of the assembly. A member who doubts the vote can move for a counted vote if the vote was not counted previously and if the member doubts the accuracy of the announced result of the vote.
4. Be conscious of and sensitive to the emerging parliamentary situation. There are many clues within a meeting that the situation may potentially deteriorate. A good presiding officer recognizes these clues and is prepared to take the appropriate steps.

Process Motions Efficiently

28.12   While content of motions may not be known in advance, processing those motions and taking votes should happen in a standardized manner. The members will become familiar and more comfortable with the process if the required steps are consistently followed with the appropriate language and a steady cadence, that is, the pace and rhythm of the presiding officer's voice.

28.13   The steps of processing a motion are listed in Chapter 10. Following is a list of items the presiding officer must consider or perform when applying these steps:

1. Determine the correct wording of the motion.
2. Have the motion brought to the podium in writing. Be sure that it is worded correctly and verify with the maker, if necessary, before proceeding.
3. If not submitted in writing, write it so that it can be repeated correctly any time it needs to be restated. Remember, the presiding officer has the right to require that motions be submitted in writing.
4. Before stating the motion, determine whether the proposed motion is in order and contains a clear proposal.
5. State the motion or resolution in full. If there is a display, refer to the display and read it aloud if necessary.
6. Re-state the immediately pending motion or resolution again after significant time debating. Restating the motion will give members an opportunity to focus on the business at hand.
7. Require members to state their name before debate. This frequently leads to better behavior.
8. Make sure the debate and any amendments are germane and in order. Attempt to alternate between proponents and opponents of a measure.
9. When putting the question, prepare the members for the vote. Ask, "Is there any further discussion?" Or state, "There being no one seeking recognition, we will proceed to vote." Pause to see if any member seeks recognition or objects. If that happens, be ready to continue debate. If no one seeks recognition or objects, put the pending motion to a vote.
10. Before taking the vote, instruct the members on what their vote means. For example, the first time the assembly votes on Close Debate and Vote Immediately, remind them that if they want to end debate and vote on the immediately pending question, vote in favor, and if they want to continue debating, vote in the negative.

28.14 Mastering the order of precedence and the language of parliamentary procedure will help the presiding officer to move efficiently into the proper wording for processing the proposal. Knowing what motions can be applied to a motion will help prevent improper motions from being processed. It also allows the presiding officer to be helpful to those that do not know how to properly word their intent. The presiding officer may inform the member that their motion is "not in order at this time" and may also advise them of the procedural steps that must occur before it may be proposed, e.g., "after the pending secondary amendment has been disposed of, that amendment will be in order." Practicing a script for processing common motions will help develop a cadence and perfection of the language that can be applied to less common motions.

28.15 Learning the basic rules of motions as defined in Chapters 12–16 is a fundamental skill for a presiding officer, and proficiency in using these rules should be a priority.

28.16 If you are unsure or unclear on the rules, pause to check them before you proceed, either by consulting the parliamentarian or reviewing the motion chart included in this book or available on the website at aipstandardcode.com.

Understand Meeting Structure

28.17 Meetings where decisions are to be made are usually conducted formally. Such formality is more conducive to respectful behavior and efficiency of the meeting and requires the rules below to be followed more closely and rigorously:

1. Members must seek recognition to speak and be recognized by the presiding officer before proceeding.
2. There is no discussion without a motion being made.
3. Each step in processing a motion is followed intentionally.
4. All debates and discussion are addressed to the chair.
5. Only last names and titles are used when speaking to or of another member, or sometimes the other members may be referred to in the third person. Sometimes no names at all are used but positions or other references to identify members such as "the last member speaking," or "the delegate from Missouri." It is best to never use the words "you," "your," "I," "me," or "my," when referring to others or yourself. The words *the member* and *presiding officer* are preferred. Examples are "The member's time has expired," not "Your time has expired"; "The member's point of order is not well taken," not "Your point of order is not well taken"; and "The ruling of the chair has been appealed," not "My ruling has been appealed."
6. If unanimous consent is not used, all steps in conducting a vote are followed.

28.18 In small boards or committees, less formality may be allowed by relaxing some of the rules if it improves the functionality of the meeting and respects the rights of all members. If it is the custom of the organization:

1. Members may make motions or speak without the necessity of formal recognition.
2. Motions do not have to be seconded.
3. Any limits on debate may be relaxed if others who wish to debate have similar opportunities.
4. A member may discuss things without a motion being on the floor.
5. The chair may make motions, participate in discussion, and vote.

28.19 The presiding officer may have to increase formality when there are larger groups, the proceedings are more contentious, or the culture of the group requires it.

28.20 As a meeting progresses and the confidence and trust in the chair grows, some steps in processing motions may be condensed, especially those in announcing a vote. The presiding officer should remember that the rules are made to facilitate the meeting and trivialities may be ignored. A good example of this is when a motion has been made and debate is underway, but no second was made. Obviously more than one person is interested in discussing the motion so the second is assumed, and the meeting can proceed.

Managing Decorum

28.21 The presiding officer must be vigilant about breaches of decorum and intervene early to prevent proceedings from deteriorating. See Chapter 11, the section, Rules of Decorum and Conduct in Debate. Early intervention can be more tactful and gentler and avoid the need for more severe disciplinary measures. Decorum is acting and speaking respectfully during the meeting and listening carefully to what others are saying. Members should always speak to the merits of a motion. It is never in order to speak to the motives and personalities of members. Neither is the use of profanity or other foul language permissible. Generally speaking, if it would be considered rude in polite conversation, it is likely out of order. The presiding officer should interrupt the debate, including the member, to remind the member—and the assembly—of the rules of decorum and require adherence to them, "The chair wishes to remind the member—and all the members of this assembly—that attacking the motives or reputation of another member are not in order. Debate will be confined to the merits of the pending motion."

28.22 Members who persist in misconduct during a meeting may be removed from the meeting by vote of the assembly as follows: "Member John Smith, you must conform to the rules of this meeting and to the rules of decorum. You have been reminded of the rule once and you are now recognized for these repetitive offenses. Any further violations will be subject to further discipline."

28.23 If a member persists in breaches of the rules, or if the assembly is becoming more unruly due to contentious debate or an issue that has sharply divided the members, it may be wise to suggest a recess. The recess may provide a "cooling off" period in either circumstance and allow the opportunity for a compromise or mutually satisfactory solution to be reached.

28.24 If the member again persists in violations of decorum, the presiding officer may ask to have the member removed from the assembly hall. The presiding officer may assume or entertain the undebatable motion: "Shall the member be allowed to remain in the room?"

28.25 Finally, with regard to the general demeanor of the presiding officer:

1. Refrain from calling attention to yourself. Your behaviors should focus the attention of the members on the motions or resolutions that are coming before them. When a member poses a factual inquiry, seek out someone who has expertise to answer the question and try to refrain from answering yourself.

2. Speak only when required. Don't respond to rhetorical questions or questions that are not directed explicitly to you. Encourage others to speak, especially those who may have been silent during the proceedings, but don't continue to seek debate when the members have responded with their silence when asked, "Is there further debate?"

3. Refrain from using the words *I*, *me*, or *mine*. Use "the presiding officer," "your presiding officer," "the chair," or "your chair." At times, first person plural may be used: "Are we ready to vote?"

4. When making a decision, be decisive in stating your ruling ("the chair rules that…") Speak confidently in articulating why this ruling is the right decision. Sports officials are trained to consider and confirm that they are making an informed and reasonable decision, and then to "Blow the whistle firmly and confidently and sell the call!"

CHAPTER 29. The Professional Parliamentarian

29.1 A credentialed parliamentarian can be helpful and is often essential for effective meeting management and more.

29.2 A professional parliamentarian has had training and professional experience in parliamentary law and is usually not a member of the organization. Professional parliamentarians should be credentialed by the American Institute of Parliamentarians, the National Association of Parliamentarians, or both. Accreditation is a higher standard than simple membership in these organizations and is obtained through successful demonstration of knowledge.

29.3 Unless retained to represent a specific group of members, the parliamentarian is not an advocate for causes or a representative of any group or individual within the organization but is retained to help the body accomplish the legitimate purposes of the organization.

MEETING OR CONVENTION PARLIAMENTARIAN

29.4 Traditionally, and most commonly, a professional parliamentarian serves as the meeting or convention parliamentarian. This may be a convention, a meeting of the general membership, or a meeting of a smaller body such as the board or a committee.

29.5 The meeting parliamentarian is primarily an advisor to the presiding officer. Specifically, the meeting parliamentarian advises the presiding officer on how rules and procedures can be applied properly to facilitate good decisions, allowing the presiding officer to conduct the meeting, process items of business, and make rulings. The meeting parliamentarian is, like the presiding officer, neutral regarding the issues being considered and focuses on advising that proper process is followed and that the rights of members, both as individuals and collectively as the assembly, are protected.

29.6 The meeting parliamentarian is primarily responsible to the presiding officer but may also aid and advise others outside of and in preparation for the meeting, such as the board; committees, especially committees with an active role in the organization's annual meeting or convention; other officers; staff; and members of the assembly.

29.7 Many organizations retain a parliamentarian on an annual basis, which allows for consultations on parliamentary questions at any time as well as assistance in meeting or convention planning. If this is not done, the meeting parliamentarian should be engaged early during the planning phases of the meeting to advise and assist on matters such as:

1. reviewing the proposed agenda, noting potential problems, and proposing measures to avoid or minimize them;
2. reviewing the governing documents to confirm whether the meeting plans are in compliance and that all required activities will be performed;
3. drafting or advising on the rules of order for the meeting or convention;
4. preparing the presiding officer, other leaders, and staff for their roles at the meeting; and
5. drafting or reviewing and advising on the script for the meeting, including correct procedural language for all who will be speaking or presenting from the podium.

29.8 At the meeting itself, the parliamentarian sits next to the presiding officer to unobtrusively provide advice and information or engage in a short discussion. The parliamentarian is responsible for advising that no procedural details are overlooked, for anticipating procedural strategy, and for making sure the chair is aware of parliamentary requirements to be observed. If a serious mistake is being made, the parliamentarian unobtrusively calls it to the attention of the presiding officer, who then decides what action to take. The parliamentarian often has experience that allows them to anticipate problems and suggest proactive interventions to the presiding officer.

29.9 The parliamentarian may also train members on rules and procedures before the meeting or convention. During the meeting itself, the meeting parliamentarian only engages with the members of the assembly at the direction of the presiding officer; this is uncommon and usually occurs if a particularly complicated procedural concept needs to be explained.

29.10 Because the parliamentarian advises and works at the direction of the presiding officer, the relationship between the two is vital to the success of the meeting. The presiding officer may or may not follow the advice and is responsible for the final ruling, based on the officer's knowledge of the organization, assembly, and procedures. However, the more capable presiding officer understands the value and importance of a good parliamentarian. An experienced presiding officer understands that a parliamentarian brings a professional attitude and an excellent knowledge of the details of the procedures so that the presiding officer is free to concentrate on the agenda and the overall progress and tone of the meeting. This enables the presiding officer to focus on the assembly and proceed with confidence and poise.

29.11   In some organizations, the presiding officer chooses the parliamentarian although the organization's board or staff will also likely be involved in this decision. The organization's engagement with the parliamentarian may continue over many years, even while the leadership changes, which allows for a deeper familiarity and understanding of the organization's rules and culture. At a minimum, the best practice is for the parliamentarian to meet with the presiding officer to determine the method of communication between them before and during meetings, to review the meeting script, and to prepare for contingencies that may come up during the meeting.

29.12   Occasionally, it may be advantageous for the parliamentarian to preside over portions of the meeting, and this may be prearranged if controversial topics or contentious discussion is anticipated. The provisions of the next section, Professional Presiding Officer, apply during these portions of the meeting.

29.13   Following the closing of a meeting or convention, the parliamentarian should follow up with the organization on the items of business acted upon during the meeting. The parliamentarian has the opportunity at this time to provide input to the leadership on any procedures that should be changed for the next meeting or problems that need to be addressed.

PROFESSIONAL PRESIDING OFFICER

29.14   There are circumstances where a professional neutral third party is the best option to preside over a meeting. Due to their expertise, many certified parliamentarians often function as a professional presider or a *professional presiding officer* for an organization although occasionally a well-respected individual may be invited to preside. In either case, the invited presiding officer is required to be impartial on the issues while still processing procedural rulings and any subsequent appeals.

29.15   The decision to engage a professional presiding officer may simply be a recognition that a neutral third party would best serve the needs of a particular situation. It may also arise as a result of concerns regarding, or a lack of confidence in, the current presiding officer because of a conflict of interest; perceptions of unfairness; prior attempts to exceed the authority of the position; or lack of prowess at presiding.

29.16   Even though the bylaws may state that a specific officer "will preside at all meetings," the specified officer may voluntarily yield that duty to another to preside over a specific motion or to preside over the entire meeting.

29.17   In some cases, these provisions may assign the duty of presiding to a designated successor if the specified officer does not preside. The designated successor may also delegate this duty to a professional presider or other skilled individual voluntarily.

29.18   There may be occasions when either the body has lost confidence in the designated presiding officer or simply wants to ensure that a neutral facilitator will preside over the meeting. In these instances, the body may temporarily relieve the designated presiding officer and any designated successors by a majority vote.

29.19   When using a professional presiding officer, only those duties associated with the business of the meeting are assumed by the professional presider. All the other powers, rights, duties, and responsibilities of the presiding officer enumerated in the bylaws remain with that officer. For example, the parliamentarian would not be able to vote or appoint members to committees when he or she presides over the meeting.[87]

DRAFTING/AMENDING/REVISING BYLAWS

29.20   Professional parliamentarians are consulted to create bylaws for new organizations and to compose amendments or a revised set of bylaws for existing organizations. An important objective in creating or making changes to bylaws is to ensure that the resulting document is free from conflicts within it and free from conflicts with higher level governing documents as well as the law.

29.21   Parliamentarians begin the process by meeting with the client to obtain a thorough understanding of the client's request and its needs. There may be several individuals or groups within the organization that provide input because the bylaws specify the framework for the entire organization, how it functions, and the rights and privileges of members and committees.

Frequent communications with the client during the drafting process is important. It helps to ensure that the parliamentarian and the client are in continual agreement about the course of the project, and it enhances efficiency by minimizing the amount of time spent in reworking the language.

29.22 In the process of gathering information, the parliamentarian should identify customs that would best be codified to prevent future challenges. The parliamentarian may also identify issues that could be resolved by making changes to the existing framework or functions of the organization, such as separating the functions of a secretary-treasurer into two separate offices of secretary and treasurer. Situations in which bylaw provisions stifled or hindered operations in the past, should be addressed, such as providing for an election by acclamation when there is only one candidate for office.

29.23 Parliamentarians should use plain language in drafting to help members understand the provisions and to reduce confusion. Parliamentary rules should not be included because of the possible need to quickly vary from a procedural rule. Such rules are more conveniently placed in a document other than the bylaws so that they are easier to access and change.

29.24 Prior to adopting the new document or amendments, the client should be advised of the differences in the methods for consideration and voting as described in Chapter 6.

WRITTEN OPINIONS AND EXPERT TESTIMONY

29.25 Often parliamentary problems involve several rules and principles. A parliamentarian must be able to reconcile the principles and rules of parliamentary law that may be involved in a particular situation with the documents of the organization. When asked a question, the parliamentarian must give a considered opinion as to how the rules and principles apply. Having been retained as an authority, the parliamentarian should be familiar with the organization's parliamentary authority and governing documents to the degree that it is generally unnecessary to research the documents during a meeting.

29.26 In cases where there is a dispute on procedure outside the meeting, or within a meeting of an organization without a meeting parliamentarian, a parliamentarian should be hired to write a parliamentary opinion that interprets the rules in question and recommends further action. The parliamentarian should have all relevant rules and documents before the opinion is drafted. Otherwise, additional information may change the interpretation and recommendations within the opinion. A parliamentary opinion is not the same as, or a substitute for, legal consultation.

29.27 Occasionally, a parliamentarian will be hired as an expert witness. Before providing testimony in court, the expert witness may also be asked to provide a written report. It is important to consult with the attorney first to ensure that the testimony from an expert witness can be admitted. If the organization decides to hire an expert witness, the attorney should be in close contact with the parliamentarian, providing important deadlines and the scope of the report. It is especially important that the parliamentarian be provided with full and correct information, as this may otherwise impact the testimony and its admissibility, as well as the overall case.

TEACHING

29.28 A professional parliamentarian can provide services to an organization, an individual, or groups of individuals by conducting classes or workshops on various aspects of parliamentary procedure. These can include short presentations on limited topics, up to and including workshops to teach presiding at an in-depth level of skill and knowledge.

29.29 For a target audience of members, short presentation topics are more common and can be on topics such as main motions, amendments, agendas, voting, rules of debate, bylaws, board member orientation, and others to meet the specific requested topics that are of particular interest to the organization.

29.30 For presiding officers, presiding workshops can be as short as a few hours, covering only the most basic skills and commonly encountered motions, up to a full weekend workshop covering almost all the motions in the parliamentary authority, with presiding practice opportunities, as well as topics beyond the content of books.

29.31 The American Institute of Parliamentarians provides a Teachers' Course and issues credentials in the form of the "T" designation to AIP-credentialed parliamentarians who complete that course. As with other parliamentary credentials, the *T* must be maintained and renewed at intervals based on current requirements and documentation of ongoing teaching experience.

PARLIAMENTARIANS AS CONSULTANTS

29.32 Parliamentarians can be engaged to work in several roles that may not be "traditional" parliamentary roles.

29.33 Frequently parliamentarians have consulting roles that take advantage of their specialized knowledge. Some of these specialized roles include serving as elections monitor or head teller, preparing minutes, assisting the credentials or other convention committees, and assisting with technological issues in the meeting, including serving as a "live editor" at meetings, projecting motions and amendments, or managing electronic polling or voting.

29.34 Credentialed parliamentarians are well qualified to serve as elections monitors or head tellers. These individuals' training and testing help assure their knowledge about counting ballots, and their ability to ensure that the tellers' reports are presented fairly and accurately.

29.35 Professional parliamentarians can bring in teams of individuals to serve as tellers, ensuring that the balloting process is managed by a team with both expertise and demonstrated neutrality.

29.36 Many times, parliamentarians are engaged to work with convention committees, reviewing or drafting proposed convention rules or assisting with designing and preparing the credentials committee's report. Parliamentarians may also assist with reference committees and the recommendations that they present to the assembly to ensure that they are in appropriate form.

29.37 Some professional parliamentarians are adept technically, as well, and can manage electronic meeting platforms, electronic voting systems (whether an in-room keypad system or a voting application that can be used for a hybrid or virtual meeting).

FLOOR PARLIAMENTARIAN

29.38 A credentialed parliamentarian may be asked to serve in the nontraditional role of advising a group or individual, rather than the presiding officer, on parliamentary procedure in real time during a meeting. This role is termed a floor parliamentarian. A floor parliamentarian is relieved from the obligation to be impartial; only a faction or an individual from the larger body is being represented. This service is usually requested to advise the group or individual regarding procedure and strategy. This helps ensure that those members retain their ability to fully exercise rights as a member of the assembly. This service may also include strategy and planning sessions prior to the meeting to prepare the group or individual for situations which may occur during the meeting.

29.39 In many cases, the presence of a floor parliamentarian along with a parliamentarian serving in the traditional role facilitates the orderly transaction of business. In such a situation, proponents of both sides of an issue are receiving proper parliamentary advice on how to accomplish their goals. A floor parliamentarian, like a traditional parliamentarian, has no inherent right to interject their opinion or advice upon an assembly unless asked to do so by a majority of the body. A floor parliamentarian should not be utilized to violate the rules of an assembly through procedural maneuvers.

CONTRACTUAL ISSUES

29.40 It is vital when engaging a credentialed parliamentarian to precisely define the role, duties, and reporting relationship. These provisions are definitive in determining the professional responsibilities of the parliamentarian, particularly when serving in a nontraditional role. As part of this contract, it should be clear that the parliamentarian only advises on parliamentary matters and not on legal matters.

CHAPTER 30. Boards

DEFINITION

30.1 The bylaws of many organizations provide that a smaller group, acting on behalf of all the members, shall carry on the work of the organization between meetings of the membership. The group is called the board of directors, executive board, board of trustees, or some other name meaning the governing board.

30.2 A board may have specific responsibilities and authorities detailed in the governing documents and may also have statutory obligations. Boards can vary in scope of authority and in size, depending on the characteristics of the organization; however, boards are always subject to the authority of the entire membership, except as the bylaws or statutes may provide otherwise.

MEMBERS OF THE BOARD

30.3 The bylaws must designate the membership of a board, including the size, composition, and method of selection of board members. A governing board of a voluntary organization is generally composed of the elected officers of the organization and of directors elected by the membership. Board members, including officers, may be elected at large, on a regional basis, by specific constituencies within the membership, or by other means as the bylaws provide, including combinations of such methods. Boards may not change their own membership unless authorized by the bylaws.

30.4 Many organizations give continuity to the board by staggering the terms of members of the board so that the entire membership does not turn over at the same time; this ensures that there are always experienced members on the board. Usually, the president and secretary of the parent body are the chair and secretary of the governing board. All members of the governing board are sometimes referred to as officers, but the term *officers*, as used in this book, refers to those with specific titles such as president, secretary, and treasurer and does not include the members elected or appointed to the board without further duties assigned.

30.5 Individual officers and directors have no independent capacity to make determinations on behalf of the organization except that officers or directors may have specific authority to commit the organization to certain actions within their areas of responsibility.[88]

DUTIES, POWERS, AND RESPONSIBILITIES

30.6 The duties, powers, and responsibilities of the board of directors should be clearly defined in the bylaws. Such a board is usually authorized to act for the membership in the intervals between membership meetings unless certain powers are assigned exclusively to the membership by the bylaws. In some jurisdictions, the board may have statutory powers defined, and the statute may or may not provide the authority to restrict those powers by bylaw provisions.

30.7 The final authority of any organization remains with its assembled members, except as that assembly may direct otherwise by adopting provisions in the bylaws or the adopted parliamentary authority. Any action of a governing board can be rescinded or modified by the membership unless law or the bylaws assign authority to the board, or the matter acted on no longer remains within the control of the organization. All members of a governing board share in a joint and collective authority, which exists and can be exercised only when the board is in a meeting. Individual members of a board have no greater authority than any other member of the organization except when the board is acting collectively. Officers and members to whom specific duties are assigned perform the duties of their offices or assignments in addition to sharing in the group authority and duties of the board.

PROCEDURE IN BOARDS

30.8 Depending on several factors, a board may conduct itself more or less formally as it finds appropriate. Small boards may conduct business with less formality while large boards usually require more formality. The appropriate level of formality is not determined by a specific number of members but more by the ability of the board to function efficiently and effectively with the degree of formality being followed. The formality may be established by rule or by custom, but generally if procedure is creating confusion or not allowing clear decision-making, more formality may be needed. See Chapter 31, "Committees and Committee Reports," the section Procedure in Committee Meetings, for specific ways that procedures may be relaxed.

30.9 In the same way, if a specific issue or issues in general are complex or contentious, greater formality may be needed to navigate decision-making without confusion or wasted time. The same principle may apply if one or more board members have difficulty conducting themselves in a courteous and orderly fashion. A skilled presiding officer will identify the degree of formality that is appropriate for a specific board, and this may vary from issue to issue and from meeting to meeting.

CONFIDENTIALITY AND MINUTES

30.10 Business conducted at a board meeting should not be discussed, except with other directors, unless and until the information has been issued to all members or to the public by approval of the board. The minutes of a board are available only to its members, unless the board decides otherwise, because the board considers many matters that cannot be discussed outside of the board without injury to the organization or to its members. All board members have access to minutes of board meetings, including meetings the board member did not attend or that occurred before the individual was a board member. Minutes of board meetings are not available to those members no longer on the board, even minutes of those meetings they attended.

30.11 If authorized in the bylaws, the assembly may order board minutes to be made available to all members, except for minutes of closed sessions. The motion to make minutes available should be qualified as to which minutes should be made available. Minutes for board meetings held in closed session shall not be subject to inspection by the assembly unless the board has voted to make them available. The method of distribution shall be determined by the rules of the organization.

COMMITTEES OF THE BOARD

30.12 The board has the right to establish and appoint committees of the board to which it may delegate authority and that are directly responsible to the board. The composition and duties of such committees may be governed by the bylaws or applicable statutes. If the bylaws designate the board to take specific actions, such as filling vacancies, that authority may not be delegated to a committee although a committee may recommend a final action to be taken by the board.

30.13 In some organizations, it is customary to provide for a small executive committee of the governing board, usually composed of the president, designated additional officers, and perhaps additional board members. The authority of an executive committee to take actions should usually be balanced with a consideration of the necessity of the organization to act quickly when needed, on the one hand, and with the potential risks of a small body executing substantial power, on the other hand.

30.14 The specific composition, powers, and duties of this committee must be provided for in the bylaws. In the absence of such bylaw provisions, an executive committee has no different authority than any other board committee. Some organizations give the executive committee extensive power to act for the board between its meetings, with designated exceptions, and perhaps with specific areas of independent power. Others limit it to acting on emergency matters or on recurring matters that must be disposed of promptly. In most cases, the board can rescind the action of the executive committee just as if it had taken the action itself.

30.15 An executive committee reports to the board, and its actions are reviewed by the board at each meeting and included in the minutes of the board. An executive committee should keep its own minutes, particularly if it has specific duties that it can exercise independently of the board.

CONFLICTS OF INTEREST

30.16 A director or officer of an organization is permitted to have business dealings with the organization, except when prohibited by the bylaws or by law. The director or officer has both a legal and a moral duty to disclose any interest in such a transaction and must deal fairly with and in the best interests of the organization.[89] For organizations adopting this parliamentary authority, a board member with a personal interest may not vote or debate on the matter but, if present, is counted toward the quorum unless the bylaws of the organization or applicable law requires otherwise.

30.17 Organizations may define conflicts of interest in their bylaws and provide the details of the expected or required conduct of officers and members with such conflicts, and the procedures to be followed when these bylaw provisions are violated. Before adopting such a statement in their bylaws, an organization should review applicable state law, which often includes provisions on the matter of conflict of interest and the extent to which members of a board must be excluded from debate and/or voting when a conflict of interest may exist. State law may include provisions on the matter of conflict of interest and the extent to which members of a board must be excluded from debate and/or voting.

30.18 Tax-exempt status of an organization is another reason for caution in dealings between the organization and a member of its governing board. If a transaction is found to unduly favor a director or officer, the tax-exempt status of the organization, for example, under the US Internal Revenue Code, may be jeopardized.[90]

FIDUCIARY DUTY OF BOARD MEMBERS

30.19 As previously noted, officers and directors owe a legal duty to the organization when assuming a decision-making role, and this duty supersedes all other duties, including to their specific constituencies. This responsibility is referred to by the term *fiduciary duty*. Every decision-maker, which may include officers, directors, committee members that have the power to act, and individuals with designated responsibilities, owes the organization a duty of care and a duty of loyalty. A generic overview of the duties of care and of loyalty are provided, but the specifics will vary between jurisdictions and there may be other duties required of decision-makers.

30.20 The duty of care requires that decision-makers act with the same level of care when acting on behalf of the organization that a reasonable person would use in similar circumstances.

30.21 The duty of loyalty requires decision-makers to act in the best interest of the organization and not for their own personal interests. Decision-makers that personally benefit from the actions taken by the organization have a duty to disclose the benefit but may also be tasked with proving the actions were in the best interest of the organization. Common actions that decision-makers must be aware of are:

1. the organization engaging in a transaction that the decision-maker may be involved in with another party to the transaction;
2. actions that the decision-maker could appear to benefit from whether the transaction was completed or not completed;
3. the decision-maker or a close family member receiving a personal financial benefit; or
4. action in which the decision-maker holds a personal interest.

30.22 Decision-makers should also be aware that denying the organization an opportunity and obtaining it personally or providing that same opportunity to another organization could constitute a breach of loyalty.

STATUTORY PROVISIONS RELATED TO PUBLIC BOARDS AND OTHER ORGANIZATIONS

30.23 Public bodies, and in some cases other types of organizations, such as homeowner associations or condominium boards, may be subject to statutory provisions such as notice, quorum and agenda requirements, voting requirements, or those governing their composition and actions. There may be provisions prohibiting discussion of board business outside of board meetings, sometimes referred to as sunshine laws or open meeting laws. The legislation establishing such public boards usually defines their authority and limitations, as well as how their membership is established. Procedural rules governing such boards may be specific to the particular board or derived from general statutory requirements for public boards. Nevertheless, it is almost always permissible for such boards to adopt a parliamentary authority to provide rules and guidance for matters not determined by the law, and this is advisable.

CHAPTER 31. Committees and Committee Reports

31.1 Committees are subdivisions of the membership charged with various aspects of the work of the organization. Standing committees are those that are designated in the bylaws and, as such, remain in existence if they remain in the bylaws. Special committees are created to fulfill a specific assignment and cease to exist once their final report is delivered.

IMPORTANCE OF COMMITTEES

31.2 Committees are important because they perform the bulk of the work in many organizations. One way that members can share in the work and responsibilities of their organization is through committee service. Recommendations from committees often become the final decisions of organizations. Most well-run business meetings spend considerable time on committee reports and recommendations. While the conclusions of committees are often accepted as the conclusions of the organization, committees do not have the authority to make final decisions on matters, except to the extent that the bylaws of the organization grant such authority, or the organization delegates such authority to a committee.

31.3 Committees should never become dumping grounds for issues, nor should committee membership be used to reward members or to placate troublemakers. Committees can be excellent training grounds for future leaders of an organization but should only be established if needed.

31.4 In some jurisdictions, applicable law may provide restrictions or rules regarding the composition and operation of an organization's committees.

31.5 Some of the advantages that enable a committee to work more efficiently than the larger parent organization are:

1. Greater freedom of discussion is possible.
2. More time is available for each subject assigned to the committee.
3. Informal procedure is used in committee meetings.
4. Better use can be made of experts and consultants.
5. Delicate and troublesome questions may be considered without publicity.

6. Hearings may be held giving members an opportunity to express their opinions.

STANDING COMMITTEES

31.6 A standing committee does the work within its particular area of responsibility as described in the bylaws or referred to it by the organization or the governing board. Members of standing committees serve the same terms as those of officers unless the bylaws provide otherwise. Standing committees are ready to receive referrals and to carry out ongoing or recurrent assignments. A membership committee, which investigates and forwards applications for membership, is an example of a standing committee.

31.7 An organization may provide for and fix the duties of as many standing committees as it finds useful. The name, method of selecting members and their number, quorum, duties, term of office, and requirements for reports of each standing committee are often included in the bylaws. Standing committees are created and dissolved in accordance with the bylaws.

SPECIAL COMMITTEES

31.8 A special committee performs a specific task assigned by the body creating it. Even if called by another name such as an *ad hoc committee*, a *task force*, or a commission, and unless otherwise designated by the organization, groups of members that are performing a specific task assigned by the organization or board are special committees and are subject to the same rules as special committees.

31.9 A special committee ceases to exist when its final report is issued or when its assigned actions are completed. If the body that created the committee votes to delegate additional work to a special committee, it continues until the new assignment is completed and another report is submitted. A committee created to arrange a social gathering is an example of a special committee. The body that created a special committee may also take action to dissolve it.

31.10 Special committees of an organization are created and appointed as directed by the assembly, and report to the assembly, or as the assembly otherwise directs. The need for such special committees may arise to address particular purposes, which may include but are not limited to investigating issues in need of research; gathering facts, evidence, and testimony for disciplinary matters; or implementing actions that the organization has decided to take. A special committee of a board of directors is created and appointed by action of that board, and reports to the board, or as the board otherwise directs. The motion creating a committee should include its purpose and any instructions needed, and any powers that are desired. For more information on the delegation of power and authority by officers, boards, and committees, see Chapters 27 and 30.

31.11 Committees may be established primarily for deliberation or primarily for action.

Committees for Deliberation

31.12 A committee appointed for deliberation and investigation or one that performs discretionary duties should be composed of members such that more than one point of view is examined, both when considering information and explaining the impact of that information. The report of such a representative committee will likely reflect the opinions of the whole organization and, as a result, its recommendations are more likely to be adopted. A nominating committee and a committee to recommend the location for a new building are examples of committees that should have members who represent opinions from differing perspectives within the organization.

Committees for Action

31.13 A committee for action executes a particular task already decided on. This type of committee does not function well unless composed of members who favor the job to be done. A committee established to raise an endowment fund or plan a special event is an example.

Selection of the Committee Chair

31.14 A committee chair should be chosen for the ability to plan and direct the work of the committee and to function well with its members. On a deliberative committee, this may not be the person with the most expertise but rather the one with the best facilitation skills. On an action committee, it is the one best able to lead the implementation of the action. Unlike the presiding officer of an assembly, the chair of a committee may take an active part in its discussion and deliberations and usually has all the rights of the other members, including the rights to present motions and vote.

31.15 The body or person authorized to appoint the members of a committee has the right to appoint the chair. If no committee chair is elected or appointed, the committee may select its own from among its membership. If no chair is designated, the member first named convenes the first meeting and presides during the election of a chair.

31.16 Recent practice increasingly utilizes the appointment of co-chairs of committees. However, it is rare for two or more separate individuals to be able to exercise leadership of a committee as effectively as a single member. Such appointments create uncertainty as to which roles and responsibilities of a committee chair should be carried out by which co-chair. Differences of opinion between the co-chairs can be difficult to resolve; co-chairs are not recommended.

31.17 In most situations, identification and utilization of vice-chairs, to whom specific areas of work are assigned and who operate under the direction of a single committee chair, is likely to be a more successful approach to such shared leadership.

SELECTION, REMOVAL, AND REPLACEMENT OF COMMITTEE MEMBERS

31.18 Even if the president or another officer has the power to appoint a committee, this does not include the power to establish or create such a committee under that officer's own authority.

31.19 Members of standing committees are appointed as directed in the bylaws, often by the president with the approval of the governing board or assembly. The advice and suggestions of members enable the president to utilize effectively the talents of a larger number of members.

31.20 It is often advisable to consult a prospective committee chair regarding the selection of the other committee members, and an incumbent committee chair regarding the appointment of a successor. However, a committee chair does not have the authority to add or remove members of the committee; that authority lies with the appointing person or body. Those serving on committees serve at the pleasure of those who have appointed them. Only the appointing officer or the approving body may remove a member or the chair from a committee position. No reason for removal is usually required, but it is uncommon to remove a committee member unless the member has failed to do assigned work, does not attend meetings, or is disruptive to the committee's work in some way.

31.21 In the absence of rules to the contrary, vacancies on a committee, including a vacancy in the committee chair, may be filled in the same manner as was the case for the original appointment.

EX OFFICIO MEMBERS OF COMMITTEES

31.22 Some organizations may designate specific position holders, such as an officer or a committee chair, to serve as a member of a committee while holding that position. Whether or not a member of the organization, sometimes those who hold a specific position in a parent or subordinate organization, or in other roles, are deemed members of a committee by virtue of their position. In both examples, such members are termed *ex officio members*. An ex officio member is not elected or appointed to a committee but automatically becomes a member when elected or appointed to a particular office. When an ex officio member ceases to hold the position that entitles the member to hold the ex officio position, that person's membership on the committee terminates and the new holder of the office assumes the ex officio membership. For example, the president is often an ex officio member of all committees except the nominating committee.

31.23 Unless the organization's governing documents provide otherwise, an ex officio member has all the rights, responsibilities, and duties of other members of the committee, including the right to vote. The ex officio member is a full working member of a committee and is counted in determining both what the quorum is and if a quorum exists at a meeting.

31.24 Anyone who is not expected to be a regular working member of the committee should be designated as an advisory or consultant member instead of being given ex officio status. An advisory or consultant member has the right to attend meetings and participate in debate but is not counted in determining the quorum, does not count toward the achievement of a quorum, and does not have the right to make motions or vote.

COMPOSITION, POWERS, RIGHTS, AND DUTIES OF COMMITTEES

31.25 The composition, powers, rights, and duties of each standing committee are provided for in the bylaws. The composition, powers, rights, and duties of special committees are provided for in the motions creating them or in the instructions given to them. Since no committee has inherent powers, rights, or duties, these must be delegated to it by the authority that established the committee. Even an executive committee or board of directors has no powers and no duties except those delegated to it by the bylaws or by vote of the membership, except as applicable law may provide otherwise.[91] For more information on the delegation of powers and duties to boards, see Chapter 27.

31.26 Unless otherwise provided in the bylaws or in a resolution establishing a committee, all committees are responsible to and work under the direction and control of the authority that created or established them. Standing committees are ultimately responsible to and usually under the control of the appointing body, and report to the board when the board is acting for the assembly in the intervals between membership meetings. Standing committees are responsible to the board only if the bylaws stipulate that. Special committees, no matter how appointed, are responsible to the authority establishing the special committee.

31.27 Any subject or duty that has been assigned to a special committee may be withdrawn at any time and assigned to another committee or considered by the body. Any proposal or assignment of work to a standing committee may be withdrawn by the governing body unless the subject or motion is assigned exclusively to that committee by the bylaws. Any special committee may be dissolved by the authority that created it.[92]

31.28 A committee cannot claim to represent the organization to any outside person or organization except when specifically authorized to do so. Unless there is specific authorization given to a committee to collect, hold, or disburse funds, all funds should be collected, held, and disbursed through the regular financial channels of the organization.

31.29 A committee has the right to appoint subcommittees of its own members, to which it may delegate authority. Such subcommittees are directly responsible to the committee. Subcommittees report only to the committee that created them. In committees with a heavy workload, subcommittees can assist in the completion of that work, and the work done by chairs of such subcommittees may be useful in identifying future committee chairs.

WORKING MATERIALS FOR COMMITTEES

31.30 The secretary is responsible for ensuring that each committee is furnished with specific instructions on the work it is expected to do and with all helpful information that is in the possession of the organization, including:

1. a list of the committee members and contact information, such as phone numbers, email addresses, and any other information necessary;
2. a statement of the motion, problem, or task referred to the committee;
3. any instructions to the committee from the appointing power;
4. a statement of the duties, powers, and financial limitations of the committee;
5. available information that will be helpful to the committee—for example, reports of former similar committees;
6. policies, rules, or decisions of the organization relating to the committee's work; and
7. the nature of the report desired by the appointing power and the date the report is due.

31.31   If the secretary of the organization does not provide such materials, it is the duty of the chair of the committee to obtain them for the committee members.

ATTENDANCE AT COMMITTEE MEETINGS

31.32   Committees meet in closed session. The confidentiality of committee deliberations must be protected because it is not yet the act of the assembly. No officer, member, employee, or outside person has the right to attend any meeting of a committee except by invitation of the committee or by direction of the appointing body. Committee members must maintain the confidentiality of the committee's work and should not discuss the work of the committee with those who are not committee members unless specifically authorized or instructed to do so by the committee itself.

31.33   If the committee wishes to invite a staff member, consultant, or other person, it may vote to do so, but otherwise all meetings of committees are limited strictly to its members. To further protect the privacy of the proceedings of a committee, its minutes are open only to members of the committee unless ordered to be produced by the entity establishing the committee.

PROCEDURE IN COMMITTEE MEETINGS

31.34   Committees should function under procedures that are appropriate for the applicable circumstances. While committees preferably function with relaxed procedure, greater formality may be appropriate as the committee size increases, when the issues are complex or highly controversial, or when committee members have demonstrated an inability to work cooperatively under such informal procedures. Occasionally the organization, through its rules, dictates committee procedure, but in the absence of such direction, a committee may determine its own procedures and level of formality under the guidance of the committee chair.

31.35 Unless the organization directs otherwise, the quorum in a committee meeting is a majority of the committee members, including ex officio members, but excluding any advisory or consultant members.

31.36 The committee chair is expected to provide leadership, including assigning work and calling committee meetings. If the chair fails to call a meeting, one-third of the committee members may do so, or the organization's president may call a meeting of the committee.

31.37 To ensure that a committee's meeting time is used most effectively, it is common for committee members to do preparatory work in advance of meetings. This may include discussing issues by email or other electronic means to identify areas of tentative agreement and disagreement, and doing the necessary research and data collection to facilitate final decision-making. Sharing information before an actual committee meeting may allow questions to be asked, and answered, and further research to be done, if necessary, before the meeting, so that the meeting itself has a higher likelihood of having all the information needed to make decisions. The preparatory work expedites the meeting of the full committee but cannot replace that meeting.

31.38 During committee meetings, the chair has the usual responsibilities of a presiding officer. Procedure is often relaxed by allowing discussions to occur prior to introduction of formal motions, permitting motions without seconds, permitting debate without limits on the number or length of speeches, permitting members to remain seated when speaking, and allowing the chair to participate fully in the committee deliberations, including debate and voting.

31.39 Even with these changes, decorum must be maintained, and the chair should encourage balanced participation by all committee members and discourage domination of meetings by individuals or small groups. The chair may permit discussion on the relevant subject under consideration prior to the introduction of a motion, but once a motion is under consideration, debate must be germane to the motion.

31.40 Decisions are often made by general consent, but when this is done, care should be taken that the exact wording of actions is recorded and accurately states what everyone agreed to; if this is not the case, fully worded motions and amendments and a formal vote are required to adopt an action.

31.41 If appropriate, and if not prohibited by the organization's bylaws or rules, or by law, committees may meet by electronic means. Such a meeting is as proper as a physical meeting of the members, provided the other requirements for conducting a meeting have been met: in particular, notice, quorum, and the ability of all members to hear all other members simultaneously. For guidance in conducting meetings by electronic means, see Chapter 19.

31.42 Notes may be kept on proceedings that may or may not eventually become minutes. Committee notes are often recorded for internal use by the committee. If notes are to be kept, the chair should designate a member to serve as the committee secretary for this purpose. Committee notes do not constitute the committee report, which should be a separate written document, properly approved by the full committee at an actual meeting.

31.43 For more information on committee minutes, see Chapter 23.

COMMITTEE HEARINGS

31.44 A committee may conduct an open hearing during which it listens to the viewpoints of members, and sometimes of nonmembers, consultants, or other experts, on the subject assigned to it. During the hearing, the committee members may ask questions to elicit information or merely listen to the comments offered. In either case, the committee members should not enter into debate or show bias on the subject matter of the hearing. Some organizations also encourage input by members to committees, even in the absence of hearings, to assure that the committee is aware of relevant facts and opinions; such input may be provided in writing or via electronic submission, according to the rules of the organization or the requirements of the committee. Just as with materials gathered during a hearing, this input should be shared with all committee members. At the end of the hearing, or at a future meeting, the committee, in closed session, deliberates and agrees on the conclusions and recommendations that it will present to the membership.

31.45   Most committee hearings are open to all members of the organization. However, hearings for the purpose of considering matters of discipline, finance, or other subjects that should be considered confidentially, or that might be harmful to the organization or to a member, are open only to members of the committee assigned to conduct the hearing and any staff the committee permits. Such committee meetings are, in essence, a closed session. For a discussion of reference committee hearings held in a convention, see Chapters 24 and 25.

FORM OF COMMITTEE REPORTS AND RECOMMENDATIONS

31.46   Committee reports vary widely depending on the purpose of a committee. For a committee directed to study an issue or implement a program, the report usually includes:

1. a statement of the question, subject, or work assigned to the committee and any important instructions given to it;
2. a brief explanation of how the committee carried out its work;
3. a description of the work that the committee performed or, in the case of a deliberative or investigating committee, its findings and conclusions; and
4. the committee's recommendations, if any.

31.47   A committee report should be as brief as possible, consistent with clarity. It should provide the background necessary for an understanding of any recommendations the committee is making for a decision by the assembly. Credit may be given to anyone rendering unusual or outstanding service to the committee, but the report does not give special mention to those who only perform their expected duties.

31.48   For committees charged with deliberations or actions, recommendations should be contained in a separate section in the report or attached to the report. Each recommendation should be in the form of a motion or resolution to be presented, discussed, and acted on as a separate motion by the voting body. Such motions, as with all motions, should be written clearly and should be complete, so that reference to the report is not necessary to understand the action to be taken if the motion is adopted.

31.49 Ordinarily, the assembly should act only on these motions. If opinions and recommendations are included in a report, and the report is adopted, the opinions and recommendations, as well as the balance of the report, are binding on the organization. Such a broad commitment may be unwise and is appropriate only in unusual circumstances, such as when the organization wishes to demonstrate its approval of the entire content of the report, perhaps to the public.

31.50 When a committee reports on a referred motion, with or without pending amendments or other incidental motions, the committee report should consist of recommendations for disposal of the referred motion(s). The committee's report is subject to customary content regarding the form of its report. In addition to the other elements of a committee report, when a committee reports on such a referred motion, the assembly should then begin consideration with the referred motion as the immediately pending motion, in the exact form in which it was when referred. The committee's report should consist of recommendations for disposal of the referred motion.

31.51 As an example, if a motion "to build a new headquarters building" is referred to a committee, possible recommendations from the committee might include: amendment of the motion by addition of "at a cost not to exceed $500,000" and adoption as amended.

Presiding Officer:	The committee to which was referred the motion "to build a new headquarters building" has reported back with the recommendation to amend the motion by adding "at a cost not to exceed $500,000." The motion before the assembly is to build a new headquarters building. The chair of the committee is recognized.
Committee Chair:	At the direction of the committee, I move to amend the motion by adding "at a cost not to exceed $500,000."
Presiding Officer:	The motion comes from a committee and needs no second. The motion is to amend the main motion by adding "at a cost not to exceed $500,000." If adopted, the main motion would read "to build a new headquarters building at a cost not to exceed $500,000." Is there any discussion on the motion to add "at a cost not to exceed $500,000?"

31.52 The motion would be processed as any other Motion to Amend.

31.53 As an additional example, if a motion "to build a new headquarters building" is referred to a committee, possible recommendations from the committee might include: defeat of the referred motion.

Presiding Officer:	The committee to which was referred the motion "to build a new headquarters building" has reported back with the recommendation to defeat the motion. The chair of the committee is recognized.
Committee Chair:	The committee recommends defeating this motion and suggests a "No" vote on the pending question.
Presiding Officer:	The motion before the assembly is "to build a new headquarters building." Is there any discussion?
Presiding Officer: (after debate)	The question is on the motion "to build a new headquarters building." If you are in favor of building a new headquarters building, vote "Aye." If you are opposed to building a new headquarters building, vote "No."

31.54 If a report does not provide recommendations, the presiding officer should state the motion as referred, or any amendments that were also referred with the motion, as the immediately pending question.

AGREEMENT ON COMMITTEE REPORTS

31.55 The report and the recommendations of a committee must be agreed on at a meeting of the committee. The committee members must have the opportunity to hear all the different viewpoints on the questions involved and to discuss them freely with one another. Otherwise, the report cannot state the collective judgment of the committee. The approval of a committee report or recommendation by members of the committee individually and separately, without a meeting, is not valid approval unless specifically authorized by the body creating the committee. Unless prohibited by governing documents or statutes, an exception to these requirements may occur if the unanimous written agreement of every member of the committee is given outside of a meeting.

31.56 When a report in its final form, along with the report's recommendations, has been considered and approved by a majority vote at a committee meeting, it is signed by the chair and may be signed by the members who agree with it. If the report is approved at an electronic meeting, the chair should sign the report and list the members approving it. A member who agrees to a committee report with exceptions or reservations, especially regarding the report's recommendations, may indicate the portions with which he or she does not agree and sign the report, signifying approval of the remainder. See the section, Minority Reports, later in the chapter for noting a committee member's disagreement with a submitted committee report.

PRESENTATION OF COMMITTEE REPORTS

31.57 At the time in the order of business for committee reports, the presiding officer calls for each report in the order determined by the presiding officer and placed on the agenda. The sequence of presenting reports should be flexible to meet the needs of the meeting, and the order of presentation may be varied by majority vote or by general consent. Only those committees that are required to or are prepared to report should be included in the agenda. A committee report is presented by its chair or by a member designated by the committee to report. The reporting member may introduce the report with a brief explanation if necessary. If a committee report is long, usually only a summary of it is presented orally, and copies of the full report are made available upon request. Lengthy reports may be distributed to members in advance of the meeting to provide sufficient time to read and understand the report.

31.58 In conventions or annual meetings of large organizations, committee reports usually are distributed to members in advance. In this case, the committee chair makes explanatory statements if needed and presents only the recommendations of the committee.

31.59 While advance preparation and distribution of committee reports is customary for conventions and annual meetings, it is a useful process for all meetings. Utilization of this process, if members recognize and accept their responsibility to prepare for the meeting, may reduce meeting time and permit members to give more leisurely and in-depth consideration to the reports. Advance distribution also provides an opportunity for members to obtain additional information before the meeting, perhaps preventing a delay in decision-making that might otherwise occur. If rules are adopted requiring all reports and/or resolutions to be submitted in advance, a process should be included for approval of consideration of submissions received after the deadline if the assembly feels their urgency or importance justifies such an exception.

CONSIDERATION OF COMMITTEE REPORTS

31.60   A committee report, after being presented to an assembly, is open for comment or questions. It is the content of the report and its recommendations for action that are open to discussion without regard to the authors.

31.61   A committee report cannot be amended except by the committee, since no one can make the committee's report different from what the committee approved. If the committee offers recommendations, the committee's recommendations cannot be altered in the report. However, if taken up on the floor in the form of a motion, the recommendations are subject to debate and amendment by the assembly.

31.62   A committee report, after it is presented, may be disposed of in any of the following ways:

1. The report may be filed. This is the usual method for disposing of a committee report. It may be filed automatically or ordered filed by a motion, or the presiding officer may announce, "The report will be filed," and proceed to the next item of business. A report that is filed is not binding on the assembly but is available for information and may be considered again at any time.

2. A subject or motion and the report covering it may be referred back to the committee, or to another committee, if further study, modifications, or recommendations are needed. If a submitted report is referred to another committee, the first committee's report may still be filed.

3. Consideration of a committee report may be postponed to a more convenient time.

4. A report is not adopted except in unusual circumstances applicable to the particular report. If a report is adopted, this expresses the assembly's agreement with all the findings and opinions contained in the report and to any recommendations that might be included in it but not to any recommendations submitted separately. Since the adoption of a committee report binds the assembly to everything in the report, best practice is to file reports instead of adopting them. A motion "to receive" a committee report is unnecessary.

5. A final or annual financial report from a treasurer or finance committee is referred to the auditors by the presiding officer without a motion. No final financial report is adopted without an accompanying report from the auditors certifying its correctness.

6. If a financial report concerns proposed or future expenditures only, as in a budget, it is treated as is any other financial recommendation of a committee.

7. A motion proposed by a committee is moved by the committee chair or other reporting member, or it may be stated by the presiding officer. It does not require a second and is handled as any other motion before the assembly, just as if it had been proposed from the floor and seconded.

8. If the assembly finds the report, in whole or in part, fundamentally objectionable or otherwise unsatisfactory, the assembly may:

   a. refer it back to the committee with clear instructions for correcting the deficiencies;

   b. express this disapproval by its action on any included recommendations; or

   c. adopt a separate main motion expressing its disapproval, likely with mention of the specific areas of concern. Adoption of such a main motion will ensure that the assembly is on record as not agreeing with some of or all the content of the filed report.

9. If the committee report presents information that a member feels should lead to action, but the report includes no such recommendation, a new main motion germane to the content of the report may be offered and considered.

RECORD OF COMMITTEE REPORTS

31.63 After a committee report has been presented, it is filed by the secretary. A committee report is not included in the body of the minutes unless the assembly directs otherwise.

31.64 The minutes of each meeting should state what reports were presented, by whom, and the disposition of each report. Some organizations attach copies of final reports to the official copy of the minutes as unadopted appendices.

31.65 Each organization should adopt its own policies on retention of committee reports and other records. Legal considerations and the organization's values and resources will have an impact on such policies. For example, any documents that may be required to be retained for future legal action must be retained in a retrievable form.[93] If filed electronically, similar precautions should be followed for such reports as are followed for minutes, ensuring security and backup protocols.[94]

MINORITY REPORTS

31.66   If any member of a committee disagrees with the report submitted by the committee members, the committee member may submit a minority report signed by those who agree to it. (See the section, Agreement on Committee Reports, for noting disagreement with only a portion of a committee report.) More than one minority report may be submitted. A minority report can only be presented immediately after the report. Any minority reports are filed for reference. Committee members may offer amendments to recommendations contained in the committee report.

PRESENTATION OF COMMITTEE RECOMMENDATIONS

31.67   Recommendations, which are to be presented in the form of motions, are acted on when they are presented with the committee report. When several recommendations are interrelated and have not been distributed to the members in advance, they should all be read or displayed before considering and voting on the recommended motions.

31.68   After the presentation of the report, the chair of the committee reads the first recommended motion from the committee and moves its adoption. As an alternative, the presiding officer may state the motion.

31.69   The presiding officer, not the committee chair, presides over the assembly's consideration of the committee motions although the committee chair may be recognized to answer questions. Otherwise, the committee chair's rights in debate are the same as any other member.

31.70   The motion should be stated in a form that will allow the assembly to vote directly on the proposal itself, not on whether to agree or disagree with the recommendation of the committee. For example, if a committee recommends a motion "that a membership drive be held in the spring of each year," the motion is presented to the assembly as "At the direction of the committee, I move that a membership drive be held in the spring of each year." This presentation of the proposal allows the assembly to consider the main motion, to apply all the motions to it that are ordinarily permitted, and to vote directly on the actual proposal.

31.71 A well-stated motion requiring a decision directly on the proposal prevents the confusion caused by such motions as "I move that we approve the recommendation of the finance committee rejecting the proposal of the treasurer to modify the system of keeping financial records." It is impossible to amend or affect this motion in any way that will reach the original proposal, even though the members may wish to do so. The original motion should be stated: "I move that the treasurer be authorized to modify the present system of keeping financial records." The presiding officer or the chair of the committee would then state for the information of the members that the original motion had been proposed by the treasurer and that the finance committee recommends a "No" vote on it.

31.72 After a motion embodying a recommendation has been stated to the assembly, it is considered and acted on as is any other main motion.

CHAPTER 32. **Finances**

SETTING UP FINANCIAL RECORDS

32.1 Every organization should establish and maintain an appropriate accounting system for its funds. A good system for controlling finances saves time and money. Therefore, it is wise for even a small organization to consult an accountant when it is establishing or revising its financial records. If an organization expects to receive gifts or solicit contributions for specific causes, it should take great care to comply with laws regarding solicitation of funds. Such laws may apply wherever funds are solicited, and not just in the jurisdiction of incorporation or the location of the organization's headquarters. Additionally, there must be strict adherence to legal and accounting requirements to segregate funds whose use is intended by the donor to be restricted to particular purposes.

32.2 The organization must take great care when accepting restricted funds because many jurisdictions do not allow the funds to be utilized for anything other than the specific intent of the original donation. While some restrictions may be time based or cause based, for example a contribution for a student scholarship, some restrictions can require funds be kept in perpetuity and only investment earnings can be used. Often, organizations desire to access the corpus of restricted funds but should consult the donor records to determine the appropriateness or legality of using those funds. It is recommended that organizations adopt a gift policy that outlines the process for utilizing restricted funds that is agreed to by donors at the time a gift is offered.

32.3 A useful accounting system will allow information to be organized for easy use for required tax filings, if any, and will also allow officers, the board of directors, and members to understand the organization's finances in a meaningful way.

REPORT OF THE TREASURER

32.4 At each regular meeting, the treasurer should give a brief report or summary of the revenues and expenses and call attention to any unusual items. The presiding officer should then inquire whether there are any questions about the treasurer's report.

32.5 The treasurer should make a complete report annually. All members should have access to this report and any recommendations made by the treasurer, external accountant, or internal financial review committee. The treasurer's report is filed for future reference.

32.6 If an organization has a finance committee, the committee should report at least quarterly, giving an accurate summary of the financial situation, any financial problems of the organization or significant variances from the budget, and of any contemplated proposals or plans involving finances.

REPORT OF A FINANCIAL REVIEW OR AUDIT

32.7 Organizations should have a financial review or audit at least once a year and when a new treasurer takes office. A financial review committee composed of members is helpful but is not the best financial safeguard for the organization's finances. Better results can be obtained if an independent audit or review is carried out. If an internal financial review does not or cannot develop the necessary review procedures for the organization, an independent accountant should be consulted.

32.8 An independent accountant should be selected by vote of the governing board or the membership. Members and staff with a conflict should disclose this, and should recuse themselves from the selection, to help ensure impartiality in selecting the independent audit or the type of engagement.

32.9 Certified public accountants and chartered accountants are authorized by law to express independent opinions on the financial statements of an organization. If the cost of an audit is too prohibitive, reviewed financial statements will provide limited assurance. This is a better practice than an internal financial review, as the review is being done by an independent third party. Organizations should also consult with any state, provincial, or territorial laws that may require submission of audited or reviewed financial statements and any applicable asset or gross receipt thresholds. Despite limited resources, often these requirements cannot be waived.

32.10 An independent accountant or auditor's report is an opinion on the financial statements of the organization. There are two levels of assurance that an accountant can provide:

1. A financial statement review is the first level of service in which an independent accountant provides limited assurance that there are no

material modifications required for the financial statements to be in accordance with generally accepted accounting principles. Reviews do not look at the internal control environment, nor is a fraud risk assessment performed. As a result, a review does not provide the same level of assurance as if an audit had been performed. For smaller organizations with only a handful of staff or volunteer leaders, this is usually appropriate as the organization is not of sufficient scale to have an effective operating internal control environment.

2. A financial statement audit requires an auditor to express an opinion that the financial statements are presented fairly, in all material respects, and reflect the financial position and activity of the organization in accordance with generally accepted accounting principles. To do this, an auditor conducts a series of tests of significant financial statement line items. While this is the best-known report to the public, there are significant financial hurdles to having an audit completed. For most organizations, this level of assurance isn't necessary unless there is a level of financial complexity, significant assets, or a legal or contractual requirement to have one performed.

FINANCIAL SAFEGUARDS

32.11 Organizations need to be aware of the various tax laws that apply to their activities in their jurisdiction of incorporation or, if not incorporated, those location where business is conducted. This awareness applies to requirements for submitting financial statements and financial recordkeeping. To safeguard its integrity, the organization should consult with legal and accounting professionals for advice on setting up and maintaining financial records and for advice on the reporting requirements and payment of taxes when applicable.

32.12 These financial safeguards include the adoption of a budget; the requirement of authorization for non-budgeted purchases; strict supervision of any person who collects or expends funds or incurs financial obligations on behalf of the organization; separation of the duties of recording incoming funds and recording outgoing expenditures; an annual financial review; and a surety bond covering those who have access to the organization's funds.

32.13 Most organizations prepare and adopt a budget of estimated revenues and expenses. For organizations adopting this book as their parliamentary authority, adoption of the budget is a pre-authorization for the expenses included in it unless the organization's rules explicitly provide otherwise. Organizations may require specific authorization for any expenditure not included in the budget or more than the budgeted amount. Others have more relaxed provisions that, for example, permit an over-expenditure if the net effect on the budget is even or positive. This requires ongoing monitoring of actual activity compared to the budget but minimizes the need for repeated approval of specific expenses.

32.14 A few organizations provide that proposed expenditures above a nominal amount require a purchase order or some other form of authorization, and some provide that unusual, and particularly large, expenditures require authorization by the board of directors or the membership.

32.15 Only members and employees specifically authorized should be permitted to commit the organization to expenditures. Provisions are often adopted to require expenditures above a certain amount to have an authorizing signature. If an authorized representative purchases goods or services in the name of the organization, the organization will be legally obligated to pay the bill, regardless of whether the members later vote to pay or not to pay it.

32.16 In order to ensure there is a backup in the event one signatory either resigns or is unable to perform the duties, at least two people should be designated as signatories on bank accounts. Unlike those who may be internally authorized to approve expenses, such as a committee chair or the president, the designated signatories are the individuals listed at the financial institution as being able to conduct business on behalf of the organization. These are the individuals who disburse funds that were authorized above.

32.17 Instructions to any committee should state how much money, if any, the committee is authorized to spend. Unless a committee is authorized to collect, hold, or expend funds through separate accounts, all funds should be collected, held, and expended through the regular financial channels of the organization.

32.18 If an organization has access to online banking and read-only access can be granted to additional parties, it is recommended that this access is given to any internal financial review committee to enable the independent performance of these procedures. While copies of bank statements can suffice, direct access to the bank helps establish the existence of the bank accounts, ensures the accuracy of the balances and transaction activity, and serves as a monitoring control to mitigate potential fraud.

32.19 Some larger organizations may have other financial complexities, including investments, inventory for sale, and pledged contributions among many potential items. Policies should be adopted by the board to handle the management or accounting of these matters. For example: An investment policy statement would give guidance on how to manage investments; periodic inventory count procedures would ensure that inventory is appropriately valued; and collection policies would identify at what period the organization would write off a pledge as a bad debt. In all these instances, the board should consider consulting with professionals prior to adopting procedures.

CHAPTER 33. Discipline of Members and Officers

DISCIPLINE AND EXPULSION OF MEMBERS

33.1 Procedures for the discipline and expulsion of members should be included in the bylaws. However, every organization has the inherent right to discipline, suspend, or expel a member.[95] A membership can be terminated and a member expelled because of a violation of an important duty to the organization, a breach of a fundamental rule or principle of the organization, or for any violation stated in the bylaws as grounds for expulsion.[96] However, even if rules for discipline are not included in the bylaws, action can be taken against a member who has breached important duties, fundamental rules, or principles of an organization, or who has caused harm to the organization or its reputation.

33.2 Discipline may consist of, for example, requiring a member to appear before the governing board and explain certain actions or pay a fine, if the bylaws permit imposition of a fine, or a member may be reprimanded or suspended from membership for a limited time.

33.3 In addition, an organization has the implied power to expel a member for violation of duties as a citizen.[97] For example, a member may be expelled upon being convicted of a criminal offense that would discredit the organization.[98]

33.4 These powers must be exercised in the context of fairness and with adherence to any adopted rules on such powers. A proceeding to expel a member must not violate any rule of the organization or any of the member's rights under the law. The primary requisites for expulsion proceedings are due notice and fair hearing.[99]

33.5 Unless the bylaws provide otherwise, the essential steps for imposing severe discipline or expelling a member are:

1. *Charges*: Charges made by a member stating the alleged violations and preliminary proof shall be in writing and filed with the secretary. An organization may provide in its bylaws that a member's rights may be suspended, either automatically or pursuant to a vote of the board, from the time that charges are served on the member until completion of the disciplinary action. In organizations adopting this parliamentary

authority, an officer of the organization who has been charged on a disciplinary matter may be suspended temporarily from office by a majority vote of the board.

2. *Investigation*: A committee of *disinterested*[100] members is appointed to investigate the charges thoroughly and promptly, and if it decides that a hearing is warranted, sets a date and time, and notifies the secretary.

3. *Notification*: The secretary sends the accused member a trackable communication at least fifteen days before the date of the hearing. The communication must contain a copy of the charges, the time and place of the hearing, and a statement of the member's right to be present at the hearing to present a defense, to be represented by an attorney or other party, and to receive a copy of any record of the proceedings.

4. *Hearing*: A hearing must be held either at a closed membership meeting or by a hearing committee composed of disinterested members other than those on the investigating committee. In conducting the hearing, the committee should preserve decorum and conduct the hearing impartially and in compliance with any applicable rules and procedures; restrict evidence and testimony to the written charges; and uphold the right of the accused member to present a defense, to cross-examine witnesses, and to refute the charges that have been made.

5. *Decision*: The hearing committee or membership meeting must, within a reasonable time, make findings of fact on the essential points at issue. If the hearing is held before a committee, it should make a finding of guilt or innocence and send a copy of the decision and findings of fact to the accused member and to the secretary.

6. *Penalty*: If the member is found guilty of the charges, the hearing committee reports findings to the membership meeting and may recommend a penalty to the membership meeting. The decision must then be approved by a majority vote at the meeting. The authority to impose penalties can be delegated to the hearing committee or to the board of directors by the membership in the bylaws or standing rules of order. If a body other than the membership is to be authorized to make a final decision, this must be designated in the bylaws; likewise, if an appeal process is to be allowed, this must be described in the bylaws.[101]

33.6 Some organizations permit a member who has been expelled to apply for readmission after a certain period of time. A member who is expelled does not have an automatic right to apply for readmission to membership.

33.7 An organization from which suspension or expulsion from membership may be harmful to the member's reputation or livelihood, such as some professional societies, should exercise particular care to follow its own rules in disciplinary matters. Consultation with legal counsel may be advisable in such situations.

REMOVAL OF AN OFFICER FOR CAUSE

33.8 The right to hold office is a basic right of membership and that can only be limited in the bylaws. An officer, director, or elected committee member who is removed from office is still entitled to run for future office unless the bylaws provide otherwise.

33.9 An organization has an inherent right to remove an officer, director, or other elected position from that position for valid cause.[102] Officers, directors, or committee members can only be removed by the same authority that elected or appointed them unless the law or governing documents provide an alternate procedure. This authority can be delegated to a board of directors or an executive committee either by a clause in the governing documents or a motion, but the delegation of authority must be specific regarding removal. Removal from office is not transferred to a board or executive committee with the general delegation of authority commonly granted for a board or executive committee to act on behalf of the assembly between meetings. Such a general grant of authority does authorize the board or executive committee to suspend an officer pending the outcome of a disciplinary procedure.

33.10 The bylaws should provide for procedures for removal or suspension. In the absence of an established procedure, the disciplinary body may adopt its own procedures, provided that they are reasonable.[103]

33.11 The power to select carries with it the power to remove. Unless otherwise directed in the governing documents, the body that elects a position is the only body authorized to remove a person from that position. An appointed officer or committee member may be removed by the authority that made the appointment.

33.12 An incumbent in an elected position may only be removed for valid cause using the procedures below unless otherwise provided in the bylaws. The common valid causes for removal from office include but are not limited to:

1. gross, willful, or continued neglect of the duties of the office, which include, but are not limited to, the fiduciary duties of care, loyalty, and diligence;
2. actions that intentionally violate the bylaws;
3. failure to comply with the proper direction given by the assembly or the board;
4. intentional violation of the secrecy of a closed meeting;
5. failure or refusal to disclose necessary information on matters of organization business;
6. unauthorized expenditures, signing of checks, or misuse of organization funds;
7. unwarranted attacks on any officer, member of the board of directors, or the board on an ongoing basis;
8. misrepresentation of the organization and its officers to outside persons;
9. conviction of a felony; or
10. failure to maintain the qualifications for office, such as membership requirements, payment of financial obligations, or licensure or residency requirements.

33.13 The procedures for suspending or removing officers, directors, and elected committee members must provide adequate notice to the individual to be removed, a hearing, which includes the right to counsel, and a reasonable opportunity to present a defense, including the right to present and to cross-examine witnesses. Further information about these steps may be found in the section, Discipline and Expulsion of Members, earlier in this chapter, noting that the process for officer removal may be somewhat more peremptory because loss of office is not as serious a consequence as expulsion from membership.[104]

Suspension

33.14 An officeholder may be suspended by the board or the assembly during an investigation. Any proposed suspension motion, including a Motion to Suspend Temporarily, pending investigation, should be complete, including mention of:

1. what duties and authority, if any, the suspended officer will have during the course of the suspension;

2. what requirements are necessary to terminate the suspension; and

3. appointment of a temporary officer if necessary to perform duties essential to the functioning of the organization during the suspension.[105]

Vote Required to Remove

33.15 If the law or bylaws are silent, the vote for removing an officer, director, or elected committee member is the same vote by which the position was filled, usually a majority vote, but in no case may it be less than a majority vote.

REMOVAL OF AN OFFICER WITHOUT CAUSE

33.16 Many provisions of law provide for removal of an officer, director, or other elected position without cause by a straightforward vote of the membership or the board. Many organizations also wish to avoid the somewhat cumbersome procedures to remove an ineffective and even unpopular officer or director from office. Although it is preferable to afford the officer due process and remove them for cause, an organization not otherwise bound by law may remove an officer from the office without cause by a majority vote provided the following two conditions are met:

1. Previous notice of the intent to remove the officer without cause is sent to the membership before the meeting.

2. The number of votes cast in favor of removal must be greater than or equal to the number of votes necessary to elect the officer at the meeting when elected.

OTHER DISCIPLINARY SANCTIONS

33.17 In addition to or instead of removal from a position, an officer, director, or other elected official may have their duties altered or restricted due to action by the assembly. An assembly can fine an officer or a member if such a provision is provided for in the governing documents.

33.18 A member or an officer may be censured or reprimanded by a vote of the assembly regarding their actions; this process cannot be allowed to infringe upon the individual's right to protect their reputation against false allegations. The individual may be requested to appear before an appropriate body to explain their actions.

REMEDIES FOR IMPROPER REMOVAL

33.19   An officer who complains of improper removal, or a member who believes that he or she has been disciplined improperly, should exhaust the procedures for relief afforded by the organization before appealing to the courts.[106] If proper procedures are followed, the courts will seldom interfere with the removal of an officer for valid cause.

CHAPTER 34. Glossary of Parliamentary Terms

34.1 These are brief definitions of common parliamentary or meeting procedure terms, which may or may not be covered further in this parliamentary authority. Terms that are covered in this parliamentary authority will have greater explanation and applicable rules in appropriate chapters. For references to these terms, please see the Index.

34.2 **Abstain (Abstention):** To refrain from voting.

34.3 **Acclamation:** Acceptance of a nominee or a proposal by applause or other informal signs of assent.

34.4 **Action Log:** A document that records the summary of decisions made or actions taken but is separate from the minutes.

34.5 **Ad Hoc Committee:** See *special committee*.

34.6 **Adjourn:** The process by which a formal end or conclusion of a meeting or convention occurs.

34.7 **Adjourned Meeting:** See *continued meeting*.

34.8 **Adjournment Sine Die (without day):** The final adjournment terminating a convention, series of meetings, or the body itself.

34.9 **Adopt:** To approve by vote or general consent and give effect to a motion or a report.

34.10 **Adopt in Lieu Of:** A Specific-Purpose Main Motion whose adoption is intended to dispose of one or more other main motions that are known to be coming before the assembly, such as when main motions are required to be submitted in advance of a meeting.

34.11 **Affirmative Vote:** The "Yes" or "Aye" vote supporting a motion as stated.

34.12 **Agenda:** The list of items of business to be brought before the meeting or convention, which, if adopted, is binding on the assembly.

34.13 **Amend:** A process to change the wording of a motion, bylaw, or other statement by inserting or adding, striking out, or striking out and inserting words or paragraphs.

34.14 Annual Meeting (Annual General Meeting or Annual Membership Meeting): A meeting of the members held once per year as specified in the bylaws; often requiring election of officers and annual reports.

34.15 Apply (Applies to): A motion is said to apply to another motion when it may be used to alter, dispose of, or affect the first motion.

34.16 Approval of Minutes: The process to accept the secretary's record of a meeting, thus making the record the official minutes of the organization.

34.17 Approval Voting: A method of voting where members vote in favor of each candidate that is acceptable to them with no limit on the number of "Yes" votes in an election for a number of positions of equal rank. Those candidates with the most "Yes" votes, up to the number of available positions, are elected.

34.18 Articles of Incorporation: A charter granted by government and creating an incorporated organization, also known as a *corporate charter* or *certificate of incorporation*.

34.19 Assembly: A meeting of the members of a deliberative body.

34.20 Assumed Motion: A motion that is stated by the presiding officer without being formally moved and seconded.

34.21 Ballot Vote: A system in which the voter cannot be identified with the choice expressed.

34.22 Board Meeting: An official meeting of the board of directors or board of trustees.

34.23 Board of Directors (Board of Trustees): Persons elected or appointed by the members of an organization to manage the affairs of the organization. This body is usually comprised of officers and others who represent the membership in a specifically delegated decision-making capacity. This may be referred to by a number of different names; however, the duties are generally the same.

34.24 Borda Count Voting: A point-based system in which the voter ranks each candidate or proposition. The candidate or proposition receiving the highest total points among all voters wins.

34.25 **Bullet Voting:** In an election where multiple candidates may be elected on a single ballot, a method of focusing voting power on a single candidate by choosing to place a single vote for a particular candidate and to abstain from using any additional votes for anyone else.

34.26 **Bylaws:** The set of rules adopted by an organization that defines its structure and governs its functions.

34.27 **Bylaws Interpretation:** See *canons of construction*.

34.28 **Bylaws Revision:** The replacement of the current bylaws with a new set of bylaws.

34.29 **Call to a Convention:** The notice distributed to members prior to the convention, indicating the time and place of the convention and outlining the procedure for submitting delegates and alternates.

34.30 **Call of a Meeting:** The notice distributed to members prior to the meeting, indicating the time and place of the meeting and, if required, stating the business that is to be brought up at the meeting.

34.31 **Call to Order:** A declaration by the presiding officer that the meeting is opening or resuming.

34.32 **Called Meeting:** See *special meeting*.

34.33 **Canons of Construction:** General rules of interpretation to be considered when interpreting ambiguous provisions of bylaws or rules.

34.34 **Certificate of Incorporation:** See *articles of incorporation*.

34.35 **Chair:** The presiding officer of a deliberative body or committee, or the presiding officer's position in the meeting room. In some organizations, the highest ranking officer is also referred to as the chairman.

34.36 **Chair Pro Tem (also Chair Pro Tempore):** An elected or appointed temporary presiding officer who does not have the administrative powers of the elected officer.

34.37 **Challenging an Election:** Objecting to an election on the grounds that it is not being conducted properly.

34.38 **Challenging a Vote:** Objecting to a vote on the grounds that the voter does not have the right to vote. Often confused with *challenging an election*.

34.39 Change in the Parliamentary Situation: A change in the perception of the assembly motion or the status of debate that results in essentially a different question before the assembly.

34.40 Charges: Alleged violations of conduct or the bylaws that are formally presented to a member in writing as a prelude to disciplinary proceedings.

34.41 Charter: An official grant from a parent organization of the right to operate as a constituent or component group of the parent organization. See *articles of incorporation*.

34.42 Closed Meeting: A meeting of an assembly, board, or committee that only members of the particular group may attend unless the attendance of others is invited by the body; the discussions held or actions taken are legally considered as confidential; sometimes called *executive session*.

34.43 Committee: A group of individuals who report to a deliberative body and who make recommendations to the decision-making body for action, or, if properly authorized, act for the deliberative body.

34.44 Common Parliamentary Law: The body of rules and principles that is applied widely by custom and tradition in deliberative bodies involving the procedure of organizations. It does not include law or particular rules adopted by an organization. See *parliamentary law*, a substantially equivalent term. Parliamentary common law refers to the law of meeting procedures as applied by the court in deciding litigation.[107]

34.45 Conflict of Interest: An incompatibility of interests, either real, perceived, or apparent, between one's private interest and one's fiduciary duty to the organization.

34.46 Consent Agenda (Calendar): A list of meeting business items that are routine and noncontroversial, and likely to be accepted without individual vote or debate. The list is adopted automatically en bloc when no further items are removed.

34.47 Consider by Paragraph (Seriatim): A method of consideration where the assembly focuses on one paragraph or section of a proposal at a time and perfects it through amendments before moving on to the next paragraph or section.

34.48 Constituent or Component Units: Subordinate groups making up a parent state, national, or international organization and chartered by it.

34.49 **Constitution:** The set of rules establishing the fundamental framework of the organization unless established in the bylaws.

34.50 **Continued Meeting:** A meeting that is a continuation, at a later specified time, of an earlier regular or special meeting. The continued meeting is legally a part of the original meeting. It is sometimes called an *adjourned meeting*.

34.51 **Convene:** To open a meeting or convention.

34.52 **Convention:** As used in this book, an official meeting of delegates from constituent entities that is usually held over several days in a series of meetings under a single agenda or program.

34.53 **Convention Notice:** See *call of a convention*.

34.54 **Corporate Charter:** See *articles of incorporation*.

34.55 **Creating a Tie:** A vote cast, usually by the presiding officer, that results in an equal number of affirmative and negative votes, thereby changing the outcome.

34.56 **Cumulative Voting:** A voting method where a member may place multiple votes for a single candidate when multiple candidates are being elected on a single ballot, instead of casting single votes for a number of different candidates.

34.57 **Custom:** Commonly understood and accepted unwritten methods that apply in certain governance aspects of an organization. These are also known as traditions of a particular organization.

34.58 **Deadlock:** An unresolved tie vote in an election that does not result in a completed election.

34.59 **Debate:** Formal persuasive discussion of a motion or proposal by members under the rules of parliamentary law.

34.60 **Delegate:** A member who has been chosen by an entity to represent it at a convention and who has registered in attendance at the convention and been issued credentials.

34.61 **Delegate Nominee:** A member who has been chosen by an entity to represent it at a convention before registration.

34.62 **Deliberative Assembly:** A meeting of a group of members of the organization authorized to make decisions for the organization. Boards, membership meetings, and conventions of delegates are all forms of deliberative assembly.

34.63 **Demand:** An assertion of a parliamentary right by a member.

34.64 **Dilatory Tactics:** Misuse of procedures with the intent to delay or prevent progress in a meeting.

34.65 **Directed Proxy:** A power of attorney given by the proxy giver with specific instructions on how to vote in the proxy giver's absence.

34.66 **Disinterested:** Persons who do not have a conflict of interest.

34.67 **Disposition of a Motion:** Action on a motion by voting on it, referring, postponing, tabling, withdrawing, or in some way removing it from the consideration of the assembly.

34.68 **Division of the Assembly:** A demand by a single member for the presiding officer to verify an unclear or inconclusive voice vote by taking a standing, but not necessarily a counted, vote.

34.69 **Double Threshold Vote:** A type of vote that meets a designated threshold of the individual members (delegates) and also meets a stated threshold of caucuses, constituent units, delegations, or divisions of members, or an alternative threshold of the individual members. For example, a double majority vote might require (a) a majority of the individual members voting and the majority of the number of members constituting a quorum, or (b) a majority of the individual members voting as well as a majority of the state delegations.

34.70 **Duties, Duty:** An obligation to act or perform a task that is owed to the organization or another person or entity by virtue of one's office, position, or membership.

34.71 **Election:** The process in which the membership selects a person to occupy an office or other position.

34.72 **Electronic Meeting:** An official assembly of the members of an organization, via electronic means, which may have video and audio components, during which all participants can hear one another and obtain recognition. During such meetings, there is no temporal separation of the members except for a recess and the meeting continues until adjournment. Also called a *virtual meeting*.

34.73 **En Bloc (En Masse):** A method of approval of more than one item of business all at once in a single action.

34.74 **Entity:** A particular and discrete unit recognized as having a separate legal existence, as distinct from individuals and other similar units, with certain legally recognized rights appropriate to its form. As used in this book, it is a comprehensive term for recognized organizational forms, as distinct from individual persons, that includes corporations, partnerships, limited liability companies, unincorporated associations, trusts, estates, and governmental units.

34.75 **Executive Board:** A smaller governing group empowered to act on behalf of the entire membership of the organization, also called the *board of directors* or *board of trustees*.

34.76 **Executive Committee:** A smaller governing group empowered to act on behalf of the entire board of directors.

34.77 **Executive Director:** The chief administrator of an organization, usually an employee, who is often responsible for other employees.

34.78 **Executive Session:** See *closed meeting*.

34.79 **Ex Officio Member:** One who is a member of a committee or board by reason of holding another office; a treasurer is often an ex officio member of the finance committee.

34.80 **Fiduciary Duty:** Fundamental requirements of a board member to exercise care, loyalty, and obedience to the governing documents, best interests, and directives of an organization.

34.81 **Filling blanks:** An alternative used to consider multiple options within a motion.

34.82 **Floor** (as in "have the floor"): A member that has been recognized by the presiding officer has the floor and is the only member entitled to make a motion or to speak.

34.83 **Friendly Amendment:** A proposed change made with the intent that it be satisfactory to the maker of the motion. If proposed before the motion is stated by the chair, the maker of the motion may simply agree to the change; otherwise, it must be processed in the same way as any other amendment.

34.84 **Full Debate:** Discussion of a proposal that has no limitations other than germaneness and adopted limitations of debate.

34.85 **Fundamental Principles:** Widely accepted and basic rules of parliamentary procedure based on law or centuries of democratic practice, for example, a majority vote decides.

34.86 **Gaveling Through:** See *railroading*.

34.87 **General Consent:** An informal method of approving routine motions by assuming unanimous approval unless objection is raised. Also called *unanimous consent*.

34.88 **Germane Amendment:** An amendment relating directly to the subject of the motion to which it is applied.

34.89 **Germane Debate:** Discussion that is relevant to the immediately pending motion.

34.90 **Good Faith:** Honesty, fairness, and lawfulness of purpose without any intent to defraud, act maliciously, or take unfair advantage.

34.91 **Good of the Order:** An item on agendas utilized by some organizations as a time for members to informally suggest improvements to the organization and meeting processes.

34.92 **Good Standing:** See *member in good standing*.

34.93 **Gordian Knot:** A form of the Motion to Suspend the Rules that permits the assembly to return to a point in the meeting that was less confusing, usually to the beginning of the last main motion stated by the presiding officer.

34.94 **Governing Board:** See *board of directors*.

34.95 **Hearing:** A meeting of an authorized group for the purpose of listening to testimony on a particular subject.

34.96 **Hostile Amendment:** An amendment that is opposed to the spirit or purpose of the motion to which it is applied.

34.97 **House of Delegates:** See *convention*.

34.98 **Hybrid Meeting:** A type of meeting that combines members meeting in a virtual setting with members meeting in a physical location.

34.99 **Illegal Ballot:** Ballots cast for an ineligible candidate or by an ineligible voter or in violation of the rules.

34.100 **Immediately Pending Question (Motion):** The last proposed of several pending motions and therefore open for immediate consideration.

34.101 **Incidental Motion:** Motions that arise out of the business before the assembly and are procedural in nature.

34.102 **Incomplete Election:** A scheduled election in which the assembly is unable to fill a position with a qualified person because of either a lack of qualified candidates or an indecisive repeated vote. This is not the same as a vacancy.

34.103 **Incorporate:** To form a group into a legal entity chartered by government and recognized by law as having special rights, duties, and liabilities distinct from those of its members.

34.104 **Informal Consideration:** Consideration and discussion of a problem or motion in committees without the usual limitations on debate.

34.105 **In Order:** Permissible and correct from a parliamentary standpoint at a particular time.

34.106 **Insert:** A form of amendment whereby words are placed between other words.

34.107 **Inspector of Elections:** An individual with specified duties relating to the conduct of an election and the processing of votes, typically called a teller in nonprofit organizations.

34.108 **Instant Runoff Voting:** See *preferential voting*.

34.109 **Interrupt:** The process of seeking recognition to speak or of speaking while another member has been assigned the floor to speak or while another member or the chair is speaking.

34.110 **Invalid Ballots:** See *illegal ballots*.

34.111 **Items of Business:** Headings and specific items within each heading on an order of business or meeting agenda that outline the business to be conducted at the meeting. This excludes program listings, such as invocation, guest speaker, etc.

34.112 **Legal Ballot:** Ballots cast for an eligible candidate by an eligible voter in conformance with the rules.

34.113 *Lex Majoris Partis*: The principle that a majority rules.

34.114 **Limited Debate:** Discussion that is confined to specific points relative to the purpose of the motion itself or the assembly's decision to shorten or extend the time for debate.

34.115 **Main Motion:** A motion that brings business before the assembly. A *substantive motion*. See *procedural motion*.

34.116 **Majority:** A number that is more than half of any given total.

34.117 **Majority of the Legal Votes Cast:** More than half of the votes cast for an eligible proposition or person by eligible voters.

34.118 **Majority of Those Present and Voting:** Equivalent to *majority of the legal votes cast*.

34.119 **Majority Rule:** Rule by decision of the majority of those who actually vote, regardless of whether a majority of those entitled to vote do so.

34.120 **Majority Vote:** A vote that requires more than half of the votes in the affirmative for a proposal to be adopted. By default, unless a different basis for determining the majority is specified, majority vote means a *majority of the legal votes cast*.

34.121 **Majority Vote of All the Members:** A required vote total that is more than half the total number of current members, regardless of whether the members are present or in good standing.

34.122 **Majority Vote of All the Membership Positions:** A required vote total that is more than half the total number of membership positions regardless of whether the membership positions are filled.

34.123 **Majority Vote of All the Members in Good Standing:** A required vote total that is more than half the total number of members currently in good standing regardless of whether the members are present.

34.124 **Majority Vote of the Members Present:** A required vote total that is more than half the total number of members present in the meeting regardless of whether the members vote.

34.125 **Majority Vote of the Quorum:** A required vote total that is more than half the number of members required to achieve a quorum.

34.126 **Mass Meeting:** See *organizing meeting*.

34.127 **Meeting:** An official assembly of the members of an organization where all participants can hear one another, there is no temporal separation of the participants except for a recess, and it continues until adjournment.

34.128 **Member in Good Standing:** A member who can exercise all the rights of membership. Loss of good standing usually occurs automatically or through administrative steps and is not the same as suspension or expulsion, although members who are suspended are also not in good standing.

34.129 **Minutes:** The legal history and record of official actions of an organization taken at a meeting.

34.130 **Minutes Template:** A prepared format of an organization's minutes that is used by the secretary to prepare draft minutes.

34.131 **Motion (Question):** A proposal submitted to an assembly for its consideration and decision.

34.132 **Multiple Slate:** A list of offices and candidates containing the names of more than one nominee for an office or offices. See *single slate*.

34.133 **Nomination:** The formal proposal to an assembly of a person as a candidate for an office.

34.134 **Notice of Meeting:** See *call of meeting*.

34.135 **Notice of Motion:** See *previous notice*.

34.136 **Object:** The purpose(s) for which the organization exists.

34.137 **Objection (Objects):** The formal expression of opposition to a proposed action.

34.138 **Object to the Consideration of a Question:** A motion permitted in other parliamentary authorities to kill a main motion with no debate.

34.139 **Officers:** Members of an organization who may have specific responsibilities, duties, and powers because of their elected or appointed positions. Officers are defined in the governing documents.

34.140 **Official Year:** If not prescribed in the governing documents, an official year commences at the time that an event, such as the commencement of an officer's term or annual meeting, is scheduled pursuant to a rule and runs until the time scheduled for the next such event, approximately one year later.

34.141 **Open Meeting Laws:** Laws requiring governmental entities to have procedural transparency and openness in meetings. Also known as *sunshine laws*.

34.142 **Order of Business:** The adopted order in which the various classifications of business are presented to the meetings of an assembly.

34.143 **Organizing Meeting:** The initial meeting of a group that does not have an established membership roster or rules, sometimes called a *mass meeting*.

34.144 **Out of Order:** Not permissible, from a parliamentary standpoint.

34.145 **Parliamentarian (Member):** A member of the organization who is elected or appointed to provide information on parliamentary procedure and advise the presiding officer. A member parliamentarian may be a professional parliamentarian. The parliamentarian is not responsible or allowed to make rulings; however, the parliamentarian offers advice to a presiding officer, who makes the rulings.

34.146 **Parliamentarian (Professional):** An employed or volunteer consultant who has had training and professional experience in parliamentary law is not typically a member of the organization and is usually accredited by either AIP or NAP, or both. The parliamentarian is not responsible for ruling and is not allowed to make rulings; however, the parliamentarian offers advice to a presiding officer, who makes the rulings.

34.147 **Parliamentary Authority:** The code or rulebook specified in an organization's bylaws as its authority in matters not covered by its bylaws or standing rules.

34.148 **Parliamentary Law:** Meeting procedures in common use by most organizations providing for the equal protection of the rights of every member. See *common parliamentary law*, a substantially equivalent term.

34.149 **Penalty:** Punishment imposed on a member.

34.150 **Pending Motion (Question):** Any motion that has been proposed and stated to the assembly for consideration and that is awaiting disposition.

34.151 **Permanent Organization:** An organization formed to function over a considerable amount of time. See *temporary organization*.

34.152 **Petition for Nominations:** Signed evidence of support for a particular candidate or proposition.

34.153 **Plurality Vote:** A larger vote than that received by any opposing candidate or alternative measure.

34.154 **Power(s):** The authority or ability to act granted by the instructions of the assembly or the bylaws or other governing documents.

34.155 **Power to Act:** Authority granted to a subordinate body or committee to act on behalf of the parent body.

34.156 **Preamble:** An introductory statement giving background or reasons for the action in a proposal.

34.157 **Precedence:** The rank or priority governing the proposal, consideration, and disposal of motions.

34.158 **Precedent:** A course of action or decision that may serve as a guide or rule for future similar situations in a particular organization.

34.159 **Preferential Voting:** A one-ballot voting procedure, using candidate rankings, that eliminates the need for multiple ballots by repeatedly reallocating the ballots of the candidate with the lowest vote total to the candidate of that ballot's second and subsequent choices, which results, eventually, in one candidate receiving a majority.

34.160 **Presiding:** The act of managing or conducting a meeting from the place of authority in the meeting.

34.161 **Presiding Officer:** The person who conducts and manages the meeting according to parliamentary procedure.

34.162 **Previous Notice:** A written or verbal announcement at a meeting, in the call of the meeting, or by special advance notice of a proposal to be considered at a future meeting.

34.163 **Principles:** The beliefs and philosophy of the organization.

34.164 **Priority Agenda:** A list of important business items, or items of significant consequence, that are preferentially taken up early in the meeting, immediately following the consent agenda.

34.165 **Privileged Motion:** Motions of such urgency that they are entitled under the rules to immediate consideration.

34.166 **Procedural Motion:** A motion that does not directly handle the substantive business of the organization but rather handles that substantive business indirectly by affecting the handling of the main motion or of the meeting itself, such as a Motion to Recess or Close Debate. See *substantive motion*.

34.167 **Procedural Rule:** A rule contained in the parliamentary authority, the standing rules of order or temporary rules, or other governing documents dealing with parliamentary procedure.

34.168 **Professional Presiding Officer:** A skilled individual, often a credentialed parliamentarian, engaged to preside over a meeting.

34.169 **Program:** The agenda for a convention that includes both business and nonbusiness activities. It can also be an educational presentation within a meeting.

34.170 **Proportion of the Membership:** A percentage of membership specified in governing documents, usually as a quorum or voting requirement.

34.171 **Proposal or Proposition:** A statement of a motion for consideration and action.

34.172 **Protocol:** The formal customs and traditions for honoring special guests, the flag, invocation, precedence of officers and other honorees, or other revered customs of the organization.

34.173 **Proviso:** A stipulation in the bylaws, motion, or rule indicating certain conditions affecting the motion, such as when it goes into effect and when it ceases to be in effect.

34.174 **Proxy:** A written authorization empowering another person or entity to act, in a meeting, for the member who gives the proxy. *Proxy* may also refer to the person or entity who casts the vote.

34.175 **Proxy Giver:** A member who is entitled to a vote and grants a power of attorney to another individual or entity.

34.176 **Proxy Holder:** An individual or entity who received the right to vote or an additional vote or votes via a power of attorney from another individual or individuals.

34.177   **Putting the Question:** The statement, by the presiding officer, of a motion to the assembly for the purpose of taking the vote on it.

34.178   **Qualified Quorum:** A requirement of a number or proportion of members who must be present, plus an additional requirement of a proportion or number of constituents, delegations, or divisions of members who must be present. Also known as a double quorum.

34.179   **Question:** Any proposal submitted to an assembly for decision. See *motion*.

34.180   **Quorum:** The number or proportion of members that must be present at a meeting of an organization to enable it to act legally on business.

34.181   **Quorum Call:** A request that the presence of a quorum be verified.

34.182   **Railroading:** To push a motion through so rapidly that members do not have an opportunity to exercise their parliamentary rights. Also known as *gaveling through*.

34.183   **Rank:** A priority or hierarchy of various motions and the sequence in which they must be considered and disposed of. See *precedence*.

34.184   **Ranked Choice:** See *preferential voting*.

34.185   **Recognition:** Formal acknowledgment by the presiding officer of a particular member, giving that member the sole right to speak or to present a motion.

34.186   **Reconsider:** A motion that enables an assembly to set aside the vote or disposition on a main motion taken at the same meeting or convention and to consider the motion again as though no vote or disposition had been taken on it.

34.187   **Recorded Vote:** A vote conducted using a *roll call vote* or by electronic means where each voter's name and vote are included in the minutes.

34.188   **Reference Committee:** A committee used by organizations with extensive agendas to receive and provide recommendations on all motions or resolutions before they are presented to the full assembly for disposition.

34.189   **Regular Meeting:** A recurring meeting of an organization where a normal order of business is scheduled and usually any business is in order.

34.190 **Renew a Motion:** To present again a motion previously defeated at the same meeting or convention.

34.191 **Repeal by Implication:** The indirect rescinding of all or part of a decision by the subsequent adoption of a motion that conflicts with the prior motion.

34.192 **Reports of Officers:** Written or verbal account presented to an assembly about the area of responsibility in an organization assigned to an elected or appointed officer.

34.193 **Request:** A statement to the presiding officer expressing a desire that something be done. It is usually decided by the presiding officer. The request may also be expressed as a motion.

34.194 **Resolution:** A formal motion, usually in writing, often with a preamble, and may be introduced by the word *Resolved*, that is presented to an assembly for decision.

34.195 **Revision of Bylaws:** See *bylaws revision*.

34.196 **Roll Call Vote:** A method of voting where each member or delegation votes when called upon, with their vote recorded in the minutes. See *recorded vote*.

34.197 **Ruling:** A decision of the presiding officer that relates to the procedure of the assembly.

34.198 **Scheduled Order:** A motion that has been postponed and designated as a scheduled order is a matter that must be taken up immediately when the designated time arrives, regardless of whether something else is pending at that time.

34.199 **Scope of Notice:** The range of actions that fall between the status quo and the proposed action for which notice was given.

34.200 **Second:** An indication that a member supports consideration of a motion made by another.

34.201 **Seriatim:** Consideration by sections or paragraphs.

34.202 **Serpentine Count:** A voting method where voters verbally count themselves row by row.

34.203 **Single Slate:** A list of offices and candidates containing the name of only one candidate for each office that is often elected in a single vote. Contrast with *multiple slate*.

34.204 **Slate:** A list of offices and candidates containing the name of one or more candidates that is often elected in a single vote, frequently used to mean a *single slate*.

34.205 **Special Committee:** A committee that is selected to carry out a particular task and that ceases to exist once the task is completed. Also called an *ad hoc committee* or a *task force*.

34.206 **Special Meeting (Called Meeting):** A meeting, other than a regularly scheduled meeting, called to handle one or more specific matters listed in the call to the meeting.

34.207 **Special Rules:** Rules that are adopted by the organization that supersede the parliamentary authority and are intended to be of a temporary nature. See *temporary rules*.

34.208 **Specific-Purpose Main Motion:** A category of main motions that accomplish a specific parliamentary purpose.

34.209 **Standing Committee:** A committee that has a fixed term of office and that performs any work in its field assigned to it by the bylaws or referred to it by the organization or the governing board.

34.210 **Standing Rules of Order:** Rules adopted by the organization that supersede the parliamentary authority and are intended to be of a permanent nature.

34.211 **Standing Vote:** An uncounted vote where members indicate their preference by standing.

34.212 **Stating the Motion:** The presiding officer's initial statement of the motion, opening it for consideration.

34.213 **Straw Vote:** An informal vote that is not binding.

34.214 **Strike Out:** A method of amendment where words or paragraphs are removed.

34.215 **Strike Out and Insert:** A method of amendment where words or paragraphs are removed, and other words or paragraphs replace the removed text in a single motion.

34.216 **Subsidiary Motion:** Motions that alter the main motion or delay or hasten its consideration.

34.217 **Substantive Motion:** A motion that introduces business. A *main motion*. See *procedural motion*.

34.218 **Substitute Motion:** A title applied to an amendment that strikes an entire motion and inserts a new motion on the same subject.

34.219 **Sunshine Laws:** See *open meeting laws*.

34.220 **Supermajority:** A voting requirement that is more than a majority.

34.221 **Table:** To kill a main motion without a direct vote.

34.222 **Task Force:** See *special committee*.

34.223 **Telephonic Meeting:** An *electronic meeting* held via telephonic means, which consists solely of an audio component.

34.224 **Teller:** An individual with specified duties relating to the conduct of an election and the processing of votes, typically called an *inspector of elections* in business organizations.

34.225 **Temporary Organization:** A group formed to accomplish a specific project or goal with the expectation that the group will cease to exist when the project or goal is complete.

34.226 **Temporary Rules:** An adopted rule with a definite expiration date or time period. Sometimes known as *special rules of order*.

34.227 **Term of Office:** The duration of service for which a member is elected or appointed to an office.

34.228 **Texas Ballot:** A method of voting in which voters indicate the candidate(s) that they do not wish to be elected.

34.229 **Three-Fourths Vote/Three-Quarters Vote:** A vote that requires three-fourths of the votes in the affirmative for a proposal to be adopted. By default, unless a different basis for determining three-fourths is specified, the requirement is three-fourths of the legal votes cast.

34.230 **Tie Vote:** A vote in which the affirmative and negative votes are equal on a motion, or a vote in an election in which two or more candidates receive the same number of votes.

34.231 **Two-Thirds Vote:** A vote that requires two-thirds of the votes in the affirmative for a proposal to be adopted. By default, unless a different basis for determining two-thirds is specified, the requirement is two-thirds of legal votes cast.

34.232 **Unanimous Consent:** See *general consent*.

34.233 **Unanimous Vote:** A vote without any dissenting vote.

34.234 **Unanimous Written Consent:** A written or electronic assent to an action by all the members of a body with no abstentions.

34.235 **Unfinished Business:** Any business that is postponed to a future meeting or that was pending at the adjournment of the previous meeting.

34.236 **Vacancy:** An unoccupied office that may result because of death, resignation, removal, or loss of eligibility.

34.237 **Virtual Meeting:** See *electronic meeting*.

34.238 **Voice Vote:** An oral vote; sometimes called a viva voce vote.

34.239 **Waiver of Notice:** Act of voluntarily relinquishing the requirement of notice for a proposal or meeting; may refer also to the signed written statement proving the voluntary relinquishment of the right to notice.

34.240 **Withdraw or Modify a Motion:** The request or demand by the maker of the motion to remove from consideration or modify their motion.

34.241 **Write-In Vote:** A vote on a ballot for someone who has not been nominated.

APPENDIX A. Bylaws Checklist

A.1 As noted in Chapter 4, the bylaws of an organization, by whatever name they are known, function as a contract between the organization and the members, and between the members themselves, detailing the rights and privileges of the members, and establishing the governance framework of the organization. The content of bylaws can vary greatly between organizations; however, the following information may provide guidance on the content and structure of this important governing document. All bylaws dealing with the same general subject should be grouped together under one article, which in turn is divided into sections.

NAME AND PURPOSE

A.2 In organizations that are incorporated or that are chartered subsidiaries of a parent organization, or both, the name and the purpose of the organization are found in governing documents of higher authority: either the articles of incorporation or the charter from the parent body. In either case, repeating the information in the bylaws is not necessary. If the content is repeated, it must be understood that if an inconsistency creeps in, the name or purpose as found in the higher-ranking governing document would take precedence over the bylaws.[*]

MEMBERSHIP PROVISIONS

A.3 The next article relates to the membership of the organization. The bylaws should include provisions that define classes of membership and define the eligibility and/or qualification requirements, rights, and privileges of each class of membership. Designations for classes of membership may include categories such as active, associate, and student membership. Information about applying for membership and how to join the organization are also included in bylaws.

---

[*] In the case of a lengthy or complex statement of purpose, a footnote may indicate the information is in the charter, or the purpose should be quoted with attribution to the charter to indicate that these provisions cannot be altered by bylaw amendment. Some organizations place the purpose as a preamble to the bylaws with attribution to the charter or higher governing document.

A.4 If honorary membership is desired, it should be included in the membership provisions and should include information on how honorary members are selected, and what their rights and privileges are.

A.5 A separate section should include the amount of dues for each membership class, when dues are payable, and any grace period before a member is suspended or terminated for nonpayment of dues. Additionally, if charges are permitted to be assessed by the organization, such as late fees and fines, these must be clearly permitted and defined in the bylaws.

A.6 Just as important as the protection for the rights of members in joining and being affiliated with the organization described in the previous paragraph, there should be clear provisions for membership resignation, expulsion, and suspension (for reasons other than nonpayment of dues), and, if permitted, methods of reinstatement following a member's departure from the organization.

MEMBERSHIP MEETING PROVISIONS

A.7 The next article deals with meetings of the membership. Provisions related to meetings of the membership, including the timing of regular meetings and provisions for rescheduling or canceling them, should be in a single section. The date of the annual meeting, requirements for notice, and the list of any business to be conducted go into a separate section. Provisions for special meetings, including who may call them and how, who has the power to request them and how, and notice requirements are in a separate section.

A.8 Quorum requirements for membership meetings, if different from those in the parliamentary authority, are found in this article.

GOVERNANCE PROVISIONS

A.9 The next set of articles relate to the governance and leadership of the organization: the officers, the board of directors, the executive committee (if there is one), and committees. This section may contain several articles.

A.10 The article on officers might contain information such as the following:

1. a list of the officers of the organization;

2. any unique requirements to be eligible to serve in a specific office (such as a requirement that the treasurer has previously served as a member of the finance committee);
3. provisions related to nomination and election of officers;
4. the term of office, including when it begins;
5. the duties of each officer (in addition to any listed in the defined parliamentary authority);
6. succession of officers;
7. provisions for filling vacancies; and
8. provisions related to both the resignation and removal of officers.

A.11 The article on the board of directors might contain information such as the following:
1. composition of the board;
2. a list of the positions on the board;
3. if there are directors who are not on the board as a result of holding another office or position, provisions should be included on how those directors are chosen, the basis of their selection, qualifications, and the term of office, including when it begins, provisions on vacancies, and provisions for removal;
4. if the immediate past president is to be a member of the board, specify whether the president must complete their term to become immediate past president, provide for assignment of those duties if the immediate past president is unwilling or unable to serve, or if there is no immediate past president due to death, resignation, or non membership in the organization;
5. officers of the board: usually the elected president and secretary serve in those roles for the board as well; however, should the organization wish, other provisions can be made and should include qualifications and selection processes for these roles;
6. duties and responsibilities of the board, which often include the duty and power to act for the organization between meetings of the organization, sometimes subject to the orders of the membership; alternatively, full power to manage the affairs of the organization, with the membership assigned explicit limited authority;
7. meetings of the board;

8. meeting frequency and notice requirements;
9. quorum requirements for board meetings;
10. provisions for special meetings, including who may call them and how, who has the power to request them and how, and notice requirements;
11. authorization for the board to establish rules for such meetings, including provisions for electronic meetings if desired;
12. authority and requirements for acting without a meeting if desired;
13. provisions related to reports of the board.

A.12   If there is to be an executive committee, a separate article contains provisions covering substantially the same topics as those listed above for the board.

A.13   An article on committees may include provisions on both standing and special committees. This article includes the list of standing committees and for each standing committee: the number of members, method of selection, duties, powers, meetings, and to which body or bodies the committee reports. If other standing committees may be created without amending the bylaws, this must be specified. For special committees, this article includes provisions for their creation and selection of their members.

ADMINISTRATIVE PROVISIONS

A.14   The final set of articles relate to the administrative provisions of the organization: financial provisions, staff provisions, discipline of members, emergency provisions, provisions related to legal requirements, parliamentary authority, and amendment of the bylaws.

A.15   The article on finances might contain information such as the following:

1. budget preparation and adoption;
2. provisions for financial oversight and review, whether internal, external, or both;
3. any requirement for a surety bond for officers and employees;
4. any requirement for the organization to provide directors' and officers' insurance; indemnification provisions;
5. authorization for and limitations on expenditures; and
6. compensation of officers and board members if desired.

A.16   The article on staff, if needed, might contain information such as the following:

1. if there is to be an executive director, provisions for the hiring, compensation, duties and powers, reporting relationship, and termination; and
2. reporting relationship of the staff with the board and other leaders of the organization.

A.17   The article on discipline and expulsion of members might contain information such as the following:

1. grounds for action;
2. the process required to discipline a member;
3. the types of penalties that may be applied;
4. vote requirements for disciplinary actions; and
5. provisions for reinstatement if that is to be permitted.

A.18   The article on emergency bylaws might contain information such as the following:

1. who determines that an emergency exists and in what circumstances;
2. who can cancel or postpone meetings and the procedures required;
3. relaxed method and procedures for notice if desired;
4. relaxed quorum requirements if desired;
5. delegation of additional powers to the board;
6. changes to term length/limits, vacancies, order of succession, number/list of officers;
7. allowance of proxies and electronic/telephone meetings if desired and not prohibited in the bylaws or rules;
8. procedures to notify the board and/or membership of action taken outside of the standard course; and
9. grace period for returning to normal procedures after the emergency.

A.19   See Appendix B for sample emergency bylaws.

A.20   An article containing provisions required to maintain legal status might contain information such as the following:

1. dissolution clauses; and
2. other provisions to maintain legal or tax-exempt status.

A.21 The article adopting the parliamentary authority should say:

> In all matters not covered by applicable law, its constitution, bylaws, standing rules of order, or temporary rules, this organization shall be governed by the current edition of the *American Institute of Parliamentarians Standard Code of Parliamentary Procedure*.

A.22 The final required article is the article defining the requirements to amend the bylaws, which should contain information such as the following:

1. notice required for bylaws amendments to the members;
2. form of that notice;
3. who may propose amendments and to whom they must be submitted;
4. provisions related to review by bylaws committee or reference committee; and
5. the vote required to adopt bylaws amendments.

APPENDIX B. Sample Emergency Bylaws

MODEL SET OF EMERGENCY BYLAWS

B.1   These bylaws shall become effective if an emergency is declared by a government agency in the jurisdiction where the organization is organized or in which a meeting is planned to occur.

B.2   During any emergency, for three months after the termination of the emergency, and until any meeting properly noticed during that period takes place (but not more than six months after the termination of the emergency), the following provisions apply unless terminated earlier by the board or membership:

B.3   Notice of a meeting of the board of directors only needs to be given to those directors that it is practicable to reach. Notice may be given in any manner that is practical and as soon in advance as reasonably possible. Notice may be given by any officer if the secretary is unavailable or incapacitated. The quorum consists of those directors who attend.

B.4   The highest-ranking officer who is available may call or cancel a meeting of the board. The board may call or cancel a meeting of the members. If urgent action is required and the board cannot meet, the highest-ranking officer who is available may cancel a meeting of the members. The members of the affected body should be notified of the call or cancellation as soon as possible, by any reasonable means of communication in the circumstances. The board may reschedule any membership meeting and the highest-ranking officer who is available shall reschedule any board meeting canceled under this provision. Even in case of emergency, proxies may not be used at meetings of the board or members.

B.5   Meetings of the board and members otherwise required to be held in person may be held by any means by which all directors or members may communicate simultaneously with all other directors or members in attendance. The board may set a reasonable quorum for a meeting of the members. The board may adopt rules for the conduct of meetings of the board and the members. The board may determine that any item of business otherwise to be determined by the members may be decided by mail or electronic ballot by procedures adopted by the board. If the board is incapable of meeting in a manner in which all directors may communicate simultaneously with all other directors, the board may act by a vote of two-thirds of the directors able to be notified and capable of responding within a reasonable time.

B.6 If not otherwise provided in the bylaws, officers and directors shall serve until their successors are chosen. Vacancies that would normally be filled by the members under the bylaws may be filled by the board until the next meeting of the members.

B.7 The board may change the location of the principal office, adopt temporary amendments to the bylaws to remain in effect until the next meeting of the members, or take any other action otherwise required to be taken by the members, except for election of officers to act beyond the next meeting of the members and amendment of the bylaws or corporate charter to remain in effect beyond the next meeting.

B.8 As soon as practicable during and after the termination of the emergency, the board shall notify the members of all actions taken and changes to governing documents made during the course of the emergency.

B.9 After a canceled meeting or the termination of the emergency, a special, annual, or regular meeting of the members may address any business items required by the bylaws, including any business items that were required to be addressed during the period of the emergency. The members may also rescind the remaining effect of any action taken during the emergency.

APPENDIX C. Sample Proxy Form

A. Proxy Giver Identification

C.1 Name _____, Membership # _____ (if applicable)

C.2 Address: _____

B. Proxy Holder Identification

C.3 Name _____, Membership # _____ (if applicable)

C.4 Address: _____

C. Authority to Act as Proxy

C.5 I, _____, the undersigned, hereby appoint the above-named proxy holder to attend, act, and vote in my place at the meeting of members of the _____ (association name) to be held on the _____ day of _____ (month), and at any continuation or adjournments of said meeting. This proxy may be revoked by me at any time by notice in writing to the proxy holder and to the secretary of _____ (association name). The proxy holder may not further assign the rights and duties detailed in this proxy to another. The proxy holder may act in the same manner and to the same extent, and with the same power as I, the proxy giver, could act if I were personally present at the meeting, subject to the following instructions or restrictions:

D. Instructions and Restrictions

C.6 (The proxy giver may provide any instructions or restrictions below as to how the proxy holder may act and vote at the meeting)

1. Example: The proxy holder shall vote in favor of the proposal to amend Bylaw VII.

2. Example: The proxy holder shall only vote for candidates nominated by the nominations committee.

3. Example: The proxy may only vote in my place but may not make motions or debate.

4. Example: The proxy may be counted to establish and maintain a quorum, but the proxy holder may not vote, make motions, or debate.

E. Signature of Proxy Giver

C.7 Signature _____, Dated _____

APPENDIX D. Sample Convention Rules for a Hybrid Meeting

Meeting Rules

D.1 **Log-in time.** The tech team shall provide the internet meeting service availability to begin no less than 10 minutes before the start of each meeting and workshop if possible.

D.2 **Quorum.** The presence of a quorum shall be established and announced by the chair or tech team who can observe the in-person attendees and the ability to see the online list of participating members. Thereafter, the continued presence of a quorum shall be presumed unless the tech team notifies the president of the lack of a quorum.

D.3 **Technical requirements and malfunctions.** Electronic connection to the meeting is the responsibility of each attendee; no action shall be invalidated on the grounds that the loss, or poor quality, of an attendee's individual connection prevented the attendee from participating in the meeting or workshop, nor will a refund be granted.

D.4 **Forced disconnections.** The chair may cause or direct the disconnection or muting of an attendee's connection if it is causing undue interference with the meeting.

D.5 **Recordings.** Attendees shall not record any session or workshop.

D.6 **Assignment of the floor.** To seek recognition by the chair, a virtually attending member shall type their name in the chat feature and a member attending in person shall provide their name to a microphone monitor and state: (i) the purpose for which recognition is being sought; (ii) the intention to speak for or against the motion; or (iii) the intention to make a Factual Inquiry or Parliamentary Inquiry. The microphone monitor will enter the information into the chat feature for the in-person attendee. The raise hand feature shall not be used for these purposes.

1. An in-person tech team member(s) will monitor the chat feature and collaborate to ensure equity of recognition and keep track of the speaking order. The queue shall be cleared after each new debatable motion is stated by the chair.

2. Factual and Parliamentary Inquiries shall be given priority in recognition.

D.7 **Interrupting motions.** Members wishing to make the interrupting motions Point of Order and Appeal from the Decision of the Chair shall raise their hands, either in person or virtually. No other motions will be allowed to interrupt. An in-person tech team member(s) will assist the chair to ensure interrupting motions are promptly addressed.

D.8 **Identification of speaker.** When recognized by the chair, members shall state their names and state, province, or country.

D.9 **Motions submitted in writing.** Members wishing to make a main motion or to offer an amendment shall, before being recognized, email the motion to _____.

D.10 **Display of motions.** Main motions, or the pertinent part of main motions, amendments, and other documents currently before the assembly, shall be displayed to the extent feasible.

D.11 **Debate.** Only members who are registered for the meeting shall have the right to speak on issues before the assembly. A member may speak no more than twice, for no more than two minutes each time, on a debatable motion.

D.12 **Discussion time.** Total discussion time on each main motion shall be limited to twenty minutes.

D.13 **Voting and balloting.** Only members who are registered and in compliance with the membership date of record shall have the right to vote. Votes shall be taken by general consent or by an external electronic voting service. Ballot votes, if required, shall be taken using an external electronic voting service.

D.14 **Bylaws corrections.** The bylaws committee shall be authorized to correct article and section designations, punctuation, grammar, syntax, and cross-references and to make such other technical and conforming changes as may be necessary to reflect the intent of the decisions arising from the members.

D.15 **Nominees' speeches.** At the close of nominations, each nominee (or a designee) shall have two minutes for remarks. Nominees shall speak in nomination order.

APPENDIX E. Model Minutes–Example

Call to Order

E.1 The regular meeting of the XYZ Association was called to order at 5:00 p.m., on July 25, 20__, at headquarters by President Ann Anderson. Secretary Richard Recorder was present.

Opening Ceremonies

E.2 The invocation was given by Sally Wright.

E.3 Pledge of Allegiance to the Flag of the United States of America was led by Helen Honor.

E.4 Inspiration was given by Hillary Hearing.

Roll Call

E.5 Members in attendance: President Ann Anderson, Vice President John Jones, Secretary Richard Recorder, Treasurer Milly Money, members: Molly Stone, Helen Honor, Sally Wright, Hillary Hearing, and Mary Member.

E.6 Parliamentarian: Kate Karing

E.7 Members absent: David Dodger and Milly Mentor

E.8 Guests present: Susan Samuel

Quorum

E.9 A quorum was present.

Minutes

E.10 The minutes of the June 18, 20__, meeting were approved as presented.

Report of Officers

E.11 President Anderson reported.

E.12 Vice President Jones reported.

E.13 Secretary Recorder read correspondence from XYZ Association National Headquarters concerning the dates for the convention in January.

E.14 Treasurer Money reported as follows:

Opening balance as of (date)	$1,898.50
Income	$500.00
(Donation)	
Disbursements (Expenses)	$200.00
(Printing)	
Closing balance as of (date)	$2198.50

E.15 The report of the treasurer was filed.

E.16 Bills for meeting room rental and office supplies were approved for payment.

Report of the Board

E.17 The secretary presented the report of the XYZ board as follows:

E.18 The board met by teleconference on July 4, 20__, and took the following actions:

1. Approved the appointment of Molly Stone as chair for the Spring Fling.
2. Approved the application for the *American Institute of Parliamentarians Standard Code of Parliamentary Procedure* to be sold in the XYZ bookstore.
3. Reviewed the XYZ insurance documents.

E.19 Standing Committees

1. The membership committee report was presented by Chair Mary Member. The report is attached to the minutes.
2. The scholarship committee report was presented by Chair Helen Honor. The report is attached to the minutes.
3. The committee recommended funding a scholarship to the XYZ Association Annual Education Conference for one local student in the amount of $500. The recommendation was adopted.

Special Committees

E.20 The report of the planning task force was presented by Chair Hillary Hearing. The report is attached to the minutes.

Unfinished Business

E.21 The motion relating to Fall Fair, which was pending at adjournment of the previous meeting, was adopted as amended to read "that the XYZ Association hold a potluck dinner on the first Thursday in September at 6:30 p.m. in the community center to welcome this year's new members."

New Business

E.22 John Jones moved "that the president appoint a committee of three to explore the cost of purchasing a computer for the secretary." The motion was adopted as amended to read "that the president appoint a committee of three to explore the cost of purchasing a computer and printer for the secretary and report back at the next meeting." President Jones appointed Treasurer Money, Helen Honor, and Hillary Hearing to the committee, with Treasurer Money as chair.

Announcements

E.23 The next meeting will be held at the fairgrounds on August 18, 20___.

Program

E.24 The program was presented by Susan Samuel, consultant on setting personal goals.

Adjournment

E.25 The meeting was adjourned at 8:52 p.m.

E.26 Richard Recorder_____

E.27 Secretary

E.28 Approval

E.29 Minutes approved this _____ day of _____, 20____

E.30 (Date minutes were approved)

E.31 _____

E.32 Secretary (initials or signature)

APPENDIX F. Minutes Template–Subject Format

F.1 Parenthesis provide options; square brackets give information/notations/instructions.

1. Call to Order

F.2 The (regular/special/annual/continued) meeting of the (name of organization) was called to order at (time), on (date), at (location) by (name and title of presiding officer). Secretary (or temporary secretary) (name) was present.

2. Opening Ceremonies [if applicable]

F.3 Invocation was given by (name).

F.4 Pledge of Allegiance was led by (name).

F.5 Inspiration was given by (name).

3. Roll Call [if roll call taken]

F.6 Members in attendance: (Names).

F.7 Parliamentarian: [if not a member].

F.8 [if applicable] Members absent:

F.9 [if applicable] Guests present:

4. Quorum

F.10 A quorum (was/was not) present.

5. Minutes

F.11 The minutes of the (previous or date) meeting were (approved/not approved) as (presented/read/amended/distributed). [Note: corrections are entered in the final draft of the minutes.]

6. Reports of Officers

F.12 (Elected officers: president, vice president, other elected officers) (title and last name) reported (only actions or informational items that apply to the organization; one paragraph per officer).

F.13 Secretary (last name) read correspondence from (identify source, basic information) and (action taken or to be taken if applicable).

F.14 Treasurer (last name) reported as follows:

Opening balance	$ 0,000.00
Income (May identify sources of income)	$ 000.00
Disbursements (Expenses) (May identify new disbursements)	$ 00.00
Closing balance	$ 0,000.00

F.15 The report of the treasurer was filed.

F.16 [if applicable] Bills (identify) were approved for payment.

7. Report of the Board [if applicable]

F.17 The secretary presented the report of the (identify organization) board as follows: (list actions taken).

8. Standing Committees

F.18 The (standing committee name) report was presented by (name, title if chair) and is attached to these minutes. (Include any action taken on recommendations from the report. No opinion or discussion. Use one paragraph per report.)

9. Special Committees

F.19 The (special/ad hoc committee/task force name) report was presented by (name, title if chair) and is attached to these minutes. (Include any action taken on recommendations from the report. No opinion or discussion. Use one paragraph per report.)

10. Unfinished Business [if applicable]

F.20 The motion (state motion), which was (pending at adjournment/postponed to this meeting) at the previous meeting, was (adopted/adopted as amended/defeated/referred/etc.). (If amended, use the wording as adopted. One paragraph per motion.)

11. New Business [if applicable]

F.21 (Name) moved that (exact wording of the motion as stated by the chair). The motion was (action taken). (If amended, use the wording of the motion as adopted with the notation that it was amended. One paragraph per motion.)

12. Announcements

F.22 (Announcements of information pertaining to the whole organization.)

13. Program [if applicable]

F.23 The program was presented by (name of presenter and title of subject). [No opinion or discussion.] [Note: the program may be stated prior to adjournment or at other times as determined by the organization.]

14. Adjournment

F.24 [If by motion] (Name) moved that the meeting be adjourned. The motion was adopted, and the meeting was adjourned at (time).

F.25 [If by the chair] The meeting was adjourned at (time).

F.26 _____

F.27 Secretary (or temporary secretary)

Approval

F.28 Minutes approved this ___ day of _____, 20___

F.29 (Date minutes were approved)

F.30 _____

F.31 Secretary (initials or signature)

APPENDIX G. Useful Tools for Preparing Minutes

MINUTES TEMPLATE

G.1 A *minutes template* is a format of an organization's minutes that is used by the secretary to prepare an initial version of the minutes prior to the meeting. This allows a large portion of the minutes to be set up prior to the actual meeting when the secretary will only have to edit the template. For examples of minutes templates in both column and subject formats, see information online at aipstandardcode.com.

G.2 Meetings have many common elements that are well known before the meeting begins. These include such items as the type of meeting, the location, the presiding officer, and presence of the secretary. These items in the first paragraph of the minutes may be formatted well in advance of the actual meeting.

G.3 The call to order, any routine opening ceremonies, and the quorum statement may also be formatted with a blank to fill in the actual time, names, or number. If a roll call is conducted, the names of all members may be listed and then the names of members not in attendance may be deleted and not included in the final draft.

G.4 In addition, at either a regular meeting or a convention, the agenda is generally known prior to the actual meeting. Most of the activities and names of reporting members are listed on the proposed agenda. For instance, the reports of officers, standing committees, and special committees are listed on the agenda prior to the meeting. The minutes template may list this information prior to the meeting and the actual report or item of business is added as it is presented. Any item of business for which advance notice was given may also be incorporated into the minutes template.

G.5 Utilization of a minutes template allows the secretary to easily add the motions and items of business in a consistent format as they come up during the actual meeting. This can save considerable time after the meeting and often will allow the first draft of the minutes to be ready for submission to the minutes approval committee shortly after the meeting concludes.

ACTION LOG

G.6   In addition to the minutes, the organization may develop a system of recording actions taken that is separate from the minutes. This is called an *action log* and allows an organization to quickly review previous decisions. The need for this system often comes up when a motion is made that may conflict with an action previously taken. It is not unusual, as an organization's leadership changes, to have a question about whether a proposed motion conflicts with a past action. A well-organized action log facilitates retrieval of answers.

G.7   The log identifies all decisions of the organization in a spreadsheet. It is often a list of actions organized by subject and recorded by date for quick cross-reference to the minutes. Some organizations incorporate the total wording of the adopted motion because access to the minutes may not be readily available. In some organizations, responsibility for completing the action and the date that the action was completed are also in the action log. If the documents are stored digitally, the past action may quickly be retrieved. For an example of an action log, see documents at aipstandardcode.com.

APPENDIX H. Tellers' Report–Elections

H.1	Office Vice President	
H.2	Eligible voters	345
H.3	Legal votes cast	341
H.4	Illegal votes cast	2
H.5	(2 votes for ineligible candidates)	
H.6	Blank votes	3
H.7	Votes required to elect	171
	John Smith	195
	Laurie Jones	141
	Pat Wright	5
H.8	Date ___ (current date)	
H.9	Signatures of tellers	
H.10	Nancy Norton	/s/ Nancy Norton
H.11	Chris Roark	/s/ Chris Roark
H.12	Tom Tuttle	/s/ Tom Tuttle

APPENDIX I. Adopt in Lieu of Flowchart

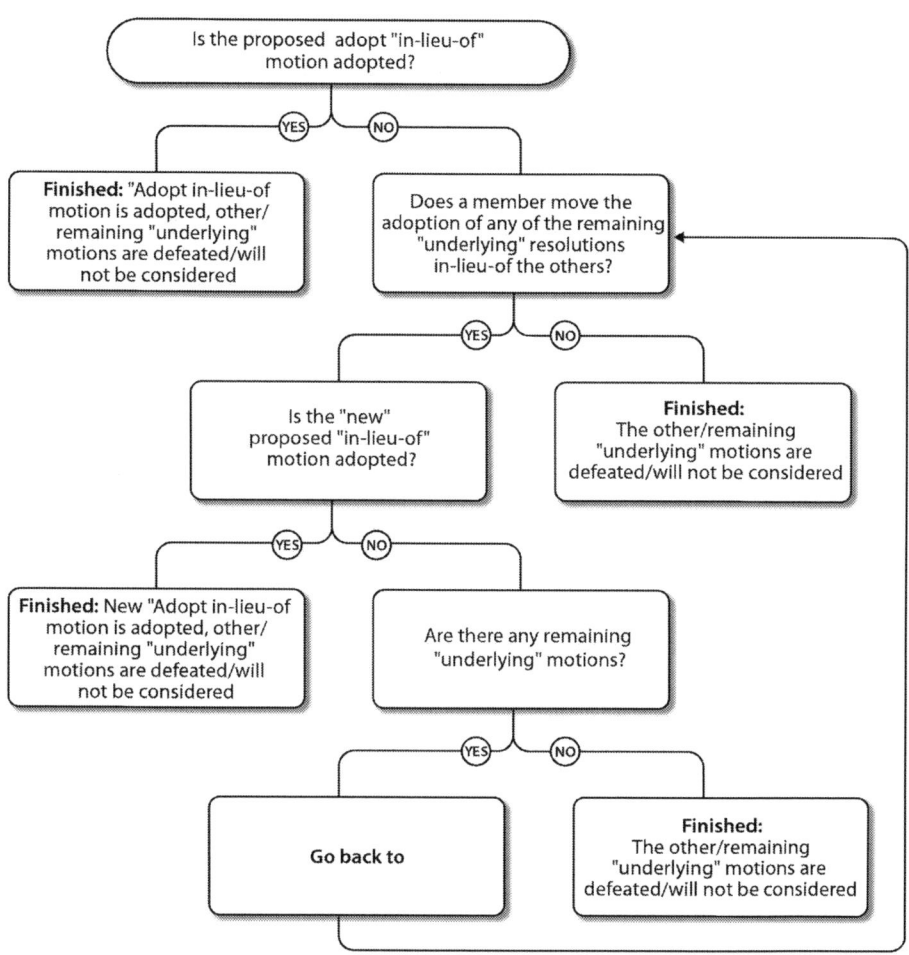

APPENDIX J. Notes and Citations

Chapter 1

1 Mr. Justice Douglas speaking before the Rhode Island Bar Association, as quoted in *Oregon State Bar Bulletin* (December 1947) at 7.

2 *McNabb v. United States*, 318 U.S. 332, 347 (1943).

Chapter 2

3 A "town meeting would very soon find itself entangled in the complicated meshes of parliamentary rules, which would effectually stop all proceedings." *Hill v. Goodwin*, 56 N.H. 441 (1876), *quoted in Bullard v. Allen*, 124 Me. 251, 261, 127 A. 722, 727 (1925).

4 "Among the rights protected by the First Amendment [of the U.S. Constitution] is the right of individuals to associate to further their personal beliefs." *Healy v. James*, 408 U.S. 169, 181 (1972).

5 "In the absence of any statutory provisions controlling the matter ...a decision of the majority will be valid and binding." *Norfolk & W. Ry. Co. v. Virginian Ry. Co.*, 110 Va. 631, 646, 66 S.E. 863, 868 (1910).

6 Thomas Jefferson, *Manual of Parliamentary Practice* § 517 (1801) (citing 2 John Hatsell, *Precedents of Proceedings in the House of Commons* 99–100 (2d ed. 1786)).

7 "The fundamental rule is that all who are entitled to take part shall be treated with fairness and good faith." *In re Election of Directors of Bushwick Sav. & Loan Ass'n.*, 189 Misc. 316, 318–19, 70 N.Y.S.2d 478, 481 (Sup. Ct. 1947).

8 Thomas Jefferson, *Manual of Parliamentary Practice* § 451 (1801).

Chapter 3

9 Howard L. Oleck & Cami Greene, *Parliamentary Law and Practice for Nonprofit Organizations* § 85, at 145–49 (American Law Institute/American Bar Association 2d Ed. 1991); See also George Demeter, *Demeter's Manual of Parliamentary Law and Procedure* 244–245 (Blue Book ed. 1969).

10 *Baron v. Fontes*, 311 Mass. 473, 476–77, 42 N.E.2d 280, 281 (1942) (former officers of an organization were entitled to injunctive relief when offices were usurped and there was no means in the bylaws to challenge such action).

11 *Snay v. Lovely*, 276 Mass. 159, 164, 176 N.E. 791, 793 (1931).

12 "It is essential that the associates shall each be able to learn from the charter... [their] rights in the corporation, and the extent to which [their] interests are involved in it." *In re National Literary Ass'n*, 30 Pa. 150, 151 (1858).

13 "It is well established that members of voluntary associations are required to exhaust their internal remedies prior to instituting legal action to enforce certain rights."

Logan v. 3750 N. Lake Shore Drive, Inc., 17 Ill. App. 3d 584, 587, 308 N.E.2d 278, 280 (1974) (citation omitted).

Chapter 4

14 *Edgar v. Mite Corp.*, 457 U.S. 624, 645 (1982) ("The internal affairs doctrine is a conflict of laws principle which recognizes that only one State should have the authority to regulate a corporation's internal affairs—matters peculiar to the relationships among or between the corporation and its current officers, directors, and shareholders—because otherwise a corporation could be faced with conflicting demands.").

15 "It is well established that 'the constitution, rules and bylaws of an unincorporated association if they are not immoral, contrary to public policy or the law of the land, or unreasonable, constitute a contract between the members which the courts will enforce.'" *Casumpang v. ILWU Local 142*, 108 Haw. 411, 422, 121 P.3d 391, 402 (2005) (quoting *Martinez v. Parado*, 35 Haw. 149, 153 (1939)) (footnote omitted).

16 *Heritage Lake Prop. Owners Assn. v. York*, 859 N.E.2d 763, 764 (Ind. App. 2009) ("[T]he articles of incorporation and bylaws of a nonprofit corporation constitute a contract between the state and the corporation, the corporation and its members, and among the members themselves.").

17 *Baldwin Cnty. Elec. Membership Corp. v. Catrett*, 942 So.2d 337, 345 (Ala. 2006) ("'It is well established that the constitution, bylaws, rules, and regulations of a voluntary association constitute a contract between an association's members....'") (quoting *Turner v. West Ridge Apts., Inc.*, 893 So.2d 332, 335 (Ala. 2004).

18 Thomas Sedgewick, *Treatise of the Rules which Govern the Interpretation of Statutory and Constitutional Law* (2d ed. 1874).

19 See *In re Koliba*, 338 B.R. 48, 50 (Bankr. N.D. Ohio 2006) (in absence of extenuating circumstances, attorney may not plead ignorance of procedural rules as a defense in proceeding to sanction him for violating such rules).

20 Luther Stearns Cushing, *Manual of Parliamentary Practice* (1844), p. 160, ¶ 315.

21 AIP Opinion 2008-527, *Reluctant, Recalcitrant, or Resigned Secretary*, 49(2) PJ 78 (April 2008).

22 Henry M. Robert, *Parliamentary Law* (1923), p. 452, q. 107.

23 Luther Stearns Cushing, Lex *Parliamentaria Americana* § 115, 43–44, § 412, at 169 (1856).

24 Thomas Jefferson, *Manual of Parliamentary Practice* § 41 (1801). (citing Hakew. 93; Towns. col. 134).

25 *Content v. Metro. St. Ry. Co.*, 37 Misc. 618, 623, 76 N.Y.S. 151, 154 (Sup. Ct. 1902) ("In the selection of officers and directors, and in all matters requiring action by the stockholders, generally, the will of the majority must govern. 'The powers of a majority to bind the whole company by their vote is derived solely from the agreement of association between the shareholders.'" (citation omitted), *aff'd sub nom. Wormsor v. Metro. St. Ry. Co.*, 73 App. Div. 626, 76 N.Y.S. 1038 (1902), and aff'd, 73 App. Div. 230, 76 N.Y.S. 749 (1902). See *God's Hope Builders, Inc. v. Mt. Zion Baptist Church, Inc.*, 321 Ga. App. 435, 440, 741 S.E.2d 185, 190 (2013) (to determine whether individuals "represent[ed]

a majority of the church's members," who could act for the church, court would "review the church's bylaws governing membership, which we must construe according to contract principles.").

26 Thomas Jefferson to Alexander von Humboldt, 13 June 1817, *The Papers of Thomas Jefferson*, Retirement Series, vol. 11, *19 January to 31 August 1817*, ed. J. Jefferson Looney. Princeton: Princeton University Press, 2014, pp. 434–435.

27 *Benintendi v. Kenton Hotel*, 294 N.Y. 112, 118 (1945).

28 *Benintendi v. Kenton Hotel*, 294 N.Y. 112, 119 (1945) (quoting *Dr. Hascard v. Dr. Somany*, 1 Freeman 503, 504 (1693)).

Chapter 6

29 "The right[s] to vote as a member …or to participate in its affairs …are personal to the member…." *Chambrella v. Rutledge*, 69 Haw. 271, 283, 740 P.2d 1008, 1015 (1987).

30 "The requirement of secrecy would seem to include not only the right to vote in secret but also the right to secrecy after the ballots are cast." *Bachowski v. Brennan*, 413 F. Supp. 147, 150 (W.D. Pa.1976), appeal dismissed, 545 F.2d 363 (3d Cir. 1976), quoted in *Donovan v. CSEA Local Union 1000*, 594 F. Supp. 188, 196–97 (N.D.N.Y. 1984), *aff'd in part, rev'd in part on other grounds*, 761 F.2d 870 (2nd Cir. 1985).

31 If, however, the chair takes the vote by a method other than by ballot and "there is objection, the vote is deemed invalid, and the vote on the proceeding or question should be taken all over again in the manner prescribed by the bylaws. Objection to such illegality, however, must be raised at the time the vote is taken." George Demeter, *Demeter's Manual of Parliamentary Law and Procedure* 244–245.

32 *Frankel v. Jewish Center*, 144 Misc. 2d 548, 552, 544 N.Y.S.2d 955, 958 (Sup. Ct. 1989).

33 "A member may be 'present' in person or by proxy…." *Herning v. Eason*, 739 P.2d 167, 169 (Alaska 1987

34 "According to Kenneth Arrow's impossibility theorem, no alternative voting method is capable of resolving all the dilemmas raised. Solving one problem often creates another." *See* William Poundstone, *Gaming the Vote: Why Elections Aren't Fair and What We Can Do about It* (Hill & Wang 2008).

35 The Standard Code (2nd ed. 1950) introduced the prior sentence, relying on *City of Chariton v. Holliday*, 60 Iowa 391, 14 N.W. 775 (1883).

36 "No presiding officer should be permitted to arbitrarily or fraudulently defeat the will of the majority of any deliberative assembly by making a knowingly false announcement of the result of a vote…." *Gipson v. Morris*, 31 Tex. Civ. App. 645, 649, 73 S.W. 85, 88 (1903).

Chapter 9

37 "Whether these forms be in all cases the most rational or not is really not of so great importance. It is much more material that there should be a rule to go by, than what the rule is; that there may be an uniformity of proceeding in business, not subject to the caprice of the Speaker, or captiousness of the members." Thomas Jefferson,

Manual of Parliamentary Practice § 1 (1801) (citing 2 John Hatsell, *Precedents of Proceedings in the House of Commons* 149–50 (2d ed. 1786)).

38 "[W]here there is no special rule on the subject, a motion to reconsider may be made at any time, or by any member, precisely like any other motion, and subject to no other rules." Luther Stearns Cushing, *Lex Parliamentaria Americana* §1266, at 506 (1856). See George Demeter, *Demeter's Manual of Parliamentary Law and Procedure*, 153 (Blue Book ed. 1969); Richard B. Johnson *et al.*, *Town Meeting Time* (3d ed. 2001) § 32, at 78; Paul Mason, Mason's *Manual of Legislative Procedure* § 464.3–5 (2020 ed.).

39 Paul Mason, *Mason's Manual of Legislative Procedure* § 157 (2020 ed.) (provides reasons why seconds are not required in legislative bodies).

40 American Bar Association, Model Nonprofit Corporation Act § 1002 (4th ed. 2022).

41 Longstanding common law supports rescission of earlier enactments by implication when directly contradicted by subsequent enactments. See Theodore Sedgwick, *A Treatise of the Rules which Govern the Interpretation of Statutory and Constitutional Law*, 97–107 (2d ed. 1874).

Chapter 11

42 The presiding officer "must relinquish the chair and should not return until after disposition of the pending question." Howard L. Oleck & Cami Green, *Parliamentary Law and Practice for Nonprofit Organizations* § 39, at 77 (2d ed.1991).

Chapter 12

43 Paul Mason, *Mason's Manual of Legislative Procedure* § 53 (2020 ed.).

Chapter 13

44 *Strader v. Haley*, 216 Minn. 315, 326 (1943) ("By ratification, the principal absolves the agent from any liability to the principal which otherwise would result from the fact that the agent acted without authority.") (citing *Triggs v. Jones*, 46 Minn. 277, 48 N.W. 1113; *Sheffield v. Ladue*, 16 Minn. 388, 16 Gil. 346, 10 Am. Rep. 145; 1 Dunnell, Dig. § 191. *Cf. Goss v. Stevens*, 32 Minn. 472, 21 N.W. 549).

45 Cushing, *Law and Practice of Legislative Assemblies* § 1266 (2d ed. 1856).

46 "The policy having been determined, and the action taken and carried out under authority of law, the power to change or rescind does not exist." *Schieffelin v. Hylan*, 106 Misc. 347, 355, 174 N.Y.S. 506, 511 (Sup. Ct. 1919), aff'd, 188 A.D. 192, 176 N.Y.S. 809, *aff'd*, 227 N.Y. 593, 125 N.E. 925 (Sup. Ct. 1919).

Chapter 14

47 Paul Mason, *Mason's Manual of Legislative Procedure* § 402.1 (2020 ed.).

48 "[I]t may be adopted by a majority vote, even when the motion to which it is applied requires more than a majority." Howard L. Oleck & Cami Green, *Parliamentary Law and Practice for Nonprofit Organizations* § 27, at 56 (2d ed. 1991).

49 "[I]t is always the duty of the presiding officer [at council meetings] to enforce the law or rules applicable to the body...." *Arrington v. Moore*, 31 Md. App. 448, 456, 358

A.2d 909, 914 (citations omitted) (quoting McQuillin's *The Law of Municipal Corporations*), *cert. denied*, 278 Md. 729 (1976).

Chapter 17

50 "Common parliamentary rules, in use by all deliberative assemblies in this country, may also be resorted to, in the absence of any made by the association itself, in considering the regularity of its proceedings." *Ostrom v. Greene*, 161 N.Y. 353, 362, 55 N.E. 919, 922 (1900).

51 "A nonprofit voluntary association …seems to occupy an anomalous position in the law. It is not a partnership, yet, in reference to the rights of the members in the property owned by it, they are to be determined to a large extent by the application of the principles of law peculiar to partnerships." *Bentley v. Hurley*, 222 Mo. App. 51, 55, 299 S.W. 604, 606 (1927).

52 National Conference of Commissioners on Uniform State Laws, Revised Uniform Unincorporated Nonprofit Associations Act (2008, rev. 2011).

53 *Kansas City Power & Light Co. v. NLRB*, 137 F.2d 77, 81 (8th Cir. 1943).

54 *See* D.C. Code § 29-401.50 (e).

55 Codified at 29 U.S.C. §§ 401 *et seq.*

56 "In concept, the term 'nonprofit' means that the net gains realized by the [entity] do not inure to the benefit of the members or principals and no distributions are made except on dissolution." Unincorporated nonprofit entity in perspective, 1 Ltd. Liab. Co.: L., Prac. and Forms § 13:2 (2021).

57 American Bar Association, Revised Model Nonprofit Corporation Act (1988); American Bar Association, Model Nonprofit Corporation Act (4th ed. 2022).

58 American Bar Association, Revised Model Nonprofit Corporation Act § 13.02 (1988); American Bar Association, Model Nonprofit Corporation Act §§ 622, 641 (4th ed. 2022).

Chapter 18

59 "No action can be taken which will be binding upon the corporation unless every stockholder has notice…." *Asbury v. Mauney*, 92 S.E. 267, 268 (1917) (citation omitted).

60 See *FDIC v. Harrington*, 844 F. Supp. 300, 305–06 (N.D. Tex. 1994); *In re Mortgage & Realty Trust*, 195 Bank. Rep. 740, 750 (Bankr. C.D. Cal. 1996) ("The fiduciary duty of loyalty of a corporate director includes a duty to preserve the confidentiality of confidential information received from the corporation during service as a director. This rule applies to all information received by a director in the course of his or her duties that is not in the public domain, and that the corporation does not presently want to have publicized.").

61 See Model Nonprofit Corporation Act §§ 704 (a), 821 (a) (4th ed. 2022).

Chapter 20

62 "If the notice failed to comply with the statutory and …by-law requirements, such omission is ground [sic] for voiding the election unless there is a clear waiver on [the]

part [of the complaining member].... Where insufficient notice of an election is given 'there is no election and justice requires no further showing.'" *Election of Directors of FDR-Woodrow Wilson Democrats, Inc.,* 57 Misc. 2d 743, 746–47, 293 N.Y.S.2d 463, 466–67 (Sup. Ct. 1968) (citations omitted).

63 "[T]he attempt ...to oust [the member] from his positions as vice president and director, without notice to him and without a vacancy having been created, in the directors' meeting of June was void." *Piedmont Press Ass'n v. Record Pub. Co.,* 156 S.C. 43, 54, 152 S.E. 721, 726 (1930).

64 *Lippman v. Kehoe Stenograph Co.,* 11 Del. Ch. 80, 88 (1915) ("Each member of a corporate body has the right to consultation with the others and has the right to be heard upon all questions considered, and it is presumed that if the absent members had been present they might have dissented and their arguments might have convinced the majority of the unwisdom of their proposed action, and thus have produced a different result. If, however, they had notice and failed to attend they waived their rights....").

65 See Opinion 2017-628, *How Specific Must Previous Notice Be Under AIPSC?* 58 (02) P.J. 36 (April 2017).

66 "There can be modifications and supplementations [to the proposal as stated in the notice of the meeting] provided that the Notice has fairly apprised its recipients of the scope of the action to be taken." *Nigro v. English,* 59 Misc. 2d 193, 196, 298 N.Y.S.2d 438, 441–42 (Sup. Ct. 1969) (citations omitted).

Chapter 22

67 "It is a fundamental rule of parliamentary procedure ...that a majority of the members of a body consisting of a definite number constitutes a quorum for the transaction of business...." *Hill v. Ponder,* 221 N.C. 58, 62, 19 S.E.2d 5, 8 (1942) (citations omitted) (emphasis added).

68 "[A] quorum of any body of an *indefinite* number for purposes of elections and voting upon questions ...consists of those who assemble at any meeting regularly called...." *In re Havender,* 181 Misc. 989, 992, 44 N.Y.S.2d 213, 215 (Sup. Ct. 1943) (citation omitted) (emphasis added).

69 *In re Application of Gilmore,* 340 N.J. Super. 303, 310, 774 A.2d 576, 580 (App. Div. 2001) (citing Paul Mason, *Mason's Manual of Legislative Procedure* § 504).

Chapter 23

70 Henry Campbell Black, *Black's Law Dictionary,* 1194 (Bryan A. Garner, ed., 11th ed. 2019) (citing Ray Keesey, *Modern Parliamentary Procedure* (rev. ed. 1994) and *Robert's Rules of Order Newly Revised* (11th ed. 2011).

71 "Corporate books and records generally subject to inspection include the transcript of charter and by-laws, minutes of meetings...." *Morton v. Rogers,* 20 Ariz. App. 581, 586, 514 P.2d 752, 757 (1973).

72 "A nonprofit corporation must keep as permanent records minutes of all meetings of its members, board of directors, and any designated body...." American Bar Association, Model Nonprofit Corporation Act §401 (a) (4th 2022).

Chapter 26

73 "We reject plaintiffs' arguments that calling for nominations from the floor at the time of an election is not a fair and effective method for nominating Board managers...." *Liberty Ct. Condo. Residential Unit Owners Coal. v. Bd. of Managers of Liberty Ct. Condo.*, 3 A.D.3d 443, 444, 772 N.Y.S.2d 6, 7 (2004).

74 "If the by-law [stating a deadline for nominations, without specifying that eligibility was restricted to those nominated timely] was intended to mean that no member should be eligible for the office of director, unless nominated as prescribed in [the provision on nominations], such a regulation would be unreasonable." *In re Farrell*, 205 A.D. 443, 445, 200 N.Y.S. 95, 96, aff'd, 236 N.Y. 603, 142 N.E. 301 (1923).

75 "Even when one is elected, there is no restriction upon his right to decline the office...." *Black v. Bd. of Supervisors of Elections*, 232 Md. 74, 79, 191 A.2d 580, 582–83 (1963).

76 *See* 29 U.S.C. § 482 (c)(20) (union elections not to be set aside unless errors could have affected the election).

77 "Because [the] nominees did not receive the required number of votes, its nominees cannot be seated as members of [the] Board of Directors." *Badlands Trust Co. v. First Financial Fund, Inc.*, 65 Fed. Appx. 876, 880 (4th Cir. 2003) (bylaw upheld despite fact that bylaw requirement resulted in a failed election).

Chapter 27

78 Felix Frankfurter, *Of Law and Men*, 119 (1956).

79 "The vice president, at meetings of the board, in the absence of the president from the meeting, should act as president of the board at such meeting ...because that right and duty devolved upon him from the very nature of his office." *Francis v. Blair*, 1 S.W. 297, 300 (1886).

80 "So little does the law take notice of the powers of this officer (vice president) that it may be said that, by virtue of his office, he is a mere locum tenens of the president, with power of presiding at meetings of the board of directors in the absence of the president, and of doing little else without special authority." *Dreeben v. First Nat'l. Bank*, 100 Tex. 344, 348, 99 S.W. 850, 852 (1907) (citations omitted); *Guy v. City of Wilmington*, No. CV N19C-11-064 AML, 2020 WL 2511122 (Del. Super. Ct. May 15, 2020) (other officers cannot appoint committee chairs when organization rules delegate that duty to the president).

81 "The president of the association was not present, and, in such case, it was the duty and the right, under the constitution, of the several vice presidents to preside in their numerical order from first to fifth." *De Zavala v. Daughters of the Republic of Texas*, 58 Tex. Civ. App. 19, 25–26, 124 S.W. 160, 163 (1909).

82 *See* Parliamentary Opinion 2009-532, *Vice-Presidential Succession, Numbered Vice-Presidents*, 50 (2) P.J. 68 (April 2009).

83 Model Nonprofit Corp. Act §§ 102, 840 (4th ed. 2022).

84 "The act of delegation …does not relieve the delegant of the ultimate responsibility to see that the obligation is performed." *Contemporary Mission, Inc. v. Famous Music Corp.*, 557 F.2d 918, 924 (2d Cir. 1977) (footnote omitted).

Chapter 28

85 "Nothing is as tedious or as distressing as a meeting that falls apart when a weak Chair loses the confidence and support of the members. This is disastrous for an organization." Hugh Cannon, *Cannon's Concise Guide to Rules of Order*, 13 (Houghton Mifflin 1992).

86 What the Chair is conveying to the members by these actions is this message: "You took your valuable time to come to this meeting. In return, I shall take time with the matters that concern you. What's important for you is important for me. I will be attentive so that you will be heard; you will know exactly what you are voting on; and the vote count will be accurate. I will not rush you or misrepresent your intentions." Hugh Cannon, *Cannon's Concise Guide to Rules of Order*, 18 (Houghton Mifflin 1992).

Chapter 29

87 *See* Parliamentary Opinion 2009-550, *The Role of the Professional Parliamentarian When Serving as Professional Presider*, 51 (3) P.J. 18 (July 2010).

Chapter 30

88 "An individual director …has no power of his own to act on the corporation's behalf, but only as one of the body of directors acting as a board." *Fleet Bank of Maine v. Druce*, 791 F. Supp. 14, 17 n.6 (D. Me. 1992) (quoting *Restatement (Second) of Agency* § 14C (1958)).

89 "The requirement that a director or officer disclose to shareholders all material facts bearing upon a particular transaction arises under the duties of care and loyalty." William Meade Fletcher, *Fletcher Cyclopedia of the Law of Corporations* § 837.70 (2020 ed.) (footnotes omitted).

90 "[T]he Church failed to carry its burden of proof in a situation where 'the potential for abuse …required open and candid disclosure of facts bearing on the exemption application.'" *Church of Scientology v. Commissioner*, 823 F.2d 1310, 1318 (9th Cir. 1987) (citation omitted), *cert. denied*, 486 U.S. 1015 (1988).

Chapter 31

91 "The Directors are …but the agents of the corporation, and where their authority is limited by the act of incorporation, have clearly no power to bind their principal beyond it. If the general power of making bylaws regulating the transactions of the corporation remain in the body at large, the power of the directors may be circumscribed by them." Joseph K. Angell & Samuel Ames, *Treatise on the Law of Private Corporations Aggregate* § 299, at 316 (4th ed. 1852).

92 "It is a well settled principle that the power to appoint generally includes the power to dismiss." *Myers v. Hartnett*, 153 Pa. Super. 228, 231, 33 A.2d 512, 513 (1943).

93 See James J. Fishman, *Stealth Preemption: The IRS's Nonprofit Corporate Governance Initiative*, 29 Va. Tax Rev. 545, 573–74 (2010); 18 U.S.C. § 1519 (provision of Sarbanes-Oxley Act of 2002, Pub. L. 107-204, 116 Stat. 745 (July 30, 2002), applying document destruction liability on nonprofit organizations).

94 "Newt Gingrich ...promised that all congressional documents ...would be filed electronically so that they would be 'available to any citizen in the country at the same moment it is available to the highest-paid Washington lobbyist.'" David S. Levine, *Secrecy and Unaccountability: Trade Secrets in Our Public Infrastructure*, 59 Fla. L. Rev. 135, 161 (2007).

Chapter 33

95 "[M]embership corporation[s] ...possess inherent power to expel or suspend members for good cause, provided ...that the member is notified of the charges and there is a hearing and an opportunity to defend." *Chisholm v. Hyattstown Volunteer Fire Dept., Inc.*, 115 Md. App. 58, 71, 691 A.2d 776, 782 (1997) (quoting 18A Am. Jur. 2d *Corporations* §§ 935–37 (1997)).

96 "[I]n every contract of association there inheres a term binding members to loyal support of the society in the attainment of its proper purposes, and that for a gross breach of this obligation the power of expulsion is impliedly conferred upon the association." *Polin v. Kaplan*, 257 N.Y. 277, 282–83, 177 N.E. 833, 834 (1931).

97 "[T]here was an inherent right of expulsion for the crime of perjury." *Cunningham v. Supreme Council of Royal Arcanum*, 165 A.D. 52, 53–54, 151 N.Y.S. 83, 84 (1914).

98 "The right of expulsion from associations of this character may be based and upheld upon two grounds: 1. A violation of such of the established rules of the association as have been subscribed or assented to by the members, and as provide expulsion for such violation; 2. For such conduct as clearly violates the fundamental objects of the association, and if persisted in and allowed would thwart those objects or bring the association into disrepute." *Otto v. Journeymen Tailors Prot. & Ben. Union*, 75 Cal. 308, 314, 17 P. 217, 219 (1888).

99 "The accused must have notice of the charges, notice of the time and place of the hearing, and a full and fair opportunity to be present and present a defense." *Davenport v. Society of Cincinnati*, 46 Conn. Supp. 411, 441, 754 A.2d 225, 241 (Super. Ct. 1999).

100 "[A] disinterested observer is not merely 'impartial' but has nothing to gain from taking a stand on the issue in question." Bryan A. Garner, *Garner's Modern English Usage* 290 (4th ed. 2016), *quoted in State Farm Fla. Ins. Co. v. Crispin*, 290 So. 3d 150, 153 (2020).

101 For additional detail on applicable procedure, see Op. 2009-534, *Default Disciplinary Procedure for a Member Under* The Standard Code, 50 (2) P.J. 72 (April 2009).

102 "The law is settled that a corporation possesses the inherent power to remove a member, officer or director for cause...." *Grace v. Grace Inst.*, 19 N.Y.2d 307, 313, 226 N.E.2d 531, 533, 279 N.Y.S.2d 721, 724 (1967).

103 "[W]e have examined the procedure [adopted by the trustees] by which the petitioner was removed and we have concluded there is no question but that he was given a reasonable opportunity to be heard and to answer the charges leveled against

him. *Grace v. Grace Inst.*, 19 N.Y.2d 307, 314, 226 N.E.2d 531, 534, 279 N.Y.S.2d 721, 725 (1967).

104 For additional detail on applicable procedure, see Op. 2009-535, *Default Disciplinary Procedure for an Officer Under* The Standard Code, 50 (3) P.J. 100 (July 2009).

105 For additional detail on applicable procedure, see Op. 2009-536, *Who Appoints a Temporary Treasurer When the Treasurer Is Suspended Under The Standard Code*, 50 (3) P.J. 103 (July 2009).

106 "It is the general and well established jurisdictional rule that a plaintiff who seeks judicial relief against an organization of which he is a member must first invoke and exhaust the remedies provided by that organization…." *Holderby v. Int'l. Union*, 45 Cal.2d 843, 846, 291 P.2d 463, 466 (1955).

Chapter 34

107 Michael E. Malamut, *Musings on General or Common Parliamentary Law*, 49 (3) P.J. 101 (July 2008).

Index

Index entries refer to paragraph locators using the paragraph number system outlined in paragraph 0.33 of the text.

A.M.P. method, 14.16–17
abstentions, 5.1, 5.12, 5.19, 5.23–24, 5.46, 5.48, 6.22, 6.53, 6.60
accountants, 32.1, 32.8, 32.11
adjournment sine die, 15.38–39
agenda, 16.8.3, 18.11, 21.8–22, 25.1, 25.6
  adoption of, 21.11–12
  approval en bloc, 21.18–19, 25.52
  changes to/flexibility, 21.10–11, 21.13–16
  consent, 2.13, 21.10, 21.17–20, 25.51–58
  preparation, 21.10, 21.19, 21.22
  priority, 21.10, 21.21–22, 25.59–62, 25.66–69
  See also under conventions
Alexander the Great, 16.13fn*
appeals, 1.5, 15.4, 15.7, 16.28, 16.30, 19.23, 23.19
  See also Motion to Appeal
articles of incorporation. *See* charters: corporate
assembly
  definition, 1.8
associations, unincorporated, 4.1, 17.4, 17.6, 17.9–17
attorneys. *See* legal counsel
audits, 32.9, 32.10.2

ballots, 26.36, 26.68
  blank, 26.44.5, 26.44.7, 26.47
  confidentiality of, 26.43, 26.54
  count of, 26.36, 26.40–41, 26.44
  folded together, 26.44.7
  illegal/invalid, 26.44, 26.47
  recount of, 26.45
  security of, 26.42, 26.54
  technical errors on, 26.44.2
boards, 1.8, 4.39, 5.17–18, 6.43, 27.51, 28.18, 30.1–23
  committees vis-à-vis, 31.10, 30.12–15, 31.26
  confidentiality and, 30.10

conflicts of interest, 5.58–59, 22.15, 30.16–18, 30.21–22
delegation of authority, 30.12, 33.9
duties and powers, 30.6–7, 30.14, 31.25
emergencies and urgent business, 18.13, 30.14
executive committee of, 30.13
fiduciary duty, 5.19, 5.58, 6.43, 30.19–22
formality and, 30.8
membership, 30.3–5
minutes, 23.8, 30.10–11, 30.15
procedures, 30.8–9
quorum, 22.10
report, 21.30
statutory provisions relating to, 30.17, 30.23
terms of, 5.56, 30.4
voting methods, 5.47–56, 6.55, 6.60–61
when members should not vote, 5.58–59
board of trustees. *See* boards
Borda, J. C., 6.57
budget, 25.57, 27.36, 32.13
  See also finances
bylaws, 4.6–40, 4.46, 4.50, 17.22
  adoption of original, 4.12–14, 17.16
  amendment of original, 4.13
  amendments to, 4.15–34, 4.38, 4.39, 5.5, 5.8, 6.46, 14.24, 25.56, 29.20–24
  conflicts between, 4.35
  consideration by paragraph, 4.13, 4.37, 16.81
  consolidation with constitution, 4.6
  drafting, 4.8–11, 17.16, 29.20–24
  effective date, 4.15–18
  emergency, 4.61–63
  interpretation of, 4.39–40
  labor unions and, 17.21
  parent body ratification, 13.21
  principles, 4.50–51
  rank, 1.9.3
  revision, 4.35–38, 20.20–24

417

rules deviating from principles within, 2.3
statement of parliamentary authority, 0.30, 4.44

"call the question," 14.112–114
call to the convention. *See* conventions: notice
candidates
   multiple slate, 26.33
   on nominating committee, 26.31
   qualifications, 6.35, 26.12, 26.25
   single slate, 26.32
canons of construction, 4.40
caucuses, 5.57
certificates of incorporation. *See* charters: corporate
chair pro tem, 27.16–18, 27.22, 27.25
charities, 17.26
charters, 1.9.2, 4.2–5, 17.21
   parent organization and, 4.1, 4.5, 17.11, 17.17
   rank, 4.1
committee reports, 31.24, 31.46–66
   amendments, 31.61
   disposition, 31.62
   distribution, 31.58–59
   filing, 31.62.1, 31.63
   minority, 31.56, 31.66
   objections to, 31.62.8
   presentation, 31.57–59
   record of, 31.63–65
   referral of, 31.62.2
committees, 4.8, 18.22, 28.18, 31.1–72
   advisory/consultant members, 31.24
   attendance, 31.32–33
   call for meetings, 31.36
   chairs, 31.14–17, 31.29, 31.36, 31.38, 31.56, 31.68
   co-chairs and vice-chairs, 31.16–17
   confidentiality and, 31.32–33, 31.45
   decorum, 31.39
   delegation of authority, 27.55, 31.25
   deliberations, 31.12, 31.14, 31.32
   empowerment of, 14.56, 23.34, 24.45–46
   ex officio members, 31.22–24
   formality and, 31.34, 31.38
   funds and, 31.28, 32.17
   general consent, 31.40
   hearings, 31.44–45
   instructions given to, 14.56, 14.59
   meetings, 31.34–43, 31.56
   membership, 31.3–4, 31.6, 31.12–13, 31.18–21
   minutes, 21.25, 23.8, 23.34–37, 23.46–47, 31.33
   motions, 31.39–40, 31.48–49, 31.61, 31.62.7, 31.67–72
   notes of, 31.24
   preparatory work, 31.37
   procedures, 31.34–43
   quorum, 22.10, 31.23, 31.24, 31.35
   recall from, 14.60
   recommendations, 31.47–48, 31.62.9, 31.67–71
   referred to, 31.50–54
   subcommittees, 31.29
   terms of members, 31.6
   vacancies, 31.21
   working materials for, 31.30–31
   See also conventions: committees; Motion to Recall from a Committee; Motion to Refer to a Committee
committees, by type
   ad hoc (*see* committees, by type: special)
   election/teller, 26.35–39, 26.44–49, 26.61
   executive, 30.13–15, 31.25
   finance, 27.36, 31.6.5, 32.6
   internal finances review, 32.7, 32.9, 32.18
   nominating, 26.3, 26.9, 26.12–24, 26.31, 26.32, 31.12
   principles, 4.50
   revision, 4.36
   special, 1.8, 4.35, 20.12, 31.1, 31.8–11, 31.25–27
   standing, 1.8, 20.12, 31.1, 31.6–7, 31.19, 31.25–27
   See also reference committees; *and individual committees under* conventions
conduct. *See* decorum
confidentiality
   closed meetings, 3.20, 18.21, 18.27–28, 19.37, 23.10, 30.10–11, 31.32–33
   voting, 6.24, 6.27, 6.36, 19.30.3, 26.43
conflicts of interest, 5.59, 22.15, 23.16, 25.9, 30.16–18
Consider by Paragraph, 16.79–85
   bylaws and, 4.13, 4.37

rules governing, 16.85
considered as a whole, 16.84
constitutions, 4.6
conventions, 4.22, 18.3, 20.8, 21.38, 24.1–46
　actions on reference committee recommendations, 25.63–75, 25.79–85
　adjournment, 15.33, 15.38, 15.45.2
　agenda, 24.36–37
　ballots, 24.38–41
　business interrupted by adjournment, 15.45
　committees, 24.12–46
　consent agenda, 25.51–58, 25.61.3, 25.63–65, 25.80
　consent agenda, items removed from, 25.61.2, 25.61.5, 25.64, 25.71–72, 25.81, 25.86
　courtesy resolutions, 25.46
　credentials, 24.15, 24.25–27, 26.62
　credentials committee and its report, 24.13, 24.15–23, 24.27, 26.62
　installation of officers, 26.60
　minutes, 23.8
　motions (*see* conventions: resolutions)
　notice, 20.7–8
　order of business, 25.61, 25.63–69, 25.71–74, 31.57
　priority agenda, 25.59–62
　program committee, 24.36–37
　quorum, 24.10–11, 24.16, 24.23, 24.27
　recesses, 15.33, 15.38, 18.3
　registration report, 24.28–29
　resolutions, 25.12–20, 25.30, 25.47, 25.76–85
　resolutions, "late," 25.12, 25.16
　resolutions, postponement of, 14.71–72
　resolutions, rejection of, 25.19
　resolutions, withdrawal of, 25.20, 25.58, 25.61.1
　rules, 4.41, 19.6, 24.30–35, 25.4
　rules committee, 24.30–31
　teller committee, 24.38–41
　timed items and scheduled orders, 21.6–7
　voting body and voting, 24.13, 24.17–18, 24.22, 24.24, 24.27, 24.38
　See also elections; reference committees
corporations, 17.18–24
　advantages of incorporation, 17.18
　board-only, 17.4
　business, 17.4, 17.6, 26.36

charters, 1.9.2, 4.3–4, 17.21
codes, 17.21–22
jurisdiction, 17.19
laws governing, 4.1, 4.3–4, 17.5–6, 17.18.4, 17.21–24
nonprofit membership, 4.3, 17.4, 17.6, 17.18, 17.25
nonprofit, 4.3, 17.4, 17.6, 17.18–20, 17.25–28, 26.36
proxies (in businesses), 6.40–41
shareholder, 17.4, 17.6
Cushing, Luther, 13.35
custom, 4.56–57

deadlocks, 5.34–36
debate, 1.2, 2.4, 2.25, 3.6.4, 3.17, 6.11, 11.1–37, 28.17.4
　bringing to vote, 11.36–38
　closing, 11.35–37
　decorum, 11.6–11, 11.20–21, 11.29, 28.21
　definition, 11.25
　extent of, 11.4–5
　germaneness, 9.12, 11.4, 11.16–18, 11.33
　non-participation in, 2.17, 5.37, 11.31, 30.16
　"not debate" speech and inquiries, 11.25–28
　recognition, 11.12–15, 11.22–24, 11.29, 16.53
　time limits, 11.33–34, 14.92, 16.50
　use of names, 11.19–20, 28.17.5
　See also Motion to Close Debate and Vote Immediately; Motion to Limit or Extend Debate; tactics
decision-making, 1.8, 2.19–23, 2.25, 2.26, 11.1, 11.8, 11.11, 11.35, 16.54, 18.33, 19.8, 19.34, 24.14, 25.1–6, 25.22
decorum, 2.27, 3.19–20, 11.6–11, 11.20–21, 11.29, 19.26, 25.29, 26.13, 27.45, 28.21–24, 31.39
delegates, 2.15, 24.1, 24.3, 24.5–11, 24.28–29, 25.17, 25.22
　alternates, 24.9, 24.26
　at-large, 24.5
　challenges to, 24.20–23, 26.62
　notices to, 20.8
　quorum, 22.8
delegate nominees. *See* delegates
delegations, 5.57
　challenges to, 24.21–22
democracy, 2.14–31, 5.1, 5.5, 6.1

Division of the Assembly, 6.13–14, 9.4, 9.11, 16.87–90
  rules governing, 16.93
Division of the Question, 9.11, 13.20, 16.69–78
  alternative proposals, 16.77
  rules governing, 16.78
duties and powers, 27.48–56
  administrative, 27.52–54
  discretionary, 27.52–53
  legislative, 27.51
  ministerial, 27.54

elections, 26.6, 26.14–15, 26.35–75
  acclamation, 26.53
  Borda Count, 6.58
  challenging the election, 26.63–69
  challenging the right to vote, 26.61–62
  computation of a two-thirds vote, 5.42–43
  computing a majority, 5.44–54
  contested, 26.56
  deadlocked, 5.35–36
  declining office, 26.15, 26.59
  dropping candidates, 4.55, 5.28, 6.53–54, 26.50.3
  incomplete, 26.29, 26.70–75
  legality, 5.48, 6.53, 26.56, 26.61–69
  majority vote, 5.11, 5.20, 5.27–28, 6.51, 26.50.1
  motions during, 4.55, 5.28
  multiple slate, 26.33
  plurality vote, 5.3–4, 5.11, 5.25, 26.50.2
  positions of equal rank, 5.47–54, 6.55, 6.60–61
  repeated voting, 4.55, 5.27–28, 5.35, 6.51, 26.50.3
  single slate, 26.32, 26.52–53
  special, 26.4, 27.66
  tie votes, 5.35–36, 6.52, 6.53fn*
  vote by mail, 6.33–34, 26.50.3
  when effective, 26.3, 26.59–60
  See also ballots; candidates; committees, by type: election/teller; committees, by type: nominating; nominations; officers; voting; voting methods
electronic meetings. See meetings, electronic
emergencies, 4.58–65, 18.13, 30.14
executive board. See boards
executive director, 27.71–73

report, 21.27
executive orders, 4.59–60
executive session. See meetings, by type: closed

factual inquiry. See Inquiries: Factual
fairness and good faith, 2.27–31, 3.19, 6.43, 19.16–20, 19.25–26, 33.4
  See also tactics: dilatory; tactics: lacking in fairness and good faith
filling blanks, 6.3, 14.41–50
  abstentions and, 14.46
  ties, 14.48–49
  voting methods, 14.50
finances, 4.10, 31.28, 32.1–19
  accounting system, 32.1, 32.3
  authorized signatures, 32.15–16
  bank accounts, 32.16, 32.18
  committees' use of funds, 31.28, 32.17
  expenditures, 32.13–15
  financial statement review, 32.9, 32.10.1
  internal review, 32.7, 32.9
  purchase orders, 32.14
  records, 32.1–3
  safeguards, 32.11–19
  See also audits; budget
Frankfurter, Felix, 27.14
friendly amendments. See Motion to Amend: accepting amendments
funds. See finances

"gaveling through." See motions: rushing
general consent, 6.8–11, 14.27, 14.30, 15.42, 16.4, 16.5, 16.65, 19.28, 21.43–44, 25.56, 25.61.3, 25.64, 31.40
  objections to, 6.9, 6.10, 14.27, 16.65
good faith. See fairness and good faith
good of the order, 21.3
good standing, 3.10–14, 5.17, 22.12
Gordian Knot, 16.13fn*
  See also Motion to "Cut the Gordian Knot"
governing board. See boards
governing documents, 4.1–65
  amendments, 3.6.7, 3.15.2, 3.15.4, 4.6
  default rules, 0.4, 0.30
  notice, 20.5
  rank, 4.1, 4.6
  See also bylaws; charters; constitutions

Hatsell, John, 2.29

"have the floor." *See* debate: recognition; meetings, recognition; meetings, electronic: recognition; motions, presentation process: recognition
Hughes, Charles Evans, 27.14

immediate past-president, 27.27
Incidental Motions, 6.2, 7.8–9, 8.7, 9.22, 16.1–94
  See also Consider by Paragraph; Division of the Assembly; Division of the Question; Inquiries; Motion for a Counted Vote; Motion to Appeal; Motion to Suspend the Rules; Point of Order; Request to Withdraw a Motion
Inquiries, 16.47–61, 21.18, 28.5
  Factual, 2.26, 9.5, 9.7, 9.11, 11.27–28, 16.59
  Parliamentary, 2.26, 9.5, 9.7–8, 9.11, 11.28, 16.56, 16.57, 16.60, 22.16
  processing of, 16.49–53
  rules governing, 16.61
inspectors of elections, 26.36
internal affairs doctrine, 4.3

Jefferson, Thomas, 2.30, 5.1, 5.7

labor unions, 17.23
Landrum-Griffin Act. *See* U.S. Labor-Management Report and Disclosure Act of 1959
laws, 1.9.1
  corporations, 4.1, 4.3–4, 17.5–6, 22.7
  emergencies and, 4.59–60
  sunshine/open meeting, 18.25, 30.23
  tax, 32.11
  See also parliamentary law
legal counsel, 4.11, 4.39, 17.8, 17.9, 17.21, 32.11
limited liability companies, 17.4, 17.6

Main Motions, 2.10, 4.27, 4.57, 7.2, 7.13–14, 9.30, 12.1–17, 14.35, 14.85, 14.96, 15.13, 15.15, 15.23, 15.30
  affirmative presentation of, 12.8
  definition, 12.1
  disposition, 12.15–17, 14.116–121
  rank, 8.5, 9.22, 12.1
  renewal, 12.16
  resolution form, 12.9–13
  rules governing, 12.17

wording of, 12.5–8
Main Motions, Specific-Purpose. *See* Specific-Purpose Main Motions
majority decision. *See* majority vote
majority vote, 1.2, 2.19–22, 3.19, 5.1–4, 5.9, 5.14–15, 5.20, 14.38, 22.14, 33.5–15
  computing, 5.12–13, 5.15–22, 5.44–56
  definition, 5.1, 5.12–14, 5.20
  elections, 5.11, 5.20, 5.27–28, 5.35–36, 6.37, 26.47, 26.50.1, 26.50.3
  exceptions, 5.4, 5.8
meetings, 1.8, 2.30–31, 28.11, 28.17–20
  actions, proposed, 20.14
  actions, validation of, 13.14–23
  actions, without meetings, 18.31–33, 19.33
  adjournment, 21.43–45
  announcements, 21.42, 21.45
  attendance, 3.6.2, 18.23, 20.2
  business, dropped, 15.45.1, 15.46
  business, new, 21.39–41
  business, unfinished, 14.81.2, 15.45.1, 15.46, 21.33–38
  call of, 17.10–11, 18.9, 18.34, 19.12
  call to order, 18.1, 21.23, 22.1
  changes to/canceling, postponing, and rescheduling, 4.62.2, 18.14–15, 19.13
  definition, 18.1
  fairness and good faith in, 2.27–31
  formality and, 1.13, 11.19–20, 27.8, 28.17–19, 31.34
  inquorate, 22.1–3
  non-voting attendees, seating of, 6.4–5
  procedures, enforcement of, 1.5, 2.15, 16.21–23
  procedures, errors in, 2.27, 2.29, 3.16
  procedures, purpose of, 0.1, 1.2, 1.3
  programs, 21.4, 27.16
  recesses, 28.23
  recognition, 3.17.3, 10.3, 10.8, 11.12–15, 11.22–24, 11.29, 14.113–114, 15.7, 16.25, 16.36, 16.51–63, 28.17.1
  reports, 21.27–32, 23.18, 23.38–39, 23.46
  rules, 28.17–20
  rules, temporary, 1.9.4, 1.14–15, 4.41–42, 4.59
  standing rules of order, 0.4, 1.9.4, 1.14–15, 4.9, 4.41–42, 5.5, 17.11, 21.1, 21.19, 2.22
  use of information gained at, 3.20
  See also agenda, committees;

confidentiality; conventions; debate; decorum; general consent; minutes; motions; notice; order of business; proxies; quorum; reports; rules; speakers: interruption of; voting; voting methods; *and individual motions*

meetings, by type, 18.1–34
　adjourned (*see* meetings: continued)
　annual, 4.21, 14.72–73, 18.2, 20.8, 21.6–7, 21.38, 23.8, 31.58
　called (*see* meetings, by type: special)
　closed, 3.20, 15.4, 18.21–28, 19.37, 23.10, 23.24–25, 31.32–33
　continued, 9.19, 5.5, 15.25.2, 15.26.2, 15.28, 15.29, 15.32, 15.36–37, 16.8.2a, 18.16–20, 20.11, 20.12, 21.16, 26.72
　hybrid, 18.5, 19.6, 19.17
　mass/organizing, 4.12, 17.10–17, 18.4, 22.6
　regular, 8.5–6, 18.5–8, 18.15, 20.9
　special, 3.16, 18.9–13, 18.17, 20.10, 21.5, 21.15, 23.13, 26.72
　telephonic (*see* meetings, electronic)
　virtual (*see* meetings, electronic)
　See also boards; committees; conventions
meetings, electronic, 0.3, 4.62.7, 18.29–30, 19.1–44
　accommodations, 19.36–38
　ballot voting, 19.30–31
　call to, 19.12
　characteristics, 19.7–10
　chat feature, use of during, 19.22, 19.26
　committees, 31.41
　confidentiality and, 19.30.3, 19.37
　debate, 19.24–26
　decorum, 19.26
　digital recognition systems, 19.17, 19.24–25
　fairness and, 19.1, 19.16–20, 19.25–26
　fatigue, 19.39, 19.41
　legal requirements, 19.32–33
　logistics, 19.34–44
　motions, 19.21–22
　notice, 19.11–13, 20.13
　platforms, 19.10, 19.29
　points of order and appeals, 19.23
　polling systems, 19.29–30
　preregistration, 19.12, 20.13
　quorum, 19.13, 19.14–15
　recognition, 10.5, 19.16–20, 19.22
　roll call, 19.14
　scheduling, 19.39–41
　technical concerns, 19.42–44
　voting and voting methods, 6.38, 6.44, 6.62, 19.12, 19.15, 19.27–31, 26.55
membership
　conflicts of interest, 5.60–62, 22.15, 30.16–18
　discipline and expulsion, 3.6.11, 5.62, 28.22, 28.24, 33.1–7, 33.18–19
　emergencies, notification of actions during, 4.62.9
　equal rights, 2.14–18, 3.4, 20.2
　ex officio, 22.13
　fixed number, 5.16
　honoring and thanking, 10.39
　in good standing, 3.10–14, 5.17, 22.12
　lists and contact information, 20.3
　minutes, access to, 23.8–10
　notice, 4.62.9, 18.11, 22.14
　obligations, 2.16, 2.20
　personal gain and, 3.20, 5.58
　personal privilege, 15.1–2, 15.4
　privileges, abuse of, 3.19–20
　property rights and, 3.5, 3.21
　quorum, computation of, 22.11–15
　relationship with organization, 2.14, 3.1–3
　removal from meetings, 28.22, 28.24, 33.19
　requirements, 3.1, 3.15.4
　resignation, 2.14, 3.6.9, 3.21–26
　rights, 3.2–10, 3.16–21, 5.21, 5.58, 6.1, 6.36, 9.20, 10.3, 11.1–3, 15.6, 16.8, 16.54, 16.90, 19.4, 19.7–8, 20.2, 30.7, 33.8
　rights, absentees, 5.8, 5.21, 6.39, 16.8.2, 19.3, 20.2
　rights, based on classification, 3.7
　rights, majority, 2.4, 2.19–22, 2.25, 3.18
　rights, minority, 2.4, 2.23–24, 2.25, 3.18, 5.8, 16.8.2
　rights, under parliamentary law, 3.6, 11.2
　when not to vote, 5.60–62
　See also conflict of interest; decorum
minutes, 18.18, 23.1–47, 31.64
　access to, 23.8–10
　accuracy of/responsibility for, 23.1–4, 23.7, 23.8
　approval, 21.24–25, 23.2, 23.26, 23.29–30, 23.33, 23.44
　approval, by minutes approval committee, 23.34–37

changes and corrections, 21.24, 23.29–32, 23.36–37
closed meetings, 23.24–25
committee, 23.46–47
contents, 6.20, 9.9, 10.21, 10.26, 10.42, 12.13, 12.15, 18.11, 22.15, 23.1–19, 27.63
contents, items not included, 23.20–23
disposition, 21.24–26, 23.26–33
electronic archiving, 23.40, 23.42
format, 23.5–6
meeting notes vis-à-vis, 23.4, 23.7, 23.35, 23.37
precedents and, 4.56, 23.19
preparation, 23.7
presentation, 23.27, 23.33
reading of, 23.43
retention, 23.40–42
review, 23.33, 23.44–45
special meetings, 18.11
templates, 23.5–6
verbatim recordings vis-à-vis, 23.3
Motion for a Counted Vote, 16.91–92
rules governing, 16.94
See also voting methods: standing and counted standing
Motion to "Cut the Gordian Knot," 16.13–17
Motion to Adjourn, 3.18, 15.25–47, 18.16, 22.1
amendment, 15.29, 15.30
business interrupted by adjournment, 15.45–46
completion of business, 15.34–35
dissolution of an assembly, 15.38–39
previously set time, 15.44
privileged or not, 15.29–30
recess vs. adjourn, 15.31–33, 18.16, 21.4
rules governing, 15.47
to a continued meeting, 15.36–37
voting on, 15.41–43
wording of, 15.43
See also adjournment sine die
Motion to Adopt in Lieu of, 2.13, 13.3–8, 25.45.5, 25.76–85
features, 13.6
rules governing, 13.8
Motion to Amend a Previous Action, 4.27, 9.29, 9.36 12.16, 13.9–13, 14.24, 18.14, 23.32
rules governing, 13.13

Motion to Amend, 2.10, 4.32, 9.23.1–4, 13.32, 14.2–53, 25.73
acceptance, 14.25–30
germaneness, 14.7–11, 14.12
hostile, 14.2
improper, 14.13–15
pending, 14.20–21
primary, 14.18, 14.22
rendering main motion out of order, 14.15
rules governing, 14.51
secondary, 14.19, 14.22
types, 14.3–6
voting on, 14.35–38
withdrawal, 14.34
wording of, 14.14
See also A.M.P. method; filling blanks
Motion to Appeal, 1.5, 9.4, 15.4, 16.32–46, 23.19
rules governing, 16.46
timeliness, 16.36
voting on, 16.40–45
withdrawal, 16.39
Motion to Close Debate and Vote Immediately, 5.8, 11.28, 14.100–115
effect on pending motions, 14.107–108
proposal of, 14.105–106
rules governing, 14.115
termination of its effect, 14.109–111
See also call the question
Motion to Close Nominations, 26.10
Motion to Limit or Extend Debate, 14.87–99
effect on pending motions, 14.94–98
rules governing, 14.99
termination of its effect, 14.97–98
types of limitations, 14.92–93
Motion to Postpone to a Certain Time, 14.63–86
consideration of, 14.83–85
limitations, 14.70–73
rules governing, 14.86
scheduled order, 7.17, 14.77–82
types of postponements, 14.74–82
voting on, 14.78, 14.80
Motion to Ratify, 13.14–23
need for, 13.19–21
rules governing, 13.23
Motion to Recall from a Committee, 13.24–27
need for, 13.26

rules governing, 13.27
Motion to Recess, 15.16–24, 15.31, 22.1
  limitations, 15.20–22
  recess vs. adjourn, 15.31–33
  rules governing, 15.24
  when not privileged, 15.23
Motion to Reconsider, 9.4, 9.28, 9.36, 12.16, 13.13.7fn**, 13.28–41, 14.123
  argument against limitation of who can propose, 13.37
  dispositions that can be reconsidered, 13.29–33, 14.121
  proposal of, 13.34
  rules governing, 13.41
  who can propose, 13.35–38
Motion to Refer to a Committee, 14.52–62, 23.20, 24.45.6, 25.73
  as a main motion, 14.61
  provisions to include in, 14.56–59
  recall of, 14.60
  rules governing, 16.62
  See also Motion to Recall from a Committee
Motion to Reopen Nominations, 26.11
Motion to Rescind, 9.29, 9.36, 12.16, 13.12, 13.42–47
  rules governing, 13.47
  what can be rescinded, 13.43–46
Motion to Suspend Temporarily, 33.14
Motion to Suspend the Rules, 16.2–18
  restrictions and duration, 16.9–12
  rules, suspendable and not suspendable, 16.6–8
  rules governing, 16.18
  See also Motion to "Cut the Gordian Knot"
Motion to Table, 14.100, 14.109, 14.116–124, 25.45.7
  proposal of, 14.118–119
  rules governing, 14.124
  use of term "to table," 14.122, 24.45.7
motions, 2.10–12, 2.26, 3.6.3–4, 4.54–55, 7.1–16.94
  approval, 5.20, 5.25, 5.34
  assuming of, 10.38, 11.10, 16.14
  classification, 7.1–14
  computing a majority for separate questions, 5.44, 5.46
  defeat, 5.34, 5.38–39, 9.30
  definition, 10.1
  grouped, 2.15

  immediately pending, 8.9, 8.15, 11.17, 31.50
  introduction of next business, 10.34–35
  minutes, record of, 23.14–15
  order considered and voted on, 8.6.2, 9.21
  pending, 2.25, 4.23, 7.14–15, 8.8–15, 10.22, 14.16–17, 14.20–21
  procedural, 9.31, 23.20
  rank, 2.8–12, 8.1–15, 9.21–22
  renewal, 9.28–31, 9.36, 12.16, 13.33
  repeal, 9.29
  repeal, by implication, 9.32–35, 9.36
  rules governing, 9.1–36
  rushing, 2.27, 10.41
  tie votes, 5.34–39
  with pending amendments, 14.39
  withdrawal, 4.23, 9.4, 12.7, 14.34, 16.39, 16.62–68, 23.16
  See also A.M.P. method; debate; notice; reference committees; speakers; voting; voting methods; *and individual motions*
motions, presentation process, 5.37, 9.30, 10.1–42, 28.12–13
  addressing the presiding officer, 10.3–5
  microphone use during, 10.4, 10.8
  processing steps, combining and skipping, 10.36–42, 28.20
  proposing/moving/stating of, 10.9–13, 12.5–8, 27.19
  recognition, 10.3–4, 10.6–8
  seconding, 9.9–11, 10.14–17, 27.19, 28.20
  stating of motion, 10.18–22, 11.28
  submission in writing, 10.13, 12.6, 12.9
motions, voting process, 10.25–30, 14.35–37
  bringing to a vote, 11.36–38
  restatement of/"putting the question," 10.26, 11.28, 11.30
  results announcement, 10.31–33
  taking the affirmative and negative vote, 10.27–30
  vote requirements, 9.20
  See also voting; voting methods

nominations, 26.3–34, 26.7, 26.15, 27.19
  closing and reopening of, 26.10–11
  debate, 26.12–13
  declining of, 26.15
  from the floor, 26.7–9, 26.12, 26.34

to more than one office, 26.26–30
by petition, 6.35
temporary presiding officer, 17.10
temporary secretary, 17.11
See also committees: nominating
nominees. *See* candidates
notice, 3.18, 4.42, 20.1–17, 22.14, 23.17
  annual meetings, 20.8
  board, 20.12
  bylaw amendments, 4.21, 4.27–33, 5.5, 5.8
  bylaw revisions, 4.35–38
  changes and, 20.4
  committees, 20.12
  continued meetings, 15.36, 18.19, 20.11
  by email, 20.3
  meetings, 3.6.1, 4.62.3, 16.8.2a, 16.8.3, 18.15, 20.3–6
  motions, 4.21, 4.23–24, 13.10, 13.46, 16.8.2b
  proposed actions, 20.7
  regular meetings, 8.5–6, 18.5–8, 18.15, 20.9
  scope, 20.15–16
  special meetings, 18.9–12, 20.10, 23.13
  statutory requirements, 20.3
  waiver of, 20.17
  See also conventions: notice; meetings, electronic: notice

officers, 3.6.6, 3.15.7, 3.24–26, 4.62.5, 21.27–29, 26.3, 27.1–73, 30.3, 30.4
  appointed, 27.38–45
  compatibility/incompatibility of offices, 26.26–30
  conflicts of interest, 5.59, 23.16
  delegation of authority, 27.49–54
  disciplinary sanctions, 33.17–18
  honorary, 27.46
  incumbent, 26.75, 27.61, 26.65
  installation of, 26.60
  liability and, 3.26
  order of succession, 4.62.6
  powers, 27.22, 27.31, 27.48
  remedies for improper removal, 33.19
  removal, for cause, 33.8–15, 33.19
  removal, without cause, 33.16
  resignations, 3.24–26
  rights, 5.37, 27.19, 27.47
  succession, 27.21, 27.23
  suspension, 33.14
  terms of, 26.64, 25.57–62
  vacancies, 26.4, 26.71, 27.23–24, 27.27, 27.31, 27.63–70
  vote to remove, 33.15–16
  See also candidates; committees: nominating; elections; nominations; *and individual types of officers*
on-screen transcription, 19.37
order of business, 15.32, 21.1–7, 21.23–44
  adjournment, 21.43–44
  announcements, 21.42, 21.45
  annual meetings, 21.6–7
  business, new, 21.36, 21.39–41
  business, unfinished, 14.81.2, 15.45.1, 15.46, 21.33–38
  call to order, 18.1, 21.23
  continued meetings, 21.16
  minutes, 21.24–26, 23.27
  programs, 21.4
  reports, 21.27–32, 31.57–59
  special meetings, 21.5, 21.15
  timed items and scheduled orders, 21.6–7
  See also conventions: order of business
organizations, 17.1–28
  administrative procedures, 4.9, 4.52–53
  assets, 4.10
  constituent/component units, 1.9.2–3
  corporate offices, 4.62.8
  customary practices, 4.40.4, 4.56–57
  delegation of powers, 1.8, 2.22, 3.15.6, 4.62.5, 14.56
  disciplinary actions, 3.6.10–11, 3.15.8, 3.19, 3.20, 3.23, 18.24, 18.28
  dissolution/merging of, 3.15.3, 4.10, 15.40, 17.18.4
  dues and membership fees, 2.14, 3.12, 3.21
  duty of care, 30.19–20
  emergencies, 4.58–65, 4.62.9, 18.13, 30.14
  enforcement of rules and parliamentary law, 3.6.8, 16.21–23
  expulsion from, 3.6.10–11
  fairness and good faith within, 2.27–31, 33.4
  forms, 17.4–8
  governance within, 1.8, 2.19–23, 2.25, 2.26, 3.19, 11.1, 11.8, 11.11, 11.35, 25.1–6
  governing documents and rules, 1.9.3, 2.14, 3.3, 4.1

governing documents and rules,
  amendment of, 3.6.7, 3.15.2, 3.15.4, 4.6
leadership, 26.1–2
legal actions against, 3.8
loyalty to, 2.14, 3.9, 30.19, 30.21–22
missions/purposes, 3.5.1–2, 17.7, 17.20
parent, 1.9.2, 4.5, 4.21, 13.21, 17.11, 17.17
parliamentary rules and, 1.9–10, 29.23
penalty clauses, 4.4.15
permanent, 17.2, 17.13–15
personnel matters, 18.24
principles, 4.48–51
privilege of the assembly, 15.1–2, 15.4
property rights, 3.5, 3.15.9, 3.21, 5.8, 17.18.5
proposed actions, 20.14
protection of, 1.5, 2.15
ranking of governing documents, 4.1
ranking of parliamentary rules, 1.9–10
records, inspection and receipt of, 3.6.12
relationship between members and, 2.14, 3.1–3, 3.16–20, 5.2
resignations, 2.14, 3. 3.6.9, 3.24–26, 6.9, 3.21–26
right of assembly, 2.15
right of association, 2.14
rights, 2.14–15, 3.15, 3.17
staff, 25.101
staying in, 3.6.10
subordinate, 1.9.2, 4.5, 13.21
tax-exemptions, 17.28, 30.18
temporary, 17.1–2, 17.12, 17.15
See also boards, budget; bylaws, charters; committees; constitutions; elections; finances; meetings; membership; nominations; officers; parliamentary authority; parliamentary law; parliamentary rules; *and individual types of officers and organizations*

parliamentarians, 27.39–44, 29.14–40
  advisory role to presiding officer, 16.58, 29.5–10
  bylaws writing and, 4.8, 4.11, 4.39
  contracting with, 29.40
  credentialing of, 29.2
  floor, 29.38–39
  meeting/convention, 29.4–13, 29.34
  impartiality and, 29.3, 29.5, 29.38
  member, 27.41–44

professional, 27.40, 29.1–40
  as professional presiding officer, 29.12, 29.14–19
  services, 19.9, 29.20–37
parliamentary authority, 1.14, 4.1, 4.47
  adoption of, 0.30, 1.9.4, 1.15, 4.43–47, 17.11
  definition, 1.14
  force and effect of, 4.46
  overriding, 1.9.4, 1.14, 4.41
parliamentary inquiry. *See* Inquiries: Parliamentary
parliamentary law, 1.1–15, 4.43, 17.5, 17.11
  definition, 1.1–2
  deviations from/addition to, 4.41
  enforcement, 3.6.8
  misconceptions about, 1.12–13
  order of business established by, 21.2
  organizations using, 1.6–8
  philosophy, 2.6
  principles, 1.5, 2.1–31, 4.47, 4.48–51, 12.1, 19.7–9, 20.2
  as procedural safeguard, 1.4
  purposes, 1.4, 2.6–13, 2.20
  quorum requirements according to, 22.4
  rights of members under, 3.6
  rules, 1.9, 11.3, 29.23
  writing of opinions regarding, 29.25–26
parliamentary procedure. *See* parliamentary law
partnerships, 17.4, 17.6
plurality vote. *See* voting: plurality
point of information, 16.53
Point of Order, 1.5, 9.5–6, 9.11, 10.18, 10.26, 11.9, 11.15, 16.19–31, 23.19
  appeals, 16.28, 16.30, 23.19
  raising, 16.24–26, 22.16
  referred to assembly, 16.29
  rules governing, 16.31
  ruling on, 16.20, 16.23, 16.27–30
powers. *See* duties and powers
preamble clauses. *See* resolutions: preamble/whereas clauses
president, 27.3–15
  as administrator, 27.4
  report, 21.27
  vacancy, 27.21, 27.23–24
  See also presiding officer
president-elect, 27.20–22

presiding officer, 27.5–19, 28.1–28.5
  debate and, 2.17, 5.37, 11.31, 16.39, 27.17, 28.21–24
  demeanor/nonverbal image, 28.9, 28.25
  enforcing rules, 16.21–23, 19.20, 27.11
  helpfulness of, 28.4–6
  impartiality and, 2.17–18, 5.37, 10.12, 10.30, 11.19, 11.31, 11.32, 16.59, 27.9, 27.18, 28.3
  inquiries addressed to, 16.58–60, 28.25.2
  leading competently, 28.7–11
  managing decorum, 28.21–24
  official title, 10.3
  processing motions, 28.12–13
  skill and art of presiding, 27.5–15, 28.1–25
  temporary, 17.10
  understanding meeting structure, 28.11, 28.17–20
  verbal image, 28.10
  voting and, 5.37–41
  yielding of role, 29.14–19
Privileged Motions, 7.6–7, 15.1–47
  rank, 8.3, 9.22
  types, 7.7
  See also Motion to Adjourn; Motion to Recess; Question of Privilege
provisos, 4.16
proxies, 4.62.7, 6.39–50
  authentication of, 6.48–49
  business corporations and, 6.40
  directed, 6.44
  general, 6.44
  nonprofit corporations and, 6.41
  nonprofit organizations and, 6.42, 6.45
  revocation of, 6.45
proxy givers, 6.39, 6.45
proxy holders, 6.39, 6.41, 6.44, 6.46, 6.48–50
"putting the question," 10.26

Question of Privilege, 9.5–6, 9.11, 15.2–15
  appeals, 15.4, 15.7
  of the assembly, 15.4, 15.9
  denial, 15.5, 15.7
  forms, 15.6
  as motions, 7.20, 15.4, 15.11–13
  personal privilege, 15.4, 15.10
  rules governing, 15.14–15
quorum, 3.18, 4.62.4, 6.22, 6.47, 13.14, 13.19, 16.8.2c, 22.1–21, 30.16
  boards, 22.10
  by fixed number, 22.5–7
  by proportion of membership, 22.5
  call, 22.16
  committees, 22.10
  computation of, 22.11–15
  conventions, 22.8
  inquorate meetings, 22.1–3
  majority and, 22.4.1, 22.6, 22.8, 22.10
  presumption of, 22.19–21
  qualified, 22.9
  questioning of, 22.16–21
  requirements, 22.4–10

railroading. *See* motions: rushing
rank
  bylaws, 1.9.3, 4.6
  governing documents, 4.1, 4.6
  motions, 2.10
  parliamentary rules, 1.9–10
ratification, 13.14–23
reference committees, 4.21, 21.20, 24.14, 25.1–88
  advisors to, 25.10
  appointments and composition, 25.8–11
  conduct of members, 25.29, 25.32–33
  courtesy resolutions, 25.46
  explanations within reports, 25.48–50, 25.70
  hearings, 24.14, 25.3, 25.21–37
  influence of, 25.86–88
  limitations on testimony, 25.26–28, 25.36
  recommendations, 25.21, 25.31, 25.38–50, 25.71–85
  referrals to, 25.14–16, 25.17
  reports, 25.30, 25.42–50, 25.60.2, 25.70
  use of Motion to Adopt in Lieu of, 25.45.5, 25.76–85
  use of Motion to Refer to a Committee, 25.45.6, 25.73
  use of Motion to Table, 25.45.7
repeal by implication, 9.32–35, 9.36
reports, 23.18
  boards, 21.30
  committees, 21.30–32, 31.42, 41.46–66
  election/tellers committee, 26.46–49
  executive director, 21.27
  filing of, 21.30
  president, 21.27, 25.30
  recommendations within, 21.32, 31.47–48, 31.62.9, 31.67–71

secretary, 21.29
treasurer, 21.27–28, 27.34–35, 31.62.5–6, 32.4–6
See also committees, reports of; reference committees: reports; *and individual committee reports under* conventions
Request to Withdraw a Motion, 4.23, 9.4, 9.11, 14.34, 15.35, 16.17, 16.62–68
  permission to withdraw or modify a motion, 16.65–66
  objections to, 16.63, 16.65
  record of, 16.67
  right to withdraw or modify a motion, 16.64
  rules governing, 16.68
resignations, 2.14, 3.69, 3.21–26
  effective time of, 3.22
  with pending disciplinary action, 3.23
  withdrawal of, 3.25–26
resolutions, 12.9–13, 25.47
  preamble/whereas clauses, 12.10–13
  resolved clauses, 12.10, 12.12–13
resolutions committees. See reference committees
resolved clauses. *See* resolutions: resolved clauses
rights, 1.3, 1.4–5
  of assembly, 1.4, 2.15
  of association, 2.14
  of debate/discussion, 2.25, 3.6.4, 3.17
  equality of, 2.14, 2.16–18, 20.2
  to information, 2.26, 3.20
  protection of, 1.5, 2.15, 2.17, 2.23–24
  to rise to an inquiry, 2.26
  to run for office, hold office, and nominate officers, 3.6.6, 33.8
  to voice opposition/approval and seek to persuade others, 2.20, 2.25
  voting, 3.6.5, 6.37
  vested, 3.2
  See also membership: rights; officers; rights; organizations: rights
rules, 4.64
  custom and, 4.56–57
  emergency, 4.58–65
  enforcement of, 1.5, 1.13, 2.15, 3.6.8., 3.16–17, 16.21–23, 19.20, 27.11
  interpretation of, 4.39–40
  precedent and, 4.56–57
  See also conventions: rules; Point of Order; meetings: standing rules

of order; meetings: temporary rules; motions: rules governing; parliamentary law; *and rules under individual motions*
runoff system, 5.28

secret ballots. *See* ballots
secretary, 4.33, 6.44fn*, 27.28–33
  corresponding, 27.33
  duties, 21.10, 21.19, 23.2–4, 23.8, 26.49, 27.28–30, 31.30
  recording, 27.33
  report, 21.29
  temporary, 17.10, 23.4
  vacancy, 27.31
sergeant at arms, 27.45
serpentine count, 6.17
sign language interpreters, 19.36
speakers
  addressed during inquiries, 16.48, 16.50–51
  addressing presiding officer, 10.3–5
  interruption of, 9.3–8, 11.15, 15.7–8, 16.25, 16.36, 16.48, 16.49–52, 16.55–57
special rules. *See* meetings: temporary rules
Specific-Purpose Main Motions, 7.3, 13.1–47
  rank, 8.5, 9.22, 13.2
  See also Motion to Adopt in Lieu of; Motion to Amend a Previous Action; Motion to Ratify, Motion to Recall from a Committee; Motion to Reconsider; Motion to Rescind
Sturgis, Alice, 0.2
Sturgis' Standard Code of Parliamentary Procedure, 0.2
Subsidiary Motions, 7.4–5, 9.23, 14.1–124
  rank, 8.4, 9.22
  See also Motion to Amend; Motion to Close Debate and Vote Immediately; Motion to Limit or Extend Debate; Motion to Postpone to a Certain Time; Motion to Refer to a Committee; Motion to Table
supermajority. *See* voting: more than a majority
surety bonds, 32.12

tabling. *See* Motion to Table: use of
tactics, 3.19

dilatory, 1.11, 2.27, 9.7, 11.21, 13.37, 14.23, 16.5, 22.18, 27.1
   lacking in fairness and good faith, 2.27, 3.19, 16.57, 16.92
   parliamentary, 2.28
tally sheets, 26.49
task forces. *See* committees: special
technology support, 19.44, 20.13
tellers, 6.16, 26.36, 26.57, 29.34–35
temporary rules. *See* meetings: temporary rules
treasurer, 27.34–37
   report, 21.27–28, 27.37
trusts, 17.4, 17.6
two-thirds vote, 5.5
   computation of, 5.42–43
   taken by standing vote, 6.14
   See also voting: more than a majority

U.S. Labor-Management Report and Disclosure Act of 1959, 17.23
unanimous consent. *See* general consent
unanimous written consent, 18.31–33

vice president, 27.23–27
   ranking of, 27.27
voting, 3.6.5, 5.1–6.64, 10.27–32, 16.8.4, 28.17.6
   absentee, 6.39, 6.44fn*
   affirmative, 5.18, 5.19, 5.22, 5.24, 6.6, 10.27–29
   binding nature, 6.64–65
   board members and, 30.16
   cards, 6.19
   changing, 6.62
   counts and recounts, 26.40–41, 26.44–45, 25.56–57
   courtesy, 6.7
   deadlocked, 5.34–36
   double threshold, 5.57
   electronic, 26.54
   failure to, 5.21, 5.23
   less than a majority, 5.3–4, 5.10–11
   minority control of, 5.3–6, 5.33
   minutes, recording of, 23.16
   more than a majority, 2.4, 2.21, 2.23, 2.25, 3.18, 5.3–9
   negative, 6.6–7, 10.30
   plurality, 5.3–4, 5.11, 5.25–28

   presiding officer and, 5.37–41
   protection of minority and, 5.4, 5.8
   quorum and, 22.14
   repeated, 5.27–28, 5.35–36
   results, announcement of, 6.63, 10.31–32
   threshold, 5.24, 6.22
   tie (elections), 5.35–36, 5.41
   tie (motions), 5.34, 5.38–39
   unanimous, 5.6, 5.29–33, 26.58
   verification, 16.86–94
   write-in, 6.32, 19.31.1, 26.14, 26.47, 26.54
   See also abstentions; ballots; confidentiality; elections; general consent; majority vote; Motion for a Counted Vote; motions, two-thirds vote
voting methods, 6.1–65, 16.8.5, 26.37–38
   acting by proxy, 6.39–50
   approval, 6.29
   ballot, 5.41, 6.23, 6.24–38, 6.62
   Borda Count, 6.57–59
   bullet, 6.60
   cumulative, 6.61
   determination of type, 6.2–3, 6.20
   electronic, 6.38, 6.44, 6.62, 19.27–31, 26.40, 26.67–68
   informal (*see* voting methods: straw)
   instant runoff (*see* voting methods: preferential)
   by mail, 6.31–38, 6.44
   preferential, 5.28, 6.27, 6.51–56
   ranked choice (*see* voting methods: preferential)
   recorded, 6.20–23
   rising (*see* voting methods: standing and counted standing)
   roll call, 6.5, 6.20–23, 6.62, 26.55
   show of hands, 6.12, 6.18–19, 6.62, 26.56–57
   signed ballot, 6.23
   standing and counted standing, 6.12–18, 6.62, 10.31, 14.43, 26.56–57
   straw, 6.64, 25.31
   Texas ballot, 6.28
   voice, 6.12–13, 16.87, 16.90, 26.56

whereas clauses. *See* resolutions: preamble/whereas clauses

BASIC RULES GOVERNING MOTIONS

Order of precedence[1]	Can interrupt?	Requires a second?	Debatable?[2]	Amendable?	Vote Required?	Applies to what other motions	Can have what other motions applied to it?[3]	Renewable?
PRIVILEGED MOTIONS								
1. Adjourn	No	Yes	No	No	Majority	None	Amend, close debate	Yes
2. Recess	No	Yes	No	Yes	Majority	None	Amend, close debate	Yes
3. Question of privilege	Yes	No	No	No	None	None	None	Yes
SUBSIDIARY MOTIONS								
4. Table	No	Yes	No	No	Majority	Main motion	None	No
5. Close debate & vote immediately	No	Yes	No	No	2/3	Amend, debateable motions	Amend	Yes
6. Limit or extend debate	No	Yes	No	Yes	2/3	Amendable, debateable motions	Amend, close debate	Yes
7. Postpone to a certain time	No	Yes	Yes	Yes	Majority[4]	Main motion with pending subsidiary motions	Amend, limit debate, close debate	Yes
8. Refer to committee	No	Yes	Yes	Yes	Majority	Main motion with pending amendments	Amend, limit debate, close debate	Yes
9. Amend	No	Yes	Yes[5]	Yes	Majority	Rewordable motions	Amend, limit debate, close debate	Yes[6]
MAIN MOTIONS								
10. a. The main motion	No	Yes	Yes	Yes	Majority	None	Subsidiary motions	No
b. Specific-purpose main motions								
Adopt in lieu of	No	Yes	Yes	Yes	Majority	Designated motions	Subsidiary motions	No
Amend a previous action	No	Yes	Yes	Yes	Same Vote	Adopted main motion	Subsidiary motions	No
Ratify	No	Yes	Yes	No	Same Vote	Adopted main motion	Subsidiary motions except amend	No
Recall from a committee	No	Yes	Yes	No	Majority	Referred main motion	Close debate, limit debate	Yes
Reconsider	Yes[7]	Yes	Yes	No	Majority	Main motion, some specific-purpose main motions[8]	Close debate, limit debate	No
Rescind	No	Yes	Yes	No	Same Vote	Adopted main motion	Subsidiary motions except amend	No
INCIDENTAL MOTIONS								
No order of precedence								
MOTIONS								
Appeal	Yes[7]	Yes	Yes	No	Majority	Ruling of chair	Close debate, limit debate	No
Suspend the rules	No	Yes	No	No	2/3	Procedural rules	None	Yes
Consider by paragraph	No	Yes	No	No	Majority	Main motion	None	Yes
Counted Vote	Yes	Yes	No	No	Majority	Vote with an unclear outcome	None	No
REQUESTS								
Point of order	Yes	No	No	No	None	Procedural error	None	No
Inquiries	Yes[9]	No	No	No	None	All motions	None	Yes
Withdraw a motion	Yes	No	No	No	None	All motions	None	No
Division of question	No	No	No	No	None	Divisible motions	None	No
Division of assembly	Yes	No	No	No	None	Vote with an unclear outcome	None	No

---

[1] Motions are in order only if no motion higher on the list is pending.
[2] Debate must always be germane to the pending motion
[3] Note that the Motion to Withdraw can be applied to all motions.
[4] Postpone and make a special order requires 2/3 vote
[5] Is not debatable when applied to an undebatable motion
[6] At the discretion of the presiding officer
[7] Can interrupt proceedings, but not a speaker
[8] Adopt in Lieu of, Amend a Previous Action, Ratify, and Rescind
[9] Only if it requires an immediate answer

Made in the USA
Columbia, SC
18 October 2023

24619399R00243